ANCIENT RELIGIONS

ANCIENT RELIGIONS

Sarah Iles Johnston

GENERAL EDITOR

The Belknap Press of Harvard University Press

Cambridge, Massachusetts, and London, England

2007

Library of Congress Cataloging-in-Publication Data

Ancient religions / Sarah Iles Johnston, general editor.
p.   cm.
Includes bibliographical references and index.
ISBN-13: 978-0-674-02548-6 (pbk. : alk. paper)
1. Religions.   2. Civilization, Ancient.   I. Johnston, Sara Iles, 1957–
BL96.A53   2007
200.93—dc22   2007016512

Contents

Introduction

Sarah Iles Johnston

W hen Croesus, the king of Lydia, was debating about whether to attack the Persian Empire, he decided to seek advice from the gods. Being a cautious man, however, he decided first to determine which source of divine advice was the most reliable. He sent envoys to each of the famous oracles in the ancient world (which happened to be in Greece and Libya) and instructed them to ask the gods what he was doing in faraway Lydia one hundred days after the envoys had left his court. He then devised an activity that he was confident no one could guess: he boiled the meat of a tortoise and the flesh of a rabbit together in a bronze cauldron, covered by a bronze lid. When the envoys returned with written records of what each oracle's god had said, Croesus discovered that only two of them—Delphic Apollo and Amphiaraus—had correctly described his strange culinary experiment. He proceeded to make enormously rich offerings to Apollo (and lesser offerings to Amphiaraus, whose oracle was not as prestigious) and then asked Apollo's advice. Upon receiving it, Croesus attacked Persia (Herodotus 1.46ff).

Croesus's experiment serves as an apt parable for this volume because it is one of the earliest examples of what might be called religious comparison shopping: rather than simply asking his own experts to obtain the gods' advice, Croesus checked out all the divine resources within his reach and staked his future on the one that looked best. The general concept should be familiar enough to readers who live in America or western Europe, where religious plurality offers a spectrum of deities, practices, and beliefs to which one might pledge allegiance. Our immediate environments (in sad contrast to more distant parts of our world, including some where Croesus once walked) offer us easy access to numerous variations of Christianity, Judaism, Islam, Hinduism, and Buddhism, as well as a plethora of newer religions such as Wicca and Scientology. Some of these are imports from other cultures; others are combinations of previously existing religions.

Only relatively recently, however, have scholars recognized the extent to which ancient peoples, as well, were exposed to a diversity of religions, both indigenous and imported—or even, indeed, acknowledged that ancient peoples were exposed to a diversity of cultural influences of any kind. The historical reasons for this failure are political and ideological, as well as intellectual, among which three are especially interesting, as Walter Burkert and other scholars have shown (see esp. Burkert, *The Orientalizing Revolution*). First, in the late 18th and early 19th centuries, following a long period during which scholars of the Bible and of classical antiquity had taken cultural interaction in the ancient Mediterranean for granted, the boundaries between academic fields were redrawn in universities, and what we now call classics and theology strove to assert themselves as independent entities. As they did so, each one naturally stressed the grandeur and achievements of the cultures it represented—respectively, ancient Greece and Rome, and the ancient Near East. Second, at about the same time, Romantic nationalism developed. In their desire to show that particular myths, literatures, and forms of religion could be tied to particular ancient cultures that served as models for contemporary nation-states, Romantic nationalists not only discouraged any assumption of cross-cultural influences within the ancient Mediterranean, but also brought new energy to the old quest of tracking the specific, discrete origins of each culture's practices and ideas. Finally, and also at about the same time, notions about a lost "pre-language," shared by the Greeks, Romans, Germans, and other "Aryan" peoples—but not by the Semites—crystallized into the proposal for the language we now call "Indo-European." Linguistics provided another reason for separating the (Indo-European) western Mediterranean from the (non–Indo-European) eastern regions.

One might have expected the scholarly barrier between east and west to erode during the later 19th and early 20th centuries, which brought such advancements as the deciphering of hieroglyphs and cuneiform writing and of the Hittite language (an Indo-European language attached to an "oriental" culture), along with the discovery of Mycenaean civilizations and of orientalizing elements in Greek art. Some erosion did in fact begin to occur, especially in the fields of art history, ancient history, and the study of ancient magic (a field that was itself only in its infancy). Yet during the period between World War I and World War II, scholars, particularly in Germany, once again sought to assert the unique character of each Mediterranean culture. In 1946, publication of the Hittite creation myth, which offered significant thematic parallels to Hesiod's Theogony, reopened consideration of the question of cultural exchange in the ancient world. Slowly but surely, a new consensus emerged: the Mediterranean Sea had been not a barrier between disparate cultures after all, but rather a conduit, through which both material goods and ideas were easily transported. No ancient culture was left untouched by its neighbors. In the mid-1960s, scholarly publications based on this now widely accepted understanding began to appear, and have continued ever since.

Religious beliefs and practices, which permeated all aspects of human life in antiquity, were inevitably transmitted throughout the Mediterranean along with everything else: itinerant charismatic practitioners journeyed from place to place, selling their skills as healers, purifiers, cursers, and initiators; vessels decorated with illustrations of myths traveled along with the goods they contained; new gods were encountered in foreign lands by merchants and conquerors and, when useful, were taken home to be adapted and adopted.

The essays in this volume are drawn from *Religions of the Ancient World,* a larger reference work that both collected information about religions in the ancient world and organized it in such a way as to encourage readers to investigate those religions within the comparative framework that is now considered essential for their comprehension. By presenting material from the ten cultures and traditions that it investigated side-by-side, *Religions of the Ancient World* strove to inform its readers and generate comparative thought in complementary ways.

The first part of that work reprinted here, "Encountering Ancient Religions," consists of eleven essays whose topics cut across cultural boundaries, such as Cosmology, Myth, and Law and Ethics. The authors of these essays were charged with stepping back from the particular cultures on which their own scholarship usually focuses and taking a broader look at the given phenomena as they were found throughout the Mediterranean: What remains consistent as we cross from one culture or tradition to another? What changes, and why? What, if anything, can we say about the core functions and expressive modes that the phenomena manifest across several millennia of ancient Mediterranean history? The authors also were asked to consider what essential theoretical or methodological problems confront us as we approach these topics: How can we define "magic" in contrast to "religion," for example—or should we even try to do so? How does the transition from an orally based religious culture to one that is scripturally based affect not only the practices and beliefs themselves, but also our approach to the evidence for them? The first essay in this part asks a question that stands behind all the others: What counts as "Mediterranean religion" anyway? Or to put it otherwise: In spite of the long history of Mediterranean cultural interaction that scholars now accept, what aspects of the disparate religions most closely coalesced to form a sort of *koinē,* or common language, that could have been understood by anyone traveling through the ancient landscape?

The second part, "Histories," includes essays that trace the histories of religions in each of the cultures and traditions between about the 3rd millennium BCE and the 5th century CE, offering accounts of how each of the cultures and its political, social, artistic, and religious institutions changed over time. Here readers will find, for example, a description of the Greek polis system and its effect on civic religion, a discussion of the centrality of *maʿat* (justice, order) within Egyptian thought, a description of how Zoroastrianism developed within earlier Iranian religions, and a discussion of literary sources for Ugaritic religion. The Epilogue is an important complement to the entire volume. It poses and begins to answer questions that earlier essays, which focused on discrete topics, were unable to tackle. By asking what the phrase "ancient world" signifies, for example, the Epilogue compels us to recognize another aspect of the concern with definitions that first was broached in "What Is Ancient Mediterranean Religion?": once we have arrived at a working definition of Mediterranean religions and have investigated them as fully as possible, what can we then say about the way they differed from religions of later periods? Are the common assumptions that we make about ancient religions serviceable or misleading in understanding the transition? And was there a definitive transition at all—can we even identify behaviors that are more characteristic of ancient religions than post-ancient?

Some hundred and forty scholars contributed to *Religions of the Ancient World,* nineteen of whom are represented in this volume. Each brought his or her own methodology, style, and interests to the topics assigned. Rather than attempt to impose an artificial consistency on their contributions, the book's editors left them alone as much as possible. Thus, some essays concentrate primarily on conveying facts, whereas others produce a synoptic view of the topic at hand, adducing facts only as necessary.

To some degree, these variations reflect differences in the state of research among the fields: most of the texts and many of the archeological remains of Greece and Rome have been available for two millennia; the texts of biblical religion have been around for about the same length of time, while its monuments have come to light more slowly; both the texts and the monuments of other Near Eastern cultures were almost completely hidden until recently. Egypt stands somewhere in the middle: its monuments have always loomed on the landscape, but the languages of Pharaonic Egypt were unreadable until about two hundred years ago. Fashions in scholarship and ideological agendas also helped to condemn some cultures and their religions to near-obscurity for most of the modern era. Some fields have been more eager than others, too, to embrace new theoretical methods of study—to their benefit or sometimes their detriment. Although the editors have worked to ensure that each essay presents the basic facts that are salient to its topic, we have left the overall design and approach of discussions to individual authors. We have even allowed occasional disagreements between authors to stand, as indications of ongoing debate within the larger scholarly community.

When Croesus asked Apollo whether he should attack Persia, the god answered that if he did, "a great empire would fall." Assuming this meant the Persian Empire, Croesus attacked. But Apollo really meant the Lydian Empire, and so Croesus eventually found himself standing on a pyre in front of Cyrus, the Persian king, condemned to be burned alive.

Interpreting what someone else says is always a risky business, even if the speaker is not a god famous for enigmatic pronouncements. Comparative work is particularly fraught with risks because, try as we might, those of us who are not trained in the languages and history of a given culture can never quite understand its complexities or catch its nuances. We are apt to make innocent but grievous errors, assuming, for instance, that the sacrificial act in Egypt had the same resonance as it did in Greece, or that the professional priesthoods found in many ancient Mediterranean cultures had correlates in the rest. To carry off a project such as this volume requires a team of people who are not only excellent scholars but also excellent communicators.

Throughout *Religions of the Ancient World*'s development, the exchange of ideas was vital, and I could not have asked for better colleagues in this respect than the members of the Editorial Board. Members of the Board of Advisors—Elizabeth Clark, David Frankfurter, Albert Henrichs, Gregory Nagy, John Scheid, and Claus Wilcke—were crucial to this process as well; all of them have contributed their expertise to the project and some of them were called on frequently. The contributors, some of whom wrote more than one essay, are to be thanked both for their scholarly efforts and for their patience.

I cannot leave Croesus on his pyre. Just as the flames were licking at its edges, Cyrus engaged Croesus in a debate about the meaning of happiness. Impressed with his captive's answer—Croesus held to a dictum he had learned from the Greek statesman Solon, according to which no human life could be counted as happy until one saw how it ended—Cyrus ordered that the pyre be extinguished. It was too late, however, for human intervention to quench the flames; only through Croesus's earnest prayers to Apollo did help arrive, in the form of a sudden rain shower. Stepping down from the pyre, Croesus went on to become Cyrus's staunch friend and advisor. And so ended Croesus's experiment in religious comparison shopping. Led astray through his misinterpretation of a Greek god's advice, saved when he adduced the words of a Greek sage and prayed once again to the Greek god, Croesus the Lydian finished out his life helping Cyrus (who was himself half Mede and half Persian) carry Persian rule throughout much of the ancient world: Croesus became a true Mediterranean cosmopolite. May the present experiment in religious comparison prove to be just as inclusive in its embrace and just as fortunate in its fate.

Note on Translation and Transliteration

Personal, divine, and geographical names are given throughout in familiar or simplified forms, using no diacritical marks or special characters (Astarte, Nike, Zarathustra). Transliteration of special terms follows standard scholarly practice for the discipline involved *(nawrūz, eschatiē, pesaḥ)*.

Greek names are given in their Latinate form, except for those that are best known in their Greek forms (such as Knossos) and cultic terms or epithets (such as Hekatombaia and Zeus Ktesios).

Quotations from the Hebrew Bible and the New Testament follow the Revised Standard Version.

Translations of passages from other works, unless credited to a published source, may be assumed to be by the article's author.

Abbreviations

ANET   J. B. Pritchard (ed.), *Ancient Near Eastern Texts Relating to the Old Testament* (3rd ed.; Princeton: Princeton University Press, 1969)

CAT   M. Dietrich, O. Loretz, and J. Sanmartín, *The Cuneiform Alphabetic Texts from Ugarit, Ras Ibn Hani, and Other Places* (Münster: Ugarit-Verlag, 1995) (= second edition of *KTU*)

CIL   *Corpus Inscriptionum Latinarum*

CTH   Emmanuel Laroche, *Catalogue des textes hittites* (Études et commentaires 75; Paris: Klincksieck, 1971)

FGrH   F. Jacoby (ed.), *Die Fragmente der griechischen Historiker* (Leiden: Brill, 1923–)

IG   *Inscriptiones Graecae*

ILS   *Inscriptiones Latinae Selectae*

KAI   H. Donner and W. Röllig, *Kanaänaische und aramäische Inschriften* (3rd ed.; 3 vols.; Wiesbaden: Harrassowitz, 1971–1976)

KAR   *Keilschrifttexte aus Assur religiösen Inhalts*

KBo   Keilschrifttexte aus Boghazköi (1916–)

KTU   M. Dietrich, O. Loretz, and J. Sanmartín, *Die keilalphabetischen Texte aus Ugarit* (Alter Orient und Altes Testament 24.1; Kevelaer: Butzon & Bercker/ Neukirchen-Vluyn: Neukirchener Verlag, 1976)

KUB   Keilschrifturkunden aus Boghazköi (1921–)

PDM   *Papyri Demoticae Magicae*

PGM   K. Preisendanz (ed.), *Papyri Graecae Magicae: Die griechischen Zauberpapyri* (Berlin, 1928); 2nd ed., 2 vols., ed. A. Henrichs (Berlin, 1973–1974)

SEG   *Supplementum Epigraphicum Graecum*

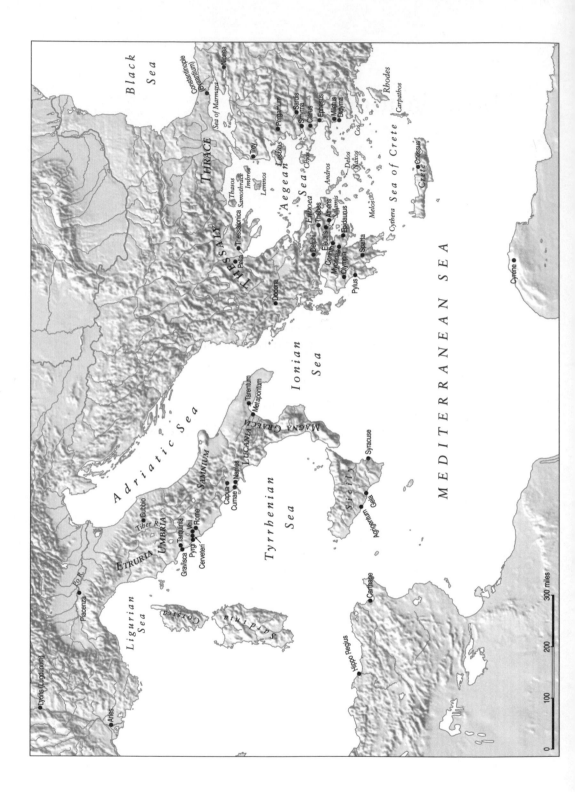

Black
Sea

Nicaea

Constantinople
(Byzantium)

Sea of Marmara

THRACE

Pergamum
Sardis
Smyrna
Clazos
Ephesus
Miletus
Didyma
Rhodes
Carpathos

Troy

Lesbos
Chios

THESSALY

Thasos
Samothrace
Imbros
Lemnos

Aegean Sea
Euboea

Delos
Andros
Naxos

Sea of Crete

Thessalonica
Pella

Delphi
Thebes
Eleusis
Athens
Corinth
Mycenae
Olympia
Pylus
Epidaurus
Sparta

Melos
Cythera
Sea of Crete
Crete
Cnossus

Dodona

Lyons (Lugdunum)

Po R.

Placenza

Ligurian
Sea

Corsica

Sardinia

Ionian
Sea

Adriatic Sea

Gubbio
Tiber R.
UMBRIA
Tarquinia
Veii
ETRURIA
Graviisca
Pyrgi
Rome
Cerveteri

SAMNIUM

Capua
Cumae Naples

LUCANIA
MAGNA GRAECIA

Tarentum
Metapontum

Syracuse

Sicily
Agrigentum Gela

Tyrrhenian
Sea

MEDITERRANEAN SEA

Carthage

Hippo Regius

Cyrene

Arles

0   100   200   300 miles

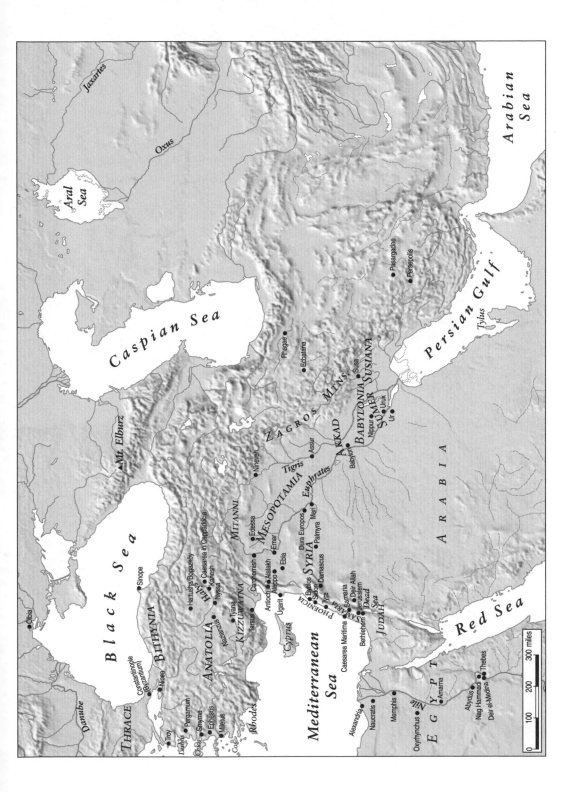

ENCOUNTERING ANCIENT RELIGIONS

What Is Ancient Mediterranean Religion?

Fritz Graf

*I*n the darkest hour of his life, Lucius, the human-turned-donkey in Apuleius's novel *The Golden Ass,* is sleeping in the sand of a Mediterranean beach. He has barely escaped from yet another humiliation, public copulation with a woman in Corinth's circus, and he is at the very end of his considerable wits. He awakens to a brilliant full moon rising over the dark waters of the Corinthian Gulf. He addresses a prayer to the moon and its goddess. And lo and behold! a beautiful woman rises out of the silvery path on the water; she consoles Lucius and introduces her astonishingly multiple personality: "The Phrygians, earliest of humans, call me the Pessinuntian Mother of the Gods; the Athenians, sprung from their own soil, call me Cecropian Minerva; the sea-tossed Cyprians call me Venus of Paphus, the arrow-bearing Cretans Dictynna, the trilingual Sicilians Ortygian Proserpina; to the Eleusinians I am the ancient goddess Ceres, to others Juno, to yet others Bellona, Hecate, or the Rhamnusian Goddess; and the Ethiopians who are illuminated by the first rays of the sun, the Africans, and the Egyptians full of ancient lore and wisdom honor me with the true rites and call me with the true name: Isis" (*Golden Ass* 11.1–5). When making these claims in Apuleius's novel, Isis is well aware of the discordant unity of Mediterranean religions. She identifies herself with most of the great goddesses of pagan antiquity, from Rome and Sicily to Cyprus and Phrygia: despite different local names and different local rituals, all people worship the same divinity. Soon enough, the Virgin Mary would top—and topple—them all.

When Apuleius wrote these lines in the latter part of the 2nd century CE, most of the geographical area we assign to the religions of the ancient Mediterranean was united as part of the *Imperium Romanum* that stretched from the Rhine to the Euphrates and from Britain to Libya and Upper Egypt; the lands east of the Euphrates—Mesopotamia, Persia, Arabia—belonged to the

Parthians, who alternated between war and diplomacy with Rome. Many inhabitants of the empire were aware of its diverse and rich religious traditions, and an exchange among these traditions had been going on for some time already. Although mountains and deserts divided the land around the Mediterranean Sea into many small and distinct units (which accounted for the astounding variety of local cultures), the sea connected rather than separated the cultures along its shore; each river valley was a unit that was open to the sea as a common interface (see Horden and Purcell 2000).

The imperial capital itself attracted not only countless immigrants, but also their gods. Roman colonists in their turn carried Jupiter, Juno, and Minerva far east—Gaza in the corner between Palestine and Egypt even celebrated the Consualia, with its horse races in honor of the old and shadowy Roman god Consus (Jerome, *Life of Hilarion* 11). The Celtic goddess of horses, Epona, spread as far south as African Mauretania and as far east as Greek Corinth (Apuleius, *Golden Ass* 3.27); the Egyptian Isis had sanctuaries in Italy, Gaul, and Britain; and a recently invented mystery cult that borrowed elements from the myth and cult of Persian Mitra/Varuna spread all over the empire. More was to come. A small Jewish messianic sect that claimed one Christus as its founder was slowly conquering the empire, to be seriously challenged only by the followers of an Arabian merchant-turned-prophet from Mecca. If this cross-fertilization of religious traditions in the ancient Mediterranean is so highly visible in this period, how much further does it reach into the past?

The kaleidoscope of power

History helps to understand the area's character. The Mediterranean was not the only connecting factor: empire building had been going on for a long time already, and empires, even unloved ones, facilitate communication. Going backward in time, the Roman and Parthian empires appear as the heirs to the Hellenistic kingdoms that were carved out of Alexander's conquest—the kingdoms of the Ptolemies, the Seleucids, the Attalids of Pergamum—and that allowed Macedonian troops and Greek artists to dominate almost the entire region associated with the religions discussed in this volume. Before Alexander, the vast eastern regions, from Anatolia to Iran, Afghanistan, and Egypt, had been part of the Persian Empire, founded by Cyrus the Great. Cyrus had wrested it away from the Assyrians, whose empire had risen in the 9th and early 8th centuries, to embrace the entire region between Persia and the Mediterranean and even, for some time, Egypt. In the centuries immediately preceding the rise of the Assyrians—the "Dark Age" that separated the Bronze Age from the Iron Age—this space had been fragmented, with the sole exception of Egypt: at the very end of the Bronze Age, natural catastrophes and invaders (the somewhat enigmatic Sea Peoples) had destroyed the seemingly stable power structure of the Late Bronze Age. The city-states of Mesopotamia and the Levantine coast—not the least those of Phoenicia, the Neo-Hittite kingdoms along the modern border between Syria and Turkey, the small towns of mainland Greece, and the kingdoms of Phrygia and Urartu in central and eastern Anatolia—all led a more-or-less independent existence during these centuries. The 2nd millennium, "centuries of unity" in Braudel's words, owed its unity and stability to a few large powers. Earlier in the millennium, the Babylonians had ruled in Mesopotamia and the adjacent areas, the Hittites in central Anatolia, while Egypt kept inside the Nile Valley; after about 1400 BCE, the Hittites pushed south toward Syria and Palestine and the Egyptians came north to meet them in the Battle of Carchemish, which settled the balance of power for a while. Smaller western Asiatic states such as Ugarit flourished, owing changing allegiances to the current dominant power, and the Minoan and Mycenaean kinglets in Greece kept their political independence at the margins of the larger powers, all the while eagerly absorbing their dazzling cultural achievements. Only Persia—the Empire of Elam in the hills east of the Tigris— was relatively isolated; its time would come later. The picture is somewhat hazier before that; the 3rd millennium was dominated by the splendor of Egypt's Old Kingdom and the many thriving and rival cities of the Sumerians and Akkadians between the Tigris and the Euphrates.

The one and the many

Political geography is not irrelevant for the history of religion. The existence of large, more-or-less unified regions, which characterized the eastern Mediterranean from the late 3rd millennium onward, made inland communication relatively easy long before the Persians used the famous Royal Road that led from the western shore of Turkey well beyond Mesopotamia. The coasts had always been in easy communication with each other: the Mediterranean encouraged travel and contact, either along the shore or, hopping from island to island, over vaster bodies of water, even from the south coast of Crete to the Nile Delta or from Sicily and Sardinia to Spain. The epochs during which communication was slow in the eastern Mediterranean were short and transitory, and relatively intensive communication must be at least as old as the 7th and 6th millennia, when agriculture and urban structures rapidly spread throughout the entire Fertile Crescent. This argues for a relative homogeneity—or at least an osmotic similarity—of cultural space, which has an important consequence for historical methodology: whenever we spot parallels and agreements in ritual and mythology, diffusion, however complex, is as likely an explanation as is parallel origin.

The means of transmission, however, are numerous and not always clear. Commerce, diplomacy, and exile led individuals to travel or live abroad. "Send this boy to Yamhad or to Qatna, as you see fit," ordered Hammurabi, according to a letter from Mari; and the Egyptian Sinuhe was living quite comfortably as a local dignitary among the Asians before the pharaoh recalled him; we are not told whether he took a god back with him. Sometimes, however, even gods paid diplomatic visits, as did Shaushka "of Nineveh, mistress of all land," who visited Amunhotep IV after 1350 BCE. Foreign wives were another matter. Dynastic marriages were common among the elite of the ancient Near East, as not only the Amarna Letters demonstrate. "The LORD was angry with Solomon" because he not only married many foreign wives (bad in itself) but because he followed their gods—"Ashtoreth [Astarte] the goddess of the Sidonians, . . . Milcom the loathsome god of the Ammonites, . . . Chemosh the loathsome god of Moab"—and even built shrines for them (1 Kings 11.5–9). Much later, the empress Julia Domna still favored her local Syrian gods while in Rome. There is no way of telling how transitory an influence the gods and cults had that these wives brought with them; the Syrian gods, however, backed by an immigrant community, did last some time. Conquerors brought gods with them, as did merchant communities and colonists. In the 2nd century CE, someone in Lydian Sardis renewed a sacred law written under the occupation of Artaxerxes II that regulated a Persian cult. The Thracian goddess Bendis, the Egyptian Isis, and the Sidonian Astarte arrived in Athens with the community of foreign traders that established itself in Piraeus.

The ease of communication had, from early on, worked to smooth over differences inside the wider region; and common socioeconomic conditions helped. All of the major players, even when speaking very different languages, were inhabitants of city-states, sharing a rather similar outlook on the world and comparable ideals and lifestyles. Whether ruled by a priest, a king, a group of aristocrats, or the city council and the citizens' assembly—all were living in urban centers that usually were walled, had a main temple and (when ruled by kings) a palace, with a high degree of commercial exchange and a rural hinterland controlled by the city; further outside were the nomadic pastoralists in the deserts of Syria and Judea or the mountains of Anatolia and Persia. The cities in turn had grown on the foundation of agriculture that defined the region since the Neolithic revolution and set it against the nomadic pastoralists. The city-states might be united under a powerful ruler, as they were under Egypt's god-king or the Hittite or Iranian conquering warrior caste; they might be conquered and sometimes destroyed by a powerful neighbor; or they might flourish by establishing changing coalitions: this only marginally affected their function as unities that were more-or-less self-sufficient. In religious terms, this meant that each city had its own pantheon, its own calendar of festivals, and its own mythology; alliances or political dependence on another power could express themselves in additional cultic elements that did not fundamentally alter the overall appearance of the cults.

The relative homogeneity is mirrored in the history of the writing systems. Egypt invented its own complex system and stuck to it for almost three millennia; knowledge of hieroglyphic writing petered out only during Roman imperial times, at about the time when the Copts began to develop their own alphabetic system. Throughout the Bronze Age, the rest of the region almost universally used the cuneiform system invented in Mesopotamia and now proving adaptable to all sorts of languages, including, albeit somewhat clumsily, Indo-European Hittite. Only the marginal Minoans had their own syllabic system for internal use, which they handed over to the Mycenaeans for use in yet a different language, Greek. The collapse of the Late Bronze Age empires destroyed this unity, but also opened the chance for the spread of a vastly improved system; whereas Cyprus adapted the Mycenaean syllabic systems and the late Hittite kingdoms developed their own hieroglyphs, the West Semites invented a much better alphabetic script. It adapted itself to every language, its twenty-odd signs were easily mastered, and so it spread rapidly to Greece, Anatolia, and Italy, in local variations whose vestiges are still with us today. The persistence of these variations—including Hebrew, Phoenician, and Aramaic in the east—should warn us against overrating the cultural and religious homogeneity and neglecting the force of local identities even in the 1st millennium of the Iron Age: it is a homogeneity of broad outlines, not of details.

Musical divinities

The give and take among religious traditions easily reaches back to even before the Mediterranean Bronze Age. This at least is what an emblematic case, the cult of the goddess Cybele, the "Great Mother" *(Magna Mater)* of Greeks and Romans, suggests (Borgeaud 1996; Roller 1999). Ancient worshipers and modern scholars alike agree that the goddess as we know her was Phrygian in origin. Her city, Pessinus, remained a theocracy under the archpriest of the Great Mother well into Roman times; her priests were eunuchs who had initiated themselves into the cult through self-castration. In early Iron Age Phrygia, the goddess was omnipresent. Inscriptions called her *Matar* (Mother), sometimes adding the epithet *kubileya,* which ancient Greek authors derived from the Phrygian word for "mountain."

The goddess arrived in Greece in the 8th or 7th century BCE, first on the eastern islands, but very soon as far west as southern Italy. The Greeks called her "Mountain Mother" *(Meter Oreia),* in a close translation of her Phrygian name, but also turned her epithet into the proper noun Cybele—and identified her with Rhea, the mother of Zeus, thus turning the foreigner into a native of venerable antiquity. In Phrygia and in Greece, she had cults on mountains, where her images or altars were directly sculpted from living rock. Such images in Phrygia, carved into mountain cliffs, represent her frontally and standing; the Greeks partly adopted this, but soon abandoned it in favor of showing her on a throne between two standing felines (lionesses or panthers). This image appears so often in archaic eastern Greece that it must cover a variety of local goddesses, all perceived by their worshipers as being akin to the Phrygian goddess. Eastern Greeks also called her Kybebe: as such, she had a cult in Lydian Sardis and in many cities further east. Kybebe is the Hellenization of another Anatolian divine name, Kubaba, the main goddess of Carchemish, an age-old city-state in northern Syria and the main link between Mesopotamia and Anatolia, an influential power after 1000 BCE. Kubaba's animal was the lion;

her cult in Sardis was ecstatic, like the cult of Cybele, but it lacked the eunuchs and castration that were typical of the cult of the Phrygian Lady. Although Greeks and Romans identified Cybele and Kybebe, the eastern Greeks sometimes perceived a difference and Hellenized Kybebe/Kubaba as Artemis or Aphrodite, the former identification stressing her nature as mistress of wild animals, the latter her erotic power.

Cybele's mythology was very rich. In the Pessinuntian myth that was given a Greek form in the late 4th century BCE (Arnobius, *Against the Pagans* 5.5–7), Cybele's companion is Agdistis, a goddess born from Zeus's intercourse with a rock—a story that is very close to the Hittite myth of Ullikummi from the Cycle of Kumarbi: the diorite monster Ullikummi is born from Kumarbi's intercourse with a rock and is as destructive as Agdistis. More common is the story of Cybele's love affair with the prince and shepherd Attis, which resulted in Attis's self-castration and death. Many stories narrated the terrible fate that befell a lover of the Great Goddess, beginning with the Sumerian poem of Inanna and Dumuzi and ending with the Homeric *Hymn to Aphrodite* (Inanna too, like Kybebe, was understood to be identical to Aphrodite). Gilgamesh was able to recite a long *leporello* of Ishtar's damaged lovers, in an episode that resonates in Diomedes' attack on Aphrodite in book 5 of Homer's *Iliad*. The stories thus lead back toward the Anatolian and Mesopotamian Bronze Age.

In archeology and cult, however, the Great Mother is difficult to grasp during the Bronze Age—but her iconography is already attested in late Neolithic Anatolia: a mother-goddess is highly visible in Neolithic Çatal Höyük in central Anatolia (ca. 6200–5400 BCE), represented in a statuette of an enthroned and naked motherly goddess with felines at her side, which looks tantalizingly close to the iconography of the Great Mother from early Iron Age Greece. In the same Neolithic settlement, a mother-goddess is closely associated with bulls—a symbolism that has been connected with the agricultural revolution of the region and its concomitant "revolution of symbols" (Cauvin) and that resonates, millennia later, especially in Minoan religious iconography.

This situation is complex, but typical. A neat unilinear derivation, dear to scholars, is impossible: Greek Cybele/Kybebe looks back to Pessinus and to Carchemish, and it is highly probable that the cult entered the Greek world from Anatolia from at least two sanctuaries: a sanctuary near Colophon in Ionia and another one in Cyzicus on the Hellespont are likely candidates. During the Bronze Age, the cult never really surfaces for us. This must have to do with the nature of our tradition, which is concentrated on the Hittite capital and the ritual world of the court: Kubaba, "Queen of Carchemish," becomes highly visible as soon as the Hittite power collapses. But there were stories, traditions both in Anatolia and in Mesopotamia, that were close to her. And she made her first appearance, quite impressively, in late Neolithic times: one suspects that this, too, is connected with the nature and social function of her cult in these very first urban agricultural settlements. There must have been religious traditions as old as the Neolithic Age, tenaciously preserved and distributed throughout much of western Asia, whose visibility for us depends fundamentally on the nature of the sources that are, before the epigraphic and textual explosion of the Iron Age, very narrow windows on the past indeed.

The Phrygian Matar Kubileya is not the only migrating divinity, although her story might be more complex than many, and such migration is not confined to the 1st millennium when, among others, the Etruscans and Romans adopted Greek gods such as Apollo or Asclepius. In the late Bronze Age, some Babylonian divinities such as Ea also gained a place in the pantheon of the Hittites, at the side of original Hittite and immigrant Hurrian divinities. Anat, the female companion of Baal in Ugarit, became popular in Egypt, especially during the 19th and 20th Dynasties; her consort Baal is present from the 18th Dynasty onward. Among the casualties of war were many divine images—the Hittites, we hear, abducted the image of Shimigi from Qatna in Syria (El Amarna no. 55), and the Persian conquerors took the statues of the gods together with all kinds of cult equipment and sacred writing from Egyptian shrines. While it is not clear whether this happened for religious reasons or because those statues were made of precious materials, at least the Romans had a habit of transferring the cults of conquered neighboring cities to their own.

One consequence of this general awareness, at least among Greeks and Romans, was what scholars call, with a term borrowed from Tacitus, *interpretatio*—to treat the divine names of other religious systems as translations of one's own: a divine name, in this reading, is nothing more than a linguistic marker, different in each individual culture, for a divine entity whose existence transcends those cultures. When informing his readers about the gods of other peoples, Herodotus consistently uses the Greek names, as when he talks about the Scythians: "They adore only the following gods: mostly Hestia, then Zeus and Gaea (they have the tradition that Gaea is Zeus's wife), after them Apollo, Aphrodite Urania, Heracles, and Ares" (*Histories* 4.59). Later historians repeat the procedure: "Among the gods, they adore especially Mercurius . . . , after him Apollo, Mars, Jupiter, and Minerva," Caesar writes about the Gauls (*Gallic Wars* 6.17). This reflects the attitude of worshipers as well, from Lydians and Lycians of Herodotus's time to the inhabitants of imperial Syria or Gaul. Votive inscriptions and sacred laws use the divine name in the language they are written in, and even theophoric names are translated: the same person who is Dionysicles in a Greek document turns into Bakivalis in a Lydian one. The list of the homologues of Isis in Apuleius follows this tradition. The habit of interpretation, however, is much older: in Hesiod's *Theogony*, Uranus (Sky) corresponds to Akkadian Anu (Sky); Cronus to Hurrian Kumarbi, Sumerian Ea, and Akkadian Enki in the Babylonian succession myth. Whoever brought those stories to Greece translated the names. And he must simply have repeated what his bilingual Near Eastern informers, long accustomed to this, told him; the translating habit goes far back. The Sumerian-Akkadian bilingual lists of divine names must be the result of bureaucratic interest in a Mesopotamia where, in the 3rd millennium, the two languages coexisted. Again, it is Egypt that seems to remain somewhat isolated during the Bronze Age and gives the impression of being different even later. It is not by chance that Herodotus—who otherwise makes constant use of Greek names everywhere—uses the Egyptian names Osiris for what "the Egyptians say is Dionysus" (2.42) and Isis for she who is "Demeter in the language of the Greeks" (2.59; see Monotheism and Polytheism).

This linguistic habit, however, has consequences. Hellenistic Isis can be depicted with the attributes of Demeter, take over her epithets, such as "bringer of wealth" *(ploutodoteira)* or "lawgiver" *(thesmophoros),* and be described with qualities that come from Greece: "Among Greek cities, you love most Athens: there, you brought forth grain for the first time, and Triptolemus distributed it to the Greeks, riding a chariot drawn by your sacred snakes." This statement, from an aretalogy of Isis (i.e., a long list of her accomplishments), transfers elements of Eleusinian Demeter to the Egyptian goddess. In the Late Bronze Age, Assur, the main god of the Assyrians, was not only identified with the Akkadian Enlil, but also took over Enlil's role as the god of destiny. Canaanite Baal, present in Egypt after the 18th Dynasty as a warlike and aggressive divinity, sometimes took over the iconography of Seth: that might explain why an Egyptian myth makes Seth lust after Anat, the Ugaritic consort of Baal. In Hittite Anatolia, sun-divinities were important; scholars point out that a Hurrian and Hittite sun-god were identified and that the Akkadian Shamash lent them details of mythology and iconography, whereas the sun-goddess of Arinna was identified with Hepat, a goddess whom the Greeks later knew as Lydian Hipta, nurse of Dionysus.

Earlier scholars called all this "syncretism." More recently, this term has come under scrutiny: originally, it was a term of Christian missionary theology, censuring the admixture of native religious traditions to Christian belief and practice in a colonial setting; thus, it was a normative term. The use of similarly normative terms in the history of religion—in a project that can be only descriptive—has always created problems, most famously in the case of the term *magic,* not the least because the necessary redefinition of the term proved difficult and contentious, as the divergences in its use even in this volume show (see Magic). Thus, more recently, syncretism was replaced by the more-fashionable term *hybridity.* This term originated in colonial history and was also adopted to describe immigrant cultures; it always refers to the result of adaptations and assimilation of either native or immigrant cultures or languages to the dominant culture or language. Neither term describes accurately the processes of transfer and assimilation that have been going on in Mediterranean religions over the millennia, from the late Neolithic period to the rise of Christianity. Sometimes, a dominant culture was the origin of religious features—the Hittites were influenced by the Mesopotamian cultures, the Minoan and Mycenaeans by Egypt and the Levant, the Etruscans and Romans by the Greeks who arrived in southern Italy as colonists. Sometimes, items of a conqueror's religion were taken over by the conquered—the West Semite Hyksos brought Baal and Anat to Egypt, the Persians brought Anaitis and the fire cult to Anatolia. Sometimes, the conquerors adopted large parts of the religious system already in place—most famously the Hittites, although the evidence is

so closely focused on the king that it might distort the facts: the king had political reasons for concentrating the empire's religious traditions in his own hand.
In other places, the natives resisted the pressure of conquerors or colonizers:
the eastern Greeks turned the Persian term for a religious functionary, *magu-*,
into a term of abuse, while the Scythians on the northern shore of the Black Sea
killed their king when he became infected with the cult of Dionysus in Greek
Olbia (Herodotus, *Histories* 4.79). The Egyptians kept their distance from the
Greek settlers in Naucratis, who continued their local cults of Athena or Dionysus; if anything, the settlers shaped details of their cult after impressive
Egyptian rituals that they witnessed.

Inhabitants of the ancient Mediterranean, it seems, thus could travel wherever they wanted and almost always meet the gods they knew; sometimes,
there might have been different stories attached to them—the Scythians, according to Herodotus, thought that Zeus's wife was Gaea; the Babylonians
narrated, as a citizen of Ugarit might have realized with some surprise, that
their Astarte, whom the Babylonians called Ishtar and the Sumerians Inanna,
once had been taken prisoner by her sister, the queen of the dead. But when
Hittites imagined that their Zeus, the storm-god Teshub, had been born from
his father's body, some Greek traveler or merchant brought this back in a
somewhat garbled form, as the story that ended with Cronus vomiting up the
five siblings of Zeus together with the stone that he had swallowed instead of
his youngest son.

There were, of course, exceptions, where theological centralization im-
printed believers with the uniqueness of their own god—most prominent in
Judaism after its turn toward monotheism and then of course in Christianity.
But neither denied the existence of gods of the others—it was an ongoing concern of Israel's religious elite to prevent the cult of all those Baalim. The Christians quickly turned the many gods of the others into *daimonia* (1 Cor. 10.20–
21), to be fought and exorcised. And the polytheists refused to recognize the
uniqueness of the one God and, continuing their interpretative mood, turned
YHWH into yet another form of Dionysus or of Baal.

Rituals and places

If, thus, travelers in the Mediterranean world found their own gods everywhere, albeit somewhat disguised at times and speaking in foreign tongues,
would they also have been able to participate comfortably in another culture's
cults or at least have recognized places of cult and understood most of the
things they saw being performed? And, as a possible consequence of this: is the
process of osmosis and assimilation that is visible with regard to the divine
world also visible in the forms of rituals and their physical surroundings?

The basic forms of cult seem to have been recognizable enough. When, in an
Ovidian tale, a young traveler from Greek Thebes passes an altar somewhere
in Lycia, "black with soot and ashes," he imitates his local companion who is

mumbling a short prayer—nothing more than "bless me"—and then wants to know "whether this altar belongs to the nymphs, to Pan, or to a local divinity" (*Metamorphoses* 6.325–30). In other words, this foreigner recognizes the altar as a marker of sacred space and a focus of the rituals connected with it, but he is unable to name the recipient of the cult. Similarly, Herodotus had no problem identifying processions, sacrifices, festivals, temples, images, and altars when traveling in Egypt—to the extent that he derived Greek religion from Egyptian, as some centuries later Dionysius of Halicarnassus derived Roman religion from Greek.

Prayer and sacrifice, but also libation, procession, and votive gift, are the elements of cult that, in manifold combinations, made up the impressive festivals of ancient cities or were performed, alone or in combination, by individuals on their own behalf; altar, temple, and image were markers of space where cult took place. These ritual and architectural forms are almost ubiquitous elements of religion—this must be the reason that a foreigner could recognize them and understand their basic message.

When thus, on this very basic level, ritual might have been understandable throughout human societies, the question begins to be much more complex once we look into transfer and assimilation, and not only because of the problem of attestation. While one's own gods certainly were part of what defined one's identity—as was one's city, one's language, and one's family—the rituals in which one participated and their very specific forms, which were learned from early youth, defined identity even more so. Changing rituals can be understood to threaten loss of identity, as the debate about reforming the Catholic liturgy after the Second Vatican Council made clear. And over and over again, religious innovation and protest resulted in new rituals—the sacrifices of Pythagoreans or Zoroastrians, the strictness of Jewish ritual rules, the specific forms of baptism or Eucharist in early Christian groups all defined in-groups against outsiders. And even outside this conscious step of distancing one's group from all the others, differentiation through behavior is vital because it is behavior—not belief—that is visible. Meuli (1975: I.336) tells the story of the German woman who attended a funeral in a neighboring village and inquired solicitously whether one should start weeping already in the funeral home or only when in the cemetery—local customs matter, and if they did even in the highly normative world of Christian ritual, all the more so in the much more diverse and much less normative world of the early Mediterranean cultures. Pausanias's guidebook, the sacred laws, and the many etiological stories can teach us how many varieties of the basic sacrificial ritual existed even in the linguistically and culturally rather uniform world of Hellenistic Greece.

Furthermore, even small differences can carry significance and express social function, which makes assimilations much harder—or makes borrowing a highly selective and conscious process. Libation, the visible pouring out of an often valuable liquid such as oil or wine, is a ritual act that some scholars have traced back to prehuman origins. Whereas in Greek and Roman cult, libations are usually part of an overall sacrificial ritual or else confined to small gestures such as the one that opened and closed the symposium, they were much more visible in the eastern monarchies; this has been seen as asserting social superiority through the royal gesture of conspicuously squandering wealth. Libation vessels with elegant long spouts thus become important items in Bronze Age Anatolia and Mesopotamia—but also, at about the same time, at the royal courts of Shang and Chou China. This should teach us how easily a similar function—to turn libation into a conspicuous act—generates a similar form.

Still, transmission and borrowing are well attested in the sphere of ritual. Not all cases are as straightforward as the case of scapegoat rituals. To drive out an animal or a person charged with all the negative forces of the community is something that West Semitic and Greek cities shared, and it seems to have drifted west in the early Iron Age; this is benignly simple (see Ritual). The case of hepatoscopy—the practice of using the liver of a sacrificial sheep to divine the future—is more intriguing. It is attested in Mesopotamia, Syria-Palestine, Anatolia, and Etruria, not the least by the existence of surprisingly similar liver models that were used to help the diviner's memory. Again, a movement from east to west is highly likely, despite the intriguing and unexplained absence of the technique in Greece, the natural interface between the Levantine east and Italy.

More complex still is sacrifice. Everywhere in the Mediterranean world, sacrifice was at the center of cult. Its ostensible purpose was to feed the gods or the dead: most often, from Ur to Rome, sacrifice was understood as a common banquet of gods and humans. Thus, as in human diet, the meat of freshly slaughtered domestic animals was the choice dish, but all other food, from bread and fruit to wine, water, and oil, was used as well. Refusal to participate in animal sacrifice is always the result of theology and, in some sense, a protest against the killing, be it the Zoroastrians' cult of pure fire or the Pythagoreans' vegetarianism, which was grounded in their eschatological beliefs in reincarnation. Beyond this very general agreement, which again goes well beyond the Mediterranean world, things become complex and diverse. To convey the food to the gods by burning—to take one of the most conspicuous traits in Greek and Roman sacrifice—was no universal practice: in the large and rich Mesopotamian and Egyptian temples, the priests of the king received the food and presented it to the gods; then, the priest and their human guests ate it themselves. This is why the ritual of "Opening the Mouth" is the fundamental ritual for installing a cultic image in Mesopotamia and Egypt: "This statue without its mouth opened cannot smell incense, cannot eat food, nor drink water," as a ritual incantation has it. But the prerogative of priests to feed on the sacrifice is widespread even where burning dominates. When the newly conscripted Delphic priests of Apollo despair about living high up on a barren mountain, the god comforts them: "Each of you, a knife in his right hand, will continuously slaughter sheep, and you will have plenty, since the mortals will bring always them to me" (Homeric *Hymn to Apollo* 535–37). West Semites, in marked difference from the Mesopotamians and Egyptians, burnt the gods' parts on their altars, as did the Greeks already in the Mycenaean age and later

the Romans and Etruscans; they did not feed the images but the gods themselves. Hebrews, after all, had no cult images at all, whereas Greeks and
Romans consecrated them in a different way or not at all. The sequence of
burning and banquet is common to all of them, as is the presence of both
"whole offering" and "shared offering," the rite of entirely burning the animal
and the rite of sharing it in a banquet. Lines of transmission can be guessed at,
but they are complex: while the correspondence of Hebrew *bāmâ* (high place
of cult) and Greek *bōmos* (altar) seems to point to a derivation of the western
rite from the West Semitic world—with perhaps Cyprus as an interface—the
most conspicuous form of altar in Greece, the ever-growing heap of ashes and
remains of burnt animals, has parallels in central Europe already in the Late
Bronze Age. The practice of burning animals could have arrived in Greece
from several sides and is perhaps an Indo-European heritage reinforced from
the West Semitic east.

In other cases again, a common phenomenon does not necessarily call for
an explanation of transfer and assimilation. Ecstatic or "intuitive" prophecy
is known all over the globe, and it is well at home in the ancient Mediterranean. Ecstatic prophets were widely attested in Mari during the epoch of
Hammurabi, and their similarity to more recent biblical prophecy has been
noted; the temporal distance, however, forbids the assumption of a simple
transfer. Female ecstatics are well attested in the cult of Ishtar at Arbela in the
Assyrian epoch; not much later, the Greeks have their Sibyl and the Delphic
Pythia, but also the male prophet Bacis; the fame of the Sibyl survives the
Christianization of the Roman Empire. While specialists like this can be imagined as itinerant and thus as easy agents of transfer, it is impossible to indicate
simple lines of development, and there might be no necessity for it: suffice it to
indicate, once again, a common religious matrix.

In this essay, I have regarded the religions of the ancient Mediterranean world
as being in constant contact with each other—a contact that, similar to that of
languages in contact, resulted both in assimilation and in dissimilation. I have
not looked for specific characteristics of "the" religions of the ancient Mediterranean world, beyond their being in almost constant contact; in fact, this, to
me, seems their main characteristic. This is a rather minimalist approach. I am
not looking for unique characteristics, those traits that would differentiate the
religions of the ancient Mediterranean from, say, the religions of Southeast
Asia or of Mesoamerica. To look for such unique traits in cultural studies too
often proves elusive and is motivated as often by ideological longings as by dis-
interested scholarly concerns. Rather, I am looking for characteristics that confirm the relative unity that would justify the enterprise of studying these different religious cultures together in one vast project. Already the political and
social histories of the world between the Italian peninsula and the mountains
east of the Tigris argue for a high degree of interpenetration that began well before the Late Bronze Age, and the same is true for cultural history, although
here, research has barely begun. The margins, as always, might be somewhat

hazy and permeable to an outsider—ancient Iran also looks toward India, Celtic northern Italy toward Gaul and Spain: there are no sharp boundaries in cultural history. But the space in itself is clearly defined.

Nor have I given in to the temptation to sketch a typology of religions according to the major sociopolitical forms, the opposition between city-states and nomadic tribes being the main divide. But while the different concerns of these groups certainly were reflected by the different functions of their divinities and their rites, any more constant and fundamental difference in the religious systems is elusive. Jewish monotheism cannot be explained by nomadic pastoralism alone, but is the result of a complex constellation of social, economical, and political forces. Many city-states such as Mari combined city dwellers and nomads or developed their sedentary city life from a former nomadic life. This double origin was easily visible in lifestyle choices, but proves considerably more elusive in religion. We lack a clear religious parallel to the exhortation of a prophet in Mari to his king "to ride in a chariot or on a mule" and not to ride a horse, to follow the example of the "Akkadians," not the nomads—both lifestyles were available, but with different values attached (*Archives Royales de Mari,* Tabl. VI.76.20). Cultural systems, furthermore, can retain (and sometimes resemanticize) elements that belong to former sociopolitical systems—the pastoralist's reed hut remains prominent in Mesopotamian rituals well into the Iron Age, and the Greek pantheon remains organized as a royal court even under Athenian democracy. No theory up to now convincingly correlates social and religious systems, and most attempts by sociologists such as Max Weber or Niklaus Luhmann have concentrated on Christianity and sometimes naively generalized Christian conceptions of religion. Other possible differences, such as the difference between the religion of a city-state and of a kingdom that unites many city-states, are even less relevant: we do not deal with different religious systems but with rituals designed to express the status of the king. These rituals are, on the king's side, rituals of his court, and, on the city's side, additions to the already existing body of rituals and beliefs, but they do not change the system.

Bibliography

Borgeaud, Philippe. *La mère des dieux: De Cybèle à la Vierge Marie.* Paris: Seuil, 1996.

Braudel, Fernand. *Les mémoires de la Méditerranée: Préhistoire et antiquité.* Paris: Fallois, 1998. English translation: *Memory and the Mediterranean.* Tr. Siân Reynolds. New York: Knopf, 2001.

Burkert, Walter. "Opfertypen und antike Gesellschaftsstruktur." In *Der Religionswandel unserer Zeit im Spiegel der Religionswissenschaft,* ed. Günther Stephenson. Darmstadt: Wissenschaftliche Buchgesellschaft, 1976.

Cauvin, Jacques. *Naissance de divinités, naissance de l'agriculture: La révolution des symboles au néolithique.* Paris: CNRS, 1998. English translation: *The Birth of the Gods and the Origins of Agriculture.* Tr. Trevor Watkins. Cambridge: Cambridge University Press, 2000.

Dick, Michael B., ed. *Born in Heaven, Made on Earth: The Making of the Cult Image in the Ancient Near East.* Winona Lake, Ind.: Eisenbrauns, 1999.

Horden, Peregrin, and Nicholas Purcell. *The Corrupting Sea: A Study of Mediterranean History.* Oxford: Blackwell, 2000.

Meuli, Karl. *Gesammelte Schriften,* ed. Thomas Gelzer. Basel, 1975.

Porter, Barbara Nevling, ed. *One God or Many? Concepts of Divinity in the Ancient World.* [Chebeague, Maine:] Casco Bay Assyriological Institute, 2000.

Ribichini, Sergio, Maria Rocchi, and Paolo Xella, eds. *La questione delle influenze vicino-orientali sulla religione greca: Stato degli studi e prospettive della ricerca.* Atti del Colloquio Internazionale, Roma, 20–22 maggio 1999. Rome: Consiglio nazionale delle ricerche, 2001.

Roller, Lynn E. *In Search of God the Mother: The Cult of Anatolian Cybele.* Berkeley: University of California Press, 1999.

Monotheism and Polytheism

Jan Assmann

What is polytheism?

"Monotheism" and "polytheism" are recent words, not older than the 17th century CE, and they have different statuses. Monotheism is a general term for religions that confess to and worship only one god. "One God!" *(Heis Theos)* or "No other gods!" (first commandment)—these are the central mottos of monotheism. The religions subsumed under the term *polytheism* cannot, however, be reduced to a single motto of opposite meaning, such as "Many gods!" or "No exclusion of other gods!" On the contrary, the unity or oneness of the divine is an important topic in Egyptian, Babylonian, Indian, Greek, and other polytheistic traditions. Polytheism is simply a less polemical substitute for what monotheistic traditions formerly called "idolatry" and "paganism" (Hebrew *ăbôdâ zārâ*, Arabic *shirk* or *jahiliya*). Whereas monotheism constitutes a self-description of religions subsumed under that term, no such self-description exists for polytheistic religions. Monotheism asserts its identity by opposing itself to polytheism, whereas no polytheistic religion ever asserted itself in contradistinction to monotheism, for the simple reason that polytheism is always the older or "primary" and monotheism the newer or "secondary" type of religion. Monotheism is self-description, polytheism is construction of the other. However, although polytheistic religions include a concept of divine unity, these religions undoubtedly do worship a plethora of gods, which justifies applying a word built on the element *poly* (many) to them. Unity in this case does not mean the exclusive worship of one god, but the structure and coherence of the divine world, which is not just an accumulation of deities, but a structured whole, a pantheon.

Theologia tripertita

The most cogent theory of polytheism comes from an ancient author. Varro's concept of a "tripartite theology" refers to a general structure that is perfectly well applicable not only to the Roman and Greek religions that Varro had in mind, but also to ancient Egyptian and Babylonian religions. These religions know three spheres or dimensions of divine presence and religious experience, which closely correspond to Varro's three theologies, showing that we are dealing here with a rather general structure of polytheism. His *theologia naturalis* (Greek *theologia kosmikē*, cosmic theology) corresponds to the cosmic dimension of divine manifestation; his *theologia civilis* (Greek *theologia politikē*, political theology) corresponds to the cultic dimension; and his *theologia fabularis* (Greek *theologia mythikē*, mythical or narrative theology) corresponds to the dimension of *historia divina*, the stories about the gods, their names, epithets, and genealogies (*Antiquitates rerum divinarum*, frags. 6–10 Cardauns).

Cosmos. The first dimension of divine presence or manifestation is the cosmos or nature. Polytheistic cosmology views the cosmos as a cooperative process: the deities cooperate in creating and maintaining the world. In Egypt, the sun-god and his daily course across the sky and the underworld beneath the earth form the center of this processual cosmology. In Babylonia and Greece, the gods seem to be less involved in maintaining the cosmic process and freer to intervene in human affairs. There, the aspect of unity and coherence is expressed above all in social and political terms, especially in the model of a royal court. However, the idea of a highest god who rules as a king over the world of gods is common to all polytheisms of the ancient world. Political philosopher Eric Voegelin has coined the term *Summo-Deism* in order to emphasize the hierarchical structure of polytheism. Typically, the highest god is also the creator (Marduk in Babylonia; Re, later Amun-Re, in Egypt; although in Greece and Rome, according to the best-known cosmologies, neither Zeus/Jupiter nor any other god creates the world; it simply develops out of Chaos on its own).

In Egypt, the highest god combines the aspects of creator, sun, and king. Here, the idea of unity seems most prominent. Before the monotheistic revolution of Akhenaten, however, the fundamental plurality of the divine world in its cosmic manifestation was never questioned. The cosmic process was viewed as an interplay of convergent and divergent powers. Two otherwise antagonistic powers, Horus, the god of royal legitimacy, and Seth, the god of anarchic violence and force, cooperated in defending the sun-god against Apopis, a water-dragon personifying chaos. The order must always be defended against a gravitation toward disorder or entropy. Order is time or movement, and it would come to an immediate standstill if the foe were definitely annihilated once and for all.

In the eyes of the Egyptians, the success of the cosmic process was always at risk. In the same way as the Mesopotamians, the Chinese, and the Romans, Egyptians were constantly occupied in watching the sky and in observing all kinds of natural phenomena with the greatest attention. But whereas in Mesopotamia, China, and Rome this attention was associated with various forms of divination that served to reveal the will of the gods and to foretell the future, in Egypt it was connected with the daily ritual that served to assist the gods in maintaining the world, supplementing divine action with ritual action. Thus, the Egyptians observed the regular and the recurrent, whereas cultures that focused on divination observed the exceptional and deviant. In the context of this task and their intellectual preoccupation with it, the Egyptians accumulated an incredible amount of knowledge, a kind of sacred cosmology, whereas the Sumerians and Babylonians, in the context of their preoccupation with divination, accumulated a similar mass of omen literature, which established connections between divine signs and historical or biographical events.

The cosmic dimension provides evidence of the gods through the natural world and its phenomena. Nobody would dream of denying the existence of the divine powers: they are overwhelmingly present in the shape of sun and moon; air, water, fire, and earth; life and death; war and peace; and so on. It is possible to neglect them, to break one of their specific taboos, to miss the correct performance of their rites, but it is impossible to either enter or leave a relationship which is always already established, into which we are born, and which is never the matter of a personal decision.

Cult and political organization. The second dimension consists of the various forms of terrestrial governance in which the gods of a polytheistic pantheon typically participate. The more important deities of a pantheon are "town-gods," and the more important urban centers of a country are a god's cities in the sense that they are strongly associated with the name of a deity whose temple is the chief temple of that town: Marduk and Babylon, Assur and the city Assur, Athena and Athens, Ptah and Memphis, and so on. The pantheon is an assembly of town lords and temple owners, headed, in some cases, by a god whose temple is in the capital and who, for this reason, rules not only his city but the whole country (e.g., Marduk and Babylon) or, in other cases, who has important cults in virtually every city, even if the city worships another divinity as its own (e.g., Zeus is prominent even in Athens). Aspects both of unity and of diversity are prominent in the political and geographical dimensions of godhead as well. The aspect of unity can be represented by the unity of a country and its hierarchical structure of center and periphery (as in Egypt) or by the periodic gathering together of different towns' citizens at centralized cult places such as Olympia (as in Greece), whereas the aspect of diversity finds its expression in the specific identity and profile of the individual towns and regions.

The political dimension of the divine world may also be called cultic, because it is in their function as town lords and ladies that the deities receive cultic worship. The cult is the service that a lord or lady requires and resembles in many respects a royal ceremonial. The feasts are typically celebrated in the form of a procession and have the clear political meaning of territorial ownership and its annual confirmation.

Myth. The third dimension may be called the personal or biographical aspect of the divine world. In a polytheistic religion, a deity cannot be spoken about without reference to other deities. The gods live, act, and display their personalities and characters in interaction, not only or even primarily with humans, but with one another, in relation to other gods, in "constellations" that find their expression in myths, genealogies, epithets, names—in short, in everything that can be said about a deity. Divine constellations reflect the fundamental order and elementary structure of human society—husband and wife, brother and sister, mother and son, mother and daughter, father and son, father and daughter, lover and beloved, lord and slave, hero and enemy, and so on. These constellations unfold in stories (myths) of equally fundamental character, founding and modeling the basic structures of human life, institutions, hopes, and experience: love and death, war and peace, identity and transformation, suffering and salvation. The relation between the divine and the human world is anthropomorphic rather than anthropocentric. The natural partner of a deity is another deity, not humanity. The gods of a polytheistic pantheon care above all for themselves, in the second place for their cities and their followers, and only exceptionally for humankind at large. But this relative distance between the divine and the human worlds is compensated for by intense analogy and a relationship of mutual modeling. The structures of the divine world and the stories about the gods reflect the fundamentals of human existence, but they function as models, and not as mirrors. The gods live and die, rule and serve, suffer and enjoy, win and are defeated: they set the norms and forms of human life, which repeats and reflects the timeless models and follows the traces of *historia divina*.

The "theologization" of history: Anthropomorphism and anthropocentrism

The tripartite structure of polytheism establishes a rather indirect relation between gods and humans. The sphere of direct encounters and interventions, which plays such an important role in Greek, Roman, and Babylonian mythology, seems to be missing. How shall we account for the widespread belief that illness and misfortune are expressions of divine wrath and that the gods intervene in various forms in human affairs? There seems to be a fourth dimension of divine manifestation and religious experience, which comprises human life and history.

In Egypt, we actually observe the emergence of history as a fourth parameter or dimension of the divine world, starting with the 18th Dynasty and gaining predominance in the Ramesside age (ca. 1300–1100 BCE). With the emergence of the dimension of history, the relationship between the divine and the human worlds changes from anthropomorphism to anthropocentrism. The gods not only maintain the cosmic process, not only dwell and rule on earth in their temples, and are not only involved in stories that take place in their own sphere among the gods—they also determine the course of human history on earth, the welfare of the state and the people; they do this by sending victories and defeats, health and illness, prosperity and disaster. In Egypt, this "theologization of history" is a new development. In Mesopotamia, however, as in Greece, Rome, and Bronze Age Anatolia, the religious meaning of history seems to have been a concept that was in place from the start. Gods supervise the observance of treaties and help to protect the integrity of their sanctuaries and cities. In Mesopotamia we also find the concept of a "personal god," which brings the worlds of gods and humans into closer relationship, while at the same time preserving the principle of plurality and diversity. Each human being has a specific personal god among the lesser gods, who cares for him or her and intercedes on his or her behalf with the greater gods.

Unlike Egypt, where any forms of historiography dealing with longer periods of the past are missing until the Greco-Roman period, Mesopotamia yields many royal inscriptions that narrate the entire extension of a reign and even texts that stretch back over a series of different reigns into the remote past. The Curse on Agade, for example, narrates the history of the rise and fall of the Sargonid Dynasty during the 23rd and 22nd centuries BCE. Among other events it relates how King Naram-Sin destroyed the temple of Enlil in Nippur and how Enlil responded to this crime by sending forth the Guteans, who put an end to the Sargonid Empire. Similarly, the fall of the Empire of Ur is traced back, in another text, to certain transgressions committed by King Shulgi. The theological and juridical concept of religious guilt and divine punishment gives meaning to history and coherence to the chain of events and sequence of dynasties. In Egypt, disaster is a manifestation of chaos and blind contingency. In Mesopotamia, however, it is read as the manifestation of the punishing will of a divinity whose anger has been stirred by the king. In yet other cultures, such as Greece, a disaster can be understood as preordained by fate *(moira)*, although fate's decrees are often carried out by the gods. An event such as the Trojan War, therefore, which was viewed as historical by the Greeks, can be given meaning within a larger context of ongoing human culture.

The apex of the theologization of history is reached with biblical, especially Deuteronomistic, historiography (see Van Seters 1983). The idea of forming an alliance with God instead of only appointing certain deities as supervisors of political alliances draws God much more closely into the ups and downs of human affairs than had been the case in Mesopotamia and its neighboring civilizations. There, history was just a field of possible interventions by the gods, favorable or punitive; now it turns into *one* coherent connection of events stretching from creation until the end of the world, a sequence known as *historia sacra* in the Judeo-Christian tradition.

However, the idea of divine verdict and intervention was not totally absent even in Egypt. On the contrary, the typically Egyptian idea of a judgment after death appears as the strongest possible manifestation of the principle of divine verdict. But the concept of postmortem human immortality provides a horizon of fulfillment beyond history, whereas in Mesopotamia and Israel, where the concept of human immortality is unknown, every account has to be settled on earth. Here, the horizon of fulfillment is confined to the terrestrial world, but stretched into the future, over generations and dynasties.

In Israel, this fourth dimension of theology tends to prevail over and, in the course of time, to replace the three others. With the rise of monotheism, the cosmos ceases to appear as a manifestation of divine presence and comes to be seen merely as the creation, the work of God. The geographical and cultic dimension is reduced, after the reform of King Josiah at the end of the 7th century, to the temple at Jerusalem and no longer reflects the pluralistic identity of various centers and regions. *Historia divina,* the stories that are told about the gods and that display their characters and their vicissitudes, is turned into *historia sacra,* the story of the One God and his chosen people. *Historia sacra* is the successor of both the third or mythic dimension of narrative articulation of divine constellations and the fourth dimension in the traditional Mesopotamian sense of divine intervention in human affairs. YHWH intervenes in human affairs not only occasionally; in entering the covenant with Israel, concern with human affairs becomes YHWH's dominant trait.

Historia sacra is a dimension of divine presence that excludes the principle of plurality. There can be but one lord of history, one divine partner in a story shared by god and humans. There are, however, surprising parallels to such an extremely anthropocentric conception of the divine even in Egypt. A passage in the Instruction for Merikare speaks of the ways that God cares for humans as his cattle or herd, in terms strongly reminiscent of biblical anthropocentrism:

> Humans are well cared for,
> the livestock of god:
> he made heaven and earth for their sake,
> he pushed the greediness of the waters back
> and created the air so that their nostrils might live.
> His images are they, having come forth from his body.
>
> For their sake he rises to heaven;
> it is for them that he has made plants and animals,
> birds and fish,
> so that they might have food.
> If he killed his enemies and went against his children,
> this was only because they thought of rebellion.
>
> For their sake he causes there to be light.
> To see them he travels [the heavens].
> He established for himself a chapel at their back.
> When they weep, he hears.
> He created for them a ruler in the egg
> and a commander to strengthen the backbone of the weak.
>
> He made for them magic as a weapon
> to ward off the blow of fate,
> watching over them night and day.
> He thrashed the cowardly among them,
> as a man beats his son for the sake of his brother.
> God knows every name.

This is not only an extremely anthropocentric view of creation, it is also a monotheistic view of the divine. The text speaks of God; other gods are not mentioned. This kind of monotheism, however, is not a matter of religion, but of genre and perspective. If one looks at the world in the way that this text does, the principles of plurality and differentiation disappear, and the ultimate unity of the divine appears. This perspective is characteristic of the genre of wisdom literature, a forerunner of moral philosophy that reflects in a very general way on the fundamentals of human existence. Egyptian wisdom literature generally speaks of god instead of specific gods. This is not only a generic term, to be filled in by a specific god as the case may be (*a* god instead of *the* god), but a specific term referring to the sun-god and creator, as in the Instruction of Merikare. In the perspective of moral philosophy, this is the only god that really counts, the one god on which everything else (including the other gods) depends. Such a "monotheism of perspective" is conventionally termed henotheism to distinguish it from monolatry as a monotheism of cult, worship, and commitment, whereas the term *monotheism* is reserved for a combination of both: the transformation of a henotheistic perspective into a full-fledged religion or vice versa, the transformation of a monolatrous cult (which recognizes the existence of other gods but worships only one) into a religion adopting the henotheistic perspective in which the other gods do not exist at all.

In Egypt, the henotheistic perspective of wisdom literature and the polytheism of cult coexist without any apparent conflict. During the New Kingdom, however, the henotheistic perspective starts to affect certain domains of temple literature as well, especially hymns to Amun-Re, the god of the capital, Thebes, who becomes identified with the sun-god of Heliopolis. An early hymn to this god, dating back perhaps even before the New Kingdom, adopts the anthropocentric and henotheistic perspective of Merikare:

> Hail, Re, lord of justice,
> whose chapel is hidden, lord of the gods,
> Khepri in his boat,
> at whose command the gods emerge,
> Atum, creator of human beings,
> who differentiates them and makes them live,
> who distinguishes people by the color of their skin,
> who hears the prayers of those in distress,
> and is well disposed to those who call on him,
> who rescues the fearful from the overbearing,
> who judges between rich and poor,
> lord of perception, on whose lips is the creative word,
> it is for his sake that Hapi has come,
> lord of sweetness, great of love,
> it is to make people live that he has come.

To be sure, the gods, plural, are mentioned in this text, which is still a far cry from real monotheism and even henotheism. Yet the gods are put on a level with humans and every other creature, and the general view is clearly anthropocentric and henotheistic. Akhenaten's monotheistic Amarna revolution is the radical consequence of this shift from mythical anthropomorphism to philosophical anthropocentrism. It realizes the henotheistic perspective in terms of cult and religious institutions, turning the sun- and creator-god into the sole and only one and denying the other gods any worship and even existence. In the aftermath of this revolutionary step, the gods are readmitted into cult and general worldview; the henotheistic perspective, however, still prevails, and the gods tend now to be demoted, especially in hymns to Amun, to "names," "manifestations," "symbols," "limbs," and so on, of the One. This post-Amarna theology is closer to pantheism than to monotheism; however, the tripartite structure of divine presence—the cosmic, cultic, and mythic dimensions—is again fully expressed in the religious life of the country, and the new concept of a fourth dimension, history, does not in any way invalidate the importance of the other three.

What is monotheism?

Evolutionary monotheism

The idea of unity is not alien to polytheistic religions. On the contrary, the emphasis on the oneness or uniqueness of God or the ultimate unity of the divine world with its plethora of deities is obvious in Mesopotamian and Egyptian texts and increases over time.

Translating gods. In polytheistic religions, the deities are clearly differentiated and personalized by name, shape, and function. The great achievement of polytheism is the articulation of a common semantic universe. It is this semantic dimension that makes the names translatable—that is, makes it possible for gods from different cultures or parts of a culture to be equated with one another. Tribal religions are ethnocentric. The powers and ancestral spirits worshiped by one tribe are different from those worshiped by another tribe. In contrast, the highly differentiated members of polytheistic pantheons lend themselves easily to cross-cultural translation or "interpretation." Translation functions because the names not only have a reference, but also a meaning, namely, the god's specific character as it is unfolded in cosmological speculation, myths, hymns, rites, and so on. This character makes a deity comparable to other deities with similar traits. The similarity of gods makes their names mutually translatable. But in historical reality, this correlation has to be reversed. The practice of translating the names of the gods created a concept of similarity and produced the idea or conviction that gods are international.

The tradition of translating or interpreting foreign divine names goes back to the innumerable glossaries equating Sumerian and Akkadian words, among which appear lists of divine names in two or even three languages, such as Emesal (women's language, used as a literary dialect), Sumerian, and Akkadian. The most interesting of these sources is the explanatory list *Anu sa ameli,* which contains three columns, the first giving the Sumerian name, the second the Akkadian name, and the third the functional definition of the deity. This explanatory list gives what may be called the meaning of divine names, making explicit the principle that underlies the equation or translation of divine names. In the Kassite period of the Late Bronze Age, the lists are extended to include languages such as Amorite, Hurrian, Elamite, and Kassite in addition to Sumerian and Akkadian. In these cases, the practice of translating divine names was applied to very different cultures and religions. The origin of this practice may be identified in the field of international law. Treaties had to be sealed by solemn oaths, and the gods invoked in these oaths had to be recognized by both parties. The list of these gods conventionally closes the treaty. They necessarily had to be equivalent as to their function and in particular as to their rank. Intercultural theology became a concern of international law.

The growing political and commercial interconnectedness of the ancient world and the practice of cross-cultural translation of everything, including divine names, gradually led to the concept of a common religion. The names, iconographies, and rites—in short, the cultures—differ, but the gods are the same. This concept of religion as the common background of cultural diversity and the principle of cultural translatability eventually led to the late Hellenistic mentality, for which the names of the gods mattered little in view of the overwhelming natural evidence for their existence and presence in the world.

Hyphenating gods. Scholars conventionally refer to an Egyptian phenomenon that might be compared to the Mesopotamian technique of translating gods as syncretism. It involves the collocation of two or three different gods, leading to hyphenated names such as Amun-Re, Amun-Re-Harakhty, Ptah-Sokar-Osiris, Hathor-Tefnut, Min-Horus, Atum-Khepri, Sobek-Re, and so on. As a rule, the first name refers to the cultic/local dimension, the actual temple owner and lord of the town, whereas the second name refers to a translocal, preferably cosmic deity. Thus, Amun is the lord of Thebes, in whom the sun-god, Re, becomes manifest. Ptah is the lord of Memphis, Sokar the god of its necropolis, Osiris the god of the underworld and the dead whose Memphite representation is to be seen in Ptah-Sokar. This relationship between deities does not mean equation or fusion; the gods retain their individuality. Re does not merge into Amun or vice versa. The gods enter into a relationship of mutual determination and complementation: Re becomes the cosmic aspect of Amun, Amun the cultic and local aspect of Re; Atum refers to the nocturnal, and Khepri to the diurnal aspect of the sun-god. Hyphenation implies neither identification nor subordination; Amun has no precedence over Re, nor Re over Amun. In the course of time, however, this practice of "hyphenating" gods fosters the idea of a kind of deep structure identity.

A similar practice occurs in Greece, although with very different ramifications. A god worshiped throughout Greece, such as Artemis, may become associated with a local god whose traits are similar (thus in Arcadia we find Artemis Callisto). In these cases, however, an originally independent god—even a god who continues to be worshiped independently in some cases—is subordinated to the Panhellenic god both in the sense that the lesser god's altar is smaller than the greater god's and in the sense that myth makes the lesser god a "heroic" companion of the greater god.

"*All gods are One.*" In Mesopotamia, the pantheon is structured by strong hierarchical relations of subordination, and this, in the long run, fosters similar ideas of deep structural identity. The creation epic, the *Enuma Elish*, ends with a hymn to the chief god, Marduk, calling him by fifty names. The gods who are subordinated to Marduk become his names, aspects of his all-encompassing essence. Another text assembles a group of major deities, identifying them with roles of Marduk:

> Ninirta is Marduk of the hoe,
> Nergal is Marduk of the attack,
> Zababa is Marduk of the hand-to-hand fight,
> Enlil is Marduk of lordship and counsel,
> Nabium is Marduk of accounting,
> Sin is Marduk, the illuminator of the night,
> Shamash is Marduk of justice,
> Adad is Marduk of rains.

A hymn of Assurbanipal addresses Marduk as carrying the identity of the three highest gods as personal properties: "You hold the Anu-ship, the Enlil-ship, the Ea-ship." The culmination of these tendencies is reached when the whole pantheon comes to be seen as just aspects of one supreme god. "All gods are three," we read in an Egyptian text (Papyrus Leiden 1.350), which moreover states that these three gods are just aspects of one god:

> All gods are three:
> AMUN, RE, and PTAH, whom none equals.
> He who hides his name as Amun,
> he appears to the face as Re,
> his body is PTAH.

We easily discern here the three "dimensions" of polytheistic theology: name, cosmic appearance, and cultic "embodiment" in a statue, dwelling in a temple, ruling a city. These three dimensions, however, are encompassed and transcended by a god who is referred to as only "He." Amun is just a name screening the true and hidden name of this god, of whom another hymn states:

> People fall down immediately for fear
> if his name is uttered knowingly or unknowingly.
> There is no god able to call him by it.

In Egypt, this concept of a Supreme Being comprising in his essence the whole pantheon goes back to the Ramesside period (13th century BCE) and seems to be a reaction to Akhenaten's monotheistic revolution. It stresses the oneness of god while retaining the multiplicity of the divine. In the last instance, all gods are but One, the immanent manifold manifestation and diversification of a hidden and transcendent unity.

Hypsistos: belief in a Supreme Being. The idea that the various nations worshiped basically the same deities but under different names and in different forms eventually led to the belief in a Supreme Being (the Greek expression is *Hypsistos,* the Highest One) comprising in its essence not only all the myriads of known and unknown deities, but above all those three or four gods who, in the context of different religions, play the role of the highest god (usually Zeus, Sarapis, Helios, and Iao = YHWH). This superdeity is addressed by appellations such as *Hypsistos* (Supreme) and the widespread "One-God" predication *Heis Theos.* Oracles typically proclaim particular gods to be one and the same together with other gods:

> One Zeus, one Hades, one Helios, one Dionysus,
> One god in all gods.
> Pseudo-Justin, *Exhortation against the Greeks* 15 = Orphic frag. 239 (Macrobius, *Saturnalia* 1.18.17 quotes the first verse)

In one of these oracles, Iao, the god of the Jews, is proclaimed to be the god of time (Olam-Aion), appearing as Hades in winter, Zeus in springtime, Helios in summer, and "Habros Iao" in autumn. (Macrobius, *Saturnalia* 1.18.20; see Peterson 1926: 243–44; Hengel 1969: 476–77; and the inscription *Heîs Zeùs Sérapis Iaó* [CIL 2 suppl. 5665 = Dunand 1975: 170]). These oracles and predications manifest a quest for the sole and supreme divine principle beyond the innumerable multitude of specific deities. This is typical of the "ecumenical age" and seems to correspond to efforts toward political unification (see Peterson 1935, 1951; Schindler 1978; Momigliano 1987; Dunand 1975; and Fowden 1993). The belief in the Supreme Being (Hypsistos) has a distinctly universalist character:

> The sons of Ogyges call me Bacchus,
> Egyptians think me Osiris,
> Mysians name me Phanaces,
> Indians regard me as Dionysus,
> Roman rites make me Liber,
> The Arab race thinks me Adoneus,
> Lucaniacus the Universal God.
> Ausonius, *Epigrammata* #48 (trans. White 1985)

This tradition of invoking the Highest God by the names given him by the various nations expresses a general conviction in late antiquity about the universality of religious truth and the relativity of religious institutions and denominations and the conventionality of divine names. According to Servius, the Stoics taught that there is only one god, whose names merely differ according to actions and offices. Varro (116–27 BCE), who knew about the Jews from Poseidonius, was unwilling to make any differentiation between Jove and YHWH because he was of the opinion that it mattered little by which name he was called as long as only the same thing was meant ("nihil interesse censens quo nomine nuncupetur, dum eadem res intelligatur"; *Antiquitates rerum divinarum,* frag. 16* Cardauns). Porphyry held the opinion that the names of the gods were purely conventional. Celsus argued that "it makes no difference whether one calls god 'Supreme' [*Hypsistos*] or Zeus or Adonai or Sabaoth or Ammon such as the Egyptians do or Papaios as the Scythians." The name does not matter when it is evident what or who is meant.

In his treatise on Isis and Osiris, Plutarch brings this general conviction to the point, stating that no one would "regard the gods as different among different nations nor as barbarian and Greek and as southern and northern. But just as the sun, moon, heaven, earth, and sea are common to all, although they are given various names by the varying nations, so it is with the one reason [*logos*] which orders these things and the one providence which has charge of them" (*On Isis and Osiris* 67.377f–378a). Seneca stressed that this conviction was based on natural evidence: "This All, which you see, which encompasses divine and human, is One, and we are but members of a great body."

Revolutionary monotheism

Negative or counterreligion. Whereas evolutionary monotheism may be seen as the final stage of polytheism, there is no evolutionary line leading from polytheism to revolutionary monotheism. This form of monotheism manifests itself in the first place as a negative or counterreligion, defining what god is *not* and how god should *not* be worshiped. Revolutionary monotheism is based on the distinction between true and false, between one true god and the rest of forbidden, false, or nonexistent gods. The introduction of this distinction into the realm of religion constitutes a radical break. Polytheistic or "primary" religions generally are not concerned with questions of what to believe, but how to act. Not the truth of the beliefs but the correctness of the ritual performances and recitations is what matters: orthopraxy instead of orthodoxy. No primary religion is concerned with the danger of worshiping "false" gods; their concern is, rather, not to neglect any gods requiring worship.

The first to establish a revolutionary monotheism was Akhenaten of Egypt (ca. 1360–1340 BCE). Here, the negative energy of monotheism manifested itself not in explicit prohibitions ("No other gods! No images!"), but in practical destruction. The temples were closed, the cults abolished, the images destroyed, the names erased. Akhenaten's monotheism was based on a physical discovery: the sun was found to generate not only light and warmth, but also time. Light and time were held to be sufficient principles to explain the whole phenomenology of existence; the traditional pantheon was simply deemed superfluous. Its abolition was the logical consequence of a new cosmology. Akhenaten's monotheism was a matter not of revelation but of natural evidence. In this respect, it is closer to polytheism and to evolutionary monotheism than to revolutionary monotheism in its biblical and postbiblical manifestations.

Biblical monotheism is based not on evidence but on revelation. It is not a matter of cognition but of commitment. It requires adherents to make a conscious decision to accept revealed truth and reject deceitful evidence. Natural evidence is debunked as seduction, as luring people away from revealed truth into the traps and pitfalls of the false gods, that is, the world. The distinction between true and false refers, in its ultimate meaning, to the distinction between god and world. Revolutionary monotheism worships an extramundane or transcendent god, whereas the deities of both polytheism and evolutionary monotheism create and animate the world from within and constitute its life. These religions may be termed "cosmotheism," because they worship the world as a divine being. Biblical monotheism is based on an extramundane truth that cannot be seen or otherwise sensually experienced but only believed "with all your heart, with all your soul, and with all your power," and so is revolutionary as well.

The negative or antagonistic energy of revolutionary monotheism finds its expression, not perhaps in (f)actual history but in textual memory, in scenes of violence such as the story of the golden calf (when 3,000 men and women were cruelly executed), Elijah's competition with the priests of Baal (when the priests were massacred), Josiah's reform (when not only the "high places" [bāmôt] were destroyed but also the priests persecuted and killed), and the forced divorce under Ezra of Israelites married to Canaanites (which was a less bloody but equally violent act). This violence is not a matter of history but of semantics. However, there were always situations when textual semantics led to political action.

Canonization. Revealed truth that cannot be reexperienced in any natural way must be codified in order to be transmittable to future generations. Revolutionary monotheism appeals to memory and transmission rather than to observation, attention, divination, and diligent maintenance. In order to transmit its revolutionary message beyond the first generations of founders and followers, it must develop a body of highly normative and canonized scripture. This applies to Judaism, Christianity, and Islam as well as to Zoroastrianism, Buddhism, Jainism, Sikhism, Confucianism, Daoism, and other religions of the East, all of which are based on a canon. The revolutionary break between cosmotheism and monotheism is everywhere dependent on the invention of writing. It is an "advance in intellectuality" as Freud called it, based on a new cultural technology.

The appeal to memory and the prohibition of forgetting usually assume the form of reading, learning, and interpreting. Remembering means a form of reactualization of the normative impulses as they are laid down in the canon. The texts have not only to be learned by heart but they have to be understood and followed. This implies both believing in the truth of what the texts say and the determination to organize the collective culture and the individual lifestyle according to the codified rules, laws, and norms of scripture.

Idolatry, sin, and the construction of paganism. In consequence of its determination to distinguish between true and false, revolutionary monotheism constructs the outside world of former and foreign religions as paganism, a concept completely alien to primary religions. The Greeks knew "barbarians" but no "pagans." However, the distinction is primarily applied within the group itself; it addresses the "pagan within" and cuts right through its own community and even through the individual heart, which now becomes the theater of inner conflicts and religious dynamics. The concept of idolatry became psychologized and turned into a new concept of sin. Among the various innovations brought into the world by revolutionary monotheism, the invention of the "inner person" is of particular importance. Religion becomes a matter of the heart and soul: "The sacrifice acceptable to God is a broken spirit; a broken and a contrite heart, O God, thou wilt not despise" (Ps. 51.19 [= 51.17 Hebrew]). "And you shall love the LORD your God with all your heart, and with all your soul, and with all your might" (Deut. 6.5).

The distinction between true and false religion has not only a cognitive, but also a moral meaning. In this early stage of monotheism, the "false gods" are conceived of as fully existent and powerful beings who constitute a constant temptation and lure the human heart into the pitfalls of idolatry. Idolatry is seen not only as an error but also as infidelity and immorality. Without the existence of other gods, the commandment to be faithful to the one god would have little meaning. The gods of polytheistic religions, in their need of social bonds, formed constellations within their own sphere and were not dependent on humanity. The god of the Bible is a "jealous god," having to count on the love and loyalty of his chosen people, which inevitably fails in fulfilling his expectations. Thus, together with counterreligion, the concept of "sin" is born as the awareness of having failed in requiting God's love and of having given in to the temptations of the false gods.

The theologization of justice. Revolutionary monotheism is a religion in which the idea of justice holds the central position. Whereas in polytheistic religions such as in Egypt, the spheres of cult and justice are carefully separated (justice is for humans, and cult is for the gods and the dead), in the Bible they are emphatically connected. God does not want sacrifice, but justice. Justice becomes the most prominent way of fulfilling the will of God. This led to the still widespread conviction that justice and morals were brought into the world only by monotheism and could not be maintained without it. The construction of paganism implies the idea of lawlessness and immorality. This is, of course, a polemical distortion. The gods, above all the sun-gods (Shamash in Mesopotamia, Re in Egypt), watched over the keeping of the laws and acted as judges. In Egypt, moreover, there is the idea of a general judgment of the dead, which constitutes a first step toward a theologization of justice. But it is true that no god other than YHWH or Allah ever acted as legislator. The idea of justice is divine, but the formulation and promulgation of specific laws is the task of the king. In Egypt, the laws were never codified, and Mesopotamia had law books but no law codes. Every new king was free to promulgate his own laws and was not bound to an existing legislation. The Torah was the first attempt at creating a real law code not to be superseded by any future legislation. This was a revolutionary step by which the law—and with it religion itself, whose center the law constituted—became independent of any political government. The ideas of divine legislation, and not only codification but also revelation and canonization, are closely connected. The law formed the content of the Sinai revelation, and its codification in the various law codes in Exodus, Leviticus, Numbers, and Deuteronomy formed the core of the evolving canon.

Bibliography

Dunand, F. "Les syncrétismes dans la religion de l'Égypte gréco-romaine." In *Les syncrétismes dans les religions de l'antiquité,* ed. F. Dunand and P. Levêque. Études préliminaires aux religions orientales dans l'empire romain 46. Leiden: Brill, 1975.

Fowden, Garth. *Empire to Commonwealth: Consequences of Monotheism in Late Antiquity.* Princeton: Princeton University Press, 1993.

Hengel, M. *Judentum und Hellenismus: Studien zu ihrer Begegnung unter besonderer Berücksichtigung Palästinas bis zur Mitte des 2. Jh. v. Chr.* Tübingen: Mohr, 1969.

Momigliano, Arnaldo. "The Disadvantages of Monotheism for a Universal State." In Momigliano, *On Pagans, Jews, and Christians.* Middletown, Conn.: Wesleyan University Press, 1987.

Peterson, E. *Heis Theos: Epigraphische, formgeschichtliche und religionsgeschichtliche Untersuchungen.* Göttingen: Vandenhoeck & Ruprecht, 1926.

———. *Monotheismus als politisches Problem.* Leipzig: Hegner, 1935.

———. *Theologische Traktate.* Munich: Kösel, 1951.

Porter, Barbara Nevling, ed. *One God or Many? Concepts of Divinity in the Ancient World.* [Chebeague, Maine:] Casco Bay Assyriological Institute, 2000.

Schindler, Alfred, ed. *Monotheismus als politisches Problem: Erik Peterson und die Kritik der politischen Theologie.* Studien zur evangelischen Ethik 14. Gütersloh: Gütersloher Verlagshaus, 1978.

Van Seters, J. *In Search of History: Historiography in the Ancient World and the Origins of Biblical History.* New Haven: Yale University Press, 1983.

White, H. G. E., ed. and trans. *Ausonius.* 2 vols. Cambridge: Harvard University Press, 1985.

Ritual

Jan Bremmer

*R*eaders of this book would, of course, expect a chapter on ritual. Yet they may well be surprised that such expectations would not have been shared by most 19th-century readers. In fact, our modern usage of the term *ritual* is barely older than just one century. During most of the 19th century, ritual signified a text, a scenario, or even a liturgy. As such, it was regularly used in connection with the books of the Veda or the *Rituale Romanum,* the standard manual for the Roman Catholic mass. It was only toward the end of that century, around 1890, that the term started to be used in its modern meaning of repetitive, symbolic behavior. This development coincided with a general shift in anthropology and classics toward the observation of behavior instead of an interest in myth and origins.

Yet in the first decades of "the ritual turn," the main semantic content of the term remained the notion of fixity and routine, although it now was also realized that ritual need not always be religious. This gradual development of the notion of ritual is perhaps the reason that no consensus has been reached about its content. It is used for acts, such as initiation, that can last many years, but also for acts that may last only a few minutes, such as a short prayer. Moreover, as it is a modern term, there are no clear equivalents in the areas we are interested in. We have therefore always to keep in mind that our approach is a typically modern one, and not one necessarily recognized by the ancients themselves.

Recent studies increasingly show that the ancient Mediterranean and Near Eastern world was one where rituals and myths regularly traveled from one culture to the next. Yet whoever tries to survey rituals in the whole of this area will soon notice that it is impossible to work from the same basis in every area. It is fairly clear that the enormous philological challenges in the ancient Near East, such as the study of Sumerian, Akkadian, Eblaite, Ugaritic, Lycian, Luvian, Hurrian, and Hittite materials constitutes, have induced scholars to concentrate much more on the decipherment of their texts than on the applica-

tion of anthropological models to their meanings. Moreover, in the case of ancient Israel and Egypt, the largely prescriptive character of their ritual texts
generally prevents us from seeing how ritual worked in concrete everyday life.
And our information about Roman ritual is often dependent on scattered no-
tices of only a few authors, with the honorable exception of the *Acts* of the
fratres Arvales. Elsewhere in Italy several longer ritual texts have turned up
but, unfortunately, they are very hard to read, such as the Umbrian *Tabulae
Iguvinae* from Gubbio or the even harder to read Etruscan *liber linteus* found
in Croatian Zagreb.

In contrast, we are extremely well informed regarding ancient Greece. Epic
and lyric, comedy and tragedy, lexicography and travelers' accounts, archeology and epigraphy—all have contributed to our knowledge of the various
Greek rituals, which we can sometimes follow over many centuries. Yet even in
ancient Greece we can regularly see a ritual only through a glass darkly, since
public rituals received more attention in our sources than private rituals, and
the tradition often concentrated on the less "normal" aspects of rituals. Still, it
is especially the study of Greek ritual that has been most innovative in recent
decades, with Walter Burkert leading the way. From the middle of the 1960s
onward, he started an approach to ritual that in the course of time would combine a variety of approaches, such as functionalism and structuralism as well as
narrative and symbolic modes of analyses—an eclectic tradition also embraced
by the present author.

An immense number of rituals in our area could be studied, such as the rites
of passages of the life cycle (birth, maturity, wedding, death), the seasonal rituals (New Year), or the crossing of one area into the next. Naturally it is impossible to look at all of them in the limited space at our disposal. Instead, I will
concentrate on those rituals that have traveled from one culture to the next or
that have given rise to comments by members of a different culture. In this
way, we can see something of a shared ritual landscape between the Mediterranean and the ancient Near East. We will first look at some more extended rituals, the so-called scapegoat rituals and the Old and New Year festivals. Subsequently, we will pay attention to the "simpler" rituals of processions and
purifications, and we will conclude with some observations on the much-
discussed relationship between ritual and myth.

Scapegoat rituals from Ebla to Rome

Let us start with a ritual that nicely illustrates the permeability of ancient Mediterranean and Near Eastern cultures. Although some recently published cuneiform tablets seem to suggest that the scapegoat ritual was already practiced in
Ebla in the 3rd millennium BCE, it is only in Hittite texts that we can start to
read a fully elaborated ritual. A fine example is the prescription of Ashella, a
man of Hapalla (a city-state in southeast Anatolia), which dates to the 13th
century BCE:

When evening comes, whoever the army commanders are, each of them prepares a ram—whether it is a white ram or a black ram does not matter at all. Then I twine a cord of white wool, red wool, and green wool, and the officer twists it together, and I bring a necklace, a ring, and a chalcedony stone and I hang them on the ram's neck and horns, and at night they tie them in front of the tents and say: "Whatever deity is prowling about(?), whatever deity has caused this pestilence, now I have tied up these rams for you, be appeased!" And in the morning I drive them out to the plain, and with each ram they take 1 jug of beer, 1 loaf, and 1 cup of milk(?). Then in front of the king's tent he makes a finely dressed woman sit and puts with her a jar of beer and 3 loaves. Then the officers lay their hands on the rams and say: "Whatever deity has caused this pestilence, now see! These rams are standing here and they are very fat in liver, heart, and loins. Let human flesh be hateful to him, let him be appeased by these rams." And the officers point at the rams and the king points at the decorated woman, and the rams and the woman carry the loaves and the beer through the army and they chase them out to the plain. And they go running on to the enemy's frontier without coming to any place of ours, and the people say: "Look! Whatever illness there was among men, oxen, sheep, horses, mules, and donkeys in this camp, these rams and this woman have carried it away from the camp. And the country that finds them shall take over this evil pestilence." (Trans. Gurney 1977: 49)

This is not the place to analyze the ritual in great detail, but we may note the following characteristics. First, the cause of the ritual is pestilence. Second, the ritual is not tied to a specific date in the calendar, but is executed ad hoc. Third, the means of transfer can be either an animal or a woman. Fourth, the scapegoat is not sent off without decoration, but the animal is adorned with a necklace, a ring, and a precious stone and the woman is finely dressed. Fifth, the scapegoat is sent away to the land of the enemies and offered to the hostile deity who caused the pestilence. Finally, it is the king and the army commanders who play the main roles in the ritual.

It is highly interesting to note that this ritual spread in various directions in the ancient Near East. It traveled south, where we find it in the Old Testament in Lev. 16, with its description of the Day of Atonement, which has also given us the modern term *scapegoat ritual*. According to this description, the high priest Aaron selects two goats (v. 5), the cheapest of the domesticated animals. After a lottery, one of them is assigned to YHWH, whereas the other is meant for Azazel, an obscure deity or demon (vv. 7–10). Aaron then transfers the sins of the Israelites onto the goat by laying his hands on it (v. 21). Finally, somebody (not further specified) brings the goat to the desert (v. 21). We owe a few additional details to the Mishnah, treatise *Yoma* (4.2a; 6.6a), including the goat's adornment with a crimson thread around its head.

It is not difficult to see the parallels between the Hittite and Israelite rituals. Yet at the same time, we also notice that the Israelites appropriated the ritual into their own sacrificial, theological, and calendaric system. The ritual is now supervised by the high priest, not the king; the object to be removed no longer is pestilence or another illness, but the sins of the people; the victim is only an animal, since the Israelites did not sacrifice adult humans; the mention of YHWH *and* Azazel seems to point to the earlier polytheism of the Israelites; and, last but not least, the occasion is not an incidental event, such as a pestilence, but the ritual instead is attached to a fixed point in the religious year.

Due to our poor knowledge of the prehistory of the Old Testament, we have no idea when the Israelites took over this specific sacrifice, but we are better informed regarding the Greeks. It probably was in the earlier archaic age (700 BCE?), at a time of intensive contacts with northern Syria and late Hittite states, that the Greeks appropriated the scapegoat ritual. Our best testimony derives from a passage in Harpocration, where the so-called *pharmakos* ritual is described:

> They used to lead out at Athens two men to be purifications for the city at the Thargelia, the one for the men, the other for the women. [The historian] Istros [ca. 250 BCE] has said in Book 1 of his *Epiphanies of Apollo* that the word derives from a proper name, Pharmakos [Scapegoat], and that he stole the sacred bowls of Apollo and was caught and stoned by Achilles' men and that the rites performed at the [festival of the] Thargelia are a representation of this. (Harpocration, s.v. *pharmakos* = 334 *FGrH*, frag. 50)

The very late, but reliable rhetorician Helladius (ca. 400 CE) adds:

> It was the custom at Athens to lead out two scapegoats, one for the men and the other for the women, for purification. And the men's scapegoat had black dried figs round his neck and the other had white [figs]. He (the source) says that they were called *symbakchoi*. This purification was an aversion of pestilential diseases. It took its start from Androgeos the Cretan, after whose unlawful killing a pestilential disease fell upon the Athenians, and the custom prevailed always to purify the city with scapegoats. (*Apud* Photius, *Bibliotheca* 534a Henry, trans. D. Ogden)

Other examples, such as those from the cities of Colophon, Abdera, and Massilia, help us to see that the Athenian scapegoat ritual was somewhat closer to the Hittite example than the Israelite ritual was. First, the scapegoats were human. Second, the ritual was directed against the plague. Apparently, it could be performed ad hoc, but it had also been incorporated into the calendar, as the ritual was performed yearly in early summer on the first day of a two-day festival of firstfruit offering and seasonal renewal for Apollo, the

Thargelia. Third, in the city of Colophon the scapegoat carried dried figs, bread, and cheese. Fourth, the scapegoat was led by fellow citizens out of the city in a procession, but the Greeks did not send their scapegoats into enemy country or offer them to a hostile deity. Our sources are curiously uninformative about the final fate of the historical victims, but in some cases we hear of the scapegoats being chased over the city's border or thrown down a cliff into the sea. The most important difference, however, is the Greek stress on the purification of the polis. Whereas among the Hittites the king and the army commanders play the main role in the ritual, in Greece it is the city that needs to be cleansed.

Our final example derives from Rome. Roman history tells of three members of the family Decius (father, son, and grandson) who dedicated themselves and the lives of their enemies to the gods of the netherworld in three successive battles (340, 295, and 279 BCE). This so-called *devotio* took place when the battle threatened to turn against the Romans. At those critical moments, the commander-in-chief offered his life together with that of his enemies as a ransom for the whole of the Roman army. However, the historicity of all three examples is somewhat debated, and the information given by the historian Livy (8.10.11) that a commander could offer a common soldier to die for all has much to recommend it as the usual practice. Still, throughout Roman history, the image remained prevalent that at some time in the past, army commanders did sacrifice themselves in order to save the army and with it the Roman community. It is clear that the Roman example is not only geographically but also ritually furthest removed from the Hittite example, since we no longer have to do with a plague or famine and there is no calendaric aspect to the ritual. Yet, once again the community is saved by the sending away of one element of that community.

These rituals can be approached in several different ways. We can look into their origins and work out the similarities and differences. We can also look into their functions. What did the participants expect would result from their actions? In this respect, we notice that similarity in structure need not mean similarity in meaning: for example, the sending away of an animal can imply the removal of a pestilence, but also the removal of sins. Yet the rituals are also expressions of gender and class: the Hittites send away a woman or an animal, but not a man, whereas in Greece the human scapegoat often was a male slave or a male member of the lowest classes. Moreover, we can see the varying loci of power in the respective societies. Among the Hittites the king and army commanders (as in Rome) play the leading role, but in Israel it is the high priest, and in Greece the city as a whole acts out the ritual. Finally, the ritual reflects the distinction us/them (we and the enemy), but also the opposition culture/nature (the goat is sent into the desert). Ritual thus not only communicates information about society, its values, and its power structures, but it also socializes the members of a community, since through its representations (however implicit) they learn what is important for the community as a whole.

Old and New Year festivals

Let us continue with a brief look at the rituals that accompanied the transition into a new year. Even in our own Western, ever-rationalizing world, this transition is often accompanied by ritual acts, such as the production of noise and fireworks or the organization of parades. Yet, equally, for many people the transition will hardly be noticeable, and life carries on as usual. In the ancient world, on the contrary, the transition was dramatized through some striking ritual acts. During the Sacaea, a Babylonian festival that apparently was taken over by the Persians (but the reverse cannot be excluded: our sources are too scanty to decide the matter), something rather odd took place: the masters served their slaves, a criminal acted for five days as king and even had access to the legitimate king's harem. Perhaps not surprisingly, the criminal was hanged at the end of the festival.

A comparable humiliation of the king took place at the Mesopotamian *Akitu* festival, the New Year festival that goes back to at least the middle of the 3rd millennium BCE; this strongly suggests that the Sacaea was also some kind of New Year festival. The *Akitu* festival was celebrated in the main cities of the ancient Near East, such as Uruk, Nippur, and Babylon. On the fifth day of this festival, which lasted the first eleven days (a clear indication of its importance) of the first month, Nissan, the king was led into the main temple complex of Babylon, where his regalia were taken away by the high priest. After the king had stated that he had not neglected the gods, the priest brought out his scepter, loop, mace, and crown from the cella of the god Bel/Marduk and returned them to the king. The next day the king brought the gods out of the temple to a special house (the so-called *Akitu* house) outside the city in a procession, before returning at the end of the festival. This procession was evidently so important that after the defeat of the Persian Empire the Seleucid kings continued this ritual tradition. Yet rituals are rarely kept unchanged over long periods of time, and a recently published fragment of an astronomical diary from the time of King Antiochus III (ca. 242–187 BCE) shows that the ritual had been adapted to the Hellenistic ruler cult, since on the eighth day the king performed "offerings for Ishtar of Babylon and the life of King Antiochus."

As in the Mesopotamian ritual of royal humiliation, the role reversal between slaves and masters also took place elsewhere. In 1983 a Hurrian-Hittite bilingual text (ca. 1400 BCE) was found in Hattusha that contained an Epic of Release, that is, the release of slaves and the remission of debts, such as we know from the Hebrew Jubilee festival (Lev. 25). The bilingual text does not mention the ritual itself, but only supplies the accompanying myth in which the highest god of heaven, Teshub, meets with the sun-goddess of the earth, Allani, for a meal in which the primeval gods, who had been banished to the underworld, also participate; they even sit at the right hand of Teshub. The celebration of the temporary suspension of the cosmic order surely accompanied the temporary suspension of the social order on earth. In other words, the myth about the primeval gods was associated with a ritual of reversal between masters and slaves.

Our inference of a role reversal is supported by a Greek ritual during which masters and slaves reversed roles. In a poem on Greek origins for Roman festivals, the Roman playwright Accius (ca. 170–86 BCE; frag. 3) tells us about the Athenian Kronia, a festival celebrated on the twelfth day of the first Athenian month: "In nearly all fields and towns they happily feast upon banquets, and everyone waits upon his own servants. From this has originated also our custom that the servants eat with their masters in the same place." Accius evidently wanted to give the etiology of the Roman Saturnalia, but by doing so he also related an interesting element of the Athenian Kronia, the festival in honor of Cronus, one of the Titans. As was the case with the Hurrite/Hittite festival, the Athenians clearly practiced a reversal of roles between slaves and masters; moreover, as other sources tell us, on this day the slaves had a wonderful time. Now we know that Attic comedy used expressions such as "older than Cronus" and "older than Cronus and the Titans." Evidently, the antiquity of this divine generation became proverbial at a relatively early stage of Greek tradition. Cronus and his fellow Titans thus can be legitimately compared to the "primeval" gods in the Hurrian/Hittite epic. The mention of the city of Ebla in this epic shows that the origin of this ritual of reversal has to be looked for again in northern Syria, from where it traveled to the Hittites and, in a different way, to the Israelites, as was the case with the scapegoat ritual.

The Kronia, in turn, influenced the Roman Saturnalia, in which on December 17 the god Saturnus was freed from his usual chains. The fettering of a god was not unusual in the Mediterranean world and was concomitant with a loosening of the social order, often by creating a carnivalesque atmosphere. This was also the case in Rome, where during the Saturnalia the masters waited upon the slaves, who could also put on the clothes of their masters. Moreover, during the festival all Romans wore the *pilleus,* a cap that was symbolic of manumission, thus indicating, in other words, a status raising of the slaves and a status diminishment of the owners.

Yet such a status reversal was not limited to Roman males only. During the Matronalia of March 1, the old Roman New Year, mistresses served dinner to their slaves, and perhaps on that same day the Salian maidens, the obscure pendant of the aristocratic Salii priests, performed a sacrifice, dressed with important articles of clothes of the Salii. Finally, and perhaps more clearly, during the Nonae Capratinae, a festival held on July 5, Roman handmaidens put on the clothes of their mistresses and dined in huts, while their mistresses waited upon them. Moreover, mistresses and handmaidens sacrificed together, which was normally unheard of in Roman society. Finally, handmaidens also mocked passersby (who were frequently more important) and asked them for money.

These different dates point to an important phenomenon in the ritual year of the ancient Mediterranean and ancient Near East: winter, spring, summer, and autumn all had festivals that were to some extent New Year festivals. In most cases a change from scarcity to plenty or a period of leisure after laborious efforts will have sparked this feeling of a new beginning. And evidently, in no way could the transition be better and more clearly marked than by a reversal of the normal social order. This reversal could be expressed in different ways. In the autocratic societies of the Near East the most illuminating way was the temporary deposition of the king; in the more aristocratic and (relatively) democratic slave-owning societies of Greece and Rome, the main reversal was between masters and slaves or between mistresses and handmaidens. In the latter case and in the wearing of the *pilleus,* we noticed a change of clothes. As even today we change clothes for weddings and rituals, graduations and installations, so also in antiquity change of clothing was one of the most important ritual markers.

What was the function of such a reversal of roles? Undoubtedly, earlier generations of scholars were often too generalizing in their analysis. Against scholars' natural inclination to look for profound causes, we must always keep in mind that, in the absence of a leisure industry, rituals in antiquity were often one of the most important sources of entertainment and fun. These reversals must have provided slaves and women with a highly welcome break in their often monotonous lives. At the same time, masters and mistresses must have played along, as they knew that the normal order would be restored at the end of these festivals and thus their place in society would be confirmed once more. The festivals will therefore have had a different meaning for the varying social actors, although our sources are totally silent about their feelings. On the other hand, the temporary reversal of roles could also tempt people to try a permanent change of social roles. The Greeks in particular noticed that festivals were often occasions for revolution and regularly guarded their cities during the festivals of Dionysus, a god particularly connected with reversals. It is not surprising, then, that the end of this period was dramatized by certain ritual exclamations or, as in the case of the Athenian Anthesteria, by the burning of the phallus that had been carried along during the main procession.

Processions and purifications

Having looked at some larger and more complicated rituals, let us conclude with two kinds of rituals of a more limited scope: processions and purifications (especially purification as a physical act that employs blood, water, or fumigations). Processions are a phenomenon found all over the world and a good example of a more limited ritual, which often does not last longer than a few hours. Yet it is rarely a ritual in its own right. Processions are usually "framed" (Erving Goffman's term) by a special occasion that lends them their importance and atmosphere. Just as there is an "atmospheric" difference between a wedding and a funerary procession, so also as pure show the procession of a Roman triumph was evidently far superior to a procession for a Greek sacrifice. Two aspects are particularly important in processions: (1) the spatial arrangement, which often takes the form of leaving the city or entering the city;

and (2) the ability of processions, the major ones in particular, both to serve as a means of self-definition for a community and to articulate power relations between the full members of a community and those with fewer rights.

Let us look at a few examples. Herodotus (2.58) thought that compared with the Egyptians, the Greeks had only recently introduced processions. This is hardly correct, since processions are often portrayed in Mycenaean iconography and are even mentioned on Linear B tablets, but the reason that Herodotus thinks so perhaps is (in addition to the usual claim of Egyptian priority) the unusual splendor of some of the Egyptian processions. For example, he was clearly greatly impressed by the boat procession at Bubastis (near modern Tell Basta in the eastern Delta), during which men and women arrived in separate barges in honor of the goddess Bastet. The boat procession is a good example of what Graf (1996) calls a centripetal procession—a procession toward a religious center (processions could also be centrifugal, leading away from the center, as in the case of the Babylonian New Year festival). On the boats, some women continuously clattered their castanets, whereas some men, as was usual in ancient Egypt, played flutes—an interesting gender distinction in music! Moreover, the women, when passing a town, brought their barges close to shore in order to shout abuse at other women and to lift their skirts, which indicates that this procession was framed by the atmosphere of a New Year festival with its concomitant temporary subversion of the social order. Interestingly, however, the men apparently did not participate in this kind of (sexual) banter and preserved their dignity. Could the relation between the sexes in Egypt not tolerate a mocking of the males?

The Greek term for festive procession was *pompē*, the procession that usually culminated in an important sacrifice. The most impressive example was undoubtedly the procession during the Athenian Panathenaea festival. During this procession the Athenian citizens traversed the most important points of their town, such as the commercial center, the Kerameikos, and the Agora, and finally reached the great altar of Athena on the Acropolis. The procession was mainly organized on egalitarian principles in groups according to deme and thus constituted a display of the unity of the Athenian population; those who were unable to participate undoubtedly lined the streets to admire the procession. At the same time, however, the procession demonstrated the power and status of the Athenians, since their colonies and allies had to parade a cow and panoply, whereas the daughters of metics (immigrants without citizen rights) carried parasols for the upper-class females. Yet processions could also demonstrate modesty. When, during the most important Spartan festival, the Hyacinthia, aristocratic girls rode in race-carts or carriages made in the shapes of griffins or goat-stags, the daughter of King Agesilaus traveled in a vehicle that was "no more elaborate than that of any other maiden" (Xenophon).

At some point, the Greek *pompē* was taken over by the Romans, who called many of their processions *pompae*, such as the funerary procession *(pompa funebris)*, the circus procession *(pompa circensis)*, and the triumphal procession *(pompa triumphalis)*. Yet these processions, especially the last, lacked the egalitarian character of the *pompē,* which must have struck some non-Greeks as rather special, as seen in an astronomical diary from Hellenistic Babylon: "In that month I heard as follows: King Antiochus went victoriously into the cities of Meluhha [i.e., Egypt: ca. 169 BCE], the citizens performed a *pompē* [Babylonian *pu-up-pe*] and ritual acts according to Greek custom."

Let us conclude our exploration of ritual with some examples of purification on a small scale. Even today, purity is a highly esteemed value in Judaism and Islam. They clearly continue a preoccupation with pollution that can be followed via the Qur'an and the Old Testament into the earliest-known stages of religion in the ancient Near East. Purity was also a highly important value in ancient Greece, but the Romans were clearly much less concerned with it, and their more reticent attitude in this case has been continued by Western Christianity, where, as a whole, the problems of purity and pollution have been relegated to a minor role on the religious stage.

Purification is often concerned with uncontrollable events in human life, such as birth and death, illness and bloodshed. Sex, too, is an area where purity regulations circumscribe activity. In Israel contact with a person suffering from a venereal disease meant washing one's clothes and taking a bath (Lev. 15). Water was, indeed, the most common means of purification in the ancient world, as it is still today with the ritual baths for Moslems and Jews. However, there were also other, more unusual means of purification, which apparently traveled across religious boundaries, such as the use of blood and fumigations. The Old Testament prescribed blood to purify a house that was infected with spots of green or red mold, just as purifying blood was applied to people suffering from leprosy, also a type of mold (Lev. 14). In Babylon, the blood of a suckling pig was spattered on the bed of a person possessed by an evil spirit, whereas in Greece deranged people themselves could apparently be showered with the blood of a slaughtered piglet. Perhaps we find here the idea of blood as a life-giving substance that could revive people or houses in a controlled ritual context. As with the ritual of the scapegoat, one can hardly escape the impression that ritual purification with blood also traveled from West Semitic peoples to the Greeks.

This transfer also seems to have been the case with the use of sulfur as a means of purification. In Babylon, people possessed by ghosts could be treated by fumigation with a mixture of all kinds of substances, ranging from jackal dung and human bone to sulfur, but we find the latter substance also in ancient Greece: in the *Odyssey* 22.481–94 sulfur is used to purify Odysseus's blood-stained house after the murder of the suitors, and in the Hippocratic corpus it is ritually applied to heal breathing problems and problems in the womb. Once again, Babylonian influence is probable.

With these examples we come to the end of our discussion of rituals. It seems clear that the ancient Near East was an important generator of rituals for the rest of the Mediterranean. At the same time, we also notice that Egypt remained outside the Near Eastern sphere of ritual influence. Its geographical and, perhaps, political position enabled it to remain virtually untouched by

Anatolian and Mesopotamian influence in this respect. As in other aspects of its religion, such as its fascination with the afterlife, Egypt remained very much a loner in the world of the ancient Mediterranean and Near East.

Ritual and myth

The nature of the connection between ritual and myth is a complicated problem, which has only gradually become better understood. In the 19th century, scholars concentrated virtually completely on myth, but after the "ritual turn" at the end of that century the relationship between myth and ritual became a problem that had to be explained. The first to do so seriously was British classicist Jane Harrison, who suggested several possibilities. In 1890 she stated that myth is mostly "ritual practice misunderstood"; in her *Themis,* however, she not only suggested that myth and ritual "arise *pari passu*" but also that myth "is the plot of the *drōmenon*" (the thing acted out or ritual) (1912: 16, 331). This latter statement was developed by the so-called English-Scandinavian Myth and Ritual School, which concentrated on the Old Testament and the ancient Near East. These scholars thought that myth and ritual were so closely related that one could reconstruct a ritual from a myth, even when the ritual was no longer known. Finally, the last quarter of the 20th century witnessed two new, converging approaches. Burkert claimed that initiation rituals are "demonstrative accentuations of biologically programmed crises, menstruation, defloration, pregnancy, and birth. . . . The roots of the tales go back to verbalized action, whether ritualized or not" (1979). As both myth and ritual go back to "action programs," they cannot be reduced to one another but originate *pari passu*. This suggestion was taken up by H. S. Versnel (1993: 135) and applied to seasonal festivals. From an analysis of the Kronia he inferred not only a *pari passu* origin but also a correspondence in structure and atmosphere of myth and ritual.

This stress on the correspondence and *pari passu* origin of myth and ritual rightly points out that neither symbolic process can be separated from the other. Yet as soon as we look at specific complexes of myth and ritual, it becomes clear that these claims not only go too far—we do not know anything about the actual beginning of the myth and ritual of the Kronia—but also neglect to isolate important differences between myth and ritual, of which I will mention three briefly.

First, myth is never a complete reflection of ritual but only selectively focuses on certain parts of it. During the Babylonian New Year ritual, when the king was temporarily dethroned, a version of the *Enuma Elish,* the epic of creation, was recited, telling of how Marduk, the supreme god of Babylon, was imprisoned, beaten, and wounded. Clearly, the myth does not mention the details of the ritual, neither does its structure completely correspond with the much longer ritual. Yet the myth corresponds in mood with the ritual, highlights its most dramatic part (the dethronement of the king), and gives it added meaning by closely identifying the king with Marduk.

Second, the myths of the scapegoat ritual in Greece usually speak about the death of a scapegoat, whereas the ritual enacted only its expulsion from the community: what is symbolic and reversible in ritual often becomes realistic and irreversible in myth.

Finally, myths are more mobile than rituals. Although we have seen several migrating rituals, it is clear that myths can travel much more easily than rituals. A good example is the Sumerian myth of the flood, which not only was appropriated by the Greeks and Israelites but even traveled to India, before being spread all over the world by Christianity. One myth can even be attached to several rituals. In ancient Greece the myth of the conveyance by Orestes and Iphigeneia of a very ancient statue of Artemis was told in places as far apart as mainland Greece, Sicily, and Latium. In all of these cases, the myths also become attached to preexisting rituals. In fact, despite claims made to the contrary, myths virtually always appear to be later than the rituals they are connected with, wherever we have sufficient evidence to determine their priority (further see Myth).

Bibliography

Auffarth, C. *Der drohende Untergang.* Berlin: de Gruyter, 1991.
Bremmer, J. N. *Greek Religion.* 2nd edition. Oxford: Oxford University Press, 1994.
———. "'Religion,' 'Ritual' and the Opposition 'Sacred vs. Profane': Notes Towards a Terminological 'Genealogy.'" In *Ansichten griechischer Rituale: Festschrift für Walter Burkert,* ed. F. Graf. Stuttgart and Leipzig: Teubner, 1998.
———. "The Scapegoat between Hittites, Greeks, Israelites and Christians." In *Kult, Konflikt und Versöhnung,* ed. R. Albertz. Münster: Ugarit-Verlag, 2001.
Burkert, W. *Homo necans.* Berkeley: University of California Press, 1983.
———. *Structure and History in Greek Mythology and Ritual.* Berkeley: University of California Press, 1979.
Graf, F. *Nordionische Kulte.* Rome: Institut Suisse de Rome, 1985.
———. "*Pompai* in Greece: Some Considerations about Space and Ritual in the Greek Polis." In *The Role of Religion in the Early Greek Polis: Proceedings of the Third International Seminar on Ancient Greek Cult,* ed. R. Hägg. Swedish Institute at Athens. Stockholm: Paul Åströms Förlag, 1996.
Gurney, O. R. *Some Aspects of Hittite Religion.* Schweich Lectures 1976. Oxford: Oxford University Press for the British Academy, 1977.
Harrison, Jane Ellen. *Mythology and Monuments of Ancient Athens.* London and New York: Macmillan, 1890.
———. *Themis: A Study of the Social Origins of Greek Religion,* 1912. 2nd ed., Cambridge: Cambridge University Press, 1927. Rept., Cleveland, Ohio: World Publishing Company, 1962.
Helck, W., and E. Otto, eds. *Lexikon der Ägyptologie.* 7 vols. Wiesbaden: Harrassowitz, 1972–92.
Hoessly, F. *Katharsis: Reinigung als Heilsverfahren.* Göttingen: Vandenhoeck & Ruprecht, 2001.

Linssen, M. J. H. "The Cults of Uruk and Babylon." Diss., University of Amsterdam, 2002.

Parker, Robert. *Miasma: Pollution and Purification in Early Greek Religion.* Oxford: Clarendon, 1983.

Pongratz-Leisten, B. *Ina sulmi irub: Die kulttopographische und ideologische Programmatik der* akītu-*Prozession in Babylonien und Assyrien im 1. Jahrtausend v. Chr.* Mainz: Zabern, 1994.

Rix, H. *Kleine Schriften.* Bremen: Hempen, 2001.

Versnel, H. S. *Inconsistencies in Greek and Roman Religion,* II: *Transition and Reversal in Myth and Ritual.* Studies in Greek and Roman Religion 6.2. Leiden: Brill, 1993.

Myth

Fritz Graf

*M*yth is, at a first glance, the English derivative of a Greek word, *mythos* (word, utterance)—yet another legacy from the classical world, or so it seems. This often has made Greek mythology not simply paradigmatic, but even normative as to what myth is: whatever stories from a growing range of cultures came into scholarly consciousness between the Renaissance and the early 20th century were measured and classified against this background. But things are not as simple as this. Applied to narratives, the Greek word as used in the late 5th century BCE most often denoted invented, fictional stories. Plato opposed these stories to the truth, which could be verified or falsified by logic. This became the dominant meaning: rhetorical theorists turned it into their term for "fiction that lacks any resemblance to empirical reality," and Roman theory translated it as *fabula;* this became the term current in most European languages until the 18th century. It is immediately clear that this ancient meaning of the word is not ours: whatever our definition of myth—and there are more than we would wish or care for (Doty 1986: 9–10)—we understand myths as relevant and, in some deeper sense, true stories. Most scholarly attempts to understand myth try to filter this truth, be it historical, psychological, religious, ritualistic, scientific, or even biological, from the stories in an operation first described by the Greek philosopher and essayist Plutarch of Chaeronea (ca. 50–120 CE): "Our aim is to purify the mythic, making it yield to reason" (*Life of Theseus* 1; cf. Detienne 1981). This considerable semantic gap between ancient and modern meaning is easily explained: myth is a term of modern scholarship, invented by 18th-century German Hellenist Gottlieb Christian Heyne, who latinized the Greek word to *mythus* and radically changed its semantics.

The western Asiatic mythological *koinē*

When, in 1764, Heyne created our term, Greek mythology was the only known mythology of any Mediterranean culture: in this respect, it was the paradigm and norm for what myth was understood to be. The process that culminated in Heyne's new terminology and its concomitant radical reevaluation of mythical narrative had started with the confrontation of Greek myths with the traditional stories of newly discovered ethnological cultures, and it had found its first result in the rejection of Greek myths as "a heap of chimeras, dreams, and absurdities" ("un amas de chimères, de rêveries et d'absurdités"; Fontenelle 1724: 187). Heyne reacted to this by giving these same narratives a radically different status—no more absurd inventions *(fabulae),* but the result of primeval human thinking about the world and the container of age-old human memories *(mythi).* His contemporary Johann Gottfried Herder made the specific mythology into one of the defining characteristics of each ethnic group *(Volk)* and moved away from Greek mythology to his native Germans. All three—Fontenelle, Heyne, Herder—are exponents of the modernization of Europe that came with the Enlightenment, its trust in reason as the highest authority, and its struggle against a culture that was dominated by religion. The labeling of mythical narratives as fiction in later antiquity had successfully neutralized the stories of the pagan gods in the new Christian world, where there was only one story that dealt with the divine, and that was revealed truth. Fontenelle's rejection was the rational reaction to such stories; Heyne's reevaluation turned myths into a new sort of truth, not revealed by God but formulated by the budding reason of early humans, and it invested myth with the dignity of an ancestral heirloom; Herder's move clad them with the halo of being a nation's autochthonous truth, starting mythology on a pernicious path the led to the synthetic national mythologies of the 20th century. The romantics discovered and promoted Indian mythology as yet another and much older mythology than the Greek. Greek mythology, however, remained in its splendid isolation; whoever believed, as did Herder and the German romantics, that mythology was the creation of the *Volksgeist* did not care about diffusion and influences anyway. With the exceptions of Creuzer's easily and quickly refuted theories of an Indian missionary movement and of some diffusionist theories in the 18th century, scholars did not try to connect Greek myths with other mythologies, not the least because the mythical narratives of the neighboring Bronze Age Near East were still unknown and the Old Testament was still read as history. With the quasi-simultaneous publication of Max Müller's and Adalbert Kuhn's essays on comparative mythology in the mid-1850s, the Indo-European hypothesis—the derivation of most Western languages, from Indian Sanskrit to Irish, from a common ancestor, the hypothetical "Old Indo-European"—began to move Greek mythology out of its historical isolation: Greek myths were read as related to the myths of other Old Indo-European cultures, such as Vedic India or the Iran of the Avesta. Whereas the symbolistic interpretations of Müller and Kuhn were quickly dismissed by their contemporaries, the wider assumption of Indo-European mythology was developed by scholars as different as Georges Dumézil and Jan Puhvel (Puhvel 1987), and it is still very much alive.

With the discovery of the ancient Near Eastern cultures, the decipherment of

cuneiform writing, and the growing understanding of the languages involved—
Akkadian and Sumerian in the 19th century, West Semitic languages and
Hittite in the early 20th century—an entirely new body of texts came to be
known; as a corollary, the Old Testament began to be read as yet another collection of traditional stories. But these new discoveries rarely have affected the
study of myth and the normative status of the Greek stories; Egyptian mythology always stood somewhat apart—not the least because of the absence of
long mythological narratives—and the Mesopotamian literary texts were of
exclusive interest to biblical scholars and never to the specialists of Greek mythology. It is symptomatic that the two major collections of translations—
Hugo Gressmann's (1909) and James B. Pritchard's (1950)—presented those
texts as relevant for the study of the Old Testament only. Only after it became
clear, through Hrozný's decipherment in the 1920s, that Hittite, the language
of the Late Bronze Age rulers of Anatolia, was an Indo-European language did
Hittite mythological texts begin to become visible outside their narrow discipline, and this in turn has kindled interest in the other west Asiatic mythologies. The decisive step was when Hans Gustav Güterbock published the narration about Kumarbi, whom he provocatively named "the Hurrian Cronus"
(Güterbock 1946): this alerted some students of Hesiod to Near Eastern mythology (it certainly helped somewhat that, after all, the Hittites were Indo-Europeans). In the half century since then, insight has been growing that Late
Bronze Age and early Iron Age Greece participated at the margins of the great
ancient Near Eastern cultures (most impressively West 1997); in the last couple
of years, serious research into this field finally has begun.

West Asiatic mythology crystallized into often impressively long written
texts: narratives from Sumerian and Akkadian Mesopotamia, turned classics
and preserved, among other places, in the splendid library of Assurbanipal
at Nineveh, with the Gilgamesh Epic as the most brilliant example; Hurrian
and Hittite texts, among them the Cycle of Kumarbi, from the Hittite capital
Bogazköy (ancient Hattusha), but also a much-earlier version of Gilgamesh;
the Baal cycle and other narratives from Ugarit; and finally the Greek texts of
Homer and Hesiod, not to mention other lost epic poems from archaic Greece.
They form a significant and still-growing body of texts. They share not only
themes, scenes, and often enough structures, but also, on a more elementary
level, the fact that behind these written texts there must be a vast continent of
formalized oral storytelling—an insight less important because, in the understanding of many scholars since Heyne and Herder, myth is a mainly oral phenomenon than because oral transmission between the cultures and language
groups best explains the wide diffusion of and the somewhat fuzzy correspon-
dences between these stories.

Whereas it is firmly established that there was a long oral tradition immediately behind the poems of Homer and Hesiod, whatever their exact origin, the
oral background of western Asiatic narrative texts is less well researched. But
some Hurrian texts set out with the singer's announcement "I (will) sing"
(Schuol 2002), as do a few Akkadian texts (Dalley 1989: 204), while the stan-

dard version of Gilgamesh opens with the promise of the singer: "I shall tell . . . , I shall teach. . . ." Although this does not necessarily point to a contemporary oral culture, as the opening of Vergil's *Aeneid* teaches us, in this case it might do just that: in all the west Asiatic cultures, literacy was not widespread enough to serve as a vehicle of diffusion for these stories. Another Akkadian text opens with a dialogue between the singer and audience in which the bard offers a choice of themes for selection (Wilcke 1977). This looks even more like the literarization of a common oral situation—which is not to deny the strongly scribal character of many of the texts that have been handed down from scribe to scribe and that contain that archetypical scribal phenomenon, the list, as does the long conclusion of the *Enuma Elish*.

Not all similarities between the stories inside this narrative *koinē*, however, need to be explained by diffusion. The Mesopotamian primeval deity Tiamat is split in two to create sky and earth; Egyptian Nut (Sky) is lifted high above her consort Geb (Earth); Hesiod's Uranus (Sky) is violently separated from his wife Gaea (Earth): these are local variations of the much more widely attested theme of separation of earth and sky (Staudacher 1942), and the local variations are widely different from each other. This, then, is a certain example of a nearly universal motif; less certain is another one, the flood story. Although attested in widely different cultures (Dundes 1988), the extant stories in Mesopotamia (Atrahasis, the Nineveh version of Gilgamesh), the Old Testament (Gen. 6–9), Syria (Berossus, *FGrH* 680; Lucian, *On the Syrian Goddess* 12–13), Anatolia (Ovid, *Metamorphoses* 8.624–700), and Greece (Caduff 1986; no trace in Homer or Hesiod) share so many details that diffusion is a more economical hypothesis, despite the marked local variations.

Even less doubtful is the closeness between versions of what is called the Succession Myth, which is present in the Hurrian Kumarbi Cycle, several Mesopotamian stories (the best known being the Babylonian creation epic, *Enuma Elish*), narrations about Baal in Ugarit and other West Semitic cultures, and several Greek narrations, most prominently Hesiod's *Theogony*. In Hesiod's familiar version, primordial Chaos (Void) is succeeded by Gaea (Earth). Chaos becomes the parent of Erebus (Deep Underworld) and Night, the dark roots of the cosmos; Gaea gives birth to Sea, Mountains, Nymphs, and Uranus (Sky, the upper levels of the cosmos). Gaea makes Uranus her consort, but when he begins to prevent their offspring from leaving her womb, she persuades her youngest son, Cronus, to castrate his father. Cronus takes over the kingship; in order to stay in power, he swallows all the children that his wife Rhea bears him, until Rhea, frustrated, feeds him a stone disguised as a baby in swaddling clothes and secretly gives birth to Zeus. Again, the youngest son deposes his father and, together with his siblings, takes over the world. But before establishing his own kingship, Zeus is challenged by the Titans, his father's siblings, and by Typhon, a monster created by Gaea herself and sent against her grandson (whom she previously had helped in his fight against the Titans). Both times, Zeus is victorious and then proceeds to "attribute the honors to the gods." (It is likely that the battle with Typhon is an addition to Hesiod's story, and in later accounts Zeus is also attacked by the Giants, other sons of Gaea, before he is able to establish his own rule.)

In the Cycle of Kumarbi (Hoffner 1998: 40–42) the generation of gods who are ruling under their king, who is the supreme god of the actual pantheon, is preceded by several earlier generations of heavenly kings; the succession of these kings was often violent, and the rule of the present supreme god has to be defended against attackers: the Succession Myth narrates how the present order of things came into being and notes that this order did not go unchallenged. In the Hittite Song of Kumarbi, the primeval King Alalu is deposed by Anu (Sky), his vizier; Anu's son and vizier, Kumarbi, then deposes Anu. During the struggle with Anu, Kumarbi bites off Anu's testicles and swallows them, thus impregnating himself; in a complex action that is only partially understood, he gives birth to Teshub (the storm-god), Teshub's vizier Tasmisu, the Aranzah River, and several other gods. From that moment on, the rivalry between the ruling Kumarbi and the pretender Teshub dominates the song cycle. Kumarbi seems to have tried to swallow Teshub again but was tricked into eating an object, perhaps a stone. Teshub might have become king already in the Song of Kumarbi, but in other narratives, Kumarbi challenges him through several intermediaries, among them the monstrous sea serpent Hedammu (Song of Hedammu) and the stone giant Ullikummi, fathered by Kumarbi through intercourse with a huge rock.

There are other succession stories as well. The Hellenistic author Philo of Byblos told a complex Phoenician version, allegedly translated from the Phoenician, which leads from Elioun and Beruth to Gaea and Uranus, whose son El deposes him, to be succeeded (not necessarily violently) by a triad of gods who dominated the actual pantheon, Astarte, Zeus Demaros, and Adodos (Hadad/Baal) (Eusebius, *Preparation for the Gospel* 1.10). Hellenization is obvious, although its exact extent is difficult to determine. The Ugaritic Baal Cycle knows at least the last two generations: El and Baal enter into a violent conflict, and Baal fights and kills Yamm (Sea), El's ally. Baal fights other monsters as well, among them Mot (Death); this fight seems to end in a tie (Wyatt 1998: 34–146). Zeus's battles echo these fights, but they resonate also with the Babylonian creation epic that pits Marduk, the Lord of Babylon, against Tiamat, at the end of a succession of several divine kings (Dalley 1989: 228–77). Some of these fights—Marduk against Tiamat, Baal against a dragon, Teshub against Illuyanka, Zeus against Typhon, YHWH against Leviathan—make use of yet another story pattern, the fight against a dragonlike monster. This motif has also an Indo-European pedigree, but is more universal.

The complexity of this web of mythological narratives is obvious; no simple explanation will do. But it is also obvious that it can be the result of only a very long and very intricate process of communication—of stories heard in marketplaces, in caravanserais, in royal courts and the wide spaces around the temples, which were adapted by their singers to ever-new conditions and then more-or-less accurately remembered by travelers and merchants, brought home and fed into yet another local network of storytelling, with its own pressures and laws.

It was not only the contingencies of human memory and linguistic competence that shaped those stories. They had to respond to their societies' needs and values. Noah "was a righteous man," and he "walked with God" (Gen. 6.9), and Atrahasis was one "whose ear was open to his god Enki, he would speak with his god and his god would speak with him" (Atrahasis 4.18–20): both theocratic Babylon and priestly Israel focused on the hero's piety. In Ovid's Rome, however, Deucalion is a lover of justice, and piety in the sense of punctual ritualism ("god-fearing"; *Metamorphoses* 1.322) is reserved for his wife, Pyrrha. The *Enuma Elish* puts much emphasis on Marduk, his temple, his cult, and all the honors that the gods decree for him, and its narrative is more interested in diplomacy among the gods than in the battle: the poem was recited during the annual festival of Marduk in Babylon, and the urban audience had little interest in deeds of war—in marked contrast to Gilgamesh. Hesiod's *Theogony*, on the other hand, avoids any reference to specific cults, puts heavy emphasis on the systematic construction of the world through the relevant genealogies, and describes in detail how Cronus castrated Uranus and how Zeus fought Typhon: its intended audience must have varied, but shared an interest in battle scenes, as did the audience of the *Iliad*. If a traditional tale were to survive, it either had to be tied to a very specific, recurrent occasion, such as a festival, or it had to adapt to ever-new conditions; presumably, it was not the most successfully adapted stories that made it into the frozen state of a written text, but rather those that offered enough semantic gaps for new interpretations that aimed at opening up the now unchangeable story to its new audience.

The way that these stories are conditioned by their societies is even more visible in anthropogonical myths, stories about how humans came into being; after all, these mythical narratives aimed at explaining the *condition humaine* in a given society at a given time. In the priestly account of Genesis, God created humans "in our image, after our likeness, to have dominion" over all other living beings (Gen. 1.26), or God created man "from the dust of the ground" and put him in paradise, where the first couple swiftly transgressed limits and was sent out to suffer toils and death (2): whether guilty or not, humans are very close to God. In both the Babylonian Atrahasis story and the *Enuma Elish*, humans are created from clay and "flesh and blood" of a slaughtered god (Qingu, Tiamat's evil vizier, in the *Enuma Elish*) in order to "bear the load of the gods." In the theocratic state, humans, although by their nature akin to the gods, are supposed to be their servants and slaves. In Hesiod's *Theogony*, humans simply appear at some point, break away from the gods, and challenge Zeus through the trickster Prometheus. Zeus, however, creates woman, "the evil good" without whom man cannot live: humans, although deeply indebted to Zeus for their paradoxical stand in life, keep their distance and take a proud stance against the gods. In the late 5th century BCE, we begin to hear that Prometheus shaped humans from clay: although now the Greek trickster follows even more closely the paradigm of Mesopotamian Ea/Enki, humans owe their existence not to Zeus, but to his cunning adversary (see Cosmology, Time, and History).

Myth and ritual

The Babylonian creation epic was recited (or even enacted) at least once during the New Year festival: on a surface level, the myth talks about the foundation of the temple in which the audience was assembled—as the Homeric *Hymn to Apollo* narrates the foundation of Apollo's temples on Delos and in Delphi (it presumably was composed from two hymns, one addressed to an audience on the island of Delos, a second one in Delphi). The Delphic myth also explains the lavish sacrifices connected with the performance of the oracle: Apollo instituted them in order to feed his priests. Somewhat more complex is the ritual connection of the Hittite myth of Telipinu (Hoffner 1998: 15–20). For some unknown reason, Telipinu disappeared and "removed grain, animal, fecundity, luxuriance, growth, and abundance." A catastrophe ensues: "Humans and gods are dying of hunger." The gods search for him, finally find him, and seem to perform a rite to make him come back ("I have just sprinkled your paths with sweet oil"). Telipinu returns, seething with anger: a second ritual is needed to banish his anger into bronze vats in the underworld: "That which goes into them doesn't come up again." Finally, prosperity and peace return, and Telipinu again "looks after the king and the queen." The text ends with what looks like a further description of ritual: before the god stands a pole or tree on which a sheepskin bag is suspended; it contains every desirable thing, from "animal fecundity and wine" to "plenty, abundance, and satiety." We lack information as to the circumstances in which the text was recited, but it seems obvious that it gives a divine history to a set of rituals performed in connection with the royal couple.

In all these cases, as in many others, myth provides ritual with a divine foundation: the ritual is explained, legitimated, and removed from human influence. In some cases, such as the Delphic part of the *Hymn to Apollo,* the mythical narration is etiological, giving what Malinowski memorably called a charter. But this is not what the "Myth-and-Ritual School" meant to do (and Malinowski had developed his insight in reaction to this school): Frazer and his Cambridge colleagues and followers who were later designated by that nickname went considerably further. In their reading, every myth was generated and shaped by a ritual; furthermore, as Frazer and, in his wake, the biblical scholar Samuel H. Hooke theorized, the ritual in turn reacted to early human preoccupation with fertility of fields, animals, and humans and intended to promote it (Hooke 1933). The Babylonian creation myth was not only generated by the Babylonian New Year ritual; the ritual intended to preserve nature's fertility through the crisis of the year's end. Fertility as sole and only horizon of ritual and myth was questioned rather quickly, and Jane Ellen Harrison, whose first book (1903/1922) on Greek ritual had firmly adhered to Frazer's paradigm, replaced this in her second book (1911/1927) with Durkheimian society and its collective concerns of cohesion and continuity. The link between ritual and myth, however, remained, although its theoretization became more and more complex (Versnel 1993).

Some facts, however, seem undisputed. Rituals and myths often are connected: countless etiological stories explain the origin of a ritual or a festival. Storytelling, however, follows very different rules from ritual performance, and both motifs and entire stories migrate from culture to culture, seemingly without any ritual, and they can attach themselves to new rituals in other cultures. This, then, argues against any genetic connection between myth and ritual; if ever there was one, this was so far distant in prehistory that we cannot even guess at it. But attach to each other they do, and often such myths follow a narrative structure that is comparable to the ritual structure: the recombination of myth and ritual does not seem entirely arbitrary. A handful of structural patterns seem to dominate most rituals as well as most myths, such as the Quest Pattern (Propp 1928). The explanation that makes such structures genetically independent from each other and sees them as basic structures of human experience (Burkert 1979) is as good as any other and elegantly moves the question away from any genetic relationship between myth and ritual.

The ritual performance of the Babylonian creation myth during the New Year festival has always been crucially important for any myth-and-ritual theory. This performance dramatizes the implications of the ritual cycle in which it was embedded. The beginning of the new annual cycle is marked by a ritual process that moves from the dissolution of the old order to the onset of the new one: the mythical narrative turns this into a beginning on a cosmic scale that is not only felt as the success of creation but as the euphoria of "catastrophe survived": the Babylonian narration highlights Marduk's victory, not the coming-into-being of the cosmos. The Athenian festival cycle that surrounds the beginning of the year expresses a similar transition, although in a more complex way. Two of its festivals, the Kronia and the Panathenaia, focus on Cronus, the god whom Zeus deposed and who ruled in the Golden Age, before culture, work, and society; and on Athena, the goddess who gained Athens (thanks to her benefactions) and who will forever protect her city. In this instance, there is no public performance of mythical narration comparable to that in Babylon, but Athena's winning of the city is represented on the west pediment of the Parthenon and thus was visible as soon as the festive procession entered the sacred precinct. This procession prominently displayed and carried up to the goddess a sacred tapestry *(peplos)* embroidered with an image of Zeus's victory over the Giants, a battle nearly as decisive for Zeus's reign as Marduk's against Tiamat was for his, and one in which Athena played a prominent part at the side of her father. In yet another way, the Israelite Sukkot festival combines the specific ritual forms of inversion and dissolution at the turn of the year (Exod. 34.22)—erecting temporary twig huts, dancing, and wine drinking—and the agricultural horizon of harvesting ("when you gather in from the field the fruit of your labor"; 23.16) with the narration of Israel's stay in the desert during the return from Egypt: a detail of the foundation story of Israel serves as explanation and legitimation of the rite and, at the same time, puts it into the wider horizon of a fundamental new beginning. The Roman Parilia, yet another festival where ritual inversion and a focus on agrarian life are dominant (this time the purification of the sheep), is explained with the story of how Romulus founded Rome.

In a more performative reading, the recitation of the creation myth during the New Year ritual makes the renewal happen, as it does in certain ("magical") healing rites. An Akkadian incantation against toothache starts with a long narrative of creation, and many Egyptian and Greco-Egyptian spells make use of either a known or an otherwise unknown mythical story that serves as the powerful antecedent and parallel to the problem in hand: the narration of the one paradigmatic past event, when the gods easily solved the problem at hand, once again will solve it. The memory of a powerful past event carries its own performative power (see further Ritual and Magic).

Myth, history, and memory

In the cases of Israelite Sukkot and Roman Parilia, the myth that accompanies the rite is no cosmogonical myth—the creation myth will become important only for Rosh Hashanah, a New Year festival in postexilic Israel—but an event that is, at least in its indigenous reading, part of Israel's and Rome's histories: the exodus from Egypt and the foundation of the *urbs*.

Mythical narratives were often supposed to be closely connected with historical events. In the view of many indigenous cultures, what we call myth is really history: the Muses, patrons of storytelling, are daughters of Mnemosyne (Memory), after all. In the view of many interpreters of myth, whether native or not, mythical stories contain memories of historical events, albeit in a very distorted form, and it was seen as the task of interpretation to formulate general laws that would undo the distortion. This view is as old as Greek historiography (Hecataeus, *FGrH* 1F1), and the methods of turning myth into history varied widely, from simple rationalization to complex symbolical operations.

In monotheistic Israel, every intervention of God in the visible world—from the creation to the ongoing protection of God's people—is understood as history: where God reveals the past, there is no place for myth. In contrast to this, the surrounding polytheistic cultures knew stories that were similar to Greek myths of gods and heroes: narratives featuring the gods only—such as the Babylonian creation myth and the *Theogony* of Hesiod, the Kumarbi or Baal cycles, or the Egyptian narrative of Isis and Osiris—and narratives that show humans, often as protagonists, interacting with the gods—such as the Gilgamesh poem in Mesopotamia, the story of Keret in Ugarit, the tale of Appu in Anatolia, and the *Iliad* and *Odyssey* in early Greece. This is a function of the fundamental dichotomy between immortal gods and mortal humans, and in the figures of both Gilgamesh and Homer's Achilles human mortality is explicitly problematized. In many narratives, the human protagonists are kings of old or otherwise powerful people: only past humans of high distinction were worthy of being retained in memory. Gilgamesh, "son of Lugulbanda, perfect in strength," is the king who built Uruk's walls; the names of Lugulbanda and Gilgamesh appear in the Sumerian King List of Uruk (although separated by another name), and Gilgamesh is given a different father there, a high priest: whatever the historical facts, already the Sumerians regarded Gilgamesh as king of old (Dalley 1989: 40). Keret in the story from Ugarit is king of Khabur and seen as an ancestor of the ruling dynasty of Ugarit (Wyatt 1998: 177), as perhaps is Danel in the story of Aqhat. Priam is king of Troy; Agamemnon is king of Mycenae, and his contingents are led by a host of local kings; Theseus is king of Athens. Romulus, Numa, and Servius Tullius are kings in Rome, and it reflects the insistence of the Romans that historians still believe in their historicity, not on the basis of any factual evidence—Plutarch, at least, made no difference between Theseus and Romulus. Only the Hittite narration of Appu has a protagonist who is an ordinary citizen, albeit a very wealthy one. All these protagonists directly interact with the gods: Gilgamesh resists being seduced by Ishtar and suffers punishment for his temerity; Aqhat refuses to give his bow to the terrible goddess Anat and also suffers; Keret is personally protected and helped by El, who even creates a healing-goddess for him; the Trojan Paris is rewarded by Aphrodite for his judgment; and the Olympians all take parts for or against King Priam and his city. Romulus has a divine father; King Numa has a divine lover, and he does not hesitate to interact with Faunus, Picus, and even Jupiter in a battle of wits that he wins (Ovid, *Fasti* 3.275–344).

With these narratives, scholars sometimes felt at a loss about nomenclature: were they dealing with "myths," "legends," or "epic poems"? The question is irrelevant at best, misleading at worst: it is a matter of our own categories, and there is no scholarly consensus as to what these categories mean. Legend is as modern a term as myth, and it is often used for Christian stories, such as saints' lives, or for stories that claim a historical background (*Sagen* in the terminology of the Grimm brothers); neither of these associations is desirable. If myth, furthermore, is seen not as a specific narrative but as the plot structure that transcends individual narratives—a meaning that takes account of the many variations, spoken and written, of a given story—and if myth and epic poem are not mutually exclusive categories, then an epic poem is one specific concretization of a myth or of an entire cluster of myths, as is the case with Gilgamesh and the *Iliad,* compositions in the prehistory of which shorter individual songs *(Einzellieder)* are still preserved or recoverable. The difference between myth and epic poem, then, is the result of the creative power with which the individual narrator reacted to his myths and the pressures of the performative situation. In other words: both the Middle High German *Nibelungenlied* and Wagner's Ring Cycle are concretizations of the same myth. Whether any myth contained historical memories or was generated by a specific historical event—as the *Nibelungenlied* contained memories of the situation of central Europe at the time of the Big Migrations or as the *Chanson de Roland* had as an origin a specific event during a campaign of Charlemagne—is very much a matter of scholarly research and debate, and recent examples also show that such a historical core does not explain much of the narrative. It would be as futile to reconstruct the history of early Sumerian kingship from Gilgamesh as it proved futile to reconstruct the Trojan War from the *Iliad*, despite our growing awareness of Troy as a historical city-state at the margins of the Hittite Empire. Mythical narratives are no faithful memories of things past; they are construed according to the memory that every generation believes it needs for its own purposes.

Triumph and demise of mythology

Some narratives had a larger impact than others and traveled from one culture to another—not just as story patterns, but as story plots that included both specific actions and specific actors. Versions of Gilgamesh were widespread around Mesopotamia; Akkadian, Hurrite, and Hittite versions were kept in the Hittite capital Hattusha-Bogazköy in the later 2nd millennium, and the best-known version belonged to Assurbanipal's library in Nineveh. Another story, Nergal and Ereshkigal, was found in widely different versions in Akhenaten's Egyptian capital (modern Tell el-Amarna) and, several centuries younger, in Mesopotamia. We might be tempted, in these cases, to talk about literature, not mythology, and compare the fate of Homer's poems: copies of the *Iliad* and the *Odyssey* made their way to Alexandria and Rome, with the Latin translation of the *Odyssey* being the first Latin literary text, the *Odusia* of Livius Andronicus (ca. 240 BCE); and we could point out that most modern libraries have copies and translations of all three epics. But the distinction between mythology and literature is tenuous and somewhat arbitrary: modern writers still generate versions of these stories, following once again the story plot (or myth) that transcends an individual version. And while most modern versions never attain long-standing societal relevance, some achieve at least a short-lived relevance, such as Christa Wolf's *Cassandra* or Joyce's *Ulysses*.

But this only, once again, points to the transitory character of most scholarly categories. More urgent, in the present context, is another phenomenon: the migration and wholesale acceptance not of a single story, but of an entire body of stories, a mythology. The archives of Hattusha not only contained the different versions and translations of Gilgamesh, they presented an extraordinary collection of mythical texts written in Hittite, Hurrian, and Akkadian and concerning divinities who were Hittite (such as Telipinu), Hurrian (such as Kumarbi), Mesopotamian (such as Anu or Enki/Ea), and Ugaritic (such as Baal or Anat). One reason for this variety seems to lie in the character of Hittite domination: the empire was multicultural, and the cults that the king attended to were not just his own ancestral cults, they comprised the worship of various divinities all over his kingdom. Myths were indispensable for the performance of cult—hence their presence in the royal archives. Not that this explains everything; the versions of the Gilgamesh story, for example, must have been collected for reasons not very different from those that make the story still worth reading and thinking about some millennia later: the story has no connection whatsoever with cult but talks about general themes—the quest for friendship and the urge to overcome mortality.

The surprising western expansion of Greek mythology had different reasons. Not much after 800 BCE, the first Greek settlers arrived on Ischia, off the coast of Campania, and in the next two centuries they built their cities around the southern coast of the Italian mainland and on Sicily. The colonists exploited Italy's fertile soil and rich metal deposits; merchants must have preceded the colonists. The first images of Greek myths appear not much later, as do the first examples of writing. Before 500 BCE, Etruscan cities had taken over Greek gods such as Apollo, both his name and his iconography; the Romans had built a temple to the Dioscuri, the Castores, in their Forum, adorned another temple with pedimental sculptures presenting Athena and Heracles, and equated their Volcanus with the Greek Hephaestus: the fragment of a vase image showing how Hephaestus introduced the drunken Dionysus to Olympus was found on the Forum next to the Volcanal, Volcanus's cult site. By 300, Etruscan bronze mirrors depict countless scenes from Greek mythology, often with the names of the persons added, in native alphabet and native spelling: gods and heroes of the Greeks had become a firm part of the Etruscan imaginary world, and scenes that depict not a Greek but a (presumably) Etruscan myth are rare indeed. When Roman literacy sets in, the staggering extent of the takeover becomes visible. Whereas many Roman gods retain their Latin names—in Ennius's famous list of the twelve Olympians (*Annales* 62–63), only Apollo is Greek—their iconography and their stories derive from Greece. Roman mythology presents itself mainly in the accounts of the historians: Romans read their nondivine myths as easily in a historical key as their Hellenistic Greek contemporaries did with their epic poetry. The quality of the images and the stories must have had an important hand in this expansion, as had the lifestyle of the Greeks, their architecture and technology; temple building, the symposium on couches, the writing system were adapted, as well as stories and images. The *Iliad* and the *Odyssey,* the Theban epics, and the feats of Heracles fascinated Etruscans and Romans in the same way that the Gilgamesh story had fascinated listeners in western Asia (and Gilgamesh, too, belonged to a culture that set standards for life and technology), and many stories that arrived in the West were far removed from any anchoring in cult and ritual. But they in turn could be put to use for new etiologies or serve as models for new stories: the Roman rite of praying with a covered head is explained by a story from the mythology connected with Aeneas (Dionysius Halicarnassus, *Roman Antiquities* 12.16.1), and the story of Numa, Faunus, and Picus is manifestly influenced by Greek narratives. Scholars have argued that such stories were "literary" and "poetic inventions" and therefore not "real" myths; but this argument rests on the romantic definition of myth as a story of hoary antiquity and falls flat as soon as tradition and relevance, not age, are made the main criteria.

The final test of Greek myth's resilience came with the expansion of Christianity. Confronted with the one living and revealed God, the gods of the Gentiles became demons (1 Cor. 10.20–21), and their stories were turned into exhibits in the court of public opinion: the easy life of the Greek gods, their sexual appetites, and their sometimes negligent cruelty were ready proofs of their bad character and of the satanic inspiration behind their cult. The Christians treated the mythological narratives no differently from the way they treated the Gospels: true accounts of life and exploits of the divine and human actors. Such accusations were not exactly new: moralizing Greek philosophers had condemned these same stories, from Xenophanes of Colophon and Heraclitus of Ephesus onward (late 6th century BCE). Plato joined them, advocated heavy censorship of storytelling, and created his own philosophical myths, as had well-meaning sophists. But immediately, interpretation came to the defense of the traditional stories: what counted was not so much the surface reading but an underlying philosophical or moral meaning; truth could be distilled from the myths, if only they were read in the proper way. Generations of philosophers developed allegorical readings, and by Hellenistic times, the system was well in place (Dawson 1992); it was easily turned against the Christian accusations. And once Christianity had changed from the small world of marginal sectarians into a movement ready to convert entire cities and provinces, positions were swapped once again. Mythical narratives were too well embedded in the fabric of ancient culture and daily life to be excised or exorcised, and Christian teachers used these same instruments of allegory in order to tame the pagan stories for their own use. Seemingly without effort, the mythical narratives could be made to teach the Christian message.

Bibliography

Burkert, Walter. *Structure and History in Greek Mythology and Ritual.* Berkeley: University of California Press, 1979.

Caduff, Gian Andrea. *Antike Sintflugsagen.* Hypomnemata 82. Göttingen: Vandenhoeck & Ruprecht, 1986.

Dalley, Stephanie. *Myths from Mesopotamia: Creation, the Flood, Gilgamesh, and Others.* Oxford: Clarendon, 1989.

Dawson, David. *Allegorical Readers and Cultural Revision in Ancient Alexandria.* Berkeley: University of California Press, 1992.

Detienne, Marcel. *L'invention de la mythologie.* Paris: Gallimard, 1981. English translation: *The Creation of Mythology.* Chicago: University of Chicago Press, 1986.

Doty, William G. *Mythography: The Study of Myths and Rituals.* Tuscaloosa: University of Alabama Press, 1986.

Dundes, Alan, ed. *The Flood Myth.* Berkeley: University of California Press, 1988.

Fontenelle, Bernard de. "De l'origine des fables." In *Oeuvres complètes,* ed. Alain Niderst, vol. 3. Paris: Fayard, 1989 (orig. 1724).

Gressmann, Hans. *Altorientalische Texte zum Alten Testament.* 2nd ed. Berlin: De Gruyter, 1926 (orig. 1909).

Güterbock, Hans Gustav. *Kumarbi: Mythen vom churritischen Kronos aus den hethitischen Fragmenten zusammengestellt.* Zürich: Rhein, 1946.

Harrison, Jane Ellen. *Mythology and Monuments of Ancient Athens.* London and New York: Macmillan, 1890.

——. *Prolegomena to the Study of Greek Religion,* 3rd ed. Cambridge: Cambridge University Press, 1922 (orig. 1903). Rpt. Princeton: Princeton University Press, 1991.

Hesiod. *Theogony,* ed. and commentary M. L. West. Oxford: Clarendon, 1966.

Hoffner, Harry A., Jr. *Hittite Myths.* 2nd ed. Writings from the Ancient World 2. Atlanta: Scholars Press, 1998.

Hooke, Samuel Henry, ed. *Myth and Ritual: Essays on the Myth and Ritual of the Hebrews in Relation to the Culture Pattern of the Ancient East.* London: Oxford University Press, 1933.

Malinowski, Bronislaw. *Myth in Primitive Psychology.* London: W. W. Norton, 1926.

Pritchard, James B., ed. *Ancient Near Eastern Texts Relating to the Old Testament.* 3rd ed. Princeton: Princeton University Press, 1969 (orig. 1950).

Propp, Vladimir. *Morfologiia skazki,* 1928. English translation: *The Morphology of the Folktale.* Tr. Laurence Scott and Louis A. Wagner. Austin: University of Texas Press, 1968.

Puhvel, Jan. *Comparative Mythology.* Baltimore: Johns Hopkins University Press, 1987.

Schuol, Monika. "Zur Überlieferung homerischer Epen vor dem Hintergrund altanatolischer Traditionen." In *Grenzüberschreitungen: Formen des Kontakts zwischen Orient und Okzident im Altertum,* ed. Monika Schuol, Udo Hartmann, and Andreas Luther. Oriens et Occidens 3. Stuttgart: Steiner, 2002.

Staudacher, Willibald. *Die Trennung von Himmel und Erde: Ein vorgriechischer Schöpfungsmythos bei Hesiod und den Vorsokratikem.* Tübingen, 1942. Rpt. Darmstadt: Wissenschaftliche Buchgesellschaft, 1968.

Versnel, Hendrik S. "What Is Sauce for the Goose Is Sauce for the Gander: Myth and Ritual, Old and New." In *Inconsistencies in Greek and Roman Religion,* vol. 2: *Transition and Reversal in Myth and Ritual,* pp. 16–89. Studies in Greek and Roman Religion 6.2. Leiden: Brill, 1993.

West, M. L. *The East Face of Helicon: West Asiatic Elements in Greek Poetry and Myth.* Oxford and New York: Oxford University Press, 1997.

Wilcke, C. "Die Anfänge der akkadischen Epen." *Zeitschrift für Assyriologie* 67 (1977): 153–216.

Wyatt, N. *Religious Texts from Ugarit.* 2nd ed. Biblical Seminar 53. London: Sheffield Academic Press, 2002 (orig. 1998).

Cosmology: Time and History

John J. Collins

*A*ccording to Greek tradition, Pythagoras "was the first to call the sum of the whole by the name of the cosmos, because of the order which it displayed" (Aetius 2.1.1). Cosmology, strictly speaking, is the rational discussion of the cosmos, which developed in Greece from the 6th century BCE onward. The word is used more loosely to refer to any discussion of the nature and coherence of the world. Such discussion can be found long before the beginnings of Greek science and philosophy in the myths of the ancient Near East, especially those that dealt with cosmogony or creation.

Creation myths

It is important to bear in mind that ancient religion was not dogmatic or systematic in the manner of later Western faiths. There were no creeds to which everyone subscribed. There were several creation myths in ancient Egypt. Each city that rose to power formulated its own myth of creation. In the cosmogony of Heliopolis, the creator-god was Atum; in Memphis, Ptah; in Hermopolis and Thebes, Amun. Each cosmogony, however, had only one creator-god, and he was credited with giving life to the gods as well as to humanity. The sun-god Re appears in almost every creation account, and his name is often joined with that of other creators (Amun-Re, Re-Atum). The actual process of creation was conceived by human analogy. One model supposed that the origin of life came from the creator's semen. In the Heliopolitan cosmogony, Atum generated the first divine couple from himself, either by masturbation or by spitting. Another model associated the creative power with the utterance of a word. In the Memphite Theology, Ptah creates "through what the heart plans and the tongue commands." A third model, based on the work of an artisan, was exemplified by the potter-god Khnum. Life was often thought to have originated on a primeval mound, which emerged when the primeval flood receded.

These Egyptian creation myths are remarkable for the lack of conflict in the process. Egyptian history did not lack conflict, but the myths projected a sense of stability and permanence. This stability was expressed in the concept of *ma'at,* an all-embracing principle of order that governed all aspects of nature and society. A creator-god such as Ptah and Atum was "lord of *ma'at.*" *Ma'at* was sometimes portrayed as a goddess, Maat, the daughter of the sun-god Re, who accompanied him as he sailed across the sky. The sovereignty of the creator-god had its counterpart on earth in the rule of the pharaoh. The conflict often encountered by the monarchy was acknowledged in the myth of Osiris and Seth, but this myth too ended in stability. The evil Seth was defeated by Horus, the posthumous heir of Osiris, who then became king on earth. The living pharaoh was the embodiment of Horus, while the dead king, Osiris, was ruler of the netherworld.

In contrast to the Egyptian creation myths, those of the Semitic world were stories of conflict. The best known of these myths is the Babylonian *Enuma Elish,* which casts Marduk, god of Babylon, in the role of creator. More precisely, it distinguishes two stages in creation. In the beginning was a primordial couple, Apsu and Tiamat, often understood to represent freshwater and saltwater respectively, although this distinction is not explicit in the myth. The mingling of their waters produces the other gods. The creation of the world is a separate process. The young gods kill their father Apsu, but are then endangered by the wrath of Tiamat. Marduk is the hero who does single combat with Tiamat and kills her. In return, he is made king of the gods. From the carcass of Tiamat he creates the world: He split her like a shellfish into two parts. Half of her he set up as a sky and posted guards to make sure that her waters did not escape. He further fixed the astral likenesses of the gods in the sky and determined the months and the year. Finally he made humanity, from the blood of Qingu, an ally of Tiamat, to serve the gods. Another Mesopotamian myth, Atrahasis, describes a different occasion and process for the creation of humanity, involving a mixture of the blood of a god with clay. The political overtones of the Babylonian myth are transparent. If the gods need a strong monarchy in order to ward off danger, so too does Babylon.

We do not have a story of the creation of the world from Syria or Canaan. The god El is called father and is said to have begotten other deities. We might infer that creation was conceived as a form of procreation. The closest analogues to *Enuma Elish* in the Ugaritic literature are found in the myths of Baal. These myths describe combat between Baal and Yamm (Sea) in one episode and between Baal and Mot (Death) in another. What is at stake is the kingship of the gods, under El. These myths are often viewed as cosmogonic, on the grounds that they establish order in the universe. Support for this view comes not only from the analogy with the *Enuma Elish* but from the frequent association of creation with the defeat of a monster in biblical poetry (e.g., Job 26; Ps. 89.10 [= 89.11 Hebrew]). These combat myths suggest that creation, or the order of the cosmos, is fragile and has to be reestablished periodically in the face of recurring dangers.

The canonical account of creation in the Bible (Gen. 1) is closer in spirit to the Egyptian myths where a sovereign creator creates by his word, unhindered by any opposition. (This is not necessarily to posit Egyptian influence. There is some evidence that the biblical writers were deliberately rejecting the Babylonian account of creation, as they use the word *tĕhôm*, cognate of Tiamat, to refer to the deep without personification.)

Tales of primeval conflict are also found in Hittite (Anatolian) mythology (*ANET* 120–28). One such myth tells how Kumarbi attacked the king of heaven (Anu) and bit off and swallowed his "manhood." As a result he became pregnant with three dreadful gods, including the storm-god. The end of the myth is fragmentary, but it is likely that Kumarbi was eventually challenged for the kingship by the storm-god. In another myth, the Song of Ullikummi, Kumarbi rebels against Teshub, the storm-god. In this myth, Kumarbi impregnates a rock and fathers a giant, Ullikummi, who wreaks havoc on heaven and on earth. Eventually, the giant is crippled by the god Ea. This myth tells us incidentally that the gods severed heaven from earth with a cleaver. Yet another Hittite myth tells of a battle between the storm-god and a dragon, Illuyanka.

Greek mythology provides no comprehensive creation myth such as we have in the *Enuma Elish*. Hesiod synthesizes a range of mythological traditions in his *Theogony*. In the beginning was Chaos (a yawning void). Then came Earth, Tartarus (a terrible place beneath Hades), and Eros. From Chaos came Erebus (a dark region between Earth and the netherworld) and Night. Of Night were born Aether and Day. Then Earth brought forth Heaven and the Sea. Then she lay with Heaven and bore numerous gods. In contrast to Near Eastern mythologies, Earth is begotten, not made. While it is not clear how Earth, Tartarus, and Eros emerge from Chaos, the later stages of creation are explicitly sexual. While Heaven and Earth are not absolutely primordial, they are the progenitors of the great majority of the gods. Heaven (Uranus) is father of Cronus, who in turn is father of Zeus, the eventual supreme god. Hesiod has his own combat myth: the conflict between Zeus and the Titans and Typhon, which ends with Zeus's confirmation as king of the gods. This conflict is not related to the creation of the world, however (see further Myth). The primeval character of Earth in Hesiod is consonant with the view of later Greek philosophers such as Aristotle that the world is eternal. This view was sharply at variance with the prevalent belief in creation in the ancient Near East. According to Hesiod's *Works and Days*, the gods made the first human beings in the time of Cronus.

A quite different account of the origin of the world was proposed by Plato in his dialogue the *Timaeus*. Plato reasoned that the world must be created since it is visible and tangible, and all sensible things are in a process of change. The creator, whom he calls simply "god," desired that all things should be good and nothing bad and therefore made the world as perfect as possible. Accordingly, the cosmos became a living creature, endowed with soul and intelligence, and may even be called a god itself. Because of its perfection, it was imperishable. The emphasis on the goodness of creation is reminiscent of the biblical account in Gen. 1 and made the *Timaeus* attractive to later Jewish and Christian philosophers. Plato's creator is a craftsman, a *dēmiourgos,* like many of the creator-gods of the Near East. As in the myths, creation is not fashioned out of nothing. Where the myths began with unformed matter, or the biblical "waste and void," Plato posited invisible and formless space. Plato's idea of creation, however, was exceptional in the Greek world. Aristotle was more typical in regarding the cosmos as a self-contained whole, ungenerated and imperishable. Moreover, there is always some question as to how Plato intended his myths to be understood.

Plato's view that the initial creation was good was fully in keeping with the ancient creation myths. Hesiod provides several explanations for evil in the course of his *Theogony* and *Works and Days* (e.g., Pandora's jar). Only the Persian Zoroastrians, however, attempted to account for evil in the cosmogony itself. In their account, two opposing cosmic entities existed from the beginning: Ahura Mazda (Ohrmazd), the wise lord who was god of light, and Angra Mainyu (Ahriman), the god of darkness. These gods struggled throughout history. In a variant of this myth, the opposing gods were twin offspring of one supreme good god. The idea of a devil or Satan, which appears in Judaism in the Hellenistic period and became very influential in Christianity, was probably of Persian origin. The influence of the Persian myth can also be seen in the Jewish Dead Sea Scrolls, which say that God created two spirits to govern humanity, one of light and one of darkness.

The view of the world

Throughout the eastern Mediterranean world and Near East, the basic view of the world in the earliest literature is tripartite, distinguishing heaven, earth, and netherworld. The Egyptians variously described the heavenly realm as a bird, a cow, a woman (the goddess Nut, balancing on her feet and hands), or a flat plane held up by pillars. The sun-god Re was thought to traverse the heaven by day and then journey back to the east through the netherworld at night. After death, the soul or spirit had to encounter various dangers in the netherworld, but the righteous person might hope to ascend to a blessed life, either on earth or in heaven. The blessed abode of the dead is often called the Field of Rushes or Field of Offerings. It is far removed from everyday human life, but different texts seem to imply a location in the heavens or at the ends of the earth. The hope of the righteous was also expressed in terms of joining the stars and mingling with the gods in heaven.

In Mesopotamia, too, heaven was the abode of the gods (there were also gods of the netherworld). Human beings, however, were restricted to the netherworld after death, and this was a gloomy place. The futility of the quest for immortality is the theme of the Epic of Gilgamesh. The quest takes the hero to the ends of the earth to the abode of Utnapishtim, the flood hero, who had been granted eternal life. The myth of Adapa, in contrast, tells of the ascent of its hero to heaven, where he is offered eternal life, but rejects it because of the advice given him by the god Ea. The legend of Etana also tells of an attempt to ascend to heaven, which apparently ended in failure. The general principle held true: heaven was for the gods, humanity lived on earth and descended to the netherworld after death. There is also some evidence in Mesopotamian traditions for multiple heavens, but these had no effect on human destiny.

The most important Mesopotamian contribution to the study of the cosmos was in the areas of astrology and astronomy. The Babylonians looked to the stars for clues to the intentions of the gods. The practice of astrology implied that the movements of the stars and human affairs were interconnected, as indeed were other phenomena on earth, such as the flight of birds. But the Babylonians also developed more scientific forms of astronomy, both by observation and by mathematical calculation. There was no clear distinction between astrology and astronomy. The movements of the stars were thought to be significant for events on earth. The term *Chaldean,* which originally referred to a tribe that rose to power in Babylon, was used to designate astrologers in the Hellenistic and Roman periods.

Neither Syria nor Israel contributed much to the study of the stars. Astrology was discouraged in biblical tradition because of the temptation to worship the host of heaven, although there is evidence that some Jews practiced astrology in the Hellenistic and Roman periods. Here again the world was usually seen as tripartite. In both Canaan and Israel, heaven was the abode of the heavenly host, while dead human beings descended to a gloomy netherworld. There is some evidence that exceptional individuals, including kings, might hope for immortal life with the gods. The Bible allowed that a few individuals (Enoch, Elijah) had been taken up alive to heaven. But such cases were exceptional. The stars were the heavenly host, divine or angelic beings, who were sometimes thought to intervene in human affairs.

The earliest Greek conceptions of the cosmos were very much like those of the ancient Near East. The earth was a flat circular surface, surrounded by the river Oceanus. The sky was a disk of comparable size above it, held up by pillars guarded by Atlas (so Homer) or by Atlas himself (Hesiod). The gods were variously said to live on Mount Olympus or in the aether above the sky. The dead went down to Hades, beneath the depths of the earth, where there was no joy.

Beginning in the 6th century, however, Greek cosmology was transformed by several developments that would have long-lasting consequences far beyond the borders of Greece.

First of these was the rise of a new approach to cosmology, pioneered by the pre-Socratic philosophers. This approach favored explanations in terms of matter, without positing divine interventions. Even when the philosophers spoke of gods, they were not anthropomorphic in the manner of the myths, but rather represented aspects of the cosmos. Of course the demise of the gods was neither immediate nor complete, even in the domain of Greek philosophy, as can be seen from the *Timaeus* of Plato. Plato not only defended the idea of a creator, but argued that the world had a soul and bitterly attacked the materialistic view of the universe put forward by some philosophers. Other Greek thinkers, such as the Stoics, dispensed with the creator and regarded the universe itself as divine. The Stoics supposed that the universe was animated by Pneuma (Spirit) or Logos (Reason), a fine fiery substance that represented the active element in humanity as well as in nature. These Hellenistic concepts provided a way of reconceiving older Near Eastern ideas. Egyptian *ma'at* and Israelite wisdom were traditional concepts of cosmic order. Jewish Hellenistic writings such as those of Philo show how such concepts could be given Platonic or Stoic overtones in the Hellenistic period. Even those such as Jews and Christians, who insisted on a creator-god and therefore found Plato more congenial than they found the Stoics, reconceived their understanding of deity in terms that were more cosmological and less anthropomorphic. In Hellenistic Judaism, wisdom or spirit was considered to be the divine element in the universe, which pointed beyond itself to a creator. In Stoic theology, the cosmos, animated by spirit, was itself the deity.

The development of Greek astronomy led to a new view of the universe, significantly more complex than the old three-tiered model. Pythagoras held that the earth and the heavenly bodies were spheres moving in harmony. Plato accepted the idea that the earth was a sphere and supposed that the moon, sun, planets, and fixed stars revolved around it in their own orbits (*Republic* 10. 616–17; cf. *Timaeus* 36–39). With some variations, this model became widespread in the Hellenistic period and later. Cicero, in the *Dream of Scipio,* posited nine spheres. The outermost, the starry heaven, contains the whole and is itself the supreme god. Beneath it are seven other spheres: Saturn, Jupiter, Mars, Sun, Venus, Mercury, and Moon. The ninth and central sphere, the earth, is immovable and lowest of all. The model of the geocentric universe, with various refinements, was given its classical expression by Claudius Ptolemy of Alexandria in the 2nd century CE. The attempt of Aristarchus of Samos in the 3rd century BCE to argue for a heliocentric universe had little impact.

This new view of the universe is reflected in the Near Eastern cultures in various ways, primarily in the belief in multiple heavens. An Egyptian depiction of the cosmos from the Ptolemaic era shows the goddess Nut bending over the world not once but twice. Jewish and later Christian apocalypses tell of visionaries ascending through multiple heavens, typically seven, but sometimes three and occasionally other numbers. These visionary texts are not concerned with scientific cosmology, but they reflect the assumptions of their time about the general shape of the universe.

Related to the interest in multiple heavens was the belief that the righteous dead lived on in heaven with the stars. The epitaph of soldiers fallen at the Battle of Potidaea in 432 BCE says that the aether had received their souls, the earth their bodies (*IG* I³ 1179). The idea of heavenly immortality was given philosophical nuance by Hellenistic philosophers, who associated the aether, or upper heavenly regions, with the finest, most divine substance. Eastern peoples related it to their own traditional beliefs. In Jewish apocalypses, astral immortality meant joining the host of heaven or the angels. In the Hellenistic period, even Hades was often located in the heavens. The new view of the world had no logical place for an underworld, although the old beliefs lived on in popular religion. Plato's pupil, Heracleides Ponticus, is said to have claimed that the Milky Way was the path of souls passing through Hades in the heaven. Jewish and Christian apocalypses located the torments of the damned as well as the joy of the blessed in the heavenly regions.

Celestial eschatology tended to imply a negative view of the earthly regions. The soul was weighed down by bodily existence and was liberated to rise up after death. This tendency was taken to an extreme conclusion in late antiquity in the gnostic cosmologies that saw the creator or demiurge as an evil figure and that represented the creation of the material world as a fall. The material world was then viewed as an evil place from which souls had to be saved by enlightenment and ascent to the realm of spirit. This late antique view of the world had come full circle from the insistence of the Bible and of Plato that both the creator and the creation were very good.

Time and history

The ancient creation myths had implications for the understanding of time and history, although they did not devote much explicit reflection to them. The heavenly bodies were seen to regulate time. When Marduk fixed the stars in the *Enuma Elish,* he established the months and the years. In the biblical account, the world was created in six days so that God could rest on the Sabbath, completing the week. According to Plato, who was vastly more systematic in his reflections, time and the heaven came into being at the same instant. The sun, moon, and planets were created in order to distinguish and preserve the numbers of time. The myths generally implied a cyclic view of history. They described not only the beginning of things, but paradigmatic events that could be reenacted over and over. For the Egyptians, each sunrise recapitulated the establishment of *ma'at.* For the Israelites, historical events such as the Exodus or the return from the Babylonian Exile were reenactments of the victory of the creator over the chaos dragon. From early times, Egyptians and Babylonians were aware that all the planets revolved. Plato formalized the idea of a Great Year—the period of time that it takes for the sun, moon, and five planets to complete their rotations and return simultaneously to the same positions in relation to the fixed stars. Plato suggested that the revolving Great Years were punctuated by periodic disasters of fire and flood, which were reflected in Greek mythology in the stories of the fall of Phaethon while driving the chariot of the sun and the myth of Deucalion. The Stoic doctrine of *ekpyrōsis* (conflagration) also involved the periodic return of all things to the primal substance and their subsequent renewal.

It was axiomatic in the ancient world that gods could intervene in human affairs and implement their plans in history. Mesopotamian rulers often attributed their rise to power to the plan of their patron deity. Homer's gods acted purposefully, even if they were often at odds with each other. In most cases, these divine plans concerned limited episodes. The biblical accounts of the role of YHWH in the history of Israel are exceptional in their scope, spanning several generations. Moreover, the opening chapters of Genesis provide an account of early universal history, which forms a backdrop for the emergence of Israel. Nonetheless, the biblical story of Israel stops well short of providing a comprehensive view of all history. Such a view emerges only in the apocalyptic writings of the Hellenistic period. In the Greco-Roman world, the best analogue to the early biblical history is found in Vergil's *Aeneid,* which describes the emergence of Rome as the culmination of an epic history under divine guidance.

Hesiod's myth of the successive ages of humanity, in his *Works and Days,* is important for the emergence of a concept of universal history. It is quite possible that the poet is adapting a myth of Median or Persian origin, but this is difficult to establish because of the notorious difficulty of dating the Persian sources. Hesiod (*Works and Days* 109–196) enumerates five ages: first the golden, then the silver, then the bronze. The fourth is not defined by a metal, but is that of "the godlike race of heroes who are called demigods, the race before our own." The fifth age is that of iron, of which Hesiod says that he wishes he had either died before or been born afterward. Since he allows that something will come afterward, some people have supposed that he expected a return to the golden age, but Hesiod does not say this. He leaves the future open. The return to a golden age is suggested much later in Vergil's Fourth *Eclogue,* which refers to a "last age" predicted by the Cumean Sibyl.

The division of history into epochs or *saecula* was developed by the Etruscans and taken over by the Romans. A natural *saeculum* was the highest age a human being could attain (approximately one hundred years). A civil *saeculum* began with the founding of a city or state and lasted as long as any member of the founding generation lived. The end of a *saeculum,* however, was not always obvious and had to be inferred from signs given by the gods. Ten *saecula* were allotted to the Etruscan people, after which they would disappear. In the mid-1st century BCE there was speculation about what point in the process had been reached. On one interpretation, a comet that appeared after the murder of Julius Caesar marked the end of the ninth *saeculum* and the beginning of the tenth. The grammarian Servius (4th century CE) said that the "last age" of Vergil's Fourth *Eclogue* was the tenth. Whether this final age should be understood in the context of Etruscan speculation is disputed.

The most elaborate division of history into periods in antiquity was that of the Zoroastrians. The classic form of their theology of history is found in the Middle Persian *Bundahishn.* According to this theology, the two opposing primordial spirits, Ahura Mazda and Ahriman, coexisted for three thousand years before the creation of the world in its physical state. Thereafter world history would last for nine thousand years, divided into three periods of three thousand years each. The first three thousand would pass according to the will of Ahura Mazda, and the second three thousand would be a mixture, governed by both gods. The third period is divided into three distinct millennia. The end of each millennium is marked by tribulations and disasters, followed by the coming of a new savior. The final battle would be fought at the end of the third period. The final millennium is further divided into periods. The *Bahman Yasht* reports a vision by Zarathustra of a tree with four metallic branches, gold, silver, steel, and mixed iron. These are interpreted as representing four historical periods. A variant of this vision, also in the *Bahman Yasht,* lists the ages as seven in number.

The Persian texts are preserved in Pahlavi manuscripts from the 6th to 9th centuries CE, but the division of history into periods is certainly much older than this. Plutarch, writing around the late 1st or early 2nd century CE, gives an elliptical account of the myth, which he derived from Theopompus (early 4th century BCE). One god would dominate the other and be dominated for three thousand years. For another three thousand they would fight and make war. In the end the evil power would be destroyed. It is not clear whether this is a somewhat garbled form of the myth known from later sources or whether it represents a different division of history. It is clear in any case that the division of history into millennia was known in Persian tradition before the Hellenistic age. Some scholars have supposed that the Persian tradition of four ages symbolized by metals, attested in the *Bahman Yasht,* underlies Hesiod's schema of four declining ages. Such a proposal is difficult to verify because of the late date of the Persian sources, but this kind of periodization is an integral part of Persian cosmology, while it is exceptional in Greek tradition.

In Jewish apocalyptic writings of the Hellenistic period, history is sometimes divided into ten generations, a schema most probably derived from the Persian millennium. This division is frequently found in the Jewish and Christian Sibylline Oracles. So, for example, in Sibylline Oracles books 1–2 history is divided into ten generations, punctuated by the flood in the fifth generation and culminating with a conflagration. These oracles sometimes incorporated the work of pagan Sibyls, and so the question arises whether the tenfold division of history was a feature of the Sibylline genre outside Judaism. The only evidence for this, however, is Servius's interpretation of Vergil's last age as the tenth, in the 4th century CE. The evidence suggests that the use of Sibylline Oracles to provide a comprehensive overview of history was a Jewish adaptation of the genre.

Other schematizations of history were also popular in Jewish and Christian tradition, notably the sevenfold division derived from the days of creation or from the idea of a sabbath. Christian writers such as Lactantius in the early 4th century CE held that the world was in the 6th and final millennium of its history. Lactantius drew on a wide range of ancient philosophical and mythical speculations about the cosmos, including the late Persian Oracle of Hystaspes, a work that has sometimes been regarded as Jewish. The syncretistic character of late antiquity is shown by the difficulty of distinguishing Persian, Jewish, and other traditions in texts such as this.

Cosmic eschatology

The periodization of history is closely related to the expectation of an end of history or of the world. Ancient Near Eastern myths, such as the *Enuma Elish*, saw the establishment of kingship as the end of a process. Insofar as one might speak of a goal in history, it was the establishment of a definitive, lasting kingship. In the Bible, this was provided by the Davidic dynasty, which was supposed to last forever. When the Judean monarchy was dissolved by the Babylonians in the 6th century, hopes for the future focused on the restoration of the Davidic line. Sometimes this was expected to usher in a virtual golden age (e.g., Isa. 11.6: "The wolf shall dwell with the lamb"). A Babylonian prophecy from the 6th century BCE speaks of a king who would rule the entire world and whose dynasty would stand forever and exercise authority like the gods. Later, Vergil's *Aeneid* promised Rome an *imperium* without end, and the Fourth *Eclogue* described the transformation of the earth.

One widespread motif relating to the hope for definitive kingship envisioned a sequence of four kingdoms and a fifth. Herodotus noted a sequence of empires in Asia: Assyrians, Medes, Persians. Since the Medes never ruled in the West, this sequence is probably of Persian origin and viewed the Persians as the final, definitive empire. In the Hellenistic era, the sequence was extended to include Macedonia and finally Rome. This schema could be used in the interests of imperial propaganda, but it could also be used for subversive purposes. In the *Bahman Yasht,* the fourth kingdom is identified as "the *divs* with disheveled hair," an unflattering reference to the Greeks. The implication of the vision is that this kingdom will be overthrown at the end of the millennium. The Jewish Book of Daniel is more explicit. Daniel sees a statue made of different metals representing a declining series of kingdoms. (This vision is closer to the *Bahman Yasht* than to Hesiod, insofar as the final kingdom is a mixture of iron and clay.) In the end, the statue is destroyed by a stone representing the Kingdom of God, which presumably would be represented on earth by a Jewish kingdom.

The classic expressions of cosmic eschatology are found in Jewish and Christian apocalypses. The Hebrew prophets had spoken metaphorically of the end of the world in describing the destruction of specific places. Beginning in the 2nd century BCE, however, such language is used more literally. The Apocalypse of Weeks in *1 Enoch* says that at a fixed point in the future the world will be written down for destruction, and the old heaven will be taken away and replaced with a new one. The apocalypse of *4 Ezra*, written at the end of the 1st century CE, provides for a period of primeval silence between the destruction of the old world and the new creation and resurrection of the dead. The Book of Revelation in the New Testament also predicts the destruction of this world and the creation of a new one. Revelation provides for a thousand-year reign on earth for the just before the new creation. The popular use of the word *millennialism* is derived from this motif in Revelation. The motif of a final millennium in history, however, had older roots in Persian tradition.

The final conflict in apocalypses such as Daniel and Revelation has much in common with the old creation myths of the ancient Near East. In Revelation, the angel Michael casts a dragon down from heaven, and there are also beasts on land and sea. In the new creation, the sea (which was personified in the old Canaanite myths) is no more. In these texts, imagery that was used in the myths to describe the beginnings of the cosmos are projected into the future, to describe its consummation. It is likely, however, that the apocalyptic view of history is also influenced by Persian tradition. In the Zoroastrian myth, each of the last three millennia is characterized by tribulations and disasters, followed by the coming of a new savior. At the end of the final millennium, those who are still alive will not die, and those who are dead will be raised in a general resurrection. The wicked are purified in streams of fire as part of the purification of the world. After the conflagration, all things will be made new.

The hope for resurrection at the end of a predetermined historical sequence first appears in Jewish tradition in the apocalypses of Enoch and Daniel in the Hellenistic period. The Zoroastrian myth was certainly current before this time. The most complete reflection of the Persian account of the last things in Jewish or Christian tradition is found in the Christian author Lactantius in the 4th century CE. Lactantius synthesized various traditions in his writings and incorporated lengthy passages from the Oracle of Hystaspes.

Greek tradition usually viewed the world as imperishable, despite periodic destructions by fire and water. This was true even for Plato, despite his affirmation of creation. Even Hellenized Jews, most notably Philo of Alexandria, allowed that the world may be made immortal by the providence of God, even though it is by nature destructible. The notion of cosmic conflagration *(ekpyrōsis)* held a prominent but controversial place in Stoic thought. The *ekpyrōsis* would purify the cosmos, but would not entail a judgment. Stoics disputed among themselves whether it would be followed by *palingenesia*, renewed birth and repetition of all things. The Roman Seneca, writing in the 1st century CE, spoke of the time when the world would extinguish itself in order to renew itself again. Stars would collide, and all matter would burn with a single fire. Seneca claimed support for these ideas from Berossus, a Babylonian priest who presented Babylonian tradition in Greek in the early Hellenistic period. According to Seneca, Berossus said that these things would happen in accordance with the course of the stars and even predicted the time of the conflagration. The idea of cosmic conflagration is not attested in Akkadian sources, however, and seems to have no basis in Babylonian tradition.

A rare example of cosmic eschatology in the Egyptian tradition is found in the late Apocalypse of Asclepius, which is written in Greek and associated with the Hermetic corpus. This apocalypse retains some of the characteristics of political oracles. An evil age is caused by the invasion of foreigners, and this is followed by a radical transformation of the earth. It differs from earlier Egyptian tradition by envisioning a destruction of the world by fire and flood and then its restitution to its pristine state. It reflects the syncretism of late antiquity, where ideas circulated widely and the coherence of cosmos and history was widely assumed.

Bibliography

Clifford, R. J. *Creation Accounts in the Ancient Near East and in the Bible*. Washington, D.C.: Catholic Biblical Association, 1994.

Cohn, N. *Cosmos, Chaos, and the World to Come: The Ancient Roots of Apocalyptic Faith*. New Haven: Yale University Press, 1993.

Collins, J. J., ed. *The Encyclopedia of Apocalypticism*, vol. 1: *The Origins of Apocalypticism in Judaism and Christianity*. New York: Continuum, 1998 (esp. essays by A. Hultgård and H. Cancik on Persian and Greco-Roman traditions).

Couliano (Culianu), I. P. *Expériences de l'extase: Extase, ascension et récit visionnaire de l'hellénisme au moyen âge*. Paris: Payot, 1984.

Wright, J. E. *The Early History of Heaven*. New York: Oxford University Press, 2000.

Wright, M. R. *Cosmology in Antiquity*. London: Routledge, 1995.

Pollution, Sin, Atonement, Salvation

Harold W. Attridge

*A*ncient societies, like all human groupings, set boundaries on human behavior, defining actions that disrupted human relations in various ways as wrong. Some actions such as murder, incest, or theft were almost universally condemned, although what counted as truly unjustifiable homicide or illicit sex might vary and the boundaries of the moral community within which such actions were prohibited might vary. Other actions could easily accrue to a list of wrongful acts, from the trivial (making others sad, as in Egypt) to the profound (rebellion against God, as in Israel). Whatever the faults, people of all societies found ways of committing them, either inadvertently or maliciously. Religious systems, understood here to be the complex of rituals and stories that provided a symbolic matrix for social institutions, provided mechanisms for dealing with these actions and eliminating their results. Ritual and story, however, were not the only mechanisms for dealing with wrongful acts. Legal systems also defined crimes and specified forms of punishment and restitution. Legal systems intersected with the religious at significant points in some traditions.

Within the religious sphere, the mechanisms for dealing with "sin" involve two major conceptual schemes. Sin may be conceived as an objective defilement, a form of pollution that infects the sinner and the people and places with which the sinner might come in contact. To deal with the danger presented by the sinner, mechanisms usually involve some effort to remove the pollution or the polluting agent. Alternatively, sin may be understood in more personal terms as an insult or offense to divine power. In that case, mechanisms for dealing with the sinner may involve appeasement of the offended power, either through cultic action or repentant behavior, restitution, and reconciliation. The logic of sin as an offense against a deity leads to suffering being construed as divine punishment and the possibility of vicarious suffering as a mechanism for atonement.

Each of these somewhat conceptual schemes for dealing with sin may be seen as an "ideal type," useful for heuristic purposes but seldom at work independently. Both are often at play in cultic traditions, and the logic of both will inspire attempts to develop moralizing critiques of traditional practice and, later, theologies of sin and atonement in the monotheistic religions of late antiquity.

Pollution

Pollution was a particularly weighted form of generic uncleanness. Even this category could be construed differently in different cultural systems, since "dirt" is simply matter out of place and the boundaries of "clean" places are culturally determined. Mud on a farmer's foot in the field need not be dirt; mud on the floor of the farmer's hut could be. Pollution was that form of "dirt" that prevented participation in the realm of the sacred; impurity at any level was simply incompatible with sanctity. It was necessary to be pure in order to enter a temple or engage in a ritual, although being pure might not be a sufficient condition to allow participation, which could be limited to people of a certain age, sex, or status. The requirement to maintain purity was thus more incumbent upon participants in religious rituals than it would be on nonparticipants. In cultures with a permanent priestly class, the requirements for purity would weigh more heavily on them than on the laity.

Many things could cause pollution, but the primary sources of pollution were natural substances: blood, spittle, semen, decaying flesh. Many polluting acts involved contact, willing or unwilling, with such substances, but the material stuff of polluting dirt was the paradigmatic source of pollution. Ancient Israel's extensively documented purity system defined sources of pollution, including diseases of the skin (Lev. 14); bodily discharges, such as semen or menstrual blood (Lev. 15); and corpses (Num. 19.11–16). Similar sources of pollution are attested in ancient Mesopotamian sources (van der Toorn 1985: 30–31). Birth, sex, and death are also major sources of cultic pollution in Greece. Bits of flesh from the corpse of Polynices polluted the altars of the gods (Sophocles, *Antigone* 999–1047). It was not right *(themis)* for the goddess Artemis to look upon her dead devotee (Euripides, *Hippolytus* 1437). The sacred island of Delos was kept free of pregnant women and the mortally ill. (Abundant examples may be found in Parker 1983.) In addition to such common sources of pollution, particular animals might be unclean for certain temples, as in Egypt or for a people as a whole (Lev. 11.24–47).

To encounter simple forms of impurity was thus unavoidable for most people much of the time. In fact, in some systems, such as that of ancient Israel, some ritual impurity was required. Thus, the act of sexual intercourse, required to fulfill the divine commandment to be fruitful and multiply (Gen. 1.28), would render husband and wife ritually impure. Similarly, to bury dead relatives was required even of Israelite priests (Lev. 21.1–3; Ezek. 44.25), though the act was defiling.

The paradigmatic case of pollution is contact with an offensive substance that renders a person "unclean" and not suitable for participation in cult. Sources from many different cultural traditions treat various wrongful acts under the same general rubric. Thus a Mesopotamian incantation seeks absolution for both the ritual infraction of "eat[ing] what is taboo to [a] god [or] . . . goddess" and also a wide variety of social transgressions, such as "oppress[ing] the weak woman," "estrang[ing] companion from companion," "[taking] money . . . not due," and so on (Reiner apud Milgrom 1991: 22–23). Similarly the Egyptian Book of the Dead (125) involves a negative confession, a denial that the deceased was guilty of various negative actions ("stopping a god in his procession," "eating what is *bwt*," or "making anyone weep") and transgressions (stealing, murder, adultery). The Israelite priestly manifesto demanding holiness of the people, Lev. 19, combines the moral injunctions to revere parents and avoid theft and sexual immorality with instructions about the proper eating of sacrificial food and appropriate hair trimming and body decoration. Modern categories of cultic, social, and moral infractions were simply not part of the conceptual scene at the earliest stages of the religious traditions of antiquity. Hence the use of the term *pollution* for serious moral offenses is readily understandable.

Another impetus for the understanding of serious moral infractions as polluting may have to do with the involvement of blood in some of them, at least homicide and illicit sexual activity. Murder was a special source of pollution in many cultural contexts. Even gods were required to wash themselves after killing (*Atrahasis* 1.206–7; van der Toorn 1985: 16). Mesopotamian sources consider bloodshed an abomination (Annals of Assurbanipal: *asakku*) or an offense that brings a divine curse (*Surpu* 2.49). In Israel, major infractions such as bloodshed (Num. 35.33), sexual infractions (Lev. 18.24–30), and idolatry (20.1–5; Ps. 106.34–41) polluted either the sinner (Lev. 18.24), the sanctuary (20.3; Ezek. 5.11), or the land as a whole (Lev. 18.28; Ezek. 36.19). Early Greek law codes (Draco, 7th century BCE) could invoke the category of pollution in connection with murder. This was probably not an innovation, but a vestige of a long-established cultural form. Dramatists of the 5th and 4th centuries wove concern with pollution in objective or personified (Erinyes) form into their plays. Heinous crimes such as patricide (Oedipus) or matricide (Orestes: Aeschylus, *Choephoroi* 269–96; Euripides, *Orestes* 580–84) could produce *miasma,* an objective state of pollution that isolated the perpetrator (Plato, *Euthyphro* 4c) and prevented participation in ritual (Euripides, *Orestes* 1600–1604). Such pollution had more-serious consequences, bringing destruction to nature and culture (Aeschylus, *Agamemnon* 1644–45).

Sexual offenses could be equally polluting. Sumerian law declared that a man who raped a girl publicly became impure (van der Toorn 1985: 17). Even a god such as Nergal remained impure, despite bathing, after an affair with the queen of the netherworld. In Israel, the priestly sources of Israel viewed various illicit sexual unions as abominations (tôʿēbôt; Lev. 18).

Offended deities

The appeal to the divine as the sanction of the moral order was a powerful tool of social control. Yet in many traditions, fickle and impetuous deities could be offended at various minor slights. In the ancient Near Eastern myths of Atrahasis (*ANET* 104–6), the god Enlil is enraged at noisy humans and decides to obliterate them in a flood. In Egypt the goddess Hathor/Sekhmet (*ANET* 10–11) lusts for human blood. The Greek Artemis, after having been forgotten at a sacrifice, sends the scourge of the Calydonian boar. The Roman authorities blamed the defeat of their army by Hannibal at Trasimene on the neglect of religious ceremonies, at least according to Livy (22.9).

Gods could be offended by more serious slights. The *Iliad* opens with a scene of plague besetting the Achaean army at Troy because Agamemnon has incurred the wrath of Apollo by carrying off the daughter of his priest (*Iliad* 1.8–52). More serious still was the direct affront to the dignity of a god caused by sacrilege, the transgression of the places and things sacred to the deity, a concern widely attested in ancient sources. What counted as sacrilege included purely cultic issues: the misuse of sacrificial animals, improper disposition of sacred implements or foods, or introducing pollution into sacred spaces. Thus, in the defense of the sacred, the two conceptual realms of objective pollution and divine human relation merge.

The affront of a sacrilegious act was particularly apparent when the deity's name was invoked in vain. Ancient Near Eastern political treaties or covenants often involve oaths invoking divine guarantors of the treaties and threatening severe punishments for those who do not abide by the oaths. The Tukulti-Ninurta Epic of the 13th century BCE describes the anger of the Babylonian deities caused by the king's treaty violations. Either by defiling the deity's sacred space or by dishonoring the deity's name or status, the sacrilegious transgression evoked a divine sanction. In the epic just mentioned, the result was the offended deities' defection to Assyria, which conquered Babylon. The Mesha Stele from 9th-century Moab (*ANET* 320–21) describes a similar situation, in which the god Chemosh delivered Moab into Israelite control for a time. Homer, too, knows that Zeus punishes perjury (*Iliad* 4.160–62).

Gods may have felt abhorrence at the fact of moral pollution, their honor may have been compromised, or they may have been offended by the rebellious and ungrateful character of their subjects. In any case, their wrath manifested itself in fearsome responses. Israel's God can be as fierce as other ancient deities (Deut. 32.34–43; Ezek. 36.16–19), but his wrath is not arbitrary; rather, it is focused on transgressors, on the people in covenant with him who forget their obligations (Exod. 22.21–24 [= 22.20–23 Hebrew]), particularly by committing idolatry (32:7–10; Ps. 106.37–42). This wrath at the violation of the covenant leads, in the judgment of the prophets, to national destruction (Isa. 22:1–14) and exile (27.1–11). Expectations of a major day of divine wrath, in which YHWH would wreak vengeance on his foes, developed in Israel (Amos 5.18–20). In early Christian hands, the eschatological wrath of God against the universal reality of sin forms the background for the news of salvation (Rom. 1.18; Rev. 15.7).

While the threat of divine sanction could undergird moral and legal obligations, the understanding that the divine punished transgression provided a way of interpreting human history. Human suffering in the form of plagues, droughts, or military defeats was *prima facie* evidence for sin and divine wrath. The plague that visits Thebes due to Oedipus's actions stimulates a search for the guilty party, and a storm at sea leads to the search for the sinful prophet Jonah. The prophets of Israel, and the historical works they inspired, thus often appealed to the covenant formulas as the basis for their theological assessment of history. The theology of providential divine retribution at work in history was hardly confined to Israel, but also appears in Greek (Polybius, Dionysius of Halicarnassus) and Roman (Livy) historians.

Eliminating pollution and sin

For the simple and unavoidable or required forms of pollution, there were ready remedies. Things that caused impurities could be disposed of in various ways: by being burned, buried, or simply washed away. Simple procedures—such as a ritual bath, use of special substances (natron in Egypt; wine, clay, various plants, flours, salts in Hittite sources; the ashes of a red heifer in Israel [Num. 19]), periods of abstention from social contact (e.g., for new mothers or mourners) or from contact with the realm of the sacred—would restore the polluted person to a state of purity. The impurity removed, the individual could once again cross the boundary from profane to sacred and participate in cult. Homer's heroes must wash or purify themselves before sacrifice (*Iliad* 6.266–68), and all Athenian citizens had to purify themselves before entering the sacred space of the assembly. Israelite women were excluded from touching *sacra* after menstruation or birth, for varying periods of time: seven days for a son, two weeks for a daughter (Lev. 12.1–8).

Pollution could affect larger social units and thereby require more extensive treatment. Ancient Mesopotamian (9th-century BCE Assyria under Assurnasirpal: REVIA 2.218.85; 226.26/27; and Salmanasar: RMA 3.15.26; 3.66.70) and Hittite sources report rituals for purifying armies. Places as well as people could become polluted. But cleansing was readily available through washing or "wiping" rites, such as the ancient Akkadian *kuppuru* (Wright 1987: 291). In Israel, houses as well as people could be affected with a skin disease and require extensive purification (Lev. 14). Greeks of the archaic and classical periods knew of *katharmoi* (rituals for washing, wiping, rubbing, fumigating) and professional purifiers, forebears of both magicians and physicians.

A frequent way of dealing with pollution and other undesirable substances such as disease was through rites of disposal. Such rites could involve various mechanisms for transferring the offensive pollution to a bearer of impurity, by spitting, touching, or passing through special gates. Or the pollution could be symbolically concretized through colored threads placed on a victim and then removed. The bearer of the pollution could then be either banished or destroyed. Such rituals are found in materials from ancient Ebla, 13th-century BCE Hittite texts (the Pulisa and Ashella rituals for removing plagues), the Israelite scapegoat ritual, and in various *pharmakos* rituals in Greek cities such as Abdera, Massilia, and Athens. Israel had its equivalents in the ritual for cleansing a leper, which involved the sacrifice of one bird and the expulsion of another (Lev. 14.2–7, 48–53), and above all in the scapegoat procedure, part of the ritual of the annual Day of Atonement. Part of the procedure involved sacrifice of one goat while another decorated goat was sent to the desert, to the mysterious "Azazel," bearing all the iniquities, sins, and transgressions confessed by the people (16.21). This complex ritual has given its name to the whole class of such ritual actions. The relationship among these scapegoat rituals and the differences among them have been the subject of considerable scholarly study. Although there are significant formal cross-cultural similarities, such as the use of decorated animals or human beings, specifics of goals and procedures vary considerably (see Ritual).

The manipulation of blood was frequently part of rituals designed to eliminate pollution. Actions involving blood would be particularly understandable in the case of the severe pollution caused by the shedding of blood, on the assumption that only blood, the locus of life itself (Lev. 7.26–27, 17.14), could purify the pollution caused by blood (explicitly at Num. 35.33; cf. the rite for dealing with bloodguilt when the murderer was unknown, Deut. 21.1–9). Israel's priestly code contains provisions for sacrifices connected with other purification rituals (e.g., Lev. 15.29, for an irregular discharge of blood), but there are two major blood sacrifices explicitly designed to deal with transgressions: the "purification sacrifice" (*ḥaṭṭā't*; Lev. 4) and the "reparation sacrifice" (*'āšām*; 5.14–6.7 [= 5.14–26 Hebrew]). Both are designed in order to "make expiation" *(kpr)*. The animal used for a "sin offering" varied with the status of the offerer, and its blood would be sprinkled at various sacred locations (4.5–6, 18, 25, 30, 34; 7.2). The relationship between these sacrifices and their underlying logic are unclear. The blood of these sacrifices may have been understood as a powerful cleansing agent, removing from sacred space the stain of the sin's pollution. Similarly, the blood of the sin offering of a bull on the Day of Atonement was to "make atonement for the holy place, because of the uncleannesses of the people of Israel" (16.16). The *'āšām* is distinctive in that a monetary offering could be substituted (5.15) and in that it required restitution (5.16; 6.5 [= 5.24 Hebrew]). The latter requirement indicates that, for some priestly circles, atonement involved more than ritual. In their current literary setting, both sacrifices deal with "inadvertent" sins (4.2; 5.14), although the *'āšām* also applies to swearing falsely, suggesting a broader scope.

Appeasing divine wrath

Although divine wrath may be distinguished from sinful pollution for heuristic purposes, they often appear to be intimately linked. Thus in the Hittite scapegoat rituals, gods are asked to "be appeased" by the human offerings (Wright 1987: 46, 50). But while apotropaic rituals might avert divine wrath, an offended deity might be treated as an offended human being.

Torts could be repaired by acts of restitution or the payment of a ransom. Stolen property could be restored, with an added penalty perhaps (Exod. 22:1 [= 21.37 Hebrew]), or one could pay for a gored ox (21.35–36). Serious crimes such as bloodshed required vengeance, the death of the murderer (21.12) at the hands of an "avenger of blood" (gō'ēl haddām; Num. 35.19). The Israelite legal tradition rejects the possibility that those responsible for the wrongful death of another could avoid the death penalty by payment of a ransom (Exod. 21.30; Num. 35.31), but the condemnation suggests the existence of the practice. Interestingly, the term for "ransom" (kōper; Greek lytron) derives from the same root as that used of cultic "expiation." The language of ransom was used in Israel for the sanctuary tax paid by the people (Exod. 30.12). Although they knew the mechanism, Israelite literature does not extensively exploit notions of ransom as ways of dealing with divine wrath. A stark alternative is provided in the Roman tradition of devotio, according to which a general could snatch victory from the jaws of defeat by vowing himself to the infernal gods (Livy 8.9.1–11.1; 10.28.12–29.7).

Wrongs against others could require propitiation and appeasement of the offended party. Insofar as a deity may have been involved, atonement usually included some sort of ritual of appeasement, perhaps a sacrifice or other offering to the offended deity, but also a direct appeal, in which the offending human being confessed guilt and sought reconciliation. Such appeals are found in hymns from the 2nd millennium BCE, such as one to Marduk found at Ugarit (Ras Shamra 25.460) or to Ishtar in ancient Babylonian (Iraq Museum 58424).

The notion of moral wrong as an act of rebellion (pš') against the divine lawgiver is characteristic of ancient Israel, forming the heart of the prophetic summons to repentance and renewed fidelity to the covenant relationship. The Torah (Lev. 26.40) recognizes the need for repentance and confession. The prophetic movement that achieved written form in the 8th century insists on confession and repentance (Jer. 3.11–14; 4.1–2). The pattern of confession continues with renewed vigor in the Second Temple period (Ezra 9; Dan. 9.4–19) and provided the framework for much early Christian treatment of sin and atonement.

Confessions of sinfulness and penitent appeals to divine mercy are not incompatible with notions of purification from sin's pollution. Striking versions of the pattern are found in Israel's lament psalms. Psalm 51 combines many of the metaphors, asking YHWH for mercy, for cleansing (vv. 2, 7 [= vv. 4, 9 Hebrew]) from sin, for purging from interior guilt (v. 6 [8]), leading to moral renewal (v. 7 [9])—all of which is made a condition of effective sacrificial offering (v. 16 [18]). Similarly Ezekiel, in the 6th century, proclaiming a hopeful vision for Israel's future, portrays YHWH as promising Israel purification from the uncleanness of idolatry and interior transformation with a new heart and spirit (Ezek. 36.22–33), all of which prepares for a renewed sanctuary (40–48).

Emphasizing the interpersonal character of sin, atonement could also involve the intercession of a mediator, one who, as the Hebrew tradition says, "stands in the breech," pleading for transgressors, such as Moses (Exod. 32.11–14, 30–34; Ps. 106.23), kings such as Hezekiah (2 Chron. 30.18–20), priests in general (Num. 8.19), specific priests such as Aaron (16.47 [= 17.12]) and Phineas (Ps. 106.30), or an angel (Job 33.24). A trusted mediator could avert divine wrath, as could an innocent representative of a people, whose suffering for others' transgressions brought healing (Isa. 52.13–53.12).

Criticism and resignification

Ancient rituals of purification from pollution, either ritual or moral, as well as cultic mechanisms either for dealing with the objective results of sin (expiation) or for appeasing the wrath of offended deities (propitiation), were subject to moralizing or rationalist criticism.

Israel's prophets, while calling for repentance, denounced a reliance on the mechanics of cult (1 Sam. 15.22–23; Amos 5.21–23; Isa. 1.10–15; Mic. 6.6–9), although that critique did not entail the total rejection of cult. (A similar critique seems to underlie the Zoroastrian revolution in ancient Persian religion.) Combining ritual and moral behavior was not unique to Israel. Thus Xenophon, leading his fractious Greek army, calls for both repentance and purification after some of his troops murdered local ambassadors (*Anabasis* 5.7.13–35).

Important for later developments were the admonitions of Israel's teachers of wisdom, who advocated various personal moral practices to expiate sin. Proverbs 16.6 highlights works of compassion; texts from the Second Temple or Hellenistic period suggest such things as virtuous obedience to parents (Sir. 3.3), almsgiving (3.30), and fasting (34.30–31; *Psalms of Solomon* 3.8; *Testament of Reuben* 1.10) as expiations.

In the Greek world, two significant developments occurred at the beginning of the classical period: a rationalist criticism of traditional purification rites and an insistence that moral purification was required for "salvation." Greek philosophers ridiculed purification rites—for example, Heraclitus decreed the foolishness of "trying to wipe off mud with mud" (frag. B 5). Later, Aristotle's pupil Theophrastus described those obsessed with such practices as "superstitious" (*deisidaimōn*, literally being excessively afraid of the divine world and its powers; *Characters* 16). Equally open to criticism was the notion that gods needed propitiation from human worshipers. No, argued philosophers, deity needed nothing, least of all human sacrificial gestures.

While rationalists ridiculed rites, some groups of the 5th and 4th centuries BCE, particularly Pythagoreans and those who followed teachings attributed to Orpheus, transformed purification rituals from cult-related practices to boundary markers of their own groups. Plato denounced the rituals and the books connected with Orpheus as trickery (*Republic* 364b–65a), yet appropriated their insistence that purity of the soul was a precondition for blessed immortality. Such beliefs find striking attestation in gold leaves from four 4th-century BCE burials at Thurii in southern Italy, which speak of the deceased as coming "pure from the pure" and as members of the race of blessed immortals; two of the leaves say that the deceased has done "penance for works unjust" (see Mysteries).

Plato could criticize popular purifiers yet retain vestiges of traditional notions of pollution, as in the *Laws* (9.831–73), which indicates degrees of pollution deriving from bloodshed. More importantly, his depiction in the *Phaedo* of Socrates' last hours is replete with language of purification. The soul, says Socrates, can attain to the realm of truth only if it distances itself from the contaminating imperfections of the body, with its "loves, desires, fears, and fancies." Only that which is pure *(katharon)* can attain the realm of the pure (*Phaedo* 66b–67b; 80d–81d). Plato's distinctly religious language here, as often, provides emotional support for a complex epistemological, aesthetic, and moral vision. Purification from pollution is not a ritual matter, but a distancing of the true self from the realm of physical passion. This reorientation has ultimate salvific consequences, and the combination will appeal to many later religious Neoplatonists, both pagan (Porphyry, Iamblichus, *Life of Pythagoras*) and Christian (Origen, Augustine).

Ancient notions of pollution found new homes in other spheres. Hippocratic physicians focused much of their treatment on the *katharsis* of unbalanced and hence polluting elements (Parker 1983: 213). Aristotle, perhaps inspired by the Hippocratics, applied the same notion to the effects of tragedy (*Poetics* 6.1449b28).

Heirs of the Israelite tradition in the Hellenistic period, influenced by such Greek rationalism and their own native sapiential tradition, reduced the ritual elements of their tradition to symbols of the moral (the 2nd-century BCE *Letter of Aristeas*). The Jewish philosopher of 1st-century Alexandria, Philo, who read his scriptures through Platonic lenses, insisted on the observance of ancient Israelite purification rules, but found in them Platonic ideals. Souls, that is, must be made pure before bodies can be cleansed (*Special Laws* 1.263–69), and, while eliminating the impurity of the corpse, one engages in contemplation (*On Dreams* 1.209–12).

The cosmic power of sin

As general social practice and ritual observance dealt with undesirable conditions and actions in concrete practical ways, some religious systems developed large conceptual frameworks for dealing with the realm of the undesirable in all its complexity. Ancient Egyptian sources delineated a negative realm that opposed the realm of *ma'at,* the realm of goodness, order, and sufficiency. Zoroastrian sources in 5th-century Persia, in an influential move, posited, as part of a comprehensive theodicy, an opposition of two fundamental forces, personified as the deities Ahura Mazda and Ahriman. Perhaps inspired by such dualism, Jewish sectarians of the Second Temple period envisioned a world divided into two spheres, one guided by a Spirit of Light, the other by a Spirit of Darkness, responsible for all evil. The Dead Sea Scrolls provide the primary testimony to this scheme (e.g., *Rule of the Community,* also known as 1QS or *Serek ha-Yahad*). Jewish apocalypses of the period, such as the 1st-century CE 4 *Ezra,* also decry the pervasive power of sin. Other works provide explanations for that power. Perhaps the most colorful is the tale in the 3rd-century BCE *Book of Enoch.* On the basis of Gen. 6, this Jewish apocalypse recounts the myth of the Watchers, heavenly beings who became enamored of human women, had intercourse with them, and induced them to sin (*1 Enoch* 6–9). In such a context, moral transgression became not simply a matter of an individual's failing, but part of cosmic phenomenon, a manifestation of a universally pervasive sin.

Cosmic sin required a cosmic response. Jewish sources of the Second Temple period envisioned a decisive intervention by God into human history to restore Israel, often at the hands of an anointed (hence Messiah) royal or priestly figure, either human or angelic. This action could involve the elimination of political oppression (Daniel, *Psalms of Solomon*) or the elimination of sin through the action of an angelic priest such as Michael (Dan. 12) or Melchizedek (*Melchizedek* [11Q13] from Qumran). Such apocalyptic hope resolved problems with sin and sins in a rosy eschatological future.

Along with an increasing sense of the power of sin, sectarian Jewish sources also extended the category of pollution to serve as a general description for all sin (e.g., at Qumran, the *Thanksgiving Scroll* [1QH] 19[11].10–11).

The rabbinic movement, which came to dominate Israel's religious life after the destruction of the temple in Jerusalem in 70 CE, marks a shift. Continuing the critical stance of the Jewish wisdom literature, the rabbis agree that the means of expiating sin are to be found in the moral order. In a famous anecdote, Rabbi Jochanan ben Zakkai (late 1st century CE) responded to a colleague's lament for the devastated temple by noting that expiation was possible through almsgiving (*Avot of Rabbi Nathan* 1.5.4). Other rabbis noted the power of suffering and death to effect forgiveness of sin (Tosefta, tractate *Yoma* 5.6). At the same time, the rabbis insisted on repentance as the key to finding forgiveness for sins.

The rabbis also found their own way of treating the category of pollution and the mechanisms for dealing with it. Instead of expanding the category to cover the whole of the moral order, as did earlier sectarian Jews, or finding in it a metaphorical scheme for comprehending the destiny of the soul, as did the Platonic tradition, they concentrated on the details of ritual pollution in the Torah and developed a detailed logic of the rules of purity. In doing so, they demarcated a realm of behavior for the renewed people of Israel and focused on their obedience to the divine command and their common identity.

While the rabbis constrained the realm of pollution, they also avoided the cosmic power of sin. Their equivalent to the notion of the two cosmic spirits found in the Dead Sea Scrolls is a simple psychological model. In each human heart there are two roots *(yēṣer),* one good, one evil (e.g., Jerusalem Talmud, tractate *Ta'anit 66c;* Babylonian Talmud, tractate *Sukkah* 52b; *Sifre Deuteronomy* 45 on Deut. 11.18). The individual is not a pawn of cosmic powers, but a moral agent capable of choosing good and avoiding evil.

Early Christians inherited both the Jewish scriptures and the traditions that interpreted them. The claims that Jesus was the designated Messiah, assigned to effect that eschatological salvation (Rom. 1.3), appropriated the apocalyptic hopes of contemporary Jews. Some of his followers viewed salvation more in political and social terms (Luke 1, the *Magnificat).* Others focused on how Jesus provided salvation from sin, either by declaring sins forgiven (Matt. 9.2; Mark 2.5; Luke 5.20; 7.47) or by empowering his disciples to do likewise (John 20.23). Some followers used cultic imagery to rationalize his death. In their eyes it was a sacrifice, which provided expiation for sins (Mark 14.24; Rom. 3.25; 1 Cor. 15.3; Heb. 9–10). Jesus was thus the "Lamb of God who takes away the sins of the world" (John 1.29). Such imagery was probably based on Jewish martyrological traditions and perhaps reflected the influence of Isa. 52.13–53.12 and its vision of vicarious suffering as sacrificial expiation.

Most fruitful for later Christian notions was the theology of Paul, who combined a sacrificial understanding of Jesus's death with a cosmic notion of sin as a force so pervasive that it could even disable the revealed Torah and master human hearts *(Rom.* 7.7–25). Like the apocalyptic Jewish tradition from which he emerged, Paul understood that such a cosmic force required a cosmic response. Although he hoped for a future in which all such cosmic enemies would be finally overcome and salvation thus achieved (1 Cor. 15.54–55), he felt the salvific effects already in his own experience. He rationalized the effects of Jesus's death as the provision of a new "spirit" that transforms human hearts and liberates them from the power of sin (Rom. 8). Similarly, the Epistle to the Hebrews envisions the death of Jesus as a new Day of Atonement sacrifice, which expiates the stain of guilt not on altars, but on human consciences (Heb. 9.14) and works its liberating power by providing an example of fidelity to God for followers to emulate (Heb. 10, 12). Hebrews also employs the notion of Christ as an intercessor (7.25) or mediator (8.6), evoking figures such as Moses and Melchizedek.

Early Christians did not, however, confine themselves to a single image for describing the effects of the salvation wrought by Christ. His death was also viewed as a "ransom" (Mark 10.45) or "redemption" that purchased freedom from sin at the price of his blood (1 Cor. 6.20; Eph. 1.7; 1 Pet. 1.18–19). Such language combines ancient notions of the ransom for bloodguilt with contemporary images of purchase from slavery. Alternatively, the mythic imagination of early Christians could conceive of the death of Christ as a battle against the hostile power of sin, or its personification in Satan. Christ, then, achieved salvation as the victorious warrior over the powers of evil (Col. 2.15; Heb. 2.14–15; Rev. 19.11–16). In more personal terms Christians, particularly Paul, drawing upon language of Hellenistic diplomacy, focused on the effect of reconciliation that took place between God and humankind through the death of God's son (2 Cor. 5.17–19; Rom. 5.1–11).

Later Christian authors were generally content to follow the lead of the New Testament, understanding salvation primarily in terms of a deliverance from sin effected by Christ's sacrificial death and the power of the divine spirit. This vision implied the problematic assumption that spiritually transformed human beings would no longer be subject to sin, or at least would not commit serious sins, a notion resisted in 1 John 1.8. A corollary held that for those who did sin or commit apostasy from the group forgiveness was impossible (Heb. 6.4–8). Such rigorism continued in the 2nd and 3rd centuries with Tertullian in North Africa and Hippolytus and Novatian in Rome. A more realistic attitude toward the continuing reality of sin led to the development of a penitential system.

Persecutions of the mid-3rd and early 4th centuries were a particularly important catalyst, as the church had to deal with weaker Christians who had not found the courage to embrace martyrdom and had betrayed their commitment. After the Decian persecution, Cyprian, the bishop of Carthage in North Africa, in his work *On the Lapsed,* insisted against rigorists that even such extreme sinners could find reconciliation with the church, but only under the direction of the bishop.

While some Christians wrestled with the social consequences of sinning by members of the church, others, particularly 2nd-century groups, such as the Marcionites and those labeled by their opponents as gnostic, dealt with the topic in a more theoretical way. Inspired perhaps by early Christian rigorism and by an emphasis on Jesus as revealer of esoteric wisdom, they developed a notion of cosmic sin as ignorance of the transcendent deity. A typical expression of the notion is the 2nd-century *Gospel of Truth,* a work associated with the Valentinian school, which proclaims the rule of error caused by ignorance of God. Jesus remedied that problem and "took away the sin of the world" by revealing the hidden godhead (cf. also the 3rd-century Valentinian *Tripartite Tractate*). For such thinkers, the personal notions of propitiation of an angry deity or expiation of an objective polluting stain were not relevant. As Jewish interpreters had done for their cultic and ritual traditions in the Hellenistic world, these "knowing" Christians reinterpreted traditional moral and cultic categories in their own intellectual terms.

One late-antique religious movement akin to Gnosticism that did take seriously the category of pollution was Manicheism. In a system that recalls the combination of ascetical practice and interior purification encountered in early Pythagorean circles, this 3rd-century CE system advocated, particularly for its "elect" members, a strict dietary regimen that supported the moral purification of the soul, enabling its final return to a heavenly home.

Augustine, a sometime follower of Mani, in the early 5th century brought to its culmination the ancient Christian reflection on sin. Starting from Paul's Epistle to the Romans and its notion of the cosmic power of sin, Augustine developed his own understanding of how sin worked its ways. Where Paul had pointed to the narrative of the fall in Genesis as an example by virtue of which all human beings sinned, Augustine, relying on the Latin translation of Paul's text, found a doctrine of original sin, transmitted to successive generations of humankind by the very physical act of sexual reproduction.

Bibliography

Albertz, Rainer, ed. *Kult, Konflikt und Versöhnung: Beiträge zur kultischen Sühne in religiosen, sozialen und politischen Auseinandersetzungen des antiken Mittelmeerraumes.* Alter Orient und Altes Testament 285. Münster: Ugarit-Verlag, 2001.

Breytenbach, Cilliers. *Versöhnung: Eine Studie zur paulinischen Soteriologie.* Wissenschaftliche Monographien zum Alten und Neuen Testament 60. Neukirchen: Neukirchener Verlag, 1989.

Janowski, Bernd. *Sühne als Heilsgeschehen: Traditions- und religionsgeschichtliche Studien zur Sühneteologie der Priesterschrift.* 2nd ed. Neukirchen: Neukirchener Verlag, 2000.

Milgrom, Jacob. *Cult and Conscience: The Asham and the Priestly Doctrine of Repentance.* Studies in Judaism in Late Antiquity 18. Leiden: Brill, 1976.

———. *Leviticus.* Anchor Bible 3. Garden City, N.Y.: Doubleday, 1991–.

Miller, Patrick. *Sin and Judgment in the Prophets.* Society of Biblical Literature Monograph Series 27. Chico, Calif.: Scholars Press, 1982.

Neusner, Jacob. *The Idea of Purity in Ancient Judaism.* Studies in Judaism in Late Antiquity 1. Leiden: Brill, 1976.

Parker, Robert. *Miasma: Pollution and Purification in Early Greek Religion.* Oxford: Clarendon, 1983.

Sanders, E. P. *Jewish Law from Jesus to the Mishnah: Five Studies.* London: SCM/Philadelphia: Trinity, 1990.

———. *Judaism: Practice and Belief.* London: SCM/Philadelphia: Trinity, 1992.

van der Toorn, K. *Sin and Sanction in Israel and Mesopotamia.* Studia Semitica Neerlandica 22. Assen: van Gorcum, 1985.

Wright, D. P. *The Disposal of Impurity: Elimination Rites in the Bible and in Hittite and Mesopotamian Literatures.* Society of Biblical Literature Dissertation Series 101. Atlanta: Scholars Press, 1987.

Law and Ethics

Eckart Otto

Anthropological foundations of morality in ancient culture

Ethics as a theory of morals considers maxims of conduct from the point of view of the normative good, seeking its philosophical foundations and the consequences of good action. It brings to awareness aspects that implicitly govern action, to the extent that action is morally qualifiable. In the ancient world of the eastern Mediterranean, moral action is characterized by a synthetic view of life, which assumes a correspondence between the way that people fare in life and their deeds. The distinction between "what is" and "what ought to be" is foreign to antiquity, as is any distinction between moral duty and one's fate in life. In the ancient way of thinking, people consist of their actions, so that their existence is determined by fulfilling their obligations.

In the ancient world of the eastern Mediterranean, the moral quality of an action is measured by the extent to which it is in accord with the community's values and maxims; this accord is expressed by the way that justice is defined. The West Semitic root *ṣdq* does not mean justice in the sense of a *iustitia distributiva,* but rather solidarity and loyalty to the community in one's actions, so that the noun *ṣdqh* can be formed in the plural. The Egyptian term *ma'at* also denotes a *iustitia connectiva* of active solidarity and reciprocity of action. An act in accord with *ma'at* toward a person in need is stored in the collective memory of the community and recalled when someone who displayed solidarity needs assistance; the opposite term, *'wn-yb* (greed in one's heart, avarice) denotes egotism. In the Egyptian Lament of the Farmer, this notion of reciprocity is elevated to a moral requirement: "Act for the one who acts for you." The Greek philosopher Democritus observes that a person who loves no one is loved by no one and that the person who commits an evil act against another is unhappier than the victim. In ancient shame cultures, the collective memory of society not only directs the deed reciprocally against the perpetrator, but grants an honorable reputation to those loyal to the community, while humiliating the evildoer. The gods' first task, then, is simply to guarantee a correspondence between a person's deeds and a person's fate.

In a polytheistic pantheon the function of maintaining the world order implied by this correspondence falls not only to the highest god, such as the West Semitic El or the Greek Zeus, but also to special gods such as Shamash, the sun-god of Mesopotamia; Maat, the Egyptian goddess who embodies order in the world; or Dikē, the Greek goddess whose function is to see that laws are enforced. In monolatrous and monotheistic religions such as that of the god YHWH, this function of the sun-god can be either integrated into the god's character (as in Ps. 72) or separated and personified as a substitute figure such as Wisdom (Prov. 1.20–33; 8.1–36). Only when experience runs counter to the synthetic view of a correspondence between the quality of one's deeds and one's life, and the insight gains ground that this correspondence is precarious, are gods put to use as a higher authority for direct retribution. With this development, a motif stemming from sacred law and the law of contracts, in which the divinity directly punishes infringements of sacred duties or of clauses in a sworn contract, is transferred to the broad field of moral action.

At the same time, divine intervention in the world of humans acquires a moral dimension. The arbitrary will of the gods, whose intentions human beings seek to understand through divination, is domesticated by means of its attachment to the moral standards of human action. Thus, the ancients were familiar with numerous stories in which a divinity miraculously intervened in order to rescue a good person (Lycurgus, *Lament of Leocrates* 95–96). But since the idea of divine intervention on behalf of the morally good person is not consistently verified by experience, the link between deed and life can be extended over several generations, to make it mesh better with experience. In the early 6th century, Solon taught that while divine retribution could strike evildoers quickly, it might also be delayed and strike their descendants many years later. In approximately the same period, the Decalogue of the Hebrew Bible postponed divine retribution until the third or fourth generation, to keep the possibility of reform open (Exod. 20.5). Since experience also fails to confirm these theories in every case, divine retribution can be interpreted as a judgment imposed on the dead in an afterlife as well. The notion cropped up first in Egypt during the 12th Dynasty (Merikare, Papyrus Petersburg, lines 53–57) and found its classic expression in the Egyptian Book of the Dead around 1500 BCE. It made its way to Greece by at least the first half of the 5th century (Pindar, *Olympian* 2.58–83) and in the 2nd century BCE reached the Hebrew Bible on the periphery of the canon (Dan. 12.1–3).

For ancient peoples, what counted as "the good" before all ethical theory was traditional conduct in the sense of what was customary and therefore "normal." As a concept of the morally good, the Akkadian word *išaru(m)* (Hebrew *yšr*)—meaning "normal, right, appropriate" and, in connection with the synthetic view of life, also "fortunate, favorable"—expresses the traditional character of ancient value systems. *Išaru(m)* is based on the verb *ešeru(m)* (to be straight, to go straight ahead), from which the abstract noun *mišaru(m)* (justice) also derives, containing the aspect of correcting or straightening out what deviates from the normal. The word *kittu(m)*, which often forms a hendiadys with *mišaru(m)* and derives from the verb *kânu(m)* (to be firm, lasting), also gives expression to the traditional character of the Mesopotamian value system, which guarantees the stability of expected behavior through the traditional nature of ethical and legal norms. In Mesopotamia the promotion of social cohesion was inseparably linked to the concept of justice, as is shown by the *mišaru(m)* and *(an)durāru(m)* edicts of Babylonian and Assyrian kings in the 2nd and 1st millennia BCE, which served to reduce social tensions by forgiving debts and freeing slaves. But they also confirm the traditional character of the ancient Near Eastern concept of justice, which in this respect is paradigmatic for the whole value system of the ancient world. *Mišaru(m)* does not imply the idea of justice in the sense of social equality, so that the *mišaru(m)* edicts were not promulgated with the intention of ending social inequality. Rather, they were designed to prevent expropriation as a result of debt that would drive families out of the hereditary social class. The traditional character of this mentality is underscored by a Sumerian proverb: "The man who sows crops should sow crops; the man who harvests barley should harvest barley." Thus, the good as that which is just is what has always been realized in human action, not an "ought" or obligation, separated from what is, but rather the realized ethical substance of society since time immemorial. There the "ought" is in a state of tension with the possible action and becomes an independent entity when actions deviate from what counts as normal in society. At this point, morality meshes with law, insofar as both judicial practice and the social *mišaru(m)* edicts of the king were understood as correctives or a "straightening out" (*šutēšru[m]*; causative form of the verb *ešēru[m]*) that restored normal, that is, good, conditions as the epitome of just conditions.

The values intended to guide moral action propagated in the memorial inscriptions of the dead and in the educational literature of ancient oriental and biblical wisdom literature are correspondingly traditional. They demand neither great feats nor ascetic self-denial nor martial heroics, but rather are the values of an average bourgeois morality in the modern sense, to which belong diligence, self-control, discretion, honesty, obedience to parents, teachers, and superiors, but also generosity toward inferiors and those with a low position in society, as well as patience—that is to say, above all, an awareness of one's own limitations and the need to rely on fellow human beings and the gods. From such recognition follows a proper measure in all things. In this respect, the Egyptian teaching of Ptahhotep from the first half of the 2nd millennium should be compared with the maxims in chapters 10–30 of the biblical Book of Proverbs, the core of which dates from the first half of the 1st millennium.

The canon of values reflected in memorial and wisdom literature of the ancient eastern Mediterranean remained stable from the 3rd to the 1st millennium, and particular accents were set solely with regard to the literature's function. Thus the teachings of Ptahhotep, which served to educate officials, laid stress on the virtues important for dealing with one's superiors and inferiors, whereas the biblical proverbs were not oriented toward a specific profession and sought to educate in a more general and comprehensive manner. The bourgeois character of this eastern Mediterranean value system, which propagated an ethos of compassion derived from awareness of one's own limits and need for help, had a cultural and historical foundation; in contrast to value formulations of the western Mediterranean, it did not grow out of an aristocratic ethos. Instead, an intellectual caste of priests and sages drew on proverbs based on popular morals to formulate their value system. If the values, taken by themselves, possessed an astonishing similarity from Mesopotamia to Egypt (which derives less from processes of reception than from a socially and anthropologically based fundamental morality or from the peasant and bourgeois majority in the populations of these lands), nevertheless they occupied very different positions in their respective religious systems and in the anthropologies connected with them, which gave expression to different historical experiences and the sense of life. The Middle Babylonian creation epic *Enuma Elish* dates from the close of the 2nd millennium and from at least the 8th century on was recited regularly on the fourth day of the New Year festival in Esangila, temple of Marduk in Babylon; tablet 6.31–40 describes how Marduk, the god of the Babylonian Empire, killed Tiamat, the creature of chaos who embodied everything that causes life to fail, and made the world out of her corpse. Marduk then created humanity from the blood of Qingu, Tiamat's general, as servants for the gods and to free the gods from the guilt they bore for not opposing Tiamat's claim to rule. Thus, the fate of human beings was to work off the guilt of the gods. If they were created from the material of chaos, in the form of Qingu's blood, then it becomes easy to understand why human beings are not only mortal but also grow feeble with increasing age. The myth concludes with the gods building the imperial temple Esangila out of gratitude to Marduk.

In this system, a person could lead a successful life only by following Marduk, god of the empire, who conquered chaos and was represented on earth by the king of Babylon. For a fulfilled life, it was therefore necessary to obey the laws of the Babylonian state or, in the Assyrian version, to obey the laws of the Assyrian ruler, who represented the god of that empire, Assur. An Assyrian myth about the creation of human beings and the king from the first half of the 1st millennium makes a distinction between the creation of human beings *(lullû-amēlū)*, who are supposed to relieve gods of the toil of cultivating the land, and the creation of the king as a "human being who by virtue of his superiority makes decisions [*malīku amēlū*]"—to the king is granted rule over people and the power to wage war following the gods' instructions. This synthetic view of life, in which good actions correspond to success, is linked with loyalty to the state; it is valid only in the context of state rule and is limited even there, since from the time of its creation humankind was ordained to deprivation and toil for the benefit of the gods and the state as embodied by the king.

The Hebrew Bible endorses the contrary anthropological view, which originated in Judah in the 8th century. The writing of the Aaronic priests, conceived in the time of exile as a response to the *Enuma Elish*, similarly ends with the construction of a holy shrine (here the tent of the encounter in the Sinai). It does not, however, recount the story of the creation of the world and human beings as the conclusion of a complex cosmogony and theomachy; rather it places the creation of the world and humans, in accordance with a monotheistic concept of God, at the very beginning. Humans, in this view, were not created to labor in atonement for the sins of the gods, but to give shape to the world as God's representatives. In Mesopotamian royal ideology, the motif of humanity made in the image of god *(soeloem)* was reserved for the king as god's representative *(salum)*; in the Israelite version, the priesthood opposed the negative anthropology in Mesopotamian ideology, which bound humankind to the state legitimated by God, by applying the motif to every individual and democratizing the royal ideology. Already, in the late preexilic era, the writer of Deuteronomy set absolute loyalty to the Jewish god YHWH against the Assyrian demand of absolute loyalty to the state, by subversively transferring the oath of loyalty to King Asarhaddon to YHWH in Deut. 13 and Deut. 28. In this manner, the Deuteronomist imposed limits on demands for loyalty to the state and also deprived the state, in the form of king, of its function as a channel of divine grace. For the first time in the cultural history of the ancient orient, ethical values were disengaged from loyalty to the ruler. Correspondingly, biblical wisdom could formulate criticism of rulers that fit the kingdom of Judah, which was connected with Assyria, by attacking it on the basis of observation of nature: "The locusts have no king, / yet go they forth all of them by bands" (Prov. 30.27). The emancipation of ethical thinking from the state, which was initiated by small circles of intellectuals in Judah, prevailed when the kingdom came to an end during the late Babylonian and Persian era in Judah and consequently prevailed in the Hebrew Bible as well.

This emancipation also ran counter to Egyptian ideology of the state, which still linked the possibility of overcoming the barrier of death to an individual's loyalty to the state, without resorting to the crass negative anthropology that characterizes the Mesopotamian myths of human creation. In Egypt it was held that all human beings owed their ability to breathe—their lives—to the goddess Maat, who provided order and regularity to the cosmos as she guided the course of the sun-god. However, her protective power was directed particularly toward the king, the son of the sun-god and Maat's own brother. Just as the sun-god defeated chaos on a cosmic scale as he crossed the skies and, guided by Maat, enabled *ma'at* (justice) to prevail, so the king embodied this principle in the human sphere. State rule was, thus, the prerequisite for an individual's ability to lead a just life in terms of community solidarity, the sole standard of just behavior that would permit one to pass the test on the day of judgment. But unless the king, deified as Osiris, overcame the barrier of death, an individual had no path into the afterlife. Part of the royal practice of *ma'at* consisted of rewarding subjects for conduct that conformed to it, but it also consisted of using the law courts to resolve conflict and eliminate conduct likely to cause harm *(isfet)*. The state played an indispensable role, because human actions were by their very nature not in accord with *ma'at;* the human heart followed the law of the stronger *(isfet),* that is, egotism that endangers society. *Ma'at* could reach human hearts only through the medium of the king. In Jerusalem, too, people knew that human beings could not realize "loyalty to the community" in their own actions, through their own power alone. Despite a positive theology of creation (Ps. 8), loyalty was not granted to humankind by nature; instead, a sense of loyalty to the community, and with it the ability to act for the benefit of the community, was conveyed through a sacrifice (Deut. 33.19; Ps. 4.5 [= 4.6 Hebrew]) with YHWH's blessing (24.5; 89.14–16 [= 89.15–17 Hebrew]; 99.4; Isa. 1.21–27; 33.5). In comparison with Egypt and Mesopotamia, the king in Judah was relegated to the background in the process of granting loyalty.

The ancient western Mediterranean value system differed from the eastern in being based primarily on an aristocratic ethos rather than an everyday morality of peasants and the middle classes. The aristocratic ethos was not primarily concerned with social cohesion, but rather stressed agonistic values of combat, placing defense of personal honor *(timē)* before justice (in the sense of actions that further a sense of community). The twenty-second book of the *Odyssey,* in which the poet shows Odysseus killing 108 young men who sought the hand of his wife, Penelope, during his long absence, glorifies behavior that attaches higher value to the renown of a great feat in the eyes of an aristocratic audience—even if it consists of mass murder—than to peace in the community. Hesiod, by contrast, who at about the same time questioned this traditional glorification of honor and combat, made justice *(dikaiosynē)* the core concept of his value system, in a reversion to ancient Middle Eastern wisdom literature. An ethos that declares victory in battle as the highest value was branded as unjust hubris, which the gods would avenge, and in accordance with this the nature of the gods themselves, particularly Zeus, was recast in ethical terms. Aristocrats, as judges, were made responsible for ensuring that justice prevailed, with justice being limited to punishment of injustice. The aspect of social cohesion and solidarity, which colored the concept of justice in the eastern Mediterranean, was largely absent in Greece.

Nevertheless *dikaiosynē* in Hesiod implies that peace and the well-being of the community are valued more highly than a hero's fame. It exhorts people who feel they have been wronged to resist boundless revenge and instead accept payments from the wrongdoers; thus will conflicts end. Only if the wrongdoer refuses to cooperate should one wait for an opportune moment and strike back. In contrast to ancient Middle Eastern wisdom literature, Hesiod neither required the wronged person to forgo retaliation entirely nor adopted the *lex talionis.* This role existed in ancient Babylonian law only to protect free citizens from physical injury and was limited in the biblical law of the book of the covenant (Exodus) to murder or manslaughter; in all other cases it was replaced by reparation in some form. Where Hesiod considered it appropriate to take revenge by inflicting double the injury suffered, he was taking into account the aristocratic ethos of defending one's honor. The notion of boundless revenge did remain a theme of Greek literature well into the classical period but, as the tragedies of Aeschylus and Sophocles show, this was done in order to criticize it, for one could set limits on revenge only when values higher than honor existed. Not until Plato's *Gorgias* and *Republic* was the concept of honor finally dismantled in favor of *dikaiosynē* and was it declared better to suffer injustice than to commit it.

The negative anthropology found in Mesopotamian mythology, which bound people to the state, which in turn served as mediator between them and the world of gods, was alien to Greek thought; from the archaic epoch of aristocratic rule to that of the citizen polis, Greece did not develop total subordination of every individual under the state as in the orient. In the orient, the view of chaos and order as opposites found expression in the motif of the battle against chaos, which originated in the West Semitic region and spread from there to Mesopotamia and also in Egypt in a rudimentary form. This opposition served to justify a policy of military aggression, given that the antithesis of war was not peace but chaos. In Greece the opposition between order and chaos did not lead to an expansionist imperial policy; instead it took the form of a cultural antagonism between Greeks and non-Greeks, who were labeled barbarians. It gave expression to the self-esteem of people in the region, based on culture, which could also take the form of moral superiority. In the early 5th century, a consciousness of moral superiority over the barbarians was strengthened by the successful repulsion of Xerxes' invasion. However, moral standards became differentiated within Greek culture as well. Isocrates created a moral pyramid in which Athenians stood at the top, above first the other Greeks, and then the barbarians; and Euripides alleged that barbarians commonly practiced incest and murdered relatives (*Andromache* 173–76). He also asserted that gratitude and friendship were unknown to them (*Helen* 501–2) and that this dissimilarity between Greeks and barbarians was due not to nature *(physis)* but to *nomos* (custom) and *sophia* (intelligence), that is, it represented a cultural difference.

Distinctions were also made within Greek culture. Athenians saw themselves as honest and friendly (Demosthenes, *Against Leptines* 109), but considered the Spartans treacherous (Aristophanes, *Peace* 1066–68, 1083), while the inhabitants of Phasalus were supposed to be dishonest in business dealings (Demosthenes, *Against Lacritus* 1–2). On the other hand, a Panhellenic value system was applied when Greeks distinguished themselves from barbarians. As grave inscriptions show, its central values were courage *(aretē)* and avoidance of harmful behavior *(sōphrosynē)*. The lines of demarcation separating Greek communities from the outside world arose not, as in the political theologies of the ancient Near East, from the identification of strangers with the mythical power of chaos that has to be suppressed by the political authorities, but from the Greeks' perception of their own cultural and moral superiority. As a result, Greek policies were more defensive, but there were no powerful religious impulses at work driving the creation of a large empire. They had to be borrowed from the Orient through Macedonia. But as a result, religious impulses to rationalize ethics were also lacking in Greece; they could emerge only from a philosophy that had begun to emancipate itself from traditional religion.

The realm of the gods and morality in ancient cultures

The degree of connection between human ethos and divine behavior varied in ancient cultures. The biblical world of Israel and Judah lay at one extreme and Greek culture at the other, with Mesopotamia, Syria, Egypt, and Anatolia occupying intermediate positions. In both Greek and ancient Near Eastern thinking, the key difference between human and divine beings was that the latter were immortal. But in moral terms the Greeks considered the difference between mortals and gods to be small, since their gods, unlike humans, were not morally infallible *(anarmatētos)*. Greek gods could be seduced by Eros; they were sensitive about their own honor and could feel jealousy like human beings. In both the archaic and classical periods, the most important gods could be described as indifferent to the social norms of human interaction. At the root of this religious thinking lay the archaic ethos of the aristocracy, which permitted a hero to have a direct relationship with a protective divinity, which could rupture human ties. The logic of reciprocity in dealings between mortals and gods was the same as in relationships between friends in the aristocratic ethos, so that a divinity would support human protégés even when they violated the norms of a human community, as long as they were defending their honor. Norms that furthered the cohesion of a community through solidarity of action and pursuit of conflict resolution were thus of exactly the wrong kind to be strengthened or promoted by religious impulses. Greece had no class of intellectual religious specialists to support ethical rationalization. Greek religion was a religion of sacrifices; it required the performance of sacrificial duties from everyone and thus allowed no independent caste of priests to develop alongside the political leadership, which took its models from the martial ethos of the aristocracy. As a result, the city-states also lacked a class of religious intellectuals in a position to rationalize the ethics of the religious system and propel it toward socially beneficial values, enabling religion to confront politics as political theology and achieve political standing for such norms.

A way out of traditional religion became necessary as soon as the insight grew that human beings could neither protect themselves against contingencies in life through magic nor rely on divine assistance, since the gods were not bound to any norms of behavior. The political elite thus prevented an ethical rationalization of religion in Greece. In contrast, during the late period in Egypt the priests' domination of politics allowed religion to regress to a form of personal piety with no regard for the connective norms of social justice. This late form of Egyptian religion released the gods from the norms of *ma'at* and gave them instead an arbitrary freedom of action; human beings responded with a personal piety that released the norms of connective justice from the social dimension and transferred them to the individual relationship with a god. Good fortune in life was now believed to be secured not through social behavior, but by turning toward the divinity according to the *do ut des* (I give so that you will give) principle. This also held true for the Egyptian king, who became the paradigmatic pious example to his people, while the motif of divine descent was transferred from the king to a child of a god in a holy trinity. Whenever productive tension between religion and state politics disappears, the religious system loses its power to rationalize the ethics of a society, as examples from ancient Israel and Judah in the Hebrew Bible show.

In the social crises of the Judean kingdom, priestly intellectuals turned the norms of neighborly solidarity into theology, presenting them as the will of God, and constructed models of social solidarity in Exodus (21–23) and Deuteronomy (12–26), which they offered in response to the policy that had been carried out. The scriptural prophets, and the circles of intellectuals who took their cue from them, measured the behavior of the people by the standards propagated by the priests' collections of law and informed the people what the consequences for failing to comply would be. A characteristic of priestly theology was its distance from the state; implicitly theology thus became criticism of the state, which the prophets made explicit as criticism of the king. In this way, in postexilic Judaism, YHWH, the one god who behaved ethically and required ethical behavior from followers, became the objective of a thoroughgoing process of ethical rationalization for all areas of life of his clientele, which expressed itself in the elevation of the Pentateuch to the Torah (Law) and thus could develop its power to guide conduct. No magic, which in Egypt undermined the rationalizing power of the thought of a last judgment, could liberate people from the consequences of their actions. The hostility of Judaic religion to magic (combined with monotheism's closing off the possibility of ascribing any misfortune experienced in life to adverse deities and to the negative anthropology derived from it) increased the need for an ethical shaping of life, since misfortune could be the result only of human activity. The rationalization of religion was further increased by the political experience of being at the mercy of the great powers, with all the resulting consequences for the fate of the individual; it gave rise to questions about how such experience could be reconciled with a belief in YHWH as an ethical god. As a consequence, eschatological thinking became universal, which subjected the entire population of the world to the ethical will of YHWH and sought in it the solution to the problem of theodicy for Judah. The high degree to which rationalization was achieved in the Hebrew Bible permitted Judaism and its offshoot, Christianity, to survive as world religions, whereas the religions of other ancient centers of power perished.

The history of Mesopotamian religion offers a complex picture that should be divided according to literary genres. This more differentiated interpretation replaces the notion held by scholars in the past, who thought that the conception of divinity acquired an ethical dimension at the time of Hammurabi, in the first half of the 2nd millennium. In this view, the gods developed from morally fallible figures into beings possessed of a moral perfection unattainable by humankind, with the result that human misfortune could no longer be ascribed to demons and had to be traced back to unethical human behavior instead. However, Sumerian legends dating from the late 3rd and early 2nd millennia require a more differentiated interpretation. In mythic narratives the pantheon of gods serves to reconcile phenomena in the sphere of human life that appear contradictory—such as life and death, order and chaos, peace and war, fertility and infertility, man and woman—and to render them comprehensible; this is done by personifying these occurrences as deities whose behavior follows the logic of human interaction. An ethical idealization of gods would have undermined this function of myth. The function of gods in myths must be distinguished from their task in the traditions of wisdom literature and law, where they interact primarily not with one another but with human beings and direct human behavior by establishing a code of values. In Mesopotamia, this ethical link between deities and humanity was used chiefly to provide a religious foundation for the king as the font of law (see the prologue and epilogue of the Codex Hammurabi) and in the function of deities as witnesses in the law of contracts.

In both functions—foundation and witness—the official pantheon of gods worked solely through the channel of the king, the mediator of divine action in the world, to affect individual citizens, although everyone was entitled to pray to gods such as Shamash, Marduk, or Ishtar. A citizen's personal relationship to deities was focused on a tutelary god, who was believed to accompany this person during his or her lifetime and act as an intermediary with higher-ranking gods. Since the gods had ethically ambivalent relationships with one another, the pantheon of gods had only a very limited function as a model for human action. Only magical manipulation could save human beings from the urges to exact retribution that were imputed to gods in Mesopotamian religion. And since a tutelary god was expected to take the side of the human client even if that client had failed to behave ethically, religion was the source of very few impulses toward ethical rationalization. Wisdom teachings were cultivated in the state schools for scribes, and the ethical indifference of religion offered a good basis for the emancipation of these teachings from religion as secular philosophy following the Greek pattern; however, such an emancipation prevented a close connection between religion and the state, which also prevented an emancipation of priestly specialists as champions of an ethical rationalization of religion. This connects Mesopotamian religious history with that of Egypt. It is true that the ethical values of connective justice that are supposed to guide human behavior were personified in the goddess Maat, who was connected with the order of the cosmos and thereby provided with the very highest religious authority; however, the achievement of ethical rationalization of Egyptian religion was reduced by the fact that, in the synthetic view of life, the consequences of human action could be deflected through magic. The achievement of ethical rationalization of Egyptian religion was limited chiefly by its being a state ideology, in which the king embodied *ma'at*, although in contrast to Mesopotamian religion the functions of integrating con-

tradictory experience and stabilizing human morality were united in the figure
of the goddess Maat through the aspects of connective justice, until in the late
period this process also broke down.

The realm of the gods and law in ancient culture

Every ancient society needed law to strengthen its internal cohesion, both in
order to settle conflicts and thereby minimize violence and also to enforce sanc-
tions against socially harmful behavior and violations of social norms. In societies organized as states, the state either carried out these functions of law or supervised them; in monarchies, the degree to which the king personified legal
functions determined whether laws were codified and with what function. In
Egypt, the king's personification of law as Maat's representative meant that no
restrictions could be placed on his right to decide litigation; in theory the king
handed down judgments without being bound to codified norms, although in
practice this occurred only in specific instances of capital crimes. Thus no laws
of the king are documented from predemotic times, only a decree of King
Haremheb (18th Dynasty) along with decrees to officials that regulated privi-
leges and instructions about how to carry out their duties. In Mesopotamia,
the king was regarded as having received a mandate from the gods to enforce
the law; he could delegate this task to officers of the state government. In this
system, legal principles as descriptions of legal practice could be codified for
teaching purposes, used to give religious legitimation to the king's juridical
function, or presented to the public for propagandistic purposes, as in the case
of the Code of Hammurabi.

Collections of laws could also either advertise judicial reforms, as in the
case of the Middle Assyrian laws, or document such a reform, as did the
Hittite laws. In the legal system of the Achaemenids, judgments handed down
by the king acquired the status of unalterable law for the courts. When the Persians conquered a province, imperial policy for maintaining order was to enforce any codified indigenous laws. A first step toward making the law independent of the state occurred in Anatolia in the 2nd millennium. According to
early Hittite royal ideology, the king was not the font of law, but required a divine model in order to obey the law. Then, as a result of influences from
Mesopotamian and Egyptian ideology, the king in the Hittite Empire came to
be regarded as the earthly representative of the weather-god and as such functioned as lawgiver and supreme judge. Only in Judea and Greece, where in the
long run the legal systems were separate from the king, was the law—either
granted by YHWH or voted by the citizens of a city-state—able to take an independent stand vis-à-vis the state. Whereas the laws of cuneiform justice primarily described and documented the judgments that had in fact been handed
down and prescriptive legal functions remained a royal prerogative, in Judea
and Greece the laws exercised this prescriptive royal function themselves (*nomos ho pantōn basileus*, custom is king of everyone; Pindar, frag. 169). In the

Torah, the law is declared to have originated as divine revelation received on a sacred mountain in the desert; the circumstance prevented it from being reduced to an instrument of political power. In classical Greece, the people could become the font of laws; the gods simply confirmed them. In Judea, the theory that law emanated from divine revelation, which was broadly developed in the Pentateuch from the exilic period on, prevented a similar process of democratization in formulating laws, since a class of scribes, who derived their norms from interpreting and extending the Torah, assumed an increasingly dominant intellectual leadership in Achaemenid and Hellenistic Judea. Through its consistent presentation of law in theological terms, the Hebrew Bible made the Torah into an independent counterweight to every state that became subject to Jewish law. The followers of Alexander, on the other hand, came under the influence of ancient royal ideologies; their kingdoms took on a more-oriental character, and the king came to embody the law as *nomos empsychos* (living law) in a development that aroused fierce resistance among Jews in the population.

The emancipation of ethics from traditional religion in Greek philosophy

Greece had no intellectual class of religious specialists who could rationalize traditional religion and make it able to address the need for salvation, who could develop comprehensive theories to explain the experiences of negative contingency that impeded satisfaction of this need, and who could then impart them to their clientele in combination with moral precepts in a manner that furthered social solidarity. Thus from the 6th century, new ways to satisfy these needs arose along the margins of Greek culture, such as Asia Minor (Miletus), and then also affected traditional religion in its centers (Athens). Xenophanes (570–480 BCE) took a critical stand against traditional Greek religion, declaring, "Homer and Hesiod attributed behavior to the gods that human beings consider shameful and scandalous, such as theft, adultery, and deceitful dealings" (DK 21B11). When people wished to protect themselves from the will of the gods, which they understood to be amoral and arbitrary, they called upon the synthetic view of life, as *Odyssey* 1.32–34 already put it: "All evil, men proclaim, comes from the gods, yet nevertheless these fools ignore fate and divine warnings, and cause their own ruin." In this view the gods are anthropomorphic figures and only a mirror image of limited human imagination. While Xenophanes deduced the existence of a transcendent god from this—a problematic deduction because different *nomoi* among the human cultures had then to be traced back to differences in the world of the gods—skepticism prevailed among the Sophists. Rhetorical arguments and matters of content diverged, so that different moral judgments could coexist side by side. Increased knowledge about non-Greek peoples and their laws and customs in the 5th century led to a more relative view, in which laws were thought to be mutable rather than unchanging. The Greeks learned to distinguish between what existed in nature *(physis)* and what had been established by human beings *(nomos)*. A debate then followed over whether people ought to follow their natural instincts or act in accordance with the laws and conventions of their community. Traditional *nomos* thus became open to alteration.

In the 4th century, Plato, in a debate with the Sophists, developed a concept of *nomos* that was based on new epistemological and ontological reasoning and that did not draw on existing laws. He placed *nomos* in a world of ideas from which the material world of sensory experience was derived; human beings could approach this world by means of their powers of reasoning. A lifelong striving for knowledge became the principle of moral behavior. Since the rational human soul stemmed from the intangible world of ideas before it was implanted in the body, every grasp or comprehension of an idea was held to be a memory. And since a person's worth consisted of one's soul, one acted well and justly in improving the condition of one's soul and the souls of others. Ethics became a doctrine of happiness that reformulated the popular connection between one's deeds and one's fortune in life, for justice now numbered among the things "that must be loved for their own sake and for the consequences resulting from them by everyone who wishes to be happy [*eudaimōn*]" (*Republic* 358a). Justice could be secured permanently and human happiness realized only in the framework of the polis. Concrete ethical norms were determined by membership in one of the city-state's social classes and by the condition of one's soul. Aristotelian ethics, taking this as its starting point, is a theory of human happiness *(eudaimonia)*. Since human beings are disposed by nature to live in communities, ultimately the goal of happiness could be attained only in the polis, so that ethics became one part of political theory. For Aristotle, happiness consisted in virtue *(aretē)* as a reasonable, self-controlled life and in the possession of external goods (*Nicomachean Ethics* 1099a–b), so that human happiness was not completely under human control, but remained a "gift of the gods."

The Hellenistic schools of Stoicism, Epicureanism, and Pyrrhonian skepticism sought to point out ways by which *eudaimonia,* understood as the highest goal *(telos)* of human life, could be detached from its connections with the polis and the gods and thereby brought entirely under human control. These philosophers removed from the definition of happiness all material goods that might not be available at certain times, so that the greatest good in Stoicism was virtue, and in Epicureanism it was happiness *(hēdonē);* both terms included an attitude of indifference *(apatheia/ataraxia)* toward the material sphere. The Christian ethics of antiquity held this philosophy, which sought to attain happiness through one's own efforts, to be a way of suppressing one's experience of evil and a form of arrogance. True virtue was associated with piety and hope: "For we are encompassed with evils, which we ought patiently to endure, until we come to the ineffable enjoyment of unmixed good; for there shall be no longer anything to endure. Salvation, such as it shall be in the world to come, shall itself be our final happiness" (Augustine, *City of God* 19.4).

Bibliography

Assmann, Jan. *Ma'at: Gerechtigkeit und Unsterblichkeit im Alten Ägypten*. Munich, 1990.

Dover, K. J. *Greek Popular Morality in the Time of Plato and Aristotle*. Oxford, 1974.

Ferguson, John. *Moral Values in the Ancient World*. London, 1958.

Lambert, W. G. *Babylonian Wisdom Literature*. Oxford, 1960.

Lévy, Edmond, ed. *La codification des lois dans l'antiquité*. Paris, 2000.

Otto, Eckart. *Theologische Ethik des Alten Testaments*. Stuttgart, 1994.

Mysteries

Sarah Iles Johnston

No aspect of ancient religions has evoked greater interest—and a greater range of interests—than that of mystery cults. Scholars have repeatedly combed textual and archeological evidence in attempts to uncover their secrets (what was done? by whom? to whom?), and a variety of people from outside of academia have invoked and adapted the cults for their own uses. Mozart's *Magic Flute*, which draws on 18th-century Masonic perceptions of the mystery cult of Isis, is a well-known example; today, neopagan religious groups worship the gods of mystery cults in what they believe is the way that ancient initiates did.

In the latter part of this essay, we may gain some insights as to why mystery cults are of perennial interest. But I will begin with a summary of what scholars think we can say with certainty about the most prominent cults. In the short run, this means emphasizing Greece and Rome, the homes of mystery cults in the strictest sense of the term. This eventually leads us, however, into other cultures of the ancient Mediterranean, first through a contextualization of the Greek and Roman mystery cults within a range of religious phenomena with which they share salient characteristics, notably a promise of personal transformation and a demand for secrecy; and then through examining how later religious and philosophical systems, including Christianity, adapted the word *mystery.*

Overview

Any model of mystery cults will be imperfect, both because there were variations among individual cults in antiquity and because there remain disagreements of definition among scholars. But we must start from at least a provisional model; and so before discussing the cults themselves, I first list five criteria that many cults shared:

- Mystery cults demanded secrecy; initiates were forbidden to divulge what they had experienced ("mystery" comes from Greek *myein* [to close]).
- Mystery cults promised to improve initiates' situations in the present life and/or after death.
- Initiates garnered these advantages by establishing a special relationship with divinities during initiation.
- Mystery cults were optional supplements to civic religion, rather than competing alternatives (this is why we call them "cults," rather than "religions").
- Myths were associated with the cults, which narrated tales of the cults' divinities.

Space allows detailed discussion of only two cults here; four others are sketched more briefly, and there were other, "lesser" mysteries in antiquity as well.

The Eleusinian mysteries

The myth of Demeter and her daughter, who is called both Kore (Maiden) and Persephone, was associated already in antiquity with mysteries held in Eleusis, a town fourteen miles west of Athens. The myth appears in several, slightly different versions, of which the best known is the Homeric *Hymn to Demeter*. Hades, king of the underworld, snatched Persephone away to be his wife. Demeter searched desperately for her missing daughter and, having discovered Persephone's fate, retreated in grief from the gods' company, disguised herself as an old woman, and took work as a nursemaid in the royal Eleusinian family. When her secret attempt to immortalize the family's son was interrupted, however, Demeter became angry and, throwing off her disguise, cast the earth into famine. Under pressure, Zeus compelled Hades to return Persephone to her mother, but Hades first gave Persephone pomegranate seeds to eat, which obligated her to return to the underworld for part of each year thereafter. Hades promised Persephone that as his wife, she would have power over "everything that lives and moves" and the ability to punish those who displeased her. Demeter, reunited with her daughter, restored fertility to the fields and instructed the Eleusinians in her mysteries, promising blessings to initiates both during life and after death and warning that the uninitiated would face an afterlife in dank darkness.

Ancient sources make clear the connections between this myth and the Eleusinian mysteries. But it must be emphasized that the *Hymn to Demeter* is a literary work and probably was composed for recitation in a public context. It was not the sacred text of a cult that prized secrecy as highly as the mysteries did, and we cannot assume that all the actions it narrates signify what initiates actually did within the walls of the Eleusinian precinct. The *Hymn* can be used, however, in combination with other ancient information to paint a picture of the mysteries in broad strokes. It is likely, for example, that individuals somehow imitated Demeter's experiences during initiation and in doing so passed from grief to joy (ancient sources mention such a transition)—we know that they drank a mixture called the *kykeōn,* which Demeter also is said to have drunk in the *Hymn,* and that in doing so, like Demeter, they broke a fast. It is possible that they watched a dramatic reenactment of Persephone's kidnapping and return (a cave on the site looks like a probable setting for the kidnapping, and we are told that a bronze gong was rung during the mysteries to signify Persephone's return). Some sort of ritual probably took place around a special well in the precinct, which is echoed in the *Hymn* by Demeter's encounter at a well with daughters of the Eleusinian king. Thematically, too, the *Hymn* resonates with concerns addressed in the mysteries, most prominently the hope that a special relationship with Demeter and Persephone would protect one from the direst aspects of the mortal lot.

Other pieces of information take us further. Athens controlled the mysteries (many of its priesthoods were in the hands of two Athenian families), and thus the public parts of the ceremony were held each year in Athens, after certain secret objects had been carried from Eleusis to Athens under close guard. An Athenian official called an assembly in which the opening of the mysteries was announced. The next day, at the Athenian harbor, each initiate bathed himself or herself and a piglet, which would later be sacrificed, perhaps on the third day. The fourth day was given over to latecomers who had to catch up with what they had missed. On the fifth day, initiates walked from Athens to Eleusis wearing white garments and carrying torches. At a certain point during this journey, yellow ribbons were tied on their right hands and left legs, and at another point, as they crossed the Cephisus River, insults were cast at them by former initiates (we are not sure why). The secret objects that previously had been carried from Eleusis to Athens were carried back again on this same journey.

Upon arrival at Eleusis, initiates entered a walled precinct—and it is here that our certain information dwindles; under threat of death, initiates kept their secrets well. We do know that whatever happened inside the precinct consumed three days and that it culminated at night inside a hall called the Telesterion—literally, the place of "completion" or "initiation." Something highly significant was shown to the initiates in a sudden burst of torch light (one ancient source that many scholars judge trustworthy claims that it was "just a sheaf of wheat"; the significance of the object, whatever it was, may have been largely symbolic). We know that each initiate had to have his or her own *mystagōgos*—a guide who had already been initiated and thus could ensure that the initiate completed the process correctly. We know that initiates heard and said special things and felt that they had personal contact with Demeter and Persephone. We know that, toward the end of the process, initiates poured libations to the dead. And we know that it was possible to be initiated a second time at Eleusis, into a higher level of the mysteries. But beyond this, all is conjecture. Whatever happened at Eleusis must have been highly appealing, however: the mysteries drew initiates from all over the ancient Mediterranean and operated from the archaic into the late imperial period.

The Samothracian mysteries

The Greek word *mystēria* (mysteries) properly applies only to the Eleusinian festival, but *mystēria* was also used to refer to other, similar cults, and modern scholars have followed suit. Herodotus provides our first example, in the 5th century BCE, when he describes a cult on the island of Samothrace as *mystēria* (2.51).

The Samothracian mysteries were almost as long-lived and popular as the Eleusinian (they continued till the reign of Constantine), but we know less about them. They centered on gods whose names were secret and whom ancient authors associated with a variety of other gods, including (perhaps in imitation of Eleusis) Demeter, Persephone, and Hades; other evidence, however, suggests a central goddess and two male attendants. We know only three details of Samothrace's nocturnal initiation rite: initiates had to wear purple sashes, to tell the priest what the worst deeds were that they had ever committed, and to wear iron rings once they were initiated. Protection against dangers at sea was the most famous benefit of initiation; we hear nothing about postmortem benefits and have only fragments of myths associated with the cult. In contrast to Eleusis, individuals could be initiated not only during an annual festival, but at any time.

The Bacchic mysteries

Unlike the Eleusinian and Samothracian mysteries, initiations associated with Dionysus (or Bacchus) could be performed anywhere—in fact, some Bacchic priests made their livings by wandering from place to place, performing "initiations" (*teletai*; cf. the Eleusinian Telesterion). The ability to initiate was considered a special craft, and many priests claimed inclusion in a chain of teachers and students stretching back to mythic priests of Dionysus. In spite of this, techniques of initiation varied. From Herodotus we hear about a *thiasos* (group) of Dionysiac initiates raving through the night in a sort of maddened, ecstatic release (4.79). We hear elsewhere about initiates, especially female, ascending mountains to participate in initiations that included nocturnal dancing. The phallus, symbol of generative power and sexuality, appears often in Dionysiac iconography.

Such practices and images have fueled imaginations. In Euripides' *Bacchae*, female worshipers tear apart live animals and, eventually, the king of their city. A famous Roman repression of Bacchic cults in 186 BCE followed accusations that they were fronts for murder, sodomy, and other crimes. We have no evidence that such extremes were reached by real initiates, but the note of wild abandon that such stories strike does reflect a genuine element of Dionysiac cult: Dionysus released worshipers from everyday concerns and limits. Less wild, perhaps, were initiations connected with the gold tablets, which centered on learning the story of Dionysus's birth and sufferings. The variegated picture of initiation rites is complicated further because the goals of initiation varied. In some cases, ecstatic communion with the god was foremost, with little or no thought for the afterlife. Other rites assuaged the wrath of the dead and thus protected the living from their attacks. Still others sought to ensure the initiate's own happiness in the next world. Also open to question is how many of these cults were formally called or considered mysteries.

Here I will focus on the rites involving the gold tablets, as they both align most closely with my working model of mystery cults, and use the word *mystēs*, which refers to an initiate of a mystery. The tablets, which have been found in Greek and Italian graves dating from the 5th century BCE to the 2nd century CE, are small sheets of gold inscribed with instructions that guide the soul of the dead through the underworld and ensure that it receives preferential treatment from underworld deities. They also incorporate fragments of hexameter poetry derived from poems attributed to the mythic poet Orpheus, which narrated the story of Dionysus and Persephone. Fritz Graf suggests that these texts were also read aloud during initiations, which supports the idea that the tablets served to remind the soul (which was expected to be confused after death) of what it had already learned while alive. Some tablets were placed in the corpses' mouths, as if to actually "speak" on their behalf.

The instructions on the tablets include admonitions to avoid certain paths in the underworld and to drink from waters of Memory instead of those of Forgetfulness; this probably refers to the need to remember mistakes made during the last life lest one repeat them in the next (reincarnation also is implied by mention of a "circle of grief" from which the initiate will eventually escape). The tablets also remind the soul of declarations that it must make to Persephone, stating that it is pure, that it belongs to the divine race, that it has paid the penalty for "unrighteous deeds," and that "the Bacchic one himself [Dionysus] has released" it. The reward for doing and saying everything correctly, according to the tablets, is to join other *mystai* (initiates) and *bacchoi* who feast and drink in a pleasant part of the underworld. Similar declarations must be made to guardians who otherwise would prevent access to the waters of Memory. A late-4th-century BCE funerary vase from southern Italy, now in the Toledo (Ohio) Museum of Art, illustrates the reward: at the center of the scene, Dionysus shakes hands with Hades as Persephone looks on with approval; to his side are figures who represent the joyous afterlife that Bacchic initiates win, and separated from him, cut off from pleasure, are famous mythic figures who failed to accept Dionysus.

The declarations concerning unrighteous deeds and atonement on the tablets can be explained by reference to the myth of Dionysus and Persephone. Dionysus was the son of Zeus and Persephone. While a child, he was lured away by jealous gods called Titans, who killed and consumed most of him.

Athena salvaged his heart, which Zeus fed to his lover Semele in order that Dionysus might be reconceived. In due course the god was (re)born, although
Persephone continued to mourn her loss. Meanwhile, Zeus incinerated the Titans and humanity arose from their remains. Thus human nature is predominantly wicked. Humans must strive both to overcome this and to atone to
Persephone for the Titans' crime through initiation into the Bacchic mysteries;
otherwise they will suffer after death.

The cult of Meter

Meter (Mother) referred to a variety of goddesses who were either at home in
Greece or imported from Anatolia (e.g., Cybele). Their worship included ecstatic dancing that induced insensitivity to pain; most extremely, some male
worshipers castrated themselves while in this state, dedicating their virility to
the goddess and serving her thereafter as eunuch priests. A mythic exemplar of
self-castration developed during the late Hellenistic period: Cybele maddened
her mortal consort, Attis, because he had betrayed her; he castrated himself
and bled to death. Whether such acts were always considered part of mystery
initiations is unclear, but we do hear about eunuchs and other priests of these
goddesses who, like Bacchic priests, wandered around performing initiations.
Benefits were expected to accrue during life and perhaps after death.

Cybele officially entered Rome in 205/204 BCE under the name of Magna
Mater (Great Mother), at the suggestion of the Sibylline Books. It is later, during the imperial period, that we first hear about one of the cult's most striking
features, the *taurobolium* (bull slaughtering), although something called the
taurobolium had also been practiced earlier in Anatolia. Our evidence for the
Roman *taurobolium* is incomplete, but Philippe Borgeaud has convincingly
suggested that it involved sprinkling initiates with blood from the testicles of a
freshly castrated bull. Thus, men who did not wish to castrate themselves (and
women) could partake of the goddess's benefits. Initiation could be renewed
after a number of years by repeating the *taurobolium*. The Christian author
Prudentius exemplifies the polemics directed against mysteries in later ages
when he invents a far bloodier *taurobolium* (*Peristephanon* 10.1011–50): a
bull is slaughtered atop a grate; an initiate crouches underneath in a pit, wait-
ing to be drenched in fresh blood—but this is unlikely to reflect real practices.

The cult of Mithras

Mithra was an old Indo-Iranian sun-god concerned with the making of alliances who was transformed into Mithras by Roman men in the 1st century CE
into a god of mysteries. His mysteries particularly attracted soldiers and emphasized bonds of brotherhood. This was enhanced by the small size of individual Mithraic cults, which spread throughout the Roman Empire even as far
as Britain.

Initiates met in *Mithraea*, real or artificial caves that were decorated with frescos and reliefs to serve as models of the cosmos; in some intellectualized forms of Mithraism, this is reflected in the initiates' goal of causing their souls to ascend through the heavens, but most initiates were probably more concerned with the benefits that Mithras offered in the here-and-now, and it is difficult to know what such cosmic representations meant to them. (There is evidence that Mithraic worshipers were interested in astrology, too, but we do not know why.)

On either side of a central aisle in *Mithraea* were benches on which initiates reclined to dine, imitating the meal shared by Mithras and the sun-god (who sometimes appears as a separate entity in Mithraism). We know that there were seven grades of initiation—raven, bride, soldier, lion, Persian, sun-runner, and father—but little about what they signified or required. *Tauroctony* (killing of a bull) is central to the cult: numerous altarpieces show Mithras engaged in such an act, and we can guess that it was repeated by initiates. An inscription from one Mithraeum, "you saved us with the outpouring blood," is taken to refer to Mithras's *tauroctony,* which often is supplemented in artistic representations by symbols of fertility (e.g., a sheaf of wheat springs from the dying bull's tail). We have no textual traces of Mithraic myths, which makes interpretation of these representations difficult.

The mysteries of Isis

The Greeks knew about the Egyptian goddess Isis from at least the time of Herodotus and believed that Egyptian worship of Isis and her husband Osiris was similar to that of their own mysteries. But the first clear traces of a Greek mystery cult for Isis appear in an aretology that was inscribed and displayed in Isiac sanctuaries during the last two centuries BCE (the aretology itself may be older). In it, Isis declares that she has brought agriculture, good laws, and other benefits to the human race and that she has shown humans how to perform mystery initiations; probably she is here identified with Demeter, as she often was elsewhere, and the mysteries she claims to have bestowed on humanity are those of Eleusis (Merkelbach 1995: 113–19).

Information on initiation into Isiac mysteries in the proper sense becomes available only during the imperial period; they took place either at Isiac temples or private houses. The fullest account is found in the final chapter of a 2nd-century CE novel, Apuleius's *Golden Ass.* Lucius, the hero, although eager to be initiated and frequently visited by Isis in dreams, must wait until the goddess signifies that the time is right (not all initiates had to wait to be "called"; other evidence indicates that initiation was usually available on request). He abstains from forbidden foods, bathes, and purifies himself. Secrets of the cult's holy books are explained to him, and yet further secrets narrated to him. He fasts for ten days, dons linen clothes (wool was prohibited in the cult), and at night is taken into the innermost part of her temple in Corinth. There he undergoes a process that, he claims, involves a journey to the underworld, "trial by the elements" (probably water, fire, and air), and an introduction to all the gods. The following morning he is given a new and splendid cloak, a torch, and a garland of flowers and is displayed publicly to all worshipers of Isis. After he has celebrated for several days, Isis tells him to return home, but she and Osiris subsequently instruct him in dreams to seek initiation into the mystery cult of Osiris in Rome. Eventually, he is further initiated into the *pastophoroi,* a group of priests who serve Isis and Osiris (we are told elsewhere that at least some Isiac priests, in any given place, had to be Egyptian in order for the cult to be properly conducted). The blessings that the gods confer on Lucius include not only eschatological promises but an enhanced ability to earn money as a lawyer.

The myth connected with Isiac mysteries comes to us only in the 1st centuries BCE and CE and closely mimics that of Eleusinian Demeter (Diodorus Siculus 1.21–25; Plutarch, *On Isis and Osiris* 12–19). That Isis seeks and then mourns her husband Osiris, rather than her child, underscores the close link between the two spouses, which was already important in Egypt. Other Egyptian deities, such as Horus, the son of Isis and Osiris, were also adopted by Greeks and Romans, but Isis remained the central figure in her mysteries.

Interpretations

So much for the basic facts about mystery cults, such as they are. What can be said about how the cults functioned and how they fit into the larger religious and societal climates of not only Greece and Rome but more broadly the ancient Mediterranean?

Initiation as a process

Several ancient authors emphasize that initiates into mysteries not only *did* and *said* things as part of their initiation, but *experienced* things. In other words, there was a passive aspect to initiation. This is borne out by the passive participles that are sometimes used to describe initiates: those initiated into the cult of Meter, for example, are described as *tauroboliati* (they have been "tauroboliated," to coin a word) and those in the cult of Dionysus are said to be *bebaccheumenoi* (they have been "bacchiated"). Initiates do not simply go through required motions and gain promised rewards, they are "processed" by what they experience in the mysteries and emerge as something new.

In this respect, mystery initiation has a great deal in common with Mediterranean rites of passage. The adolescent undergoes a rite from which he or she emerges as an adult; the unmarried woman emerges from the wedding ceremony not only as a married woman in the sense of having a husband, but in the sense of being, in the eyes of her society, a different sort of woman altogether, with new responsibilities and rights. Some scholars have even suggested that the Eleusinian mysteries, and perhaps other early Greek mysteries, developed out of clan-based adolescent initiation rites: the Eleusinian priesthood was controlled by two Athenian clans, the Eumolpidai and the Kerykes, and in the myths connected with some mysteries, an adolescent or child (Persephone, Dionysus) experiences the sorts of transitions that are often associated with rites of passage in myth, such as death, marriage, and rebirth. Iconography and myth, moreover, associate Demeter (and sometimes Persephone) with the care and maturation of children, both at Eleusis and elsewhere.

But the mysteries' broader similarity to rites of passage, as procedures that process individuals and enable them to emerge as something new, prompts another observation: most parts of Greece (including Athens, home of the Eleusinian mysteries) had no rites of passage that formally and explicitly changed adolescents into adults, at least during historical times; what we find instead in some places are optional rites that *celebrate* the maturation of a few individuals (which usually meant the children of the noble and the wealthy). Why earlier, more widespread rites of passage died out (if they ever existed at all) is a question we cannot consider here, but we can at least ponder the striking correlation: it was precisely in a culture from which rites of passage were missing that mysteries developed. Rome, which eagerly adopted Greek mystery cults and then went on to create some of its own, similarly shows few traces of adolescent rites of passage after the 3rd century BCE. It is tempting to see mysteries, which promised to "complete" or "perfect" *(telein)* individuals, as developing to fill a gap.

Initiation and community

Another sort of ritual in which individuals undergo experiences and then emerge with a new status are initiations into professions, such as blacksmithing, or into roles, such as priest or king. Egyptian artisans of many sorts were initiated into their professions, and Mesopotamian priests were initiated into the priesthoods of Nanna and of Enlil and Ninlil, for example. Like adolescent rites of passage, these sorts of rituals can be glimpsed behind some mysteries. The Samothracian mysteries preserve traces of blacksmiths' guild initiations (e.g., the iron rings that initiates wear and the worship of artisan divinities called Kabeiroi). The predilection of soldiers for the Mithraic mysteries may also point toward a group with guildlike bonds, and the seven grades of Mithraic initiation suggest an interest in delineation and assumption of hierarchical roles. One possible link between guild initiations and mysteries is that both promise to let the individual in on valuable secrets—secrets that will enable them, in the case of guilds, to prosper in their profession and, in the case of mysteries, to prosper in life more generally—or prosper after death. Not so long ago, indeed, the English word *mystery* could be used to refer to one's trade or occupation. Although linguists tell us that this use really derives from the Latin word *ministerium* (service, work), its development was influenced by the Greek *mystēria* and its connotations: an apprentice was understood to be initiated into the secrets of his craft by his master. Masonic mysteries straddle the two significations.

Even when contextualized within these other forms of initiations, however, one strikingly unusual characteristic of the mysteries still sets them apart: they were not mutually exclusive. One could be initiated into as many mystery cults as one desired and could afford; during the imperial period, wealthy individuals made a "grand tour" of them. Into some mysteries, moreover, one might be initiated more than once. This is different from adolescent initiations, for example, in which the transition from child to adult is singular, irreversible, and without any need (or, usually, possibility) of supplementation. It is also different from initiation into guilds insofar as individuals seldom had more than one profession and therefore more than one guild membership. By the same token, mystery initiation is different from initiation into a position such as kingship, which usually is held exclusively of other such positions.

One reason that mystery cults may have tolerated and even supported multiple memberships among initiates was that the benefits they promised were garnered not so much by entering into a community of people who would support one another (as in the case of an adolescent entering the adult community or an apprentice entering a guild) as by making the personal acquaintance of one or more gods. In a polytheistic system, the more gods one knew, the better, and particularly in a polytheistic system such as the Greeks had, where there was no concept of dualism or of orthodoxy and heresy, there was no need to avoid one god in order to please another.

Mystery initiations, then, in contrast to other forms of initiation, focused more closely on the individual as an individual than they did on the individual as a new member of a group. Even at Eleusis, where hundreds or thousands were initiated on the same night, each initiate had to have his or her own *mystagōgos* who performed the salient acts constituting initiation, whatever they were. Other mysteries, such as those of Dionysus or Meter, were promulgated partly by independent practitioners who initiated one or a few people at a time. If we believe Apuleius's account, Isiac initiation was individualized as well.

This is not to say that there was no concept of community at all among initiates: Dionysiac initiates might celebrate the god within a *thiasos* of participants that remained the same and called each other *symmystai* (fellow initiates). At some point during many mysteries, there was communal feasting—most notably in the cult of Mithras, whose places of worship included dining couches—and after death, initiates might expect to continue feasting and rejoicing with others of their kind. There is evidence for Dionysiac initiates helping to ensure that their fellows were properly buried and that the celebrations of the *thiasos* were well funded. But by and large, we lack indications that initiates felt an obligation to one another; the bond forged among them was not one of codependence, but rather of shared privilege. Plato mentions that common initiation into mysteries contributed to building a friendship, but he also makes it clear that this was just one among many other social ties that the two friends shared—it was the sort of thing that men of their stature did (*Letters* 7.333e).

The rewards of secrecy

Secrecy is the most famous and constant characteristic of mystery cults, from which the modern meaning of the word *mystery* develops.

But secrecy was not characteristic of mystery cults alone in the ancient world. The details of some adolescent rites of passage and many other gender-specific rites were kept secret both from the young people who had not yet been initiated and from all members of the opposite sex. In ancient Sparta, in fact, the name for male rites of passage was Krypteia (The Hidden [Ritual]). Guild initiations were kept secret as well. Moving outside of these two phenomena, we find plenty of others: in some societies, only the king or a certain priest might know, for example, where a particular sacred place was situated and how to tend it, or how to use and interpret the secrets in a sacred book. In Egypt, for instance, the priestly "overseer of secrets" alone knew where certain figurines were buried, and only the pharaoh, in his role as chief priest of the sun-god, had access to certain mortuary texts. In Athens, only one family, the Gephyraioi, had access to a special temple of Demeter Achaia. In Mesopotamia, the crafts of writing and reading—and therefore access to sacred documents—were closely guarded not only by limiting access to the academy but by employing cryptographic writing in some cases. Throughout the Mediterranean, practitioners of magic possessed secret methods of accomplishing remarkable things and guarded them well.

But all forms of secrecy are not the same. We must distinguish between "absolute" secrecy—that is, a situation in which the very existence of something is unknown to outsiders—and "relative" secrecy—a situation in which outsiders know that something exists but do not know all of its details (mysteries are an example of the latter). Absolute secrecy, in fact, is uncommon in religious systems that do not embrace concepts of orthodoxy and heresy for two reasons.

First, absolute secrecy is uncommon because unless a given practice or belief is outlawed, there is no need to hide it. Outside of Christianity and Judaism, concepts of orthodoxy and heresy were virtually unknown in ancient religions and so, therefore, was the need for absolute secrecy. A partial exception is the covert practice, for strategic or social reasons, of acts that are otherwise well known and accepted. For example, *silent* prayer was unusual in the ancient Mediterranean; when people prayed silently, this usually meant that they were asking for something they did not want others to know about. A charioteer might pray silently when asking a god to hobble his opponent's horses so that the opponent would not hear the prayer and counteract it with one of his own. The would-be adulterer might pray silently for help in seducing a married woman. The technique (prayer) is socially accepted even if the ends to which it is directed must be hidden.

Second, absolute secrecy is uncommon because religious systems, or cults within religious systems, need to advertise themselves and their advantages, both in order to gain converts or initiates and in order to win prestige (the two goals are closely linked). And here, ironically, secrecy helps: nothing appeals to human nature more than something that is described as secret, as contemporary advertisers know well. The appeal lies partially in the promise that those who join will garner special advantages (i.e., that the secrets are valuable) but partially in the sheer fact that in learning them one becomes part of a special group, be it the group of Bacchic initiates, adult men, stonecutters, caretakers of the hero's secret cult, or something else.

Of course, these remarks look at matters from the outside; members of secret groups have other explanations for their secrecy, such as the need to protect gender-exclusive knowledge from the potentially ruinous interference of the other gender or the need to shield a divinity's benefits from those who had not been properly prepared to receive them. Hekhalot mystics, for example, avoided discussing what they knew outside of their own circle, claiming that it could cause damage in the hands of the uninitiated; mystics in Egypt and Mesopotamia made similar statements. But this is not to say that all ancient individuals looked at mysteries from the inside; Plato and others remarked on the way in which itinerant priests of the mysteries used their claims of secret knowledge to line their own pockets. Other ancient outsiders, particularly the early Christian writers, attacked the mysteries' claim to secrecy from a different direction, charging that it cloaked behavior that was not only heretical by Christian standards, but illegal and inhuman, such as cannibalism and human sacrifice; the Romans who opposed the Bacchanalia in 186 BCE used a similar argument. This is an old trick, but a perennially effective one: those who share a secret that has been attacked cannot defend it without betraying it.

A final observation about secrecy in mystery cults takes us back to the issue of community. Most groups that share secrets share other characteristics as well: adolescents who undergo a rite of passage share not only the secrets they learn in the process but the preexisting fact that they are male (or female) and of a certain age. Guild initiates share their intention to pursue a certain craft and, typically, also share membership in the same socioeconomic class. Most mystery cults, in contrast, drew initiates from a broad socioeconomic spectrum, from both genders, and from all age groups. Mithraism is an exception, insofar as it was restricted to males. The Eleusinian mysteries are another partial exception, insofar as they did not allow the initiation of children (except for one special child initiated each year on behalf of the city), but otherwise they were markedly catholic: so long as a person had the ability to understand Greek and did not carry the stain of murder on his or her hands, he or she was welcome at Eleusis. The lack of other unifying characteristics among initiates in most mystery cults makes the demand for secrecy—and whatever it was that the demand for secrecy shielded—all the more important in defining the initiates' identities as members of the cult. This identity did not extend very far into life outside of the cult, but the very pledge that initiates gave to guard the secret for the rest of their lives (and, as far as we can tell, almost all initiates kept to this promise) would have worked to remind them thereafter of the group that they had joined and what they had gained in doing so.

Later developments

Already in the classical period, *mystēria* and cognates such as *mystēs* (initiate) could be used metaphorically to refer to matters that were difficult to grasp but important for a person's welfare. Plato, for example, often uses them to describe the process of learning philosophy (e.g., *Menexenus* 76e). Philosophical metaphor became reality in later antiquity, however, when some Platonists used *mystēria*, *mystēs*, and other terms to refer both to varieties of Platonic philosophy that emphasized spiritual development through the acquisition of esoteric knowledge and to rituals that brought the philosophers into close contact with the gods (*Chaldaean Oracles*, frag. 132). Interaction with the gods was expected to purify the philosopher's soul, enabling it to ascend into the divine realm and eventually, after death, escape the circle of reincarnation to which other souls were condemned.

Meanwhile, a singular form of the word *mystēria (mystērion)* came to denote simply a secret in the sense of something an individual wanted to keep hidden from others; we encounter this meaning frequently in the Jewish Apocrypha (e.g., Jdt. 2.2, Sir. 27.17). Partaking of all these meanings were ancient magicians' uses of the words: a "mystery" could be a special tool or technique that a magician might wish to keep hidden from other magicians in order to preserve his competitive edge; a technique that the gods had given the magician; a procedure into which one magician had to initiate another—or several of these things at the same time, as a single spell from a single magical papyrus demonstrates (*PGM* IV.723, 732–50, 794). Lingering behind some of these uses, both philosophical and magical, was the concept of ineffability—that is, the idea that something remained hidden because its divine nature simply could not be expressed by human words. To understand a mystery, one had to experience it oneself or learn it directly from the gods.

Some early Christian uses of mystery align with the developments that we have just reviewed: for instance, God's mysteries were made known to humans by divine revelation (Eph. 3.3) or by special instructions that only an inner circle would understand (Matt. 13.11); God's mysteries promised salvation to the individual soul, particularly eschatological salvation; certain aspects of God's plan for humans were ineffable mysteries (Col. 1.27). But the word developed in an interesting new direction as well and took the idea of mystery religions along with it. Christ's disciples proclaimed themselves to be eager to reveal God's mysteries to anyone who would listen; they erased any division between initiate and noninitiate and rejected the need to undergo special rituals before receiving valuable information (1 Cor. 15.51; Eph. 3.9). As Paul and Timothy said: "pray for us also, that God may open to us a door for the word, to declare the mystery of Christ . . . that I [Paul] may make it clear" (Col. 4.3–4). The use of mystery to mean a secret that must be kept, as we see it used in the Jewish Apocrypha, for example, is absent. As a proselytizing religion that aimed to build the largest possible community as quickly as possible, Christianity used the lure implicit in the word *mystery* more boldly than anyone previously had and in doing so turned one of the best-known qualities of mystery religions—privilege through exclusivity—upside down.

It is in part their air of exclusivity—and correlatively, the tantalizing chance that we might conquer exclusivity and seize knowledge that the Greeks and Romans (unlike Paul and Timothy) strove to keep hidden—that makes ancient mystery religions so attractive even now. For some, attaining that knowledge promises the same sort of spiritual benefits that it promised two thousand years ago, as a search of "mysteries" on the internet will demonstrate: throughout the world, neopagan groups busily process new initiates. For others, it promises the same sort of satisfaction that one gets from solving other scholarly puzzles, only more so—after all, knowledge of the ancient mysteries has been occluded not only by the same intervening centuries that dim our knowledge of all aspects of ancient cultures, but also by deliberate concealment. Any scholar who turns up a new bit of evidence or provides a persuasive new interpretation shares the feeling of a master cryptographer who has cracked an enemy code. And this leaves us with an interesting question: if, some day, scholarship miraculously were to reveal all of the mysteries' secrets, would they still fascinate us? Luckily, perhaps, it is a situation that we are very unlikely to confront.

Bibliography

Beck, Roger. "The Mysteries of Mithras: A New Account of Their Genesis." *Journal of Roman Studies* 88 (1998): 115–28.

Borgeaud, Philippe. *La mère des dieux: De Cybèle à la Vierge Marie.* Seuil, 1996.

Burkert, Walter. *Ancient Mystery Cults.* Harvard University Press, 1987.

Cole, Susan Guettel. *Theoi Megaloi: The Cult of the Great Gods of Samothrace.* Études préliminaires aux religions orientales dans l'empire romain 96. Brill, 1984.

Graf, Fritz. "Dionysian and Orphic Eschatology: New Texts and Old Questions of Interpretation." In *Masks of Dionysus,* ed. T. H. Carpenter and C. A. Faraone. Cornell University Press, 1993.

Kerényi, Carl. *Eleusis: Archetypical Image of Mother and Daughter.* Tr. Ralph Mannheim. Princeton University Press, 1967 (orig. 1960).

Merkelbach, Reinhold. *Isis Regina—Zeus Sarapis.* Teubner, 1995.

Religions in Contact

John Scheid

Contact among different religions and gods was a constant in the ancient world. Ancient Rome, for example, always had more than one religion, and it was only during the last period of its history that it saw the spread of exclusively monotheistic religions. The public religion of Rome involved all Roman citizens as such, but this religion was not the only one they had to deal with. In Rome itself, every citizen belonged to several other religious communities, starting with the household religion, which was autonomous with respect to the public religion; the associations or social groups to which a citizen could belong—colleges of merchants or artisans, neighborhood groups, or military units—each of which had its own religion; and, finally, specific forms of religious practice, such as those involving sorcery, magic, and divination, which continued to flourish despite occasional persecution. Moreover, citizens of a Roman colony had religious obligations within the public religion of that colony. The gradual diffusion of Christianity did not suppress this pluralism, since the various Christian communities, divided and resistant to central authority, coexisted for a long time and shared the field with the two other religions "of the book," Judaism and, eventually, Islam. In this way, the religious life of the ancient world was shaped by a plurality of overlapping religious obligations that were not mutually exclusive, but among which certain ones had precedence.

What was true inside Rome and the city-states that surrounded it was equally true outside of that circle. Because these city-states were relatively small, they themselves were surrounded by other small states in fairly close proximity, whose religious systems were nonetheless different, despite significant structural resemblances. Rome was bordered on the north by Etruscan city-states, on the south and southeast by Latin-speaking and, more generally, Italic populations. These cities and peoples had their own religions, with which their neighbors had become familiar and with which they had learned to get along. In fact, in the archaic period, influential families moved back and forth between the various city-states, and they seem to have adapted, without too much difficulty, to local religions. Etruscan families are known to have lived in Rome; there is also the story of the arrival in Rome of the Sabine Attus Clausus, ancestor of the Claudii clan, with five thousand followers who assimilated into the Roman populace.

At another level, Rome was part of the Latin League that united thirty communities; the annual foundational act of this league was a common sacrifice to Jupiter on Monte Cavo. It would be interesting to know how this sacrifice was conducted and how it was perceived by representatives of the thirty groups, whose religious customs differed significantly, despite their kinship. But the literary tradition never mentions issues of this sort—perhaps owing to the absence of consistent source material from this period and this particular religious practice and perhaps especially because, by the very nature of their religious systems, these separate groups were accustomed to practicing religious cohabitation: it was what they did every day in their homes.

Furthermore, none of these religions proselytized. A person belonged to a religious community by virtue of birth or social position, and a notion such as conversion made no sense at all. Belonging to a religion was part and parcel of having a social position, and one's ritual obligations concerned life in this world; religion did not demand an act of faith and personal conversion as a preliminary condition of membership in the body of those "faithful" to a deity, even in the mystery cults, for which initiation was required. Depending on his social situation, a citizen was subject to some kind of religious obligation, whether he liked it or not. Participation in mystery cults was, of course, a matter of choice, but, in fact, a citizen's social situation was more often the central factor, because it opened up the possibility of choice. Thus, initiates of the cult of Mithras were recruited among mid-level Roman military and administrative personnel. Taking into account, too, that all these religions were polytheistic, ritualistic, and nonexclusive, one can understand the ease with which contacts were made between adherents to the various systems of religious obligations, which overlapped and complemented one another but were not in opposition. The precise distinctions that scholars establish between public, semipublic, and domestic cults, for clarity's sake, are justified because they correspond to legal reality, but in daily life, the citizen perceived no such distinction, since everything came together for him in a set of more-or-less important and constraining religious obligations, to which he was subject depending on the time or place.

The situation was hardly any different for what gradually became the Roman world. The religious systems of Greek city-states functioned in roughly the same manner as those of Rome and Italy. And even in the Jewish nation, which practiced a monotheistic religion, the presence of "Greek" groups and city-states with their polytheistic cults was a historical and political fact that was never systematically questioned, despite the stricter conception of purity in Jewish traditions. A similar situation developed in Egypt, where the ancestral religion of the Egyptians—governed by a pharaoh whose origins were Greek, then by a Roman, the emperor—existed alongside Greek cults. In Alexandria, the powerful Jewish community and the Greek community occupying the same neighborhoods—a characteristic of Alexandrian identity—led to sporadic pogroms and conflicts, particularly in the period of Jewish uprisings; these were triggered more by rivalry, however, than by radical religious opposition.

Initially limited to areas of immediate overlap, contacts and exchanges between religions were a fundamental fact of religious life in the entire Mediterranean world. Contacts did not stop expanding even with the Macedonian and Roman conquests. Whether out of cultural inclination or as a matter of convenience, today's observer views different religions as isolated communities or else as categorically opposed. Such an approach is misleading when applied to antiquity because, with the exception of particular situations circumscribed by the historical moment, the religions of the Mediterranean world have never been isolated. Contacts and interpenetrations have never stopped taking place.

Such a religious universe could not be radically affected by changes owing to Hellenistic and Roman imperialism, at least as long as religious values were compatible, because relations with the religions and gods of others, as well as the assimilation of new gods and religious modes, constituted part of Roman religious behavior. Contacts were not always peaceful, however.

Conflicts and resistance

In the case of political or military conflict, any religion could become the evil enemy, even if it was to shed that designation once peace was reestablished. So, for the Romans, during the Third Samnite War (295 BCE), the rites of the Samnites were deemed barbarous, a judgment that had never been made before and one that was of course abandoned when the Samnites were integrated into the Roman city-state. The situation was no different in the Hellenistic world or in Syria or Egypt. Depending on the fluctuations of conflicts and truces, religions could be the object of accusations and repressions, but for political and military rather than religious motives. While the Alexandrian Greeks and Jews exchanged mutual accusations, their aim was to do the other group harm, not to destroy its practices and beliefs; for the most part, each side managed to accommodate the other's form of religion. In spite of the catastrophe attributed to the Jewish Wars (66–70, 135 CE) and the religious consequences brought on by the destruction of the temple and the Hasmonean kingdom, once peace had returned, there was no longer any fundamental enmity between Jews and Romans in the greater part of the Roman world. After the Jewish Wars, when Greek and Roman presence increased in Judea, the rabbinic schools developed rules that allowed Jews to live in the same community as non-Jews, instead of radically prohibiting such cohabitation. So, in spite of the profound changes in Judaism provoked by the destruction of the temple, the period afterward was a relatively calm and prosperous one for Jewish communities, particularly in Asia Minor and Rome.

In Rome, some cults or ritual practices, such as those of Isis and Bacchus or those of various philosophers and seers, were persecuted from time to time, but never permanently and for their own sake. The sole prevailing issue was what passed for public order, that is, the political situation. The well-known suppression of the Bacchanalia (186 BCE) reveals the Roman desire to preserve strict control over religious developments in Rome and in Italy and over the admission of new religious practices into Rome. This repression aimed at putting an end to a new form of the cult of Bacchus, imported from Campania. The Bacchic communities did not belong to the public religion, but rightly or wrongly, their sudden proselytizing, combined with other practices viewed as disruptive to the public order, seemed to reveal a desire to create an organization encompassing all of Italy; in other words, the *thiasoi* (groups of worshipers) were thought to mask a vast conspiracy. These accusations and suspicions forced the intervention of magistrates, who severely curtailed the Bacchic movement and reduced the cult to what it had been before its expansion (Pailler 1988). This incident shows that Roman society and its authorities did not always react with tolerance to the introduction of new religious practices, even where cults with private status were concerned. The state sought to exert control over the population and repressed even the slightest attempt on the part of the populace to organize outside of public structures.

Some cults offered the possibility of this kind of organization, hence the hostility of the authorities, if the political context alerted them. There is no need to dwell on the subject of the wars that sprang out of Jewish resistance to the gradual Hellenization in Judea, brought about first by the Seleucids, then by the Romans. The policy of assimilation followed, in early imperial times, by the Hasmonean kings, a policy that reflected a much more conciliatory position, could not prevent the complete rejection of Roman influence by radical groups. The Jewish Wars offer a well-documented example of insurrection against the Romans, in which motives of a religious order played a central role and constituted the basis for the rebellion. During another Jewish revolt, in 116–17 CE, pagan temples seem to have been destroyed, notably in Cyrenaica. The pogrom incited in Egypt by this revolt characterized Jews in part as enemies of the Egyptian gods (Frankfurter 1992). Furthermore, the Greeks of Alexandria, protesting against Roman tyranny, also invoked the local Sarapis cult; more generally, in Egypt, Thrace, and Gaul, indigenous priests often played a role in insurrections (Beard, North, and Price 1998: 347). At the time of such rebellions in Germany, Gaul, and Brittany, for example, Roman temples were destroyed and participation in Roman religions was terminated. We should note, however, that local cults were generally integrated into the local Roman religion and that their priests were often members of the local elite. All this tends to show that the insurgents were rejecting the Romans rather than their gods and that religions themselves changed direction depending on political events: during such conflicts, the religious practices and the gods that had once symbolized integration into the Roman world became symbols of submission or, in the case of indigenous cults, symbols of freedom.

Contacts and exchanges

In the course of antiquity, and especially under the Roman Empire, contact among peoples, ethnic groups, and religious communities gave rise to lively and lasting exchanges, leaving aside occasional revolts, wars, or pogroms. From the earliest period about which we have information, Athens, Rome, or Carthage welcomed traditions and deities whose names revealed their foreign origins.

Let us take Rome as an example: its expansion was the most spectacular of all, and it allows us to study the process of "acculturation" in detail. The religious architecture of the 6th century BCE—that of the Capitol, for example— was in large part borrowed from the Etruscans. Tradition even attributes it, along with the Capitoline triad housed in the temple, to kings and artisans from Etruria. This same tradition holds that Roman rites of divination, such as the technique of interpreting auspices and even the practice of triumphal processions, were derived from Etruscan practices, and it situates the origins of the Sibylline Books, introduced by an Etruscan king, in Campania. Whatever the value of these traditions, it is clear that the Romans were not scandalized that central elements of their religious rites came from neighboring peoples. Early-20th-century historians clearly had more difficulty understanding this openness to outsiders; Georg Wissowa expressed astonishment at the idea that the most important gods of the Roman state, Jupiter, Juno, and Minerva, were of foreign origin (1912: 40–43). The vestiges of the archaic period likewise reveal an early Hellenism, by way of the Etruscans and neighboring Italic city-states. Statues from the archaic temples of Saint Omobono are clearly derived from contemporary Greek art, as is the decor on the temple of Castor and Pollux in the Roman Forum. Furthermore, it was during this early period that Hercules, Apollo, and Castor and Pollux themselves were installed in Rome. These deities owe more to relations with the Italic city-states (Tibur, Tusculum) than to direct contacts on the part of the Romans with Magna Graecia (the parts of Italy that the Greeks had colonized), and they show in any case the extent to which all the peoples of ancient Italy were open to other religious traditions. Archeological digs show that the Carthaginians, with the Etruscans, worshiped Uni-Astarte in her temple at Pyrgi (Cerveteri), and of course it is well known that emissaries from the Italian city-states consulted the oracle at Delphi.

These cults and gods attest to cultural and political exchanges and probably to migrations of social groups. A historical example offers some information about the integration of foreign deities. During the siege of Veii (396 BCE), the Romans used the rite called *evocatio* to adopt the local goddess Juno Regina as a Roman deity; after the taking of the city, the goddess was solemnly transported to Rome, where she was given a temple and a public ceremony on the Aventine. The Carthaginian goddess Juno Caelestis was believed to have been "evoked" when Carthage was taken in 146 BCE. As Roman colonies were established in North Africa, many local Punic cults were taken up by these Roman city-states. More generally, even if a war was not going on, deities were simply invited to Rome and established there without regard to their origin. The uninterrupted series of such deities reflects the Roman expansion, first in Italy and then in the Mediterranean: Diana, Feronia, Juno Sospita, Dis Pater and Persephone, then Aesculapius, Venus Erycina, and Magna Mater—and a little later, of course, the importing of deities was not restricted to Rome. In the 4th century BCE, the Carthaginians introduced the cult of Demeter and Persephone into the city to atone for the devastation of their sanctuary in the area around Syracuse. In Athens, the Thracian deity Bendis played a role in civic cults starting in the 5th century BCE, and Isis was introduced into the city at the beginning of the 4th century BCE.

Influences and "acculturation"

The integration of these cults came about without difficulty, according to a complex system. As far as we can tell, in Rome, for example, public ceremonies were celebrated either in the Roman style or according to a "foreign" mode, and this had been true for a long time. The Capitoline triad and Castor and Pollux seem always to have been honored according to Roman rituals, while the Hercules of the Ara Maxima was honored according to different, rather more "Greek" modalities. At the beginning of the 4th century, the first celebration of a *lectisternium* (a banquet for gods) harkened back likewise to the Greek tradition of *theoxenia* (entertaining gods at a meal). Nothing is known, of course, about the domestic practices of this period, except for the slow transformation of funerary rites; we can follow their evolution throughout Italy under the influence of aristocratic traditions coming from Greece and Magna Graecia. During the historical period, the situation was much the same, although it responds to different imperatives that were at work then. From the Punic Wars on, Rome entered into direct contact with the Mediterranean world and, at the beginning of the 2nd century BCE, with the countries of Greece. The introduction of gods and religions belonging to other religious cultures, and probably new representations of Rome's relation to the rest of the world as well, shaped the evolution of Rome's relation to the gods and cults of others. The more general concept of the "cult according to the Greek ritual" was created in Rome in this context, although this type of practice was not limited to Rome. The cult of Demeter and Persephone in 4th-century BCE Carthage must have been celebrated by Greeks living in Carthage who followed the Greek rite. About the same time, a priestess of Greek origin presided over the new "Greek" cults of Ceres that had been introduced in Rome.

The concept of the "Greek rite" was not an old one, although evidence for the practice itself was already present from the beginning of the 4th century with the introduction of *lectisternia,* with their clear reference to the Greek *theoxenia.* The very term *ritus Graecus* (Greek cultic mode) appears for the first time in the 2nd century BCE in a text of Cato the Censor (*Orationum,* frag. 77 Malcovati); it remained relatively rare and somewhat surprising. If the

Romans put "ceremonies according to the Greek rite" *(sacra Graeco ritu)* or "Greek cults" *(Graeca sacra)* in this category, this does not mean that the cults of all Greek deities fell under the same rubric. The rites of the cults of Hercules, Apollo, and Saturn were "Greek," for example, but not those of the cults of Aesculapius, Bacchus, Hecate, Nemesis, or Magna Mater. The cult of Castor and Pollux could have been classified under the Greek mode, especially since Demetrius Poliorcetes cited the cult of the Castores as proof of the Romans' and the Greeks' common parentage (Strabo 5.232); but the Romans apparently never categorized it that way. On the contrary, the twins were patrons of the Roman cavalry, that is, patrons of the elite and therefore of a constitutive element of Roman identity. And this is not because they were perceived as being less Greek than, for example, Hercules, because an ancient inscription from Lavinium called them *quroi* (= Greek *kouroi,* a term often used to describe them in Greece; Degrassi 1957–63: no. 1271a). On the other hand, Hercules came from Tibur (Tivoli) and the Castores came to Rome from Tusculum, rather than from any of the Greek city-states.

The Romans classified certain festivals and one of the modalities of Roman sacrifice as being of Greek origin. In Livy, cults founded by Romulus were celebrated according to the Alban rite (from Alba Longa, the twins' homeland), but the cult of Hercules corresponded to the Greek rite because it had been founded by Evander, who came from Greek Arcadia (Livy 1.7.3). Cato asserts that the Saturnalia, the festival of Saturn, was celebrated according to the Greek rite. The cult of Apollo was viewed as the best illustration of the Roman Greek-rite cult. Early in the 2nd century BCE, part of the cult of Ceres fell into the same category. A Sibylline oracle of 125 BCE prescribed a religious service that had to be celebrated by children according to the Achaean rite; other, still older Sibylline oracles advised processions and celebrations according to the Greek rite (see, e.g., Livy 25.12.10, 13). Finally, the protocols of the Secular Games at the beginning of the empire specified that the sacrifices be celebrated "according to the Greek rite" *(Graeco Achivo ritu).* In other words, the category was complex; it was not simply limited to all the religious services concerning a deity originating in the Greek world or to all the rites belonging to the cult of these deities.

If we look closely at the literary texts, two additional phenomena stand out. In the first place, the concept of the Greek rite refers to an ethnic group (the Greeks) and not, as with the Alban rite, the Roman rite, or the *cinctus Gabinus* (the manner of draping the toga practiced by the Gabinians during the Roman-style cult), to a city-state such as Alba, Rome, or Gabii. This distinction denotes an opposition between a ritual mode belonging to a smaller group, or even to a city-state integrated within the Roman state, and a broader, less distinct group that extends well beyond any given city-state. In the second case, a different category is involved, one that is no longer institutional but almost geographic or cultural—in any event, it is quite vague. It would be interesting in this regard to know when the Romans themselves characterized certain of their rites as "Roman." At first glance, this classification makes sense only if it is contrasted to another cultic category—to the Greek-rite cults, for example.

In other words, the ritual concept of the Greek mode, invented around the time of the Second Punic War, is a good illustration of the open but complex relationship between the Romans and foreign cults and gods. In the 2nd century BCE, the major point of reference was Greece (or what passed for Greece in the Romans' eyes). This reference corresponds, on the one hand, to the second Hellenization of Rome, which was much more profound than the diffuse Greek influence of the archaic period; it transformed Roman culture. On the other hand, the reference reveals that Hellenization was actually a Roman phenomenon. From this viewpoint, the Hellenization of Rome and its religion perfectly illustrates the results of intercultural relations. When they had direct contact with the Greeks, the Romans had continuing access to the high culture of the period. From then on, it was no longer possible to think of Roman culture and institutions in a non-Greek manner. A cultivated Roman thought in ways defined by Greek philosophy, and Rome's national literature—its mythology in particular—could not help but be incorporated within the framework of a continuation of Greek literature. On the religious level, this intellectual broadening took a certain number of old or recent phenomena that were or appeared to be Greek and translated them into a cultic category. The cults themselves nevertheless unquestionably remained Roman and were not simple transpositions of Greek rites (Greek being a highly artificial category in this instance). The Greek-rite cults were much more a way for the Romans to affirm that they belonged to the Greek world, a justification for their imperialism or at least for their quest for alliances. The construction of a notion such as the Greek mode of venerating the gods was a completely Roman phenomenon, produced with no outside assistance. It is, in a manner of speaking, a fine example of self-acculturation. One can see in it, of course, a certain degree of fascination.

If admiration for Greek literature, art, and science could sufficiently justify the Hellenization of Roman culture, the same was not true for the Hellenization of Roman religion. In the latter context, it is more appropriate to speak of the way in which the Romans thought of themselves from then on. Not only did they introduce rites, such as the Matronal rites of Ceres, that created the (Greek) Eleusinian rites in Rome, in a way, but they also retrospectively Hellenized a part of their religious patrimony: at least by the time of Dionysius of Halicarnassus (1st century BCE), they discovered that they were in fact Greeks and thought of themselves as belonging to the Greek world. With this outlook, they made their own culture eminent and respectable, but they also justified their imperial ambitions. To the extent that Hellenism was thought to be the highest form of culture, whose mission was to dominate the world, Roman Hellenism could maintain uncomplicated aspirations to hegemony. A rather striking illustration of this attitude is found in the decoration of the temple dedicated to Hercules and the Muses (179 BCE), which was built by

Fulvius Nobilior beside the *via triumphalis* to celebrate his victory over the Aetolians, a rather bloody victory that verged on violating human rights. On this monument of Roman Hellenism, probably realized under the guidance of the poet Quintus Ennius, the unusual association of the hero with the Muses, as attested at the Asklepieion in Messana (Pausanius 4.31.10) and by Isocrates (*Philippus* 109–10), refers to a new type of domination to be exercised henceforth on the cultural level by the triumphant Romans, and it recalls the civilizing mission carried out by Hercules at the beginning of Roman times. In this temple, the most ancient period of Rome's past was associated with symbols of the highest knowledge, notably from the Pythagorean traditions, so as to express the superiority of Rome over the Greeks, thanks to a Herculean *imperator* in his invincibility and his culture.

Expansions

Following the end of the Social War and the integration of the Italics (inhabitants of Italy whose language was related to Latin) into the Roman city-state during the 1st century BCE, religious issues took on new dimensions. Not only did the Italics become members of the public religious community of Rome in this way, but their city-states were increasingly transformed following the Roman model. This evolution continued throughout the empire, until the moment when all free men became Roman citizens (213 CE). The expansion of the Roman city-state, combined with the continuous creation of Roman-style city-states elsewhere, profoundly changed the religious landscape of Rome and the Roman world.

Both as occasional allies and through the Latin or Roman colonies that were gradually created across Italy, the Italic peoples had long been familiar with Roman religion. Similarly, the Roman city-states that were established in Italy came into contact with other cults and gods, so that at the local level their religions functioned in the way that Rome functioned in the administrative center of the Roman state. They integrated local and public deities by taking up the particular cult practices attached to the former or by Romanizing them. For example, from the very beginning of the empire if not earlier, the city of Potentia included in its pantheon Mefitis Utiana, the patron goddess of a neighboring place of cult worship (Rossano di Vaglio), and under Augustus the colony of Hispellum became owner and manager of the old temple of Clitumnus, at the headwaters of the river with the same name. The principal deity of the colony of Lucus Feroniae was the local goddess Feronia. Nowhere was there any question of despising or destroying earlier religious forms. In turn, the Italic city-states were subject to Roman influence. Thus, in the Iguvine Tables, one can note the appearance of Roman institutional terms over the course of the 3rd century BCE. Other Italian cities, after their conquest, even had to merge their principal cult with Rome. Such was the case, for example, with Lanuvium, where the cult of Juno Sospita was celebrated in common with the Roman state from 338 BCE.

The consequence of this gradual fusion, in the context of the city-states of Roman Italy, was the gradual arrival of local Italic cults in Rome itself. At various historical moments, Diana, Juno Sospita, Feronia, and Angerona were given temples and cults in Rome. Conversely, an increasing number of Roman citizens living in Italy never went to Rome. Their lives unfolded in the "little homeland" of their city or colony, and their belonging to the Roman state was primarily a legal matter. As Roman citizens, they were all subject to the obligations of the public religion of Rome, and they profited from the benevolence of the Roman gods. But as they no longer participated in Roman institutional life, Rome became for them mainly a common reference point that they would encounter in literature or in the legends depicted on the various coins of the realm. This was clearly also true for the public religion of Rome. There was never any celebration of Roman religion at the level of the entire Roman citizenry, in a sort of religion of the empire, but it is undeniable that the cult celebrated by the magistrates and priests in Rome established a constant spiritual connection among all those who benefited from Roman citizenship. At the same time, the numerous Roman cities existing in the world, each with its own civic religion independent of Rome's, gave a diversified and still more pluralist picture of what foreigners might call Roman religion.

The golden age of religious pluralism

The peace that followed the Roman conquest of the world and the civil wars extended and accelerated the integration of peoples and city-states into the Roman world. The displacement of individuals also contributed to a mix of cultures and religions that was more intense than ever. In Rome itself and in other large cities, the flow of people from the entire world was manifest in the regular arrival of new cults and religions. But contact between them began to take place on a different level. Few new gods came into Roman public religion after the end of the Republic. The deities Isis and Sarapis, who had become public gods in the 1st century CE, were the last important foreign gods to become Roman, before the short-lived experience of Sol Elagabalus (218); then Aurelian's Sol Invictus (3rd century), likewise a god of Syrian origin; and finally, in the 4th century, the Christian god. No deities of Celtic or German origins were admitted into the religion of Rome; their integration took place on the local level, in the colonies and cities, in keeping with the overall evolution of religious practices: new cults spread at the subordinate or local level.

On the domestic and private level, a large number of new deities came into Rome, starting in the 1st century CE, at times enjoying fairly important places of worship: Jupiter Heliopolis, the Palmyrene gods, Jupiter Dolichenus, Mithras, the Jewish god, and the Christian god. Bringing together smaller or larger communities of Romans and non-Romans, these cults existed side by side in general harmony. Most of them were even established in communal sites where the collective cults of the Roman neighborhoods were practiced. Heliopolitan cults were set up in the old sacred wood of Furrina on the Janiculum, that of the Palmyrene gods in the Gardens of Caesar alongside other Roman and non-Roman cults (the sanctuary of Fors Fortuna, Hercules, Jupiter Beheleparus), and that of Jupiter Dolichenus and Mithras in some *vicus* (village or neighborhood) shrines (e.g., the famous Dolichenum of the Aventine and the Mithraeum near the *vicus* of the *Via Marmorata*).

In other words, in the various collective sanctuaries of Rome's neighborhoods, ancestral cults and new cults often came into contact, meaning that their celebrations became collective events. And as far as we know, Jewish prayer sites, like Jewish cemeteries, were not excluded from the collectivity. They belonged to the life of the neighborhood, just as other religious sites did, to the extent that, in Rome, a synagogue might serve as a topographical reference point (CIL 6.9821). Consequently, conditions were ripe for a broadening of religious experiences to include, in particular, religions whose practices differed from the ancestral ritualism. Proximity could encourage association with Jewish families and synagogues, all the more easily in that Jews could participate in the festive life of the neighborhood, in marriages and banquets, as long as they could observe the dietary rules drawn up in the 2nd century BCE by rabbinic schools; a place was likewise made for Romans who wished to pray to the god of the Jews. During periods of relative calm, Christian sanctuaries, which were more discreetly established in private domains since they were the object of latent hostility, might also attract "pagans." In the 3rd century, in any event, Christian churches were known, since their goods could be confiscated by the emperor Valerian.

The unification of the world

The unification of the world under Roman dominion also transformed the conditions of religious life in the provinces of the empire, especially in areas relatively exempt from urbanization. In the East, in Egypt, and in Africa, traditional religious life went on without much change, except that the finances of the large sanctuaries were more strictly controlled (at Ephesus, for example). Under the Republic, Greek city-states had already taken into account the eruption of Roman power in their world by creating cults dedicated to the goddess Roma or by honoring some particular Roman governor. Beginning with the empire, these provinces and city-states created cults dedicated to Roma and Augustus, in keeping with traditions going back to the Hellenistic period. In Egypt, with the exception of the cult of the emperor, Greco-Egyptian religious life continued to develop along its own lines. But from that point on, the Roman administration, following a tendency already evident in the Ptolemaic period, exercised tighter control over temple revenues and personnel. Similarly, in Jerusalem, the Romans controlled the election of the high priest, oversaw the financial matters of the temple, and restricted the functions of the Sanhedrin. In other respects, the cult continued as before, and the temple was granted the privilege of collecting the annual tax from the Jews. After the war of 66–70, this tax was allocated to the reconstruction of the temple of Jupiter on the Capitoline in Rome. This measure, intended to humiliate the Jews, actually exercised a decisive influence on the definition of Jewish identity.

In Africa, except for the prohibition against the sacrifice—real or imaginary—of children, nothing arose to disturb the religious life of the free city-states. But in Africa, more than in the Greek-speaking provinces, the creation of colonies and cities exerted an influence over the evolution of religious life. Local cults were revived within the framework of the colonies and were celebrated in Latin; but we cannot tell to what extent the cult remained in conformity with Punic traditions. The new colony of Carthage, in particular, assimilated local deities such as the Cereres (the Roman version of the Greek goddesses Demeter and Persephone), Aesculapius, Saturn, and Juno Caelestis at the end of the 1st century BCE. Along with specifically Roman deities, these gods of Punic origin from then on typified the religions of the metropolis of Roman Africa, which comprised an original mix of gods and cults. Thus both the local religions and the Roman religions became still richer and more complex. And, of course, with the opening of the world, Eastern religions, Judaism, and Christianity also took hold in Africa.

It was in the less urbanized provinces of western Europe, however, that the most significant mutations came about. Iberia had already known Greek and Punic colonization and, after centuries of fierce resistance, had adapted itself to the Roman mold. At the time of the conquest, Gaul, Germania, and the countries of the Danube were occupied by different ethnic groups that may have belonged to a single culture but that had virtually never known unity and organization into city-states of the Mediterranean type. One of the first results of the Roman conquest was to unify these different peoples and to inspire an idea of identity transcending that of clan. This was accomplished both at the level of the city-states, which were often created by the occupying Roman presence with the help of local elites, and at the level of the provinces (e.g., the altars to Augustus in Lyon, Narbonne, and Tarragon). Thanks to the process of urbanization following the model of the Mediterranean city-states, some of these groups acquired a self-awareness that they had never known before. This phenomenon became increasingly pronounced, starting with the beginning of the empire, when the Romans took peoples who had up to that point been living in small, fragmented units and regrouped them into city-states. The municipal laws discovered in Baetica make it clear that the creation of Latin or Roman cities and colonies transformed the religious life of these communities. The populations involved were often led to combine the entire set of religious practices and traditions that they viewed as collective and characteristic of their people into a single public religion, that of their city or colony. As the city-states in question were often Latin or Roman colonies, they had to conform to the common rules of Roman religious law. Unfortunately the sources currently available are of little help in showing how and to what extent older rites were integrated within the framework of local public cults.

With the exception of the prohibition against human sacrifice and druidic practices—about which we know very little—and the establishment of provincial cults, the Romans rarely intervened in this process of integration, except as advisers. Some of the local elites, in any case, had done military service with auxiliary troops of the Roman army and were thus familiar with the universe of city-states and civic religions, so they were in a position to accelerate the institutional development of their peoples. And just as the Romans themselves had reacted to their discovery of high Greek culture, these communities also aspired to their own participation in the Roman world. A large number among them gradually came to think of themselves as Roman. In this way, many Iberian, Gallic, and Dalmatian communities laid down the foundations for original local religions, which had never before had such scope. Once their opposition to Roman occupation had been surmounted, the local elites of these provinces may be said to have (re)invented their own cultures and religions under the pressure of Roman urbanization and within its formal framework.

Given that the cultural language of this new construction was Roman, it is very hard to tell to what extent the gods and cults of the northern provinces masked indigenous gods and rituals. The example of the Hellenization of the Romans can serve as a model, but it must be emphasized that the experience of military victors and rulers is different from that of defeated and subjugated peoples. On a different level, the deep transformation of Judaism resulting from the destruction of the temple provides a clear illustration of the second experience. After the Hellenizing evolution of the Jews, the catastrophe of 70 CE profoundly modified the Jewish religion.

The impetus toward interreligious exchanges prompted by the unification of the world is undeniable. The relative tolerance of the Romans and the people of the ancient world explains how religions and gods that came from all over were able to establish themselves in all the provinces without major conflict. As we have seen, plurality was the rule. With the exception of certain followers of Isis, Judaism, and Christianity, no religious group defined itself by a particular name. Furthermore, the term *Isiac* was rare, and the designation *Jew* was as much ethnic as religious. Only the label *Christian* came close to the term as it is used today. For the Jews, who never had any central authority, it was more the Jewish tax of 70 CE than ritual traditions and common memory that raised the question of Jewish identity. Without undertaking any active proselytizing, Jewish communities were open to converts who lived according to Jewish law and to "God-fearing" individuals who adhered to only some of the prescriptions.

The only lasting conflict with a religious community involved the Christians. Despite long periods of tolerance that allowed many people, especially in the cities, to associate with Christian communities and to blend certain Christian beliefs and rituals into their own domestic religions, the risk of repression was undeniably omnipresent. Before the middle of the 3rd century, the reasons for the hostility of the authorities stemmed more from concerns about disturbances of the public order than from a struggle against a religion as such. On the Christian side, hostility toward the Roman state, Roman cities, paganism, and Judaism was motivated by the Christian rejection of polytheism and the existing religions. Decidedly given to proselytizing, Christian communities tried to attract their neighbors to their religion, at least if the Christian sources are to be believed. For "pagans," this phenomenon of attraction was inscribed in the order of things from the moment they accepted the proximity of Christians in their neighborhoods or, for example, in professional associations. The Christians were able to attract the pagans because of the kinship between their religious doctrines and the issues known from pagan philosophical instruction. For many, however, their experience led not to the abandonment of their ancestral traditions but rather to an ultimately traditional practice of religion that was open to the religious practices of neighbors and social partners. Even apart from the Christians, who remained close to the Jews, a sign of such tolerance can be seen in what Christian apologetics calls *lapsi*, individuals who were not so much lukewarm Christians as people who had adopted a certain number of Christian practices and representations and made them part of their personal religion, but without wishing to belong to the Christian community in the strict sense. Another example can be found in the Naassenes, whom Hippolytus condemned and who combined, to a certain extent, Christianity with the mysteries of Magna Mater. If they were in any danger, the Naassenes abandoned the incriminating practices, as they did not see these as representing the central core of their religious experience.

The situation seems to have changed when Constantine and his sons raised Christianity to the level of a public religion. The rapidity and depth of the evolution must not be exaggerated, however. Non-Christian ancestral cults continued to be practiced for a long time at the local and domestic levels. Nor did the Christians abandon certain older practices; in the 5th century, Christians still carried out sacrifices and made vows before an image of Constantine (Philostorgius, *Ecclesiastical History* 2.17), in spite of repeated interdictions. Religious pluralism was not forcefully suppressed from one day to the next, either. Leaving aside the old cults and Judaism, let us note that Christians themselves were divided into regional and provincial communities, often far removed from one another, if we are to believe the history of heresies and doctrinal quarrels. The fact remains that this evolution ended up completely transforming the religious landscape of the Mediterranean world. From this point on, pluralism came increasingly to involve the religions of the book: Judaism, Christianity, and, as of the 7th century, Islam.

Bibliography

Beard, Mary, John North, and Simon Price. *Religions of Rome*. 2 vols. Cambridge, 1998.
Degrassi, Attilio. *Inscriptiones latinae liberae rei publicae*. 2 vols. Biblioteca di Studi Superiori 23 and 40. Florence, 1957–63.
Frankfurter, David. "Lest Egypt's City Be Deserted: Religion and Ideology in the Egyp-

tian Response to the Jewish Revolt (116–117 CE)." *Journal of Jewish Studies* 43 (1992): 203–20.

North, John. "Conservatism and Change in Roman Religion." *Papers of the British School in Rome* 44 (1974): 1–12.

———. "Religious Toleration in Republican Rome." *Proceedings of the Cambridge Philological Society* 25 (1979): 85–103.

Pailler, Jean-Marie. *Bacchanalia: La répression de 186 av. J.C. à Rome et en Italie: Vestiges, images, traditions*. Bibliothèque des Écoles Françaises d'Athènes et de Rome 270. Rome, 1988.

Scheid, John. "Aspects religieux de la municipalisation: Quelques réflexions générales." In *Cités, municipes, colonies: Les processus de municipalisation en Gaule et en Germanie sous le haut-empire romain*, ed. Monique Dondin-Payre and Marie-Thérèse Raepsaet-Charlier. Paris, 1999.

———. "Graeco Ritu: A Typically Roman Way of Honouring the Gods." *Harvard Studies in Classical Philology* 97 (1995): 15–31.

Wissowa, Georg. *Religion und Kultus der Romer.* Munich, 1912.

Writing and Religion

Mary Beard

*I*n 304 BCE, or not long before, a man by the name of Cnaeus Flavius displayed in the Forum at Rome, for the first time, the official calendar of religious festivals. Or so several Roman writers assure us. It was a revolutionary act. For up to that point, the calendar of festivals and all kinds of information that went with it (including various legal rules and formulas and details of the days on which one was allowed to bring cases) had been in the hands of a small group of priests: "hidden away in the storeroom of the *pontifices*" as the historian Livy puts it (*From the Foundation of the City* 9.46.5) and making the people as a whole dependent on secret priestly knowledge. The ancient writers disagree about exactly at which stage of his career Flavius did this. Was it while he held the office of *aedile* (a middle-ranking elected magistracy in the city)? Or was it earlier, while he was still a government clerk *(scriba)*? Cicero even debated this problem in 50 BCE, in a letter to his friend Atticus (*To Atticus* 6.1), who had raised the awkward possibility that the calendar had actually been made public more than a century before Flavius's intervention. But, details apart, this action was clearly seen as a blow against the power of the traditional priestly and governing class at Rome—Flavius himself being (in Livy's words again) "of humble birth" or, more precisely, the son of an ex-slave.

How accurate this anecdote is, we simply do not know. But, accurate or not, it brings into view some of the most important aspects of the interaction between religion and writing, not just in Rome but throughout the ancient Mediterranean world—and, indeed, more widely. First, the apparent complexity of the written document that Flavius is supposed to have revealed: an established, annual calendar of rituals, linked into a whole series of regulations about the use of different days in the year and other procedures of civil law. This kind of elaborate religious codification, with its fixed and complex rules of proper behavior, is scarcely conceivable without the resource of writing. Second, the contested political dimension. This story presents two alternative models of how written religious knowledge might be deployed: on the one hand, as the private text of an exclusive, literate priestly group, and so a formidable weapon in the armory of priestly control; on the other, as a potentially public piece of information, and so—as Flavius was to demonstrate by his posting of the calendar in the Forum—a weapon in the democratization of religious power. Third, the controversy between the ancient writers on the precise version of events is itself ultimately a product of writing. For the *history* of religion in the strictest sense, the very idea that religious history could be a subject of study and debate, separate from practice and tradition, largely depends on the "reification of the past" that comes with *written records*. We ourselves, of course, are beneficiaries of those same records; for in the absence of Roman writing, we would now know nothing of Flavius and his calendar, still less be able to explore its significance.

This chapter will reflect on the issues raised by Flavius's story, among other facets of the interaction of religion and writing in the ancient Mediterranean world. It will attempt to set these in the context of more general, theoretical, and anthropological studies of the role of written texts within cultural systems and the contested interface between traditions of "literacy" and "orality" that, since the invention of writing itself, have characterized every culture, whether ancient or modern. A particular point of reflection will be the idea of the "religion of the book." How far are ancient Judaism and Christianity, with their apparent reliance on a defining body of doctrinal texts, to be set apart from the other religions discussed in this volume?

The implications of writing

Over the last fifty years or so, the disciplines of both history and anthropology have focused intensely on the cultural history of reading and writing. For ancient historians one obvious question has been: how many people in any given ancient society were literate? It is a question that is, of course, easier to pose than to answer. Even in modern societies, with all their resources of mass survey and testing, literacy rates are notoriously hard to pin down; and they fluctuate according to the definition of literacy deployed (many more people can read than can write, many more can sign their name than can transmit even a simple message in writing). From antiquity, we have no statistical data. Our conclusions must be based on deduction from hints in ancient literature and documents, on comparison with the slightly clearer evidence from more-recent premodern societies, and, frankly, on a good deal of guesswork. For all these uncertainties, however, most scholars would now agree that throughout the ancient Mediterranean adult male literacy—in the sense of the ability to send and understand a simple written message—generally remained below 20 percent. There may have been a few, short-lived exceptions to that rule in particular communities in the ancient world. But even the apparently literate culture of the classical Greek city-states or of early imperial Rome was not founded on the mass ability to read and write. And in many societies the rate of literacy would have been considerably lower than 20 percent. A recent estimate for ancient Egypt, for example, suggests that at most periods less than 1 percent of the total population was literate. For obvious social, cultural, and political reasons, far fewer women than men could ever read and write.

Some of the consequences of this are clear and hold good for all ancient societies. Crucially for any understanding of ancient religion, the vast majority of people experienced religion orally. This is true, to some extent, even today. At least, no religious system is, or has ever been, mediated entirely in writing; oral communication, performance, and reaffirmation are always significant components of religious practice. Nonetheless in antiquity, unlike in the modern West, most of the population had access to the language of religion (whether doctrine, the word of the divine, exegesis, administration, or dissent) only orally. Modern scrutiny of the written traces of ancient religions (and—notwithstanding the importance of visual images—the history of religion is heavily dependent on written evidence) must always bear in mind the wider oral context of that writing, the interface between oral and written traditions.

Beyond that, however, the particular ramifications of restricted literacy are varied in different societies, religions, and social groups. The map of ancient illiteracy is much subtler than any raw percentage might suggest. It is linked to different political and social structures: a democratic system of government might prompt a different spread of literacy from a palace bureaucracy; while urban life was everywhere strikingly more literate than was rural life. But it may also be linked to the character of the writing system involved: syllabic or pictographic scripts often entail different patterns of literacy from alphabetic systems. In Egypt, for example, hieroglyphs—known as "the god's words"—were not only different in function from the simpler, so-called Demotic script (hieroglyphs were used predominantly in official, public inscriptions, very commonly in temples) but competence in hieroglyphic writing was confined to a much-smaller scribal or priestly group. There is no clear division between those with and those without access to the written word that operates across the religions of the Mediterranean world.

But the impact of writing on a religious system does not depend solely on the rates of literacy within any given religious community. Nor is that impact restricted to the literate minority—leaving the illiterate majority in an entirely oral culture unaffected by the strategies and conventions of literacy to which they have no direct access themselves. It is now well recognized that the existence of writing within a society (even if it is a tool that can actively be deployed by only a tiny few) can have wide cultural consequences that affect illiterate and literate alike. Quite simply, writing almost always (and, some would say, necessarily) changes the ways that societies operate and think about themselves—in religion as much as in any other sphere.

Many of the recent studies of this cultural aspect of writing owe their intellectual origins to a famous article by Jack Goody and Ian Watt entitled "The Consequences of Literacy," first published in 1963. In this theoretical essay, which took archaic and classical Greece as its prime example, Goody and Watt emphasized the intellectual and cognitive consequences of the spread of alphabetic writing systems. Part of their argument rested on the sheer permanency of writing. For them, entirely oral cultures were marked by the "unconscious operation of memory" and forgetfulness ("social amnesia"): where there is no written record, myths and traditions that no longer seem useful or appropriate are simply forgotten and pass out of the cultural memory. Practices continue in what is thought to be the traditional way ("as our ancestors did it"), but in fact are constantly adjusted—albeit tacitly and unconsciously—to new circumstances and ideas. But once writing is employed as a recording device, later generations will be faced with the written evidence of their earlier customs and thought and will need consciously to align their own behavior to it—whether in the form of rigid conservatism, explicit rejection of tradition, or self-consciously critical "historical" analysis. To take one of Goody and Watt's key examples, "once the poems of Homer and Hesiod, which contained much of the earlier history, religion and cosmology of the Greeks, had been written down, succeeding generations were faced with old distinctions in sharply exaggerated form: how far was the information about the gods and heroes literally true? How could its patent inconsistencies be explained? And how could the beliefs and attitudes implied be brought into line with those of the present?" (1963).

Similar factors lie behind the development of explicitly skeptical traditions. Every society includes men and women with unorthodox ideas, people who adopt a radically dissenting attitude to generally accepted views on religion, politics, and social order. But in an entirely oral culture, skepticism tends to die with the individual skeptic. Once the skeptic commits his or her views to the permanency of writing, however, the possibility opens of a whole *tradition* of skepticism, an alternative counterculture, parallel to society's orthodox norms. This is obviously of particular importance in the history of religion and in the development of radical, skeptical inquiry into traditional religious "truths." Goody and Watt cite the example of the Greek thinker Xenophanes in the 6th century BCE, whose surviving work includes criticism of the then-standard views on the anthropomorphic form of the gods: "If horses were able to draw, they would draw the forms of the gods like horses" (DK 21 B15). Xenophanes, we may add, in confirmation of their point, was still being read and quoted at the end of antiquity, more than a millennium later.

Goody and Watt also stress the influence of writing on the potential complexity of any organization, whether political, social, or religious. As Goody argues at greater length in his later book, *The Domestication of the Savage Mind* (1977), the ability to transcend oral memory by the apparently simple device of a written list opens up a whole series of intellectual possibilities—from the detailed classification of property (furniture, animals, or agricultural produce can be listed by type, weight, location, and so forth) to the intricate definition of calendrical time, dividing the year according to months and days and the religious obligations appropriate to each occasion (as in the calendar "published" by Cnaeus Flavius). At its most ambitious, Goody and Watt's scheme follows some earlier theorists in suggesting that the invention of writing drives a cognitive revolution, enabling for the first time certain forms of what we might call logical thinking—from the simple syllogism (if *a* then *b*, etc.) to other more complicated forms of algebraic logic.

This work has prompted considerable reaction, both favorable and—in some specific respects—dissenting. Goody himself, in response to those who objected that the phrase *consequences of literacy* appeared to suggest a too-rigid schema (in which literacy was always and necessarily followed by various social and intellectual developments) now prefers the phrase "the implications of literacy." It also remains very much an open question what level of literacy in a society, and what form of literacy, would entail the implications (or consequences) proposed. In their first article, Goody and Watt envisaged "widespread" and "alphabetic" literacy, stressing the democratic and revolutionary intellectual power of the Greek system of writing as against the scribal, narrowly restricted literacy of the syllabic or pictographic systems of ancient Babylonia or Egypt. But in his later work on lists, Goody drew as much on ancient Near Eastern material as on Greco-Roman examples (including lists and hierarchical rankings of deities from Babylonia and Egypt). In general, although the range and spread of writing differed significantly in different ancient Mediterranean societies, we can trace at least some of Goody and Watt's implications in all the (partially) literate communities covered by this volume.

Certainly, the impact of writing on ancient Mediterranean religion is evident far beyond the culture of ancient Greece, on which Goody and Watt principally drew. We have already noted the existence of a Roman calendar of festivals, whose complex and elaborately codified information would have been unthinkable without the resource of writing: in the most detailed examples of these calendars, the written data laid out include the legal and religious status of each day of the year, the divisions into months (and the main divisions within months), the traditional roster of public holidays and more recent additions to this set of festivals, plus some information on the festival concerned (the principal deity attached, the place of celebration, or the reason for its foundation). Other aspects of religion also illuminate (and are illuminated by) the Goody-Watt hypothesis. The logic of Mesopotamian divination, for example, has been linked to the particular conventions of pictographic script in which it was recorded, while in Roman cult, one of the most striking features was the preservation of archaic and apparently obsolete religious lore. By the 1st century CE, the ancient hymn sung by the Salii at their regular ritual "dance" through the streets of Rome was incomprehensible—it is reported by one Roman writer—even to the priests themselves. Likewise the hymn chanted by the Arval Brethren and recorded on one of the inscriptions documenting this priesthood's ritual activity in their sacred grove a few miles outside the city of Rome appears now (as it must have appeared to most Romans for most of their history) to be bafflingly archaic mumbo jumbo; it makes (and made) sense, if at all, only to a few specialists in the earliest form of Latin. The preservation of these ancient religious texts would have been impossible without written documents; and indeed the inscriptions from the Arval grove explicitly refer to written copies of the hymn used by the priests in their chanting.

But Goody and Watt's implications go further than that (as Gordon has argued in his 1990 study of Roman religion in the light of Goody and Watt's work). First, the incomprehensibility of these texts itself stimulated further writing, in learned commentaries that (often equally obscurely) attempted to interpret and explain their meaning. A commentary on the Salian hymn existed already in the 1st century BCE, and one of the most distinctive parts of Roman religious discourse from that time on was a whole series of specialized treatises that offered exegesis on arcane aspects of cult and cult history (e.g., *On Religious Formulas* or *On the Derivation of the Names of the Gods*). Writing, in other words, stimulated more writing. Second are the implications for religious power and control that follow from the obscurantism enshrined in this writing. For unintelligibility (which, in Gellner's words, "leaves the disciple with a secret guilt of not understanding") could be an important defense of priestly or other expert religious power. The public display of written mumbo jumbo, and the importance vested in it as hallowed tradition, was almost bound to enhance the authority of those who could claim to understand, while disadvantaging those who could not and were reliant on the interpretative skills of others. If the story of Flavius offered a popular, democratic parable of writing, other written forms offer the directly opposite message.

Influential and instructive as they are, Goody and Watt's theories can, however, be misleading if applied too rigidly, particularly in the sphere of religion. The dangers are most clearly seen in the fundamental issue of the *function* of writing. For Goody and Watt, writing is an essentially utilitarian activity. It is there to be read and to be acted on as appropriate. So, for instance, written records of procedures establish precedent and encourage conservative practice precisely because they are consulted and their example followed. But a significant part of religious writing is not utilitarian in this way. With its functions classified under the admittedly rather vague rubric of "symbolic," it may act to display, to memorialize, to reify and make permanent a variety of legitimate and illegitimate religious claims and actions—not necessarily to be read and used, at least not within the community of living mortals. The most extreme case of this is the use of writing within the varied group of religious practices we now know as magic. Spells and curses, written on lead or papyrus and deposited in tombs or wells, may well have been thought to preserve the magician's oral utterance and to take it as close as possible to the dead or chthonic powers who would mediate or bring about the desired result. More than that, the transgressive forms of writing commonly adopted in curses (e.g., words written back to front, varieties of nonsense script) served to reify the transgressions implicit in the curse itself. One Athenian spell, from the 4th century BCE, makes this link explicit. It is written backward, from right to left, and reads: "In the same way that this is cold and 'out of true,' let the words of Krates be cold and 'out of true' in the same way, his as well as those of the accusers and lawyers who accompany him" (Wünsch 1897: appendix no. 67). But even outside the particular area of "magical" practices, ancient religious writing was often not principally intended for a reader, and even some of the most extensive and detailed religious records were not systematically consulted as a guide to precedent. The records of ritual procedures made by the Arval Brethren and inscribed on stone in their sacred grove did not consistently dictate the future conduct of ritual—as the numerous changes in procedure that the texts document make clear. The inscription memorialized the rituals carried out, rather than providing a reference guide for how to act in the future. Likewise the vast majority of the many thousands of Roman inscriptions detailing vows and the performance of sacrifices can hardly have been widely consulted—or intended to be so; instead they instantiated and made permanent the ritual act itself. Writing, in other words, could be as much an integral part of religious symbolism as an external record of it.

Religions of the book?

It is conventional to draw a sharp distinction in terms of the role of writing between Judaism and Christianity on the one hand and the rest of the religions covered by this volume on the other. In Judaism and Christianity, doctrine and the word of God was defined in writing; they were—and still are—"religions of the book." This was not the case anywhere else, from Babylonia to Roman Italy; and in these other religions, so it follows, writing played a less important (or, at least, a less structurally central) part. How useful a distinction is this? Precisely how sharp should we make it?

There is no doubt at all that writing (and reading) had a particularly loaded role to play in the ancient Judeo-Christian tradition. It was not simply a question of the textual basis of religious doctrine. Writing was invested with even greater power and authority than that. So, for example, the Book of Exodus makes the radical claim that the tablets given to Moses on Sinai carried texts that were not merely the word of God in the sense of being divinely *inspired,* they were actually divinely *written:* "And he gave to Moses, when he had made an end of speaking with him upon Mount Sinai, the two tables of the testimony, tables of stone, written with the finger of God . . . And the tables were the work of God, and the writing was the writing of God, graven upon the tables" (Exod. 31.18; 32.16). And it is well known that Jews accorded considerable veneration to the physical form of their sacred texts, as if (in the words of Goodman) "religious power was enshrined within the physical object on which the divine teachings were inscribed." Torah scrolls were written according to strict rules, in carefully prescribed lettering, in ink and on the best parchment. Josephus—the Jewish priest and historian who eventually sided with the Romans in the Jewish revolt that ended in 70 CE—was well placed to observe that the destruction of a Jewish text by a Roman soldier ended in a riot (*Jewish War* 2.229–31) and that Vespasian and Titus had a scroll of the Torah carried in their triumphal procession through Rome in 71 (7.150); the scroll itself, among the other booty on show, was a powerful symbol of Roman victory over the Jews. Not surprisingly perhaps, these texts sometimes filled the symbolic role of writing that we have already noted. As Goodman and others have pointed out, the miniature texts used in phylacteries (pouches for Torah texts, bound onto the arms or forehead) "were encased in leather in such a way that they usually could not be read at all."

In early Christianity, too, the importance of writing went well beyond the existence of scripture (a word that is directly derived from the Latin for "writing": *scriptura*). The divergences between different groups of early Christians (divergences sometimes cast as the struggle of "orthodoxy" against the "heretics") were often cast in terms of the competing authority of different written texts, as well as different interpretation of the canonical Gospels. One 7th-century Christian theologian, for example, could refer to the "foul, loathsome, and unclean writings of the accursed Manicheans, gnostics, and the rest of the heretics" (John of Damascus, *Orations* 2.10). Written texts were also crucial in such cohesion as the early church could obtain. The scattered communities of early Christians depended, very largely, on written communication for any sense of group identity; the letters of Paul from the 50s and 60s CE are only the start of a tradition of epistolary exchange that aimed to reinforce and define the Christian community. And, in general, the symbolism of writing pervaded Christian discourse and visual representation. Jesus, for example, appears in early Christian sculpture displaying a book roll as his major attribute. One vivid image of heavenly power comes in the form of the "book of life," into which angels transcribe the names of good Christians for ultimate reward, while the names of sinners are listed with equal rigor elsewhere. Lane-Fox has aptly referred to these recording angels as "a literate police force, active above early Christian saints and sinners." Another image, in both Christianity and Judaism, pictures the prophet as a man who has literally consumed the written word of God. In John's visionary account in the Book of Revelation, "I took the little scroll from the hand of the angel and ate it; it was as sweet as honey in my mouth . . . And I was told, 'You must again prophesy' (Rev. 10.10–11); or as God said to Ezekiel, "Eat this scroll, and go, speak" (Ezek. 3.1).

Yet it is not quite so simple as it might seem. For a start, on the basis of what we can infer about levels of literacy throughout antiquity, most people, even in these apparently "textual" religious communities, must have had their texts mediated orally. In fact, one conservative—though not implausible—recent estimate puts the total number of Christians who were fluently literate at the end of the 1st century CE as no more than fifty at any one moment. But, even more significant than any low rate of literacy, both Judaism and Christianity embraced alternative traditions that appear to have vested as much authority in oral as in written discourse. In Judaism, for example, there was a powerful view that Moses was given the oral law, as well as written texts, on Mount Sinai; and the Mishnah, although it was authoritatively codified in writing around 200 CE, parades in form and style its oral origins as the sayings of rabbis. In Christianity, by contrast, the claims of oral authority were upheld by the simple fact that Jesus himself wrote nothing. And, for all the textual obsessions of the early church, there was an influential strand of Christian thought that positively glorified illiterate simplicity, while stressing that the Christian faithful did not need a learned (which often, in effect, meant a "pagan") education. Some early Christian saints were praised precisely because they were *sine litteris* (illiterate), as were Jesus's own disciples. John and Peter, for example, are dubbed "illiterate" *(aggrammatoi)* in the Acts of the Apostles (4.13). Predictably, perhaps, "pagan" intellectual critics of Christianity seem to have found such "holy ignorance" a further ground for mistrust of the new religion.

The picture becomes even more complicated if we start to compare the role of writing in the Judeo-Christian tradition with other religions covered in this volume. It is certainly the case that no other ancient belief system was so reliant on a group of doctrinal written texts. And it is partly for this reason—because we do not find writing where, as heirs of the Judeo-Christian tradition, we *expect* to find it—that scholars have tended to suggest that the practice of religious writing was less significant in ancient religions outside Judaism and Christianity. In fact, although there are clear differences, they are not so stark as they might appear at first sight. We have already noted the Egyptian term for hieroglyphs as "the god's words" and observed the central role of writing in those religious practices that go by the name of magic. The world of Greco-Roman "paganism" offers an even wider range of the uses of writing in cult and belief. Although the official state cults of Rome and the Greek cities were not generally founded on divinely inspired or divinely written texts, in some noncivic cults—such as those of Orpheus and the Egyptian Hermes—the word of the god, as inscribed in sacred texts, did hold a central place. At Rome itself, the major state collection of oracular texts, the Sibylline Oracles, owed its origin and its authority to the figure of the Sibyl of Cumae—a divinely inspired prophetess. The Sibylline Oracles were regularly consulted at times of danger and trouble for the city, and they were, in a sense, the word of god; they were preserved and recopied (even if conveniently amended in the process) with the full panoply of religious care. Other ancient oracles worked entirely through writing, without the involvement of even an original oral prophecy: the oracle at Praeneste (near Rome), for example, was based on the consultation of written wooden tablets, which had been discovered miraculously—already inscribed—inside a nearby rock. Although modern scholarship has tended to privilege the oral consultation of an oracle (as at the famous oracle of Apollo at Delphi), Greco-Roman gods regularly communicated in writing.

But writing pervaded the religious world of Rome in other senses. The priestly colleges were associated with so-called priestly books. Although these do not survive beyond the occasional fragmentary quotation and their exact content is still disputed, it seems very likely that they recorded details of religious formulas and procedure (or, in the case of the document that Flavius published, calendrical and legal information). More striking still, however, is the role of writing in dedications and vows in temples and sanctuaries. When Pliny the Younger visited the sanctuary of Clitumnus near modern Spoleto in the early 2nd century CE, he found a site full of the written word: "Everything there will delight you," he wrote to a friend, "and you can also find something to read. You can study the numerous inscriptions in honor of the spring [*fons*] and of the god, which many hands have written on every pillar and wall" (*Letters* 8.8.7). Even today, when almost everything inscribed on perishable material has disappeared, many Greco-Roman sanctuaries still preserve the written traces of their worshipers' activities and expressions of piety or gratitude. Although Pliny suggests that the elite visitor might find plenty to read (and, he goes on, to laugh at) in such a sanctuary, the reading visitor can hardly have been uppermost in the mind of most of those commissioning these inscriptions. Much more likely, the intention of the writing was to memorialize, or give permanence to, the ritual act commemorated. More generally, in a religion in which there were no clear articles of faith, no formal badge of belonging or ceremony of initiation, memorializing religious action in an inscription was a way of "writing oneself in" to "membership" of the religious community. This sense of "writing as belonging" took a notable twist in the conflicts between Christianity and traditional civic cults in the Roman Empire during the 3rd century CE. The emperor Decius ordered that everyone should sacrifice to the gods to prove that they were not Christian. But not just that. Once they had sacrificed in the presence of two official witnesses, they could be issued with a written certificate to authenticate their action—and, no doubt, to produce if challenged again. A few of these certificates still survive from Roman Egypt (e.g., Mitteis and Wilcken 1912: no. 124).

What underlies these different manifestations of the written word in ancient religions is not a simple clash between "religions of the book" and the rest. It is rather a series of questions about the mediation of divine power that all religions must accommodate, if not answer. What forms of communication—written or oral—carry most authority? How do you weigh the immediacy of orality against the permanency of writing? How does religious speech relate to religious text? Different religions offer different answers to these questions—and different answers at different periods and in different circumstances. In studying ancient religious systems, it is much more helpful to concentrate on that constant play-off between oral and written traditions, in all its different varieties and with all its different emphases—rather than to use the role of writing as a fixed standard against which to classify or hierarchize the different religions. This sense of religious dialectic is brilliantly captured in a Jewish story from the 6th-century CE Babylonian Talmud (tractate *Bava Metzi'a* 59a–b). In a dispute between a group of rabbis set in the 2nd century, different forms of authority were claimed for their different interpretations. One, Rabbi Eliezer, after performing a variety of miracles to support his own position, finally—in the face of continuing disagreement from his colleagues—called on heaven itself to prove his point. A supporting divine voice indeed came: "The law accords with what he says." But even this was not enough. One rabbi claimed that the voice did not really come from heaven; another claimed that, even if divine, the voice did not carry the day, for the written law must hold: "Since the Torah has already been given from Mount Sinai, we do not pay attention to heavenly voices, for You have written already at Mount Sinai"; and he went on to advise God to vote with the majority. And God's reaction to this dispute? "He laughed and said, 'My children have defeated me.'"

The religion of writing

So far I have discussed the role of writing in ancient culture and religion as if it were a topic of interest to modern anthropologists and historians of religion; and I have largely referred to writing as if it were a practice that reacted with, but was essentially separate from, religion. That is, of course, part of the story; but only a part. Writing could also be very much an integral part of religion and ritual, not simply an external influence on it. I have already mentioned briefly the symbolic role of writing within various cult practices, including magic. This should prompt us to see writing itself, potentially at least, as a ritual activity. This was certainly the case in the Arval Grove, where the inscriptions themselves document some of the rituals associated with their inscribing (iron was a prohibited substance in the grove, so the introduction of the iron tools had to be accompanied by expiatory sacrifices). In Greece the formal inscription and preservation of oaths and treaties was often similarly ritualized. In Plato's *Critias*, written in the 4th century BCE, he envisages a sacrifice in the mythical Atlantis, where the blood of a sacrificial animal is made to wash over, literally, the texts of preserved laws (119c–20c). And, as Steiner has observed (1994), the 5th-century BCE historian Herodotus projects a similar concern with ritual inscription onto illiterate barbarians. If barbarians do not use alphabetic writing, at least they "inscribe" their oaths as scars on the body of the oath taker (3.8; 4.70).

No less important is the incorporation of writing into ancient cultural commentary and myth. Plato, for example, in his dialogue *Phaedrus* has the character of Socrates argue that the invention of writing was culturally deleterious, among other reasons because it weakened the human memory (why bother to remember when you can refer to a written text?) and because it was indiscriminate in those it addressed (unlike an oral philosopher, who could choose his audience). And many ancient cultures attributed the origin of writing to divine (or heroic) invention. Egyptian hieroglyphs were said to be the brainchild of the god Thoth. Greek myths ascribed writing variously to (among others) the god Hermes, the mythical Palamedes, or the semidivine Prometheus, who brought writing to mortals as part of his civilizing mission, which also included the gift of fire. Others, however, would have backed the claims of Orpheus, legendary poet, musician, and mystic. He originated, it was said, from Thrace (in the far north of Greece), and different mythical accounts accorded him a quite different role in the history of writing: one tradition makes him its inventor; another claims that, as the Thracians were well known to be illiterate, he could not possibly be writing's ancestor. But more influential still was the idea that after his death his decapitated head continued to sing, and the words were either directly and miraculously transcribed on tablets or else copied down by faithful secretaries. "Orphic texts" (versions of which circulated widely in Greece) were thought to hold healing properties and to offer, to those who read them, the hope of life after death.

The myth of the talking head of Orpheus and the miraculous properties of Orphic texts might seem a world away from the story of Cnaeus Flavius and his practical assault on the priestly monopoly of knowledge in early Rome. But that indeed must be the range spanned by any study of religion and writing in the ancient world: from mundane record keeping to the "words of god"; from academic exegesis to magical mumbo jumbo; from writing in blood to writing in stone.

Bibliography

Baines, J. "Literacy in Ancient Egyptian Society." *Man* 18 (1983): 572–99.

Beard, M. "Writing and Religion: Ancient Literacy and the Function of the Written Word in Roman Religion." In *Literacy in the Roman World*, ed. M. Beard et al. Journal of Roman Archaeology Supplement 3. Ann Arbor, 1991.

———. "Writing and Ritual: A Study of Diversity and Expansion in the Arval Acta." *Papers of the British School at Rome* 53 (1981): 114–62.

Bottéro, J., C. Herrenschmidt, and J.-P. Vernant. *Ancestor of the West: Writing, Reasoning, and Religion in Mesopotamia, Elam, and Greece.* Chicago, 2000.

Bowman, A. K., and G. Woolf, eds. *Literacy and Power in the Ancient World.* Cambridge, 1994 (see esp. essays by M. D. Goodman and R. Lane Fox).

Goody, J. *The Domestication of the Savage Mind.* Cambridge, 1977.

Goody, J., and I. Watt. "The Consequences of Literacy." In *Comparative Studies in Society and History* 5 (1963): 304–45; reprinted in *Literacy in Traditional Societies,* ed. J. Goody. Cambridge, 1968.

Gordon, R. L. "From Republic to Principate: Priesthood, Religion, and Ideology." In *Pagan Priests*, ed. M. Beard and J. North. London, 1990.

Harris, W. V. *Ancient Literacy.* Cambridge, Mass., 1989.

Hopkins, K. *A World Full of Gods: Pagans, Jews, and Christians in the Roman Empire.* London, 1999.

Mitteis, L., and U. Wilcken. *Grundzüge und Chrestomathie der Papyruskunde,* vol. 1.2. Leipzig: Teubner, 1912.

Sawyer, J. F. A. *Sacred Languages and Sacred Texts: Religion in the First Christian Centuries.* London, 1999.

Steiner, D. Tarn. *The Tyrant's Writ: Myths and Images of Writing in Ancient Greece.* Princeton, 1994.

Wünsch, R. "Appendix continens defixionum tabellas in Attica regione repertas." In *Inscriptiones Graecae,* vol. II/III, *Corpus Inscriptionum Atticarum.* Berlin: Reimer, 1897.

Magic

Sarah Iles Johnston

A problem of definition

It was to be the greatest temple of all time—built to the glory of YHWH by King Solomon, in fulfillment of a promise that his father, King David, had made. Enormous and splendid, the temple would provide a place where the ark of the covenant could safely be stored and where all of Israel could worship.

But in the course of its construction, a problem arose. Solomon's favorite workman was attacked each night by Ornias, a vampirelike demon who stole the workman's vitality by sucking on his thumb. Solomon prayed to YHWH for help, and YHWH sent a ring to Solomon via the angel Michael. This ring, on which was engraved a device that came to be known as the "Seal of Solomon," could be used to control all the demons of the world. With help from the angel Ouriel, Solomon used the seal to stop Ornias from attacking his workman and then to order Ornias to invoke Beelzeboul, a more powerful demon who in turn invoked all the other demons. By interrogating them, Solomon learned what their names were and which plants, stones, and animal parts could be used to avert each one of them.

Solomon compelled the conquered demons to finish building the temple and afterward drove them into bottles, which he sealed shut with his ring. He buried the bottles under the temple, where they remained until the Babylonians pillaged Jerusalem many years later. Assuming that the bottles contained gold, the greedy invaders broke them open and once again let loose upon the world a host of demonic ills. Henceforth ordinary people, lacking Solomon's power to imprison the demons, could keep them at bay only by wearing amulets engraved with his seal or by using the techniques that Solomon had learned from the demons themselves. It was because he had foreseen the demons' eventual release, indeed, that Solomon had recorded the means of averting each one so carefully.

This story of Solomon and the demons, which is taken from a narrative called the *Testament of Solomon* that dates back to at least the 2nd century CE, is an apt introduction to an essay on magic, for it implicitly raises an issue that looms large in scholarly studies of the topic: namely, how can we distinguish between "magic" and "religion"? Using a special seal and other techniques to control demons makes Solomon look like what many would call a magician. This accords with other ancient portraits, where he is presented as an expert in incantations, astrology, alchemy, and other arts commonly gathered under the rubric and appears on amulets against illness and the Evil Eye. And yet, it could also be argued that several elements in the story situate Solomon within the realm of religion: the fact that the seal was a gift from YHWH, Michael and Ouriel's assistance in its delivery and deployment, and Solomon's use of the conquered demons to build YHWH's temple.

The story itself concedes nothing to this problem; the cultures in which it originated and developed simply armed Solomon with the tools that they revered as efficacious against demons and legitimated both him and those tools by linking them closely to YHWH and his angels. Nor was Solomon unusual among YHWH's devotees: Moses and Aaron performed deeds that we might call magical—not only did they turn a staff into a snake (Exod. 7.8–12) but they also devised such things as love charms and invisibility spells (*PGM* VII.619–27). Christ raised the dead and exorcised demons, feats often credited to magicians in antiquity; his name, as well as that of Iao (a variation of YHWH), empowered such things as memory charms and divinatory spells and appeared in ancient grimoires side by side with, for example, instructions for engraving silver tablets and creating (and later eating) female dolls made of bread dough (*PGM* III.410–66). The Greek hero Jason received the first *iynx* (a tool for making people fall in love) from the goddess Aphrodite (Pindar, *Pythian* 4.213–19). And on the Metternich Stele, the goddess Isis proudly claimed to teach *heka* (an Egyptian word that the ancient Greeks translated as "*mageia*" [magic]) to her favorite mortals. In other words, pagan divinities and heroes no more repudiated what we might call magic than did YHWH and his followers. In fact, far from rejecting such practices, ancient peoples enhanced their gods' and heroes' reputations by boasting that they knew more about such practices than did other cultures' gods and heroes.

And yet the modern scholarly quest to establish a division between magic and religion does have some roots in antiquity, insofar as both ancient and modern discussions hinge on terminology: what one chooses to call any particular activity (and, it follows, who is doing the choosing) determines whether the activity is understood as acceptable or discredited, pious or blasphemous, religion or magic. In antiquity, *magic* (a term that I use as a shorthand way of referring to a variety of ancient Mediterranean words) almost always referred to someone else's religious practices; it was a term that distanced those practices from the norm—that is, from one's own practices, which constituted religion. Among magicians themselves, distance could lend glamour and authority—for instance, Greek magicians claimed to one another that their spells had been invented by legendary Egyptian, Persian, or Jewish magicians—but to nonmagicians, distance usually implied charlatanry, alliances with dark gods and demons, and coercion of gods to whom other, properly reverent people prayed. Thus, in later antiquity, outsiders who feared and derided Judaism and Christianity called both Christ and Moses *goētes,* a term that had come to mean, by this time, charismatic quacks who lured their followers into illegal and immoral activities and who claimed to command armies of demons. Centuries earlier, Sophocles' Oedipus insulted Teiresias, a priest and prophet whom he no longer trusted, by calling him a "scheming *magos*" (*Oedipus Tyrannus* 387).

Thus, magic was almost always a normative, rather than a straightforwardly descriptive, term, and looking at the ancient world from our own vantage point, we can make no clean division between it and religion. Not only were many gods and religious leaders reputed to employ techniques that we might call magical (in Egypt, Persia, Mesopotamia, and Anatolia, in fact, some forms of what we call magic were in the purview of official priests), but when we examine the techniques themselves, we discover that they differ from other religious practices more in details than in substance or attitude. For example, the structure of "magical" prayers was identical to that of "religious" prayers in most Mediterranean cultures, and in cultures where sacrifice was an important part of religious practice, it stood at the center of magical practices as well. Amulets against illness and other crises invoke the aid of the same saints and holy men whom we meet in religious texts.

As for the details, we can explain many differences between magical and religious practices by noting (as some ancient authors already did) that the magician was a "technician of the sacred," someone who knew more about how to approach the superhuman world than ordinary people did. This gave him the means to innovate and improvise on established techniques. The fact that in some cultures, magicians made their livings by freelancing their skills and in others used them to supplement the incomes they earned as temple priests gave them the impetus to innovate and improvise, for the most successful practitioners would be those who confidently boasted an extensive and varied repertoire, adaptable to all occasions.

The scholarly quest to divide magic from religion, which began in earnest in the late 19th century with Sir E. B. Tylor's *Primitive Culture* and Sir James Frazer's *Golden Bough*, stems from a similar desire to divide the unacceptable from the acceptable, which in their post-Darwinian world meant not only the impious from the pious, but also the unevolved from the evolved—that is, the "primitive" from the "advanced" means of understanding the cosmos and attempting to affect it (often, "science" was brought in as a third entity to be distinguished from both magic and religion). Thus, Frazer argued that magicians' techniques developed out of an assumption that they could coerce gods and crude "prescientific" concepts such as contagion and sympathy, whereas religious practitioners, having advanced beyond this spiritually, focused on prayer and theology and scientists developed intellectually sounder means of investigation. Frazer and other armchair anthropologists used these neat (and implicitly Western, Christianocentric) divisions to distance European culture from the tribes in Africa, South America, and New Guinea, about whom missionaries sent back reports. Variations rang changes on Frazer's scheme; Malinowski, for instance, pitted magic and religion together against science (emotional phenomena against rational) but also pitted magic and science together against religion (pragmatic empiricism against nonempiricism). All such attempts, under the scrutiny of later scholarship, have been shown to rest on shaky dichotomies between "us" and "them." Most scholars of religion now concede that a reliable means of dividing magic and religion will never be found.

Does this mean that the endeavor to define magic has stopped, or should stop? No, it continues for several reasons. For one thing, scholars continue to try to identify the ways in which specific cultures internally defined magic. Although this emic approach can never be carried out perfectly—because we can never put ourselves completely into the mentality of another culture—attempts are nonetheless illuminating. Scholars of the ancient Mediterranean have another reason to pursue definitions of magic as well: we increasingly realize that religious practices and ideas traveled fluidly across cultural boundaries; it profits the Assyriologist to compare notes with the Hellenist, the scholar of Judaism with the Egyptologist, and so on. Having at least rough heuristic models under which we can categorize practices and ideas from all of these cultures, and thus compare them, facilitates discourse and analysis. As long as we keep in mind that our definitions of magic are provisional and beware of slipping into essentialist assumptions, definitions help us identify and better understand the salient features of magic in the ancient Mediterranean. It is in this spirit that the rest of this essay proceeds.

The power of words

Virtually all religious practices involve words, whether written, spoken aloud, or silently pronounced, because virtually all religious practices constitute attempts to communicate with other beings—gods, demons, angels, the dead, or the cosmos itself. (Only certain forms of mysticism, which typically stand at the margins of the religions from which they evolve, encourage worshipers to empty their minds of words completely and focus on something that lies utterly beyond language.) Distinctions between "religious" and "magical" uses of language are as elusive as any other distinctions between religion and magic.

Yet two comments can be made. First, those whom ancient cultures called magicians often were credited with extraordinary expertise in the use of words. In Egypt, temple priests, who also served as freelance magicians, were highly trained in both the written and oral use of words; *heka* itself was described as being "excellent of words"; and Thoth, the god of writing, was also a god of magic. Plato's Socrates—to take just one of many examples from the Greco-Roman sphere—said that the leaf of a certain plant would make a sick person well again, but only if special words were pronounced at the same time as the leaf was administered: "The leaf alone is nothing," he asserted (*Charmides* 155e5–8; cf. Pliny, *Natural History* 28.3.10–11). Second, particular ways of using words are commonly associated with magic, and the ancient magician tended to be marked by the power that his speech acts carried.

Curses

One characteristic shared by many magical uses of words is that they work automatically—that is, pronouncement or inscription of the words puts the statements they make into effect virtually immediately, either with or without accompanying ritual actions. Although this characteristic can be found across a range of speech acts, it is particularly common in curses—and curses, although not associated exclusively with magic, often appear in ancient collections of magical lore or in narrative descriptions of magic and its practitioners; they constitute one of the reasons that magicians were treated with respect born of fear (cf. Pliny, *Natural History* 23.4.19).

We can pursue the "automatic" nature of many curses by adapting a heuristic model developed by Christopher Faraone for study of one specific form of Greek and Roman curse, the *defixio*—a curse written on a small piece of lead or wax and deposited within a grave or other subterranean area. Faraone divides the speech acts found on *defixiones* into four groups, the third and fourth of which I combine here. (1) "Direct" formulas, in which the curser uses a first-person verb to curse or restrain the victim from performing an action ("I curse so-and-so"); this is a "performative utterance" that is expected to effect what it describes without further ado. The curser, in other words, assumes no gap between his ritualized articulation of the curse and its fulfillment. (2) Formulas in which imperative verbs direct the actions of gods, demons, and other nonhuman agents against the victim ("Restrain so-and-so!"). Although we might argue that there is no guarantee that the desire expressed by these statements will be fulfilled, the baldly imperative tone (which is less commonly found in speech acts that ancient Mediterraneans labeled "religious") leaves little doubt that the curser presumes success. (3) "Wish" formulas, which use optative verbs ("May so-and-so fail!"). Here we begin to shade into what both ancient and modern commentators often call prayer, that is, a venue in which a deity's help is sought yet never assumed to be guaranteed; but we must keep sight of two differences: a prayer is more likely than a curse to include statements intended to persuade a god or demon to cooperate with the petitioner ("I have given you sacrifices in the past"; "I will build you a temple"; etc.), the implication being that the god or demon may not, in the end, fulfill the desire. Moreover, this type of curse often includes what Stanley Tambiah has called "persuasive analogies" ("As the corpse [with which this inscribed curse is buried] is cold and lifeless, thus may so-and-so be cold and lifeless"). Similar are the vivid metaphors used in some curses: "May your root not sprout upon the earth, may your head droop at the hands of the harvester!" The use of such analogies and metaphors suggests an expectation that, if the curse is properly composed and spoken or inscribed, success will follow; although requests for divine aid are sometimes included in such curses, emphasis lies on finding the right analogies and metaphors—the right words.

I do not mean to suggest a dichotomy here, pairing magic with curses and religion with prayers (for example); nor do I mean to suggest that all curses, and only curses alone among speech acts, were understood to work automatically—although it is interesting that techniques such as persuasive analogy are found most often, outside of curses, in other speech acts associated with magic (thus a Jewish love charm, like many others from the Mediterranean, decrees, "Just as [this potsherd burns, so shall] burn the heart of so-and-so, after me"; and a Mesopotamian healing spell asks that "the illness be stripped off like these dates [are stripped from a tree]"). The pairs religion–magic and unguaranteed fulfillment–automatic fulfillment mark the end points of heuristic spectrums; if we were to plot each individual example of any type of speech act (curse, prayer, etc.) along either spectrum, we would see a spread. But the curse, a type of speech act that ancient cultures tended to place at the magic end of the first spectrum, also falls more often than other speech acts at the automatic end of the second one. The automatic nature of many curses is further demonstrated by the belief that one could instantly nullify the effects of a written curse by destroying the material on which it was written.

Secret words

Magicians frequently used special words and phrases, typically described as secret. Often, the words were understood as special names of gods or angels, names sure to catch the entity's attention; a magician who used them would not fail to gain aid. This does not necessarily represent coercion of the god or angel; although coercion is clearly intended in some cases, in others, we can better understand the use of secret names as forging a stronger bond between the magician and the addressee, as shared possession of secret knowledge typically does (see Mysteries). In yet other cases—for example, in Jewish incantations that use permutations of YHWH's name—powerful names seem to work on their own, rather than to invoke their bearers.

Notably, magicians believed that many of these secret names had been handed down from other cultures and represented other languages (which is not incorrect: Jewish names are embedded in otherwise Greek magical texts and vice versa, for example) or even the language of the gods and demons they addressed. Although the names might belong to a deity whom the magician's native language called something else, he never "translated" them—not only because they might please the god more in their original forms but also because the power of some *onomata barbara* (barbaric names) was inherent in their phonetic sounds or in the shape of the letters used to write them. Unbroken repetition of a name in some magical texts (often three, seven, or nine times, but even seventy times, in one Jewish amulet) underscores this latter point, although repetition of significant words and phrases could play other roles in magic, too. Theocritus's poetic representation of a Greek love spell includes periodic refrain of vital phrases in a manner suggesting that repetition works in the divine world just as it does in the mortal: it further guarantees divinities' cooperation (*Idyll* 2). Similarly, a spell in the Greco-Egyptian papyri tells the magician to start reciting an invocation at the seventh hour of the moon and to keep saying it until the "god hearkens to you and you make contact with him" (*PGM* II.1–64).

All of this is interesting with respect to what was said about the automatic nature of magical language above. Some magical words do work automatically insofar as they function by virtue of their inherent power alone; others can be understood as signals that immediately and unconditionally put other forces into action (what might be called the "Open Sesame" effect); but others function in the same way as ordinary speech acts among humans do, even if they have greater potential than other speech acts—that is, they may not work all of the time, or at least not immediately. One thing we can say about all of these uses of secret language is that they further demonstrate that the Mediterranean magician was someone who possessed knowledge of gods, demons, angels, and the cosmos that was deeper, more detailed, and more varied than that of the average person. It was by virtue of this knowledge, rather than by virtue of any essential difference within himself or the sorts of things he did, that he was apt to be more effective in his interactions with the supernatural entities. The magician was no Merlin, sired by a demon and thereby naturally endowed with superhuman power. Although lineage might predispose one toward magic (David, Solomon's father, was credited with exorcizing Saul of an evil spirit; Medea was the niece of Circe), most Mediterranean magicians had to be trained by their elders—Hogwarts School is just the most recent exposition of a very old idea. Even the gods' help was frequently described in terms of teaching. Aphrodite taught Jason how to use the *iynx;* and Isis taught mortals *heka* (a tradition that the satirist Lucian mocks by making his archmagician, Pancrates, spend twenty-three years under her tutelage, in secret chambers beneath the earth; *Philopseudes* 34–36).

Narrative power

Historiolae (little stories) are short narrations inserted into written or spoken spells, usually evocative of longer tales that are well known. For example, a Coptic Christian spell first sketches a story of how Jesus and the angel Michael relieved a doe's labor pains; implicit is the presumption that the patient for whom the spell is recited will similarly be relieved. The spell then goes on to sketch a tale of how Horus had stomach pains and sought the help of his mother, Isis; this is followed by explicit requests for their aid in curing the stomach pains of the child over whom the spell is recited (Meyer and Smith 1994: no. 49).

What is interesting here is not so much how easily Christianity juxtaposes itself with native Egyptian religion (Mediterranean religions were fluid, and magicians, as improvising freelancers, were more fluid than most), but rather the juxtaposition of a *historiola* whose relevance to the immediate situation is stated with one whose relevance is not. The first suggests that *historiolae* are similar to the persuasive analogies and metaphors mentioned above, insofar as the magician offers them as patterns that he wants the current situation to follow. (Some Mesopotamian examples take this idea further: they begin with a description of the patient's illness, followed by a *historiola*-type narration of a deity listening to the description and prescribing for it.) The second suggests something similar to the way in which some secret words work: power is inherent in the narration itself, and recitation calls that power into action without further ado. Again, assumptions that we tentatively made about how magical words work are challenged; again, although we can cling to some extremely broad generalizations ("ancient Mediterranean magicians were experts in using words"), we cannot go much beyond that.

Eating your words

The written word lends itself to physical manipulation and thus to methods of deployment that the oral word does not. Words inscribed on an amulet or a curse tablet remained effective as long as they physically existed, continuously averting demonic illnesses or binding enemies as if someone were speaking them over and over. What happened to a word once it had been properly inscribed, moreover, happened to what it represented as well: a Babylonian spell for eliminating an opponent prescribes writing his name on a lump of clay and casting it at midnight into a river (Abusch 1998: 63). Analogously, writing particular words down repeatedly, but each time leaving off another letter until the words disappeared completely, would make the illness that the words represented disappear. Some Greek and Latin curse tablets were inscribed with no more than the victim's name and then were folded and pierced with a nail. Although rituals were probably performed and words spoken while the tablet was pierced, the primary action, the piercing of the name, underscores how deeply the word and its referent were linked in ancient magic.

And the creativity of ancient magicians went beyond even this. Spells in the Greco-Egyptian papyri advocate writing words on natron tablets that are then dissolved in drinking water or on leaves that are subsequently licked; physically ingesting the words brings the benefits they represent. Sometimes other liquids are used to supplement the words' force: Jewish magicians spoke words over a cup of wine employed in the havdalah ceremony and then drank it (MS TS K1.117); and in a Greek spell attributed to Moses, words on a natron tablet are dissolved in a mixture of wine and the milk of a black cow (*PGM* XIII.343–646). A Hurrian physician recited incantations over oil that was to anoint the "lord of the army," his horses, chariot, and weapons before going into battle (KUB 30.42 1.8–14 = *CTH* 162).

Again we see that the power of the word is understood differently in different circumstances: sometimes as a stand-in for its referent, sometimes as carrying power in and of itself. That words could be used in a variety of (sometimes mutually exclusive) ways does not seem to have bothered magicians—they used whatever was reputed to work. Sometimes, spells even included a fallback technique ("If that doesn't work, try this instead"). This brings a further insight about ancient magic: not only did it lack an orthodoxy, as did most Mediterranean religious systems themselves, but it scarcely had anything that could be called an orthopraxy. As mentioned earlier, "magic" in a given culture typically used variations of the same main rituals used by the culture's "religion" (e.g., sacrifice, purification procedures), and if we stand back far enough, we can make certain other gross generalizations (e.g., magicians were experts in using words). But the more closely we look, the harder it is to generalize. Not only do things shift within specific cultures (Egyptian magic made greater use of written words, and Greek magic made greater use of spoken words, for instance; Frankfurter 1994), but they shift from spell to spell.

The power of images and essences

Much of what has been said about words applies to another characteristic often connected with ancient magic: the creation and manipulation of images. Thus, images (drawings, statues, etc.) often stood in for their referents. When a doll was pierced with needles by a magician, the woman whom it represented was understood to be affected as well. Binding the statue of a demon, ghost, or witch and carrying it into the wilderness or otherwise disempowering it was understood to disempower its referent as well (a particularly complex Mesopotamian example is offered by Abusch 1998: 56–58). The soles of pharaohs' sandals were engraved with images of enemies, allowing the pharaohs to crush them with every step. This strong connection between image and referent is underscored by the magical technique of making a god angry with one's intended victim by telling the god that the victim has abused the god's image (e.g., *PGM* III.110–12). Images, like inscribed words, continuously enacted what they portrayed: wearing an amulet engraved with a picture of Saint Sisinnius lancing a child-killing demon caused the saint to perform this act repeatedly on behalf of the wearer. We read about consumption of images, too. One example involves dolls made of bread dough (*PGM* III.410–66), another is a spell where images of Isis and Horus are to be drawn on the hand of an ill person, who then licks them off. Horus's healing power might also be internalized by sketching his seven eyes on natron and then dissolving them into beer (Ritner 1993: 95–96, 104).

Words and images are not mutually exclusive: many cases of manipulation involve both. Aramaic incantation bowls placed a picture of a fettered demon in the middle of concentric circles of written charms against it (examples in Lesses 2001), and some curse "tablets" were actually small, inscribed human figurines, representing their victims. But attention to images in particular raises another topic important throughout Mediterranean magic: what the Greeks called *ousia* (a participle from the Greek verb "to be"; the term might be translated as "essence"). *Ousia* comprised material taken from someone or something: hair, fingernail parings, fringe from a garment, a nail from the cross on which a criminal had been crucified, a plank from a shipwrecked vessel. *Ousia* might be understood as a special sort of image, a physical object that stood in for what was otherwise missing, making it present. In some cases, this meant the object of the spell: if you wished to curse someone or to make someone fall in love with you, it was useful to have some part of that person to manipulate. In other cases, it meant the entities on whom you relied to work the spell: nails from crucifixes and planks from fatal shipwrecks could represent the restless dead on whom magicians relied to carry out many tasks (as could actual parts of corpses). Ways of using *ousia* varied, from attaching it to an image representing the referent or to something on which the referent's name was inscribed—in both cases the *ousia* acted to connect the image or tablet more closely to the referent—to burning it, to rubbing it while you invoked the referent, or to incorporating it into an image, a statue.

Earlier generations of scholars would have called the use of *ousia* an example of sympathy: that is, what happens to the *ousia* or the object to which it has been attached happens "sympathetically" to its referent (Greek *sympatheia* literally means "experiencing [something] together"). Recent scholars have rejected this idea, along with most other Frazerian inheritances. Some of their remarks are insightful: thus Fritz Graf (1998: 137–41) emphasizes that in piercing a doll with needles a magician did not intend to make the referent feel pain in those spots, but rather feel desire. The needles should be understood as indicators of where something is to take place, rather than as miniature weapons injuring miniature flesh, and thus "sympathy" must be understood as something more complex than A:B::a:b. And yet there is no denying that sympathetic ideas were at work in antiquity. That *ousia* from a corpse could substitute for the practice of depositing or performing the spell at a grave builds on this: possession of the *ousia* brought the ghost to you instead of your going to visit the ghost. In Apuleius's story of a love spell gone wrong, a witch's house is visited by sexually aroused goatskins because her assistant gathered hairs the witch used as *ousia* from goatskins instead of from the man whom the witch desired (*Golden Ass* 3.15–18).

Late antique theorists of cosmic matters built their ideas on the same premises—although they transferred their attentions to the heavenly realms and rejected the term *magician,* calling themselves Neoplatonic philosophers, theurgists, or followers of Hermes Trismegistus instead. According to them, sympathy or *philia* (friendship, in the sense of a bond between otherwise separate entities) pervaded the cosmos, tying the higher, more-perfect, and divine realms to the lower realms of the material world, where humans dwelt. *Philia* created "chains" of existence, at the top of which were particular divinities and at the bottom of which were materials—gemstones, animals, plants, and so on—that shared the divinities' natures. Learning what these materials were and how to manipulate them enabled the worshiper to contact the divinities and thus perform many of the same feats as magicians did (they rejected such things as using the restless dead and casting love charms, but engaged in divination and control of the weather, for example). The implicit idea is the same as that behind the use of *ousia:* in order to affect or make use of something that is unobtainable, obtain something that is existentially connected to it. Ironically, it was precisely this idea that survived antiquity and was embraced by Christian Neoplatonists such as Marsilio Ficino during the Renaissance. By developing the concept of sympathy—a concept that was understood by Frazer and his followers as distinguishing magic from (Western, European) religion—Ficino and his followers found ways of bringing the ancient learning they so admired into line with Christianity.

Imagination and reality: Gender

As used in the ancient Mediterranean, magic is a normative term, but scholars have sometimes fallen prey to using it to distance groups of people or practices as well. Related to, and complicating, these issues are several others. For example, some scholars have argued that Mesopotamians worried a great deal about being attacked by witchcraft (i.e., magic deployed for injurious purposes) and thus expended effort on averting it and eliminating its sources, but did not actually practice witchcraft themselves. In other words, witchcraft was all in the Mesopotamian imagination; there was no reality behind it. This is not an argument with which I agree (nor does Tzvi Abusch, an expert on Mesopotamian witchcraft), but it serves well to demonstrate the problems that our imperfect sources cause for us, for it springs from the fact that whereas plenty of information about people averting witchcraft and accusing others of witchcraft survives from Mesopotamia, virtually none survives for the practice itself. Obviously, this could be an accident of chance—for example, if curse tablets had not been made largely of lead, we might doubt that magic was practiced in classical Greece to any significant degree; and if the Egyptian climate had not been so kind to papyri, thus preserving numerous extensive, detailed examples of magician's textbooks, we might not believe what accusing Christian authors tell us about the "pagan" practice of magic in late antiquity. We are always at the mercy of our recalcitrant sources and must learn to read through, past, and around them whenever we can.

An especially challenging set of questions in this regard involves gender. In this chapter, I have consistently used male pronouns to refer to Mediterranean magicians. In most cases, this was because the text I quoted or referred to explicitly discussed men—exceptions are the (female) Hurrian physician who recited powerful words over oil used to anoint the "lord of the army," Medea and Circe, the (female) star of Theocritus's poetic love charm, and the witch in Apuleius who accidentally attracted goatskins. But what was the reality—did more men than women really practice magic in the ancient Mediterranean?

Our sources are frustratingly lacunose on this issue; particularly frustrating is that in the Greek and Roman worlds, we tend to hear more about female magicians in literary sources than in working texts—the magical "recipe books" of the papyri, for example, scarcely mention them. This may reflect, as some scholars have suggested, a situation in which women seldom practiced magic but men (who wrote almost all of the literature) nonetheless liked to portray them as doing so—because it expressed their fear of women or because it was titillating (nor are the two mutually exclusive). It may also reflect a situation in which women's magic consisted of actions that were regarded as too trivial or female-centered to record in working texts (spells to protect children, for example). And yet, we know of two real cases in classical Athens in which women were tried on charges of magic, which suggests that even in the real world, their magic could impinge upon the world of men in threatening ways (Versnel 1990: 116–18). Another consideration is that the professional magicians (on whom this essay has focused) were likelier to be male, just as other professionals were, and in Egypt, where the sorts of magic that come to our attention were predominantly the prerogative of temple priests, we should not be surprised to hear little about women in the sources. But there was plenty of "do-it-yourself" magic going on, as well, for which we do not have good records. In this venue, women may have been just as active or even more active than men.

So much for Greece, Rome, and Egypt—but the situation seems to have been different in some other Mediterranean cultures. Royal Anatolian magic involved not only the female physicians mentioned above but other women as well: one king, for example, accuses a rival of hiring female magicians to thwart him (KUB 21.17 1.9–12), and collections of magical lore were centrally compiled in the Hurrian kingdom of Kizzuwatna by female magicians (Haas 1972: 27–29; cf. 37). Witchcraft (i.e., magic deployed for injurious purposes) was more strongly attached to women than men in early Judaism: thus, "most women are witches," said the Babylonian Talmud (tractate *Sanhedrin* 67a). Here again, we must be leery of rabbinic sources because they were created by men and make women look bad—they undoubtedly exaggerate both the degree and the evil nature of women's involvement with magic. Moreover, as Rebecca Lesses shows, there is reason to think that women in Sassanian Babylonia, including some who considered themselves Jewish, were as active as men in magic that had beneficial ends: for instance, they were sometimes involved in the creation of incantation bowls, used the bowls about as often as men, and used them against some of the same problems.

In the end, we cannot answer most of our questions about gender and magic very securely. Moreover, when we do think we have secure answers, fate often confounds us by bringing new evidence to light. After several respected scholars of Greco-Roman magic had concluded that women cast love spells to win men only in literature (i.e., in the male imagination) and that in reality love spells were cast only by men to win women, a new curse tablet from 4th-century BCE Thessaly gave us a splendid example of a woman using magic to separate the man she desired from his wife (Voutiras 1998). Similarly, Robert Daniel and Franco Maltomini (1990: 132–153) provided an undeniable example of a lesbian love charm from 3rd- or 4th-century CE Egypt, which compelled us to look again at a few similar cases that had been swept under the rug.

It may seem that this essay is full of words such as "might," "could," and "although," and phrases such as "tended to"; a reader who is new to this topic may understandably feel frustrated by the paucity of unqualified statements. I have deliberately resisted the temptation to make such statements. For one thing (this should be obvious by now), most scholars of the topic have agreed to disagree—or rather have agreed that our materials make it difficult to reach so firm a state as the word *agreement* implies. All of us have our opinions on what constituted magic in the ancient cultures we study and how magic worked in those cultures, technically, socially, and intellectually. But most of us also know that the evidence we use to support our opinions is too lacunose and its sources are too biased for any opinion to remain unchallenged very long. In other words, beyond a few precepts that are so broad as to be almost useless, there is no current consensus on the topic that I could have presented.

And yet, because this lack of consensus springs from the protean, kaleidoscopic nature of magic in the ancient Mediterranean itself, my choice to reflect it will also, I hope, convey to readers the nature of the topic. If readers leave this essay with as many questions as they had when they began it, I shall not be disappointed—so long as at least some of their questions are new.

Bibliography

Abusch, Tzvi. "The Internalization of Suffering and Illness in Mesopotamia: A Development in Mesopotamian Witchcraft Literature." In *Magic in the Ancient Near East*. Studi epigrafici e linguistici sul Vicino Oriente antico 15. Verona, 1998.
———. *Mesopotamian Witchcraft: Toward a History and Understanding of Babylonian Witchcraft Beliefs and Literature.* Leiden, 2002.
Alexander, Philip S. "Incantations and Books of Magic." In Emil Schürer's *History of the Jewish People in the Age of Jesus Christ,* ed. Geza Vermes, Fergus Millar, and Martin Goodman, vol. 3.1. Edinburgh, 1986.
Daniel, Robert, and Franco Maltomini. *Supplementum magicum.* Abhandlungen der Rheinisch-Westfälischen Akademie der Wissenschaften, Sonderreihe Papyrologica Coloniensia, vols. 16.1 and 16.2. Opladen: Westdeutscher Verlag, 1990 and 1992.
Faraone, Christopher A. "The Agonistic Context of Early Greek Binding Spells." In *Magika Hiera: Ancient Greek Magic and Religion,* ed. Christopher A. Faraone and Dirk Obbink. New York, 1991.
Frankfurter, David T. M. "Narrating Power: The Theory and Practice of the Magical

Historiola in Ritual Spells." In *Ancient Magic and Ritual Power*, ed. Marvin Meyer and Paul Mirecki. Religion in the Graeco-Roman World 129. Leiden, 1995.

———. *Religion in Roman Egypt.* Princeton, 1998.

———. "The Writing of Magic and the Magic of Writing." *Helios* 21.2 (1994): 189–221.

Graf, Fritz. *Magic in the Ancient World.* Tr. Franklin Philip. Cambridge, Mass., 1997 (orig. 1994).

Haas, Volkert. *Magie und Mythen im Reich der Hethiter,* vol. 1: *Vegetationkulte und Pflanzenmagie.* Hamburg, 1972.

Johnston, Sarah Iles. *Restless Dead: Encounters between the Living and the Dead in Ancient Greece.* Berkeley, 1999.

———. "Sacrifice in the Greek Magical Papyri." In *Magic and Ritual in the Ancient World,* ed. Paul Mirecki and Marvin Meyer. Religions in the Graeco-Roman World 141. Leiden, 2002.

Lesses, Rebecca Macy. "Exe(o)rcising Power: Women as Sorceresses, Exorcists, and Demonesses in Babylonian Jewish Society of Late Antiquity." *Journal of the American Academy of Religion* 69.2 (2001): 343–75.

Meyer, Marvin, and Richard Smith, eds. *Ancient Christian Magic: Coptic Texts of Ritual Power.* San Francisco, 1994.

Ritner, Robert Kriech. *The Mechanics of Ancient Egyptian Magical Practice.* Studies in Oriental Civilization 54. Chicago, 1993.

Smith, Morton. *Jesus the Magician.* New York, 1978.

Swartz, Michael D. "Jewish Magic." In *The Cambridge History of Judaism,* vol. 4. Ed. Steven T. Katz. Cambridge, forthcoming.

Tambiah, Stanley. "Form and Meaning of Magical Acts: A Point of View." In *Modes of Thought,* ed. R. Horton and R. Finnegan. London, 1973.

Versnel, Hendrik S. *Inconsistencies in Greek and Roman Religion,* I: *Ter Unus.* Studies in Greek and Roman Religion 6.1. Leiden: Brill, 1990.

Voutiras, E. *Dionysophontos Gamoi: Marital Life and Magic in Fourth-Century Pella.* Amsterdam, 1998.

HISTORIES

Egypt

Jan Assmann and David Frankfurter

Classical period

There is no Egyptian word for "religion," but there is a text that clarifies the Egyptian concept. According to this text, the sun-god and creator, Re, placed the king on earth in order that he might establish *ma'at* (justice/truth/order) and annihilate *isfet* (injustice/lie/disorder) by judging humankind and satisfying the gods (i.e., by giving offerings to the gods and funerary offerings to the dead).

Establishing *ma'at* and annihilating *isfet:* this formula refers to a broad concept of religion, encompassing both cult and culture. Within this broad concept, the text draws a further distinction, setting off cult (satisfying the gods) from justice (judging humankind). This distinction between the spheres of justice and cult has been consciously and emphatically destroyed in biblical monotheism, where justice moves into the center of religion. In Egypt, the question of justice is dealt with not in the context of religion proper, which is concerned with satisfying the gods, but in the comparatively secular context of judging humankind. In the broader frame of establishing *ma'at,* however, justice and morals play a central role, and almost everything that the Bible has to say on these topics is inherited from its ancient Near Eastern and Egyptian neighbors.

At the center of Egyptian religion, however, was cult. The main function of cult was to establish a connection between this world and the otherworld, where not only the gods but also the transfigured spirits of the dead were supposed to live. The basic form of this connection was an exchange of goods. The living served the gods and spirits with offerings and sacrifices and received in return all kinds of support and blessing. The ultimate aim of these offerings, therefore, was not to "feed the gods," but to support this connection, and the cultic barter was only a symbolic expression of contact and communication. Every presentation of offerings, in temples and tombs, was accompanied by a spell stressing its symbolic or sacramental meaning. However, the Egyptian concept of the divine was not restricted to the sphere of the cult. The gods were believed to dwell in the otherworlds (supernal and infernal) and to take only temporary sojourn in cultic representations such as cult images, symbols, sacred animals, trees, and objects. Cult was concerned with establishing and supporting this sojourn, to make the divine descend from heaven into the image, to transfer divine actions from the celestial to the terrestrial realm. During the offering ritual, the god or the spirit was invoked to come from all parts of the world in order to partake of the offering meal; he or she was not supposed to be simply present in the temple or tomb. The gods were believed not to dwell on but only to visit earth, and this visit would irrevocably end if cult were discontinued. Withholding offerings would make the gods not starve but only retreat into their supernal or infernal abodes.

The cult with its rituals, symbols, and recitations formed only one dimension of divine presence. Another dimension was the cosmos as a sphere where the divine manifested itself. According to the Egyptians, the world or cosmos is a process rather than a space, and the idea of order is more a matter of successfully overcoming disorder and destruction than a matter of spatial structure and beautiful arrangement. Virtually all of the gods cooperate in the project of maintaining the world, of keeping the cosmic process going. The core of this process is constituted by what the ancient Egyptians conceived of as the solar circuit, the daily course of the sun across the heavens and through the netherworld. In the eyes of the Egyptians, the success of the cosmic process was far from taken for granted—it was constantly at stake. In the same way as the Mesopotamians, the Chinese, and the Romans, the ancient Egyptians were constantly occupied in watching the sky and in observing all kinds of natural phenomena with the greatest attention. Yet unlike with the Mesopotamians, Chinese, and Romans, the goal of this attention was not divination, that is, finding out the will of the gods and foretelling the future, but to assist the gods in maintaining the world and to accompany divine action with ritual action. Thus, the Egyptians observed what was regular and recurrent in the skies, whereas cultures interested in divination watched for exceptions and deviations. In the context of this task and intellectual preoccupation, the Egyptians accumulated an incredible amount of knowledge, a kind of sacred cosmology.

In the cosmic dimension of divine presence, every major Egyptian deity had a specific cosmic manifestation and played a role in the cosmic process, in the same way as, in the cultic dimension, they had a place on earth in which to exert their terrestrial rulership. In both dimensions, the principle of diversity was irreducibly relevant: the cosmic process resulted from the synergy of a multitude of different powers, and the order and structure of Egypt found its expression in the various towns and cities ruled by deities. All of the major deities are lords or ladies of a town, and all of the major towns or cities are the realms of specific deities. The institution of divine rulership served as a representation of social and political identity. The focus of social and political identification in Egypt was the temple and its lord, a specific deity. Being citizen of a town meant being a member of a festive community, participating in the feasts that were celebrated in the form of processions. The concept of civic allocation was thus invested with religious meaning. It was a kind of covenant, where the religious tasks of the citizen corresponded to the political role of the deity. But the principle of political identity and representation was not limited to the level of villages, towns, and cities. The gods Horus and Seth represented the two parts of Egypt, Lower and Upper Egypt, and later Egypt and the foreign countries. The sun-god Re, later Amun-Re, represented the unified empire. Therefore, the cultic dimension of divine presence can also be called the political dimension. Cult and political identity are simply aspects of one and the same concept of divine presence and communication.

The third dimension of divine presence is constituted by what the Egyptians understood by the term *name*. A name in the Egyptian sense is not just a name but everything that can be said and told of a person. A name is not just an identifier but a description, a linguistic representation of a person's essence. Telling the names of a deity means reciting hymns and eulogies in his or her praise. To the linguistic dimension of divine presence belong Egyptian concepts of sacred language and sacred texts, whose recitation in the appropriate context, according to the ancient Egyptians, has magical power and contributes to the maintenance of the world.

The most important realization of the linguistic dimension of divine presence is myth. Egyptian mythology is centered on three basic myths: the myths of cosmogony, of Osiris, and of the solar circuit. In Egypt, the principle of mythical thinking is the logic of establishing analogies between three discreet realms: cosmos, state, and individual destiny (especially death). Therefore, cosmology, political philosophy, and funerary beliefs may not be separated; all three levels of reality are constantly projected onto each other in Egyptian religious texts. The myth of Osiris is centered on the problem of death; however, it is also the myth of the state, because every king plays the role of Horus, the son and avenger of his predecessor; and it has a cosmological meaning, because it clarifies the relation between heaven, earth, and netherworld. The myth of the solar circuit is basically cosmological; however, it also concerns the state and human destiny (death), because the sun-god is the model of Pharaoh in establishing *ma'at* and the model of the dead in being reborn every morning. The cosmogony is about the origin of the cosmos and of the state; it tells how, after a period of symbiosis, the gods departed to heaven and the state was established in order to organize ways of communication between the now-separated worlds of the gods and the living. Thus, establishing analogies and making the three levels of reality transparent to each other constitutes the basic principle of the linguistic articulation of divine presence. The three dimensions of divine presence correspond surprisingly well to Varro's distinction between three forms of theology: political *(civilis)*, cosmic *(naturalis)*, and poetic *(fabularis)*. Yet this correspondence does not mean that we are dealing here with a universal structure. Mesopotamian and, above all, biblical religion is different in that a fourth dimension, history, becomes more and more promi-

nent. This process has repercussions even in Egypt, and the rather erup-
tive emergence of history as a fourth dimension of divine presence after the
Amarna experience (1320 BCE) changes the structure of Egyptian religion in a
profound way. From now on, the gods are believed to intervene in the course
not only of history but also of individual biography. This means the rise of
personal piety as an attitude of deep confidence in and submission to the will
of god.

Another line of religious evolution that led to fundamental changes in the
structure of Egyptian religion is the rise of theological discourse, triggered first
by the breakdown of the Old Kingdom, when the experience of distress and
disorder posed the classical problems of theodicy. The central problem underlying the theological discourse of the New Kingdom is the relationship between
God and gods on the one hand and between God and world, or creator and
creation, on the other hand. Both of these relations are simply aspects of the
same question, because the gods and their constellations and cooperations constitute the world in Egyptian thought. Theogony and cosmogony are the same.
According to the cosmogony of Heliopolis, which played the role of a "great
tradition," the One (Arum), the personification of preexisting Oneness, creates
the world by engendering Shu and Tefnut (air and fire), who engender Geb and
Nut (heaven and earth), the parents of the five children of Nut who prolong
cosmic reality into the institutions of civilization and human history. This same
sequence of generations corresponds also to a succession of rulers: cosmogony
appears as cratogony, the emergence and evolution of power. The most important epithet of the highest god in Egypt, the quality that distinguishes the highest god from the other gods, is temporal firstness. To be the first means to be
the chief.

With the New Kingdom, the imperialistic politics of the Thutmosid Dynasty
brought about a new, universalistic cosmology. The order of creation did not
stop at the Egyptian borders but stretched far beyond, comprising many nations with whom Egypt now entered into political relations. This new image of
the world immensely enhanced the supremacy of the sun-god within the Egyptian pantheon who, from his original embeddedness in the synergetic process
of maintaining the cosmic process, moved more and more into the position of
sole creator and preserver vis-à-vis a world inhabited by both humans and
gods. Akhenaten's monotheist revolution drew but the logical consequences in
eliminating the gods altogether. His god is alone in creating and maintaining
the world, producing light and warmth by his radiation and time and development by his motion. The theology of the post-Amarna period readmits the
gods into the world, but it also stresses the distance and solitude of the solar
creator and maintainer of the world. Now, besides creation, a new model is
used to express the God-world or God-gods relationship. This is the Ba concept. Amun-Re comes to be called the "hidden Ba," whose manifestations are
either the other gods or the visible cosmos itself. God remains One, relating to
the world in a similar way to that in which the Ba relates to the body, an invisible animating principle. This new idea of god is not only a response to Amarna
but also the origin of the Hermetic idea of god, *deus mundus,* a god whose

body is the world. The Ramesside formula of "The one becoming millions" anticipates Hermetic formulations such as *hen kai pan* (one yet also many), *una quae es omnia* (you who are one and everything), and so on. The Ramesside Ba theology reaches its apex in the Late Period with the cult of the ten Bas in Thebes and El-Hibe. The idea of the world as the incorporation of a soul-like God and of God as a soul animating the world remains central in Egyptian theology even after the New Kingdom and the flourishing of the theological discourse.

BIBL.: J. Assmann, *The Search for God in Ancient Egypt* (trans. D. Lorton; Ithaca, 2001). H. Frankfort, *Ancient Egyptian Religion* (New York, 1948). E. Hornung, *The Conceptions of God in Ancient Egypt: The One and the Many* (trans. J. Baines; Ithaca, 1996). S. Quirke, *Ancient Egyptian Religion* (London, 1992). B. A. Shafer (ed.), *Religion in Ancient Egypt* (London, 1991).

J.A.

Later period

The later period of Egyptian religion, from the Greco-Roman and Coptic eras up to the Muslim conquest, involves a gradual separation and ultimate rupture between traditional Egyptian cults and foreign rulers, with consequences for cults, priestly institutions, religious literature, and popular religion. The stages of transformation can be roughly divided into the Ptolemaic period (305–30 BCE), which saw an infusion of royal patronage and the expansion of the Egyptian religious infrastructure; the early Roman period (30 BCE–early 3rd century CE), which saw the bureaucratization of Egyptian religious institutions for purposes of Roman control and taxation; the later Roman period (mid-3rd–4th century CE), which saw the economic decline of much of the Egyptian religious infrastructure and principal temple centers; and the Coptic period (late 4th–7th century CE), which saw the Christianization of Egyptian religion, involving both the persecution of traditional cults and the expansion of local forms of Egyptian Christianity.

Most of the temples visible today in Egypt—Philae, Karnak, Edfu, Kom Ombo, Kysis, and others—owe their principal expansions to Ptolemaic patronage. Ptolemaic kings styled themselves as Pharaohs according to archaic royal mythology, and they involved numerous priesthoods in the cultivation of this image. Some of this propaganda responded to a series of revolts around Thebes during the 2nd century BCE, which were sponsored and probably led by temple priests (sometimes to support a "native" Pharaoh) and in whose suppression Ptolemaic armies were often engaged. Consequently, the Ptolemaic kings were themselves presented as sons of Re and conquerors of chaos (Rosetta Stone), and they were consistently represented on temple reliefs as pious maintainers of cosmic order and fertility (Philae, Edfu).

Ptolemies also developed new cults at the center, like Sarapis (an anthropomorphic hybrid of the Apis bull and Osiris), and on the periphery, like Mandulis (based on a Nubian god). The influx of Greek language, art, and religious and philosophical ideals affected many domains of Egyptian religion. Temple scriptoria produced mythological tracts and legends in Greek, sometimes with influence from Greek literature. An already script-oriented religion absorbed Greek writing for record keeping, oracle responses, ritual spells, and even the quasi-nativist prophecies of the 2nd century BCE that paradoxically urged the expulsion of Greeks *(Oracle of the Potter)*. Encouraged by a Hellenistic romanticism of Egypt as the origin of culture and of Egyptian priests as consummate philosophers, some priests sought to convey Egyptian ideas in Greek philosophical or theosophical guise and to present their hieroglyphic systems, ritual traditions, and magical procedures as peerless in the Mediterranean world (Manetho; cf. Herodotus 2.2.5–3.1; 2.54.1–2). By the Roman period, the Egyptian wizard—an exoticized image of a lector-priest literate in hieroglyphs—would become a standard of Greek fiction, and Egypt itself would become the land of magic and mystery. Hellenistic artistic ideals influenced both domestic and public representations of gods like Isis, Amun, and Harpocrates (the Horus-child). Such representational styles—in poetry as well as art—contributed to the pantheization of certain Egyptian gods as omnipotent, Mediterranean-wide deities. Isis, for example, is hailed in inscriptions and papyri as the universal goddess, invoked in various lands by names like Aphrodite, Hecate, and Demeter. The particular center of such synthetic, multimedia activities was the new city of Alexandria, but many other cities also became centers of mixing classical and Egyptian cultures (e.g., Panopolis, Oxyrhynchus).

In none of these endeavors was Egyptian religious tradition smothered or replaced by Hellenism. Rather, Egyptian myths, deities, rites, and priestly roles were extended and developed through these various Greek expressions. As much as the god Sarapis, for example, emerged *de novo* in the 4th century BCE, he had clear Egyptian roots and had become an installation in shrines and festival calendars by the early Roman period. As much as new "foreign" gods such as Astarte, Demeter, and the Dioscuri arose as the protectors of immigrant communities, by the early Roman period they had become expressions of native gods such as Isis or Sobek, the crocodile god. Sobek himself, among the most distinctive of Egyptian deities, was the object of multiple different crocodile cults around the Fayyum region, almost all of which had thoroughly incorporated Greek language into every aspect of organization and communication.

The Roman period begins with the immediate consolidation of imperial control over priesthoods and temples. Under Augustus, the temple institutions were organized in a single bureaucracy under an imperial agent, the *Idios Logos*, their financial resources attached exclusively to imperial munificence. The annals of Egyptian religion from this period—predominantly in Greek—thus show a new determination in record keeping: priestly initiation oaths; inventories of temples, their property, and festivals; and other forms of institutional accounting, prepared for Roman supervision. Emperors continue to support Egyptian temples and priesthoods and are celebrated for it in temple reliefs; but the Roman relationship to Egyptian religion carries a distinct ambivalence. Egyptian cults have become a common feature of cities around the Mediterranean world, and Egyptian priests have grown ever more famous as court ritual experts and fictional wizards. Yet fears that such "foreign" cults might subvert political order, and fears of the revolutionary potential of indigenous priesthoods, all lead Roman officials to exert control over priestly affairs on every level: proscribing oracles, for example, in an ill-fated declaration of the late 2nd century CE.

Still, sources for this period show ever-new dimensions of Egyptian religion flourishing: a great variety of oracle shrines, producing both written and mysteriously vocal responses and attracting pilgrims' devotional graffiti; mortuary workshops in which archaic traditions of mummification and burial were extended to include gold masks (as in several oasis necropolises) or portraits of the deceased (as in Fayyum necropolises); and new forms of ancient deities, developed for local or domestic protection, such as Bes, Tutu, and Petbe, enlarging the phalanx of protector-gods that included most prominently Harpocrates-on-the-crocodiles, produced on small stone stelae to ward off dangers.

It is also at this time that the great literary syntheses of Greek and Egyptian theosophy are produced: the Hermetica (revelations of the scribal god Thoth in his Greek guise, Hermes the thrice-great) and the writings of Egyptian priests such as Chaeremon and Iamblichus. These texts articulate in Greek terms the efficacy of ritual utterance and gesture, the power of images and places, the relationship between an incomprehensible Divinity and the gods of traditional devotion, and the moral life of the one seeking communion with Divinity. The intellectual conventicles that produced such literature probably departed from temple scriptoria and took on a life of their own during the 2nd and 3rd centuries, ultimately communicating or even merging with similar scribal groups producing Christian (including gnostic) texts.

At the beginning of the 3rd century, Egyptian temples themselves were thrust officially from imperial patronage onto the diminishing financial resources of local councils; and with the declining economy of the empire over the course of the 3rd century, the infrastructure and institutions of Egyptian religion fell into decline. The sprawling precincts of Memphis, Thebes, and Edfu dwindled and were largely abandoned. Other temples, as at Douch (Kharga Oasis), Abydos, and Deir el-Bahri (Thebes), cultivated oracle cults to maintain some income; while local temples, such as those of Canopus and Menouthis near Alexandria, and peripheral complexes, like that of Isis at Philae, continued to prosper with more circumscribed catchment areas. A literature of apocalyptic decline, rooted in ancient Egyptian imagery of the liminal interregnum period (but now phrased in Greek, Hermetic, and even Christian terms), arose in the 3rd century to express utopian hopes for an eschatological kingship and the reestablishment of gods and proper worship (*Asclepius* 24–27; *Apocalypse of Elijah*). Egyptian papyri and Christian legends both record the impact of religious edicts issued by anxious 3rd-century emperors (Decius, Valerian, Diocletian) in the hope that the general decline of the empire could be averted through mass uniformity in ritual display.

The empire's official embrace of Christianity in the early 4th century touched off a series of edicts (e.g., the Theodosian Code) restricting non-Christian religion that, if not immediately repressive on traditional Egyptian piety, certainly threw some cults further onto their local-support networks. Given the centrality of image processions, shrine devotion, and divination in traditional religious expression, rather than sacrifice as the 4th-century edicts imagined heathen ritual, much active piety fell outside the edicts' scope (and was difficult to police anyway).

Traditional Egyptian religion in the 3rd and 4th centuries consequently underwent a centrifugal shift away from major temple complexes. Papyri, inscriptions, and archeological remains show the persistence of local cults to familiar avatars of Isis, Sobek, Horus, Bes, Tutu, and other deities, as well as regional pilgrimages, festivals, and oracles—all rather circumscribed expressions of communities' religious self-determination. The lives of Christian saints in the 4th through 6th centuries recall "heathen" domestic practices with ancient roots: household shrines, festival lamps, popular devotion to the Nile or a village image. From this evidence we derive less a sense of Egyptian mythology persisting than of the vitality and "place" of ancestral religious practices.

Yet among priests, such as those who collected the many spells preserved in the Greek and Demotic Magical Papyri, older myths were preserved and extended, combined with foreign names, and often directed to new types of "magic" with foreigners in mind—the priest self-styled as a wizard according to Roman expectations. These spells show the preservation of solar myths, imagery of Anubis and Thoth, and stories of the great Egyptian gods alongside Homeric verses and Syrian deities. The early forms of Coptic writing (Egyptian language transcribed in Greek letters) that appear in such texts suggest that the very writing system that Egyptian Christians would eventually appropriate began as a way for ritual experts to fix ritual pronunciation. Other priests—at the Bucheum of Armant or the Isis temple of Philae, for example—devoted themselves to more-traditional shrine duties; and it is in such places that hieroglyphic writing continued to the end of the 4th century. Well into the 4th century, one priesthood maintained an internationally renowned oracle temple of the popular fertility-god Bes at the ancient shrine of Osiris at Abydos, only to be closed when the Christian emperor feared its potential to intervene magically in imperial affairs. Egyptian priestly families remained prominent in the intellectual culture of cities such as Panopolis and Alexandria, producing poetry and philosophy and trying to maintain their priestly traditions in some form in a Christian world.

By the end of the 4th century the violent persecution of Egyptian religious places and practices seems to have reached a pitch, with bishops, monks and their abbots, village gangs, and occasionally (as at late-6th-century Philae) even armies acting to purify the landscape from a demonic heathenism. The

destruction of the Sarapeum of Alexandria in 389 CE by Christian mobs and
soldiers (under a bishop's direction) may itself have triggered further, local
destructive acts by monks around Egypt. Most evidence for the continuation of
local cults through the 5th century appears in the legends of Coptic saints,
which celebrate these cults' extirpation. The 5th through 7th centuries also
see the religious resettlement of Egyptian temples with churches and monaster-
ies. Whether the archaic holiness of these structures is maintained by virtue
of these acts of reconsecration or not, the temples' physical importance in
the landscape certainly reemerges in Christian institutional guise; and certain
graffiti, incised crosses, or image desecration in the temples suggest that the
temples were still believed to carry some ambivalent power. Shrines with cults
to Coptic saints of often murky historicity proliferate from the 5th century, offering Christians a new sacred landscape and sense of local religious identity
through processions, the recitation of martyrs' legends, the magical services of
shrine attendants, and even the development of ancient oracular services at
these shrines: incubation, written responses, private consultation. In such ways
many of the practical elements of Egyptian religion become reformulated in
Christian idiom.

Occasionally Egyptian mythological ideas are transmitted past the 4th century as well, as in some Coptic magical texts of the 7th and 8th centuries.
Coptic apocryphal texts preserved images of the underworld based on ancient
mortuary traditions; and some Coptic martyrologies, read aloud at feast days,
depicted a sacred geography based on the martyr's dismembered body that dis-
tantly recalled images of Egypt integrated through the body parts of Osiris. But
the preservation of non-Christian ideas most publicly in the Coptic period involved Hellenistic rather than Egyptian motifs: the Greek heroes and gods on
Coptic textiles, for example.

Over the Ptolemaic, Roman, and Coptic periods, then, we see the swelling
and centralization of Egyptian religious institutions; then their decline from
economic causes; and finally their persecution—dismantled or scattered—on
Christian grounds. The elaborate priestly literary production, temple
dramaturgy, and skilled artistic workshops that together supported the complex mythologies of Isis, Horus, Re, Amun, Osiris, and Seth, which we typically equate with Egyptian religion, all fell victim to historical vicissitudes. But
the more practical elements of Egyptian religious tradition—from the gestures
at domestic altars to the visits made to oracle sites and even to priests' creative
reformulation of ritual traditions—continued in local or regional form well after the official establishment of Christianity; and Coptic Christianity itself
maintained many of these elements.

BIBL.: Roger Bagnall, *Egypt in Late Antiquity* (Princeton, 1993). Heike Behlmer, "Ancient Egyptian Survivals in Coptic Literature: An Overview," in *Ancient Egyptian Literature: History and Forms* (ed. Antonio Loprieno; Leiden, 1996), 567–90. Alan K. Bowman, *Egypt after the Pharaohs* (Berkeley, 1986). Françoise Dunand and Christiane
Zivie-Coche, *Dieux et hommes en Égypte, 3000 av. J.-C.–395 apr. J.-C.: Anthropologie*

religieuse (Paris, 1991). Garth Fowden, *The Egyptian Hermes: An Historical Approach to the Late Pagan Mind* (Cambridge, 1986). David Frankfurter, *Religion in Roman Egypt: Assimilation and Resistance* (Princeton, 1998). P. M. Fraser, *Ptolemaic Alexandria* (2 vols.; Oxford, 1972). Dorothy J. Thompson, *Memphis under the Ptolemies* (Princeton, 1988).

D.F.

Mesopotamia

Paul-Alain Beaulieu

*T*he earliest detailed evidence for organized religious beliefs in the lands of southern Iraq (Sumer and Akkad, later Babylonia) comes from Eridu and Uruk. During the protohistorical period, these two sites, the earliest urban centers of Sumer, grew around cultic compounds that are already clear prototypes of later Mesopotamian temples. Created shortly after the invention of writing, the archaic texts from Uruk (ca. 3300–3100 BCE) shed light on the organization of the cult at the threshold of history. Many of them can be identified as offering lists to various forms of the goddess Inanna, including "Morning Inanna" and "Evening Inanna," the two manifestations of the planet Venus as morning and evening star. The art of the period provides compelling evidence that Uruk was ruled by a charismatic figure who acted as intermediary between the community and the city goddess. This ruler was probably a priest-king, denoted by the Sumerian word EN, which in fact appears several times in the archaic texts from Uruk.

The basic graphic and visual concepts stressing the essential nature of deities as separate from the world of mortals crystallized at a very early date. The divine determinative that precedes names of gods and goddesses in the writing system already appears in the archaic texts from Uruk and is universally used by the beginning of the 3rd millennium. Similarly, the horned headdress, which first appears in the iconography of deities during the Early Dynastic period, becomes the obligatory marker of divine status in the art by the middle of the 3rd millennium. Although Mesopotamian religion was always strongly anthropomorphic, gods could also be represented by an emblematic animal, whether real or imaginary, or a symbol, which could be a standard, a cult object, or even a completely abstract form. Some scholars espousing evolutionist views have claimed that there was a general historical tendency toward anthropomorphism from a more primitive stage of abstract or symbolic representation. The extant documentation, however, clearly indicates that all modes of divine representations existed side by side from earliest times. Indeed, during the

Uruk period purely anthropomorphic representations of Inanna existed alongside symbolic ones, including on the famous Uruk Vase, which depicts the goddess in human form, then with her standard, and possibly even with her emblematic animal, the lion. The preference for one mode of representation or the
other in a particular place or period was mainly due to fashion or to the rise of
new theological currents. During the Ur III period, for instance, cylinder seals
attest to a strong predominance of anthropomorphic representations, while
symbols and standards become more common during the ensuing Old Babylonian period and even more so during the late periods.

During the early periods, each town and village worshiped local deities—
many of them fertility-goddesses—who ensured the prosperity of the community, while the most important members of the pantheon reigned supreme in
the major political and cultural centers, such as the moon-god Nanna-Suen at
Ur, the sun-god UTU at Larsa, the mother-goddess Ninhursag in Kesh, and the
healing-goddess Nin-Isinna at Isin. The god Enlil of Nippur presided over the
entire pantheon like a remote ancestral figure, owing his prominence to the
role of his city as religious and cultural capital of Sumer. By the middle of the
3rd millennium, Enlil had clearly overshadowed other gods who filled a similar
role, notably the sky-god An, at home in Uruk, and the god of subterranean
waters Enki (later also known as Ea), the patron deity of Eridu.

Such a bewildering multiplicity of divine figures needed to be explained and
ordered hierarchically. This favored the rise of theological reflection among the
literate and priestly classes. The earliest such documents occur in the form of
lists of gods from the site of Fara and date to the Early Dynastic I period (ca.
2900–2700 BCE). That contemporary fragments of these same lists were found
at Abu Salabikh, Ur, and Uruk proves that they were not ad hoc creations reflecting the local pantheon, but compositions preserving a tradition already
common to all Sumer. Their arrangement is either hierarchical or lexical. Both
principles occur in the great list from Fara (SF1), which begins with An, Enlil,
Inanna, Enki, and six other great gods, followed by a long list of goddesses
with names formed with the initial element *nin* (lady, mistress). Lists of gods
remained one of the most productive theological genres throughout the entire
life span of Mesopotamian civilization. Sumerian hymns from the 3rd and
early 2nd millennia are also an important theological source. Prominent in this
respect is the collection of Sumerian temple hymns. The standard edition includes forty-two hymns, each of them a miniature theological treatise dedicated to one of the major temples of Sumer and Akkad. Such hymns have distant forerunners at Abu Salabikh.

Many distinctive traits developed by Mesopotamian religion during the
early periods lasted until that religion's end: the concept of deities as the real
rulers of the community served by a host of priestly attendants, the corresponding view of the temple as a princely residence where the divine rulers
hold court, the representation of gods by anthropomorphic statues brought to
life by incantations and complex rituals of animation, and the system of food
offerings redistributed to the priests and temple personnel after ritual presentation to the gods. Some hymns were still sung in the temples a thousand years

after their composition, and administrative documents from temple archives show that many festivals and cultic events occurred at the same time during the calendar year in 2000 BCE as they did in 500 BCE. Although new gods were occasionally introduced and the divine hierarchy reorganized, local deities generally retained the same attributes and survived the passing of centuries. Similarly the overall pantheon preserved its essential characteristics, with political changes being reflected mostly by the rise of new gods.

The most important catalyst for change was the intrusion of the political in the religious sphere. It is highly probable that the earliest rulers of the Sumerian city-states cumulated in their hands both secular and religious power. This type of kingship is represented by the EN, the Uruk priest-king of the archaic period. During the Early Dynastic period, however, a more secular concept of rulership emerged, expressed by the titles ENSI(K) (prince) and LUGAL (king), while the EN-ship and its female equivalents became purely religious offices. The ENSI(K) was basically the temporal ruler of the Sumerian city-state, where the land was viewed as the personal property of the god, the city ruler being only the administrator of those domains. The LUGAL represents a more personal and dictatorial type of leadership and is generally thought to have been at home originally in the north, where according to legend it had descended from heaven to Kish at the beginning of history, after the deluge. With the rise of large territorial states ruled by a LUGAL, such as the Sargonic and Ur III empires of the second half of the 3rd millennium, and the demotion of the ENSI(K) to the rank of city governor, nominations of princesses of the ruling family to high priestly offices in major cities of Sumer and Akkad became a tool of political control that survived well into the Isin-Larsa and Old Babylonian periods. The loss of the priestly function of the ruler and the increasing power wielded by him eventually led to the deification of kings. This was initiated by Naram-Sin of Akkad, was revived later by Shulgi, and then followed by the kings of the Isin-Larsa period until it died out during the First Dynasty of Babylon. The king's divine status was expressed mainly by the prefixing of the divine determinative to his name, the wearing of a horned headdress in art, and the composition of hymns extolling his divine parentage and supernatural powers.

Another important aspect of political intrusion in the religious sphere was the new symbolization of the state in the organization of the pantheon. With the rise of larger states, the gods of the capital, especially its patron deity, were often raised to a higher station reflecting the political prominence of their home. During the Sargonic period, for instance, the goddess Inanna/Ishtar enjoyed great prominence in the empire mainly because of her status as goddess of Akkad, the capital of Sargon and his successors, and this certainly explains why the native tradition attributed to his daughter Enheduanna two Sumerian hymns of great beauty and complexity to that goddess. Later in the Ur III period, the old city god of Ur, Nanna-Suen, was similarly exalted. He became the "firstborn son of Enlil," the head of the pantheon, in order to justify Ur's hegemony over Sumer and Akkad, and the composition of new hymns and myths was encouraged by kings Ur-Nammu and Shulgi to propagate this new theological concept. The most obvious, far-reaching, and lasting case of political intrusion occurred under the First Dynasty of Babylon (1894–1595 BCE), when the city god Marduk, previously a deity of no great importance except locally, was propelled to the summit of the pantheon and given the same powers as the god Enlil, the *Enlilūtu* (Enlil-ship).

Another important aspect of Mesopotamian religion during the early periods is the emergence of a synthesis of Sumerian and Semitic (Akkadian) religion. This process was certainly well under way even before the Sargonic period, when it comes into full view. Some Sumerian deities were syncretized with the Semitic gods who shared attributes with them. This was an easy process for astral and nature deities. In this manner the Sumerian sun-god UTU, worshiped at Larsa, was equated with the Semitic sun-god Shamash of Sippar, and Inanna of Uruk was identified with the Semitic Ishtar, also a Venus goddess worshiped primarily at Akkad. Generally speaking, however, the Semitic Akkadians adopted most of the Sumerian deities without any modification, although they occasionally Akkadianized their names. The Sumerian sky-god An became Anum and was provided with a wife named Antum, but such gods as Ningirsu, Ninurta, Nin-Isinna, Gula, and countless others were adopted as such. Conversely, some purely Semitic deities with no Sumerian equivalents entered the common Mesopotamian pantheon. In this category one may include such minor gods as Ishum, Shullat, and Hanish.

By and large it must be stressed that the basic structure and ideology of Mesopotamian religion was largely Sumerian in origin. As we move northward and westward, on the other hand, Sumerian influence wanes as the Semitic or local component becomes more prominent. One important center was the northern city of Asshur, where the local god of the same name, unknown in the south, was identified as the *numen loci* of the city. Various writings of the city and divine name in Old Assyrian documents indicate that the concepts of a city Asshur and a god Assur were interchangeable, from which it follows that the god Assur was originally the deified city or the location where it was built. In the south the prologue of the Code of Hammurabi sums up the official pantheon of Mesopotamia at the time when the Sumero-Akkadian synthesis has given birth to a distinctive Babylonian culture that will dominate Mesopotamia for the rest of its history. The gods Anu and Enlil have selected Babylon to be the seat of monarchy and "rule the four quarters" and its god Marduk, now promoted to the status of son of Enki/Ea, to lead humankind. Then follows a list of the great cult centers of Hammurabi's kingdom in a theological order which, significantly, still acknowledges Nippur and its god Enlil as preeminent, followed by Eridu and Enki/Ea (the father of Marduk), Babylon and Marduk, Ur and Nanna-Suen, and so on. The local theologies listed in this prologue will last until the late periods, with the important exception of the city of Borsippa, where the god Tutu, a form of Marduk, will be replaced by Nabu in the latter part of the 2nd millennium.

The Kassite kings, who by the middle of the 15th century BCE had unified Babylonia under their rule, appear to have especially favored the cult of the gods of Nippur, the ancient religious and cultural capital of Sumer. The religious buildings of their new capital Dur-Kurigalzu were all consecrated to Enlil and Ninlil, the ruling divine pair of Nippur, and to Ninurta and Gula, their son and daughter-in-law. It has been suggested that the aspect of Enlil as a mountain-god, which is often depicted in the iconography of that period, strongly appealed to the Kassites, who very probably originated from the Zagros Mountains east of Babylonia. With the exception of Suqamuna and Sumaliya, the protectors of their ruling house, the Kassites did little to impose the worship of their own deities.

During the Middle Babylonian period the worship of the personal god reached full maturity. The insistence on the intimate relation between worshiper and god favored the blossoming of a pervasive notion of sin, while the anxiety created by the frequent absence of divine response and support led to a growing awareness of the remoteness of the gods and unfathomableness of their will. These developments are evidenced by the proliferation of prayers in personal names (e.g., Sin-karabi-ishme, The god Sin heard my prayer) and on legends of cylinder seals and the composition of theodicies in which the figure of the pious sufferer appears in the forefront. Transcendental concepts of the divine are also reflected in the increasing popularity of symbolic representation of gods, especially on kudurrus (large polished stones, often used as boundary markers). The Middle Babylonian period witnessed important scholarly activity in the field of religion. Theological thinking is exemplified by the massive list of gods entitled An = Anum. Divination, magic, and medicine are introduced in the canon of scribal schools, while intellectual life becomes gradually dominated by specialists of these disciplines, whose outlook will shape religious expression and thought at the higher level until the end of Mesopotamian civilization.

In the middle of the 12th century, the Kassite Dynasty gave way to the Second Dynasty of Isin, whose rule culminated in the exaltation of Marduk, the city god of Babylon. The rise of Marduk began in the time of the First Dynasty of Babylon, when he was granted the *Enlilūtu* (power of Enlil [i.e., leadership]) over the gods. Under Kassite rule the cult of Marduk grew in importance, partly because of the continued political and cultural centrality of Babylon. The dramatic decline of Nippur during the transition to Isin II—evidenced by archeological surveys of the site—may have materially signaled the end of Enlil's supremacy. It was probably on the return to Babylon of the statue of Marduk—captured during a raid by Isin II monarch Nebuchadnezzar I (1125–1104 BCE) against neighboring Elam—that a theological reform was launched that resulted in the exaltation of Marduk, who assimilated the powers and attributes of Enlil and his son Ninurta. An inscription of King Simbar-Shipak (1025–1008 BCE) in which Marduk and Enlil are treated as the same god, provides evidence for the successful completion of this reform by the turn of the millennium.

By the 13th century, capturing the gods of the enemy had become a component of the process of war and conquest. Concomitantly, the belief developed that the ravages of war were caused by the anger of the gods at their own land,

and that the gods summoned the enemy to destroy it. Spoliation of the statue of the national god symbolized the anger of the deity, abandoning the land and people to their fates. The Epic of Tukulti-Ninurta I (1243–1207 BCE) already articulates this idea, depicting the wrath of all the city gods of Babylonia toward the Kassite King Kashtiliash. The literature describing the return of the statue of Marduk from Elam to Babylon during the reign of Nebuchadnezzar I represents the first full-fledged expression of this theology of divine anger and retribution.

The reign of Nebuchadnezzar I also seems the most probable historical setting for the composition of *Enuma Elish,* the Babylonian epic of creation. This long text describes the battle waged by Marduk against the primeval forces of chaos led by the female monster Tiamat, out of whose dismembered body he creates the world after his victory over her. Marduk is then crowned "king of the gods" by the divine assembly, and the epic ends with a long hymnic passage praising the god under his fifty names. Because of its methodic character, its description of the world from chaotic beginnings (creation was not *ex nihilo*) and its slow evolution through generations of primeval gods, its account of the creation of humankind, its eschatological projection into a future forever ruled by Marduk keeping Tiamat's evil forces in check, and its closing enjoinment to propagate the study of Marduk's names, *Enuma Elish* comes closer to being a systematic creed than any other text from Mesopotamia and thus constitutes a milestone in the history of religious thought.

The first three centuries of the 1st millennium are very poorly documented in Babylonia. One important text from that period is the sun-god tablet of King Nabu-apla-iddina (9th century BCE), which contains the earliest evidence for the *mīs pî* (washing of the mouth) ritual to transubstantiate the divine presence into the cultic image. The last great mythological composition, the myth of Erra and Isum, was created probably in the 8th century by the scholar Kabti-ili-Marduk. It portrays Marduk as an exhausted and powerless ruler, unable to stop the destructions wrought in his realm by the god Erra. The text is a theological reflection on the chaos into which Babylonia had sunk by the first half of the 8th century.

By the 14th century, Assyria had completed its transformation from a city-state into a territorial state, the *māt Aššur* (land of the god Assur). The king then extended his duties from vice-regent of the city Asshur to vice-regent of the land of Assyria, which he was now responsible for enlarging on behalf of the god. Repeated attempts to control Babylonia resulted in an influx of Babylonian learning, including the cult of Marduk, into Assyria. As in Babylonia we also see the emergence of a more transcendental concept of the deity, exemplified in the iconographic record by the altar of Tukulti-Ninurta I, which depicts the king twice in the same scene, standing and then kneeling in prayer before the altar and symbol of the god Nusku.

In spite of increased Babylonian influence, Assyria preserved some of its religious distinctiveness. The god Assur retained his original aspect of a mysterious and distant god—quite unlike that of the ubiquitous and solicitous Babylonian demiurge—which made him closer to the true character of Anu and Enlil, the ancient rulers of the Mesopotamian pantheon now displaced by younger gods. The palace decoration of Assurnasirpal II (883–859 BCE) and his son Shalmaneser III (858–824 BCE) at Kalhu, with its extensive and repetitive depiction of the king in various sacral functions and of the sacred tree tended by protective genii, underlines the distinctive role of the Assyrian ruler as high priest, intermediary between god and humankind, and mystical maintainer of the fertility and cosmic equilibrium of the land of Assyria.

With the gradual transformation of Assyria into a world-state during the Neo-Assyrian period, the need arose for a supreme god reflecting the unity and universalism of the empire. During the reign of Adad-nirari III (810–783 BCE), the god Nabu, who had reached great prominence in Babylonia by the 9th century, seemed to fulfill this function in some circles: "Trust in the god Nabu, do not trust in another god!" proclaims an inscription of the governor of Kalhu dedicated to the king and his mother Shammu-ramat (Semiramis). It is nevertheless the god Assur who ultimately became the focus of this imperial monolatry, which culminated in the theological reforms of Sennacherib (704–681 BCE), who equated Assur with the old primeval god Ansar, the logogram AN.ŠÁR then becoming the official writing of the god until the end of the empire in 612–610 BCE. From the reign of his son Esarhaddon (680–669 BCE) comes the most extensive evidence for the excessive popularity of divination, especially astrology, at the court. The library amassed by his grandson Assurbanipal (668–630 BCE) remains to this day our single most important source of Assyrian and Babylonian religious texts (rituals, incantations, prayers, myths) for the late periods, although other libraries from that period have also yielded rich material (Asshur, Sultantepe, Kalhu).

The Neo-Babylonian Dynasty (626–539 BCE) brought the cults of Marduk and his son Nabu into imperial prominence. The identity of the two gods is proclaimed in the coronation hymn of Nebuchadnezzar II (605–562 BCE), who launched a vast program of restoration of temples and cults all over Babylonia. In Babylon the ziggurat Etemenanki and the temple Esagil, both dedicated to Marduk, were rebuilt on a grand scale to reflect their new status as the navel of a vast empire. With Nabonidus (556–539 BCE) the need for a more impersonal and distant imperial deity arose once again, as earlier in the Neo-Assyrian period, this time focusing on the moon-god Sin. Under his reign the religious antiquarianism that characterizes this entire era reached a new climax, best exemplified by the consecration of his daughter as high priestess of the moon-god at Ur, an institution that had long fallen into oblivion.

The archives of the Eanna of Uruk, the temple of the goddess Ishtar (ca. 8,000 texts), and of the Ebabbar of Sippar, the sanctuary of the sun-god Shamash (ca. 35,000 texts), allow us to study the local pantheons of these Neo-Babylonian cities and the material aspects of their cult. Babylonian religion, emblematized in Judeo-Christian consciousness as mere irrational "idol worship," is there revealed in its daily routine. The main temple is the earthly abode of the city's tutelary gods and their retinue, all represented by anthropomorphic images served by numerous attendants, while secondary gods reside in the small sanctuaries located in the city and its satellite towns. Administrative texts detail the lavish offerings presented to the gods, the magnificence of their attire, the flurry of ritual activities surrounding them. This overwhelming evidence for the predominance of anthropomorphic worship of the gods stands in marked contrast to the iconography of that period—largely known from stamp and cylinder seals—in which deities are almost always depicted by their symbols.

With Babylon's fall to King Cyrus the Great of Persia, a new phase began with Mesopotamia as a mere province in a succession of far-flung multinational empires. Although the native religious institutions no longer benefited from royal patronage, there is ample archeological and epigraphic evidence that during most of the Achaemenid and Seleucid periods the traditional temples with their old gods and rituals remained the focus of civic and religious life and that their priesthood retained its elite status. With the Parthian conquest of Mesopotamia at the end of the 2nd century BCE, however, there is a drastic change. Cuneiform documentation disappears everywhere, except in Babylon, where the traditional religion appears to have survived somewhat longer, and as we reach the beginning of the common era archeological evidence for the abandonment of the old temples can be gathered from many sites. Religion in Mesopotamia then became increasingly syncretistic, a mixture of Assyrian, Babylonian, Persian, Greek, Aramean, and Jewish elements, and when the Sasanian Dynasty took over in the 3rd century CE the old religion was all but extinct. At the beginning of the 6th century CE, the Neoplatonist philosopher Damascius still accurately quotes the genealogy of primeval gods found at the beginning of the Babylonian epic of creation, but this was a final testimony to a now-vanished civilization.

BIBL.: Jeremy Black and Anthony Green, *Gods, Demons, and Symbols of Ancient Mesopotamia: An Illustrated Dictionary* (Austin, 1992). Jean Bottéro, *Religion in Ancient Mesopotamia* (Chicago, 2001). Édouard Dhorme, *Les religions de Babylonie et d'Assyrie* (Paris, 1945). Thorkild Jacobsen, *The Treasures of Darkness: A History of Mesopotamian Religion* (New Haven, 1976). A. Leo Oppenheim, *Ancient Mesopotamia: Portrait of a Dead Civilization* (rev. ed.; Chicago, 1977), chap. 4.

Syria and Canaan

David P. Wright

*T*he historical study of the religion of ancient Syria and Canaan (Syro-Canaanite, Syro-Palestinian, Northwest Semitic religion) is made difficult by the lack of documentary and material evidence from which to construct a clear and continuous image of religious ideas and practices. The textual evidence from the first three millennia BCE gives a general idea of the main ideas and their development of Northwest Semitic religion.

The earliest substantial sources pertaining to Syro-Canaanite religion come from finds at the ancient site of Ebla (modern Tell Mardikh), located halfway between the Mediterranean Sea and the Euphrates River in Syria. It was a significant city-state in the 24th century BCE. Although few of the two thousand complete or fragmentary texts discovered there pertain directly to religious matters and although the interpretation of the texts is still in flux, some basic features of Eblaite religion have emerged. About forty deities are mentioned in the tablets. A core of West Semitic deities is observable: Dagan, Hadda (the thunderer or storm-god; later Hadad), El, Belatu (the lady), Ashtar, Suinu (moon-god), UTU (sun-god), Kabkab (star), Kamish (later Chemosh), Malik, Rasap (later Rashpu/Reshep). The four city gates were named after the gods BE, Baal, Rasap, and UTU. The first two are probably to be identified as Dagan and Hadda, respectively, which shows the prominence of these deities.

The texts indicate that Ebla had several temples devoted to various gods that housed the statues of the deities. Some texts speak of the quantity of silver or gold used to make such statues. Animals as well as bread, beer, wine, and oil were offered to the gods. Objects of precious materials were also devoted to the deities. In addition, special feasts for different gods were distributed throughout the year. Some of these celebrations included processions parading the deity's statue. Besides the high liturgy of the temples and feasts, many incantations sought to bind demonic evil and to oppose serpents and scorpions.

Details about Northwest Semitic religion after the time of Ebla are lacking for almost a thousand years. Part of this gap is filled by evidence from the theophoric personal names borne by Amorites. The Amorites were pastoral groups attested at the end of the third and the beginning of the 2nd millennium BCE whose homeland appears to have been northwest of Mari along the middle Euphrates and lower Khabur rivers and in the surrounding steppe areas. While Amorite names cannot be counted on to indicate the specific religious propensity of the bearer, they can in a general way reflect the gods venerated near the time when they appear. The list of gods has resonances with the earlier Eblaite pantheon. The Amorite names from Mari around 1800 BCE, for example, show a frequent appearance of the gods Hadda, El, Dagan, and Lim (also attested earlier at Ebla). Amorite names are also found with Anat, Samas (later Shamash, the sun-god), Rasap, and perhaps Ashtar. The epithet or name Baal also appears in many names. The Ur III Amorite names from a few centuries earlier do not reflect as many West Semitic deities, but there are many with El and a few with Hadda.

Documentation of Northwest Semitic religion is much more abundant in the latter half of the 2nd millennium BCE. The major sources from this time are the texts and material finds from Ugarit (modern Ras Shamra), near the Mediterranean coast in Syria, and from surrounding areas. More than one thousand documents, dating to around the 13th century and written in Ugaritic, the native language of the region, have been unearthed. Because of the quantity of tablets, the breadth of genres, and their antiquity, this is presently the most important single corpus for the study of Northwest Semitic religion.

The main distinction in genres is between the narratives (myths and legends) and texts that describe or prescribe actual ritual practice (incantations, prayers, hymns, votive texts, god lists, festival catalogues, sacrificial lists, ritual prescriptions or descriptions). These two groups provide different kinds of information about Ugaritic religion. The longest narratives are the Baal myth cycle (*KTU* 1.1–6), a series of stories telling of Baal's rise in authority among the gods, and the stories of Aqhat (1.14–16) and Kirta (1.17–19), legends about childless patriarchal figures whom the gods bless with offspring. These stories are valuable for their insight into the context and motivation for various religious activities, such as religious feasting, sacrifice, prayer, temple building, funerary ritual, cursing, blessing, and healing. They explain the relationship between various gods, including conflicts between them, and reflect views about the gods' personalities. These texts also reflect on the nature of life, such as the importance of children, the immortality of the gods, and the mortality of humans. Because the religious practices described in the Aqhat and Kirta texts do not entirely agree with texts that describe actual ritual practice, they may reflect popular customs or customs of earlier times.

The texts pertaining to actual ritual practice reveal other dimensions of Ugaritic religion. The texts listing offerings to various gods and other lists of deities mention many more gods (probably more than one hundred) than do the narrative texts, and they show some variation in the order of the gods from one text to the next. The Sacrifice of Sapan (*CAT* 1.148) is a chief example of a royal sacrificial text. The occasion was one of about twenty "feasts of the king" (*dbú mlk;* cf. *CAT* 1.91). The text is essentially a list of sacrifices. The gods that appear at the head of the list are *ilib* (god-father, perhaps a dynastic deity), El, Dagan, and several Baal deities. Other major deities mentioned include Athirat, Sapan, Kothar, Shapsh, Yarikh, Anat, Rashp, and Yamm.

Other ritual texts are connected with the royal cult. One custom they illuminate is the revering of the dynasty's deceased kings. The kings were thought to live on as the *rapa'ūma,* associated with the underworld. They were incorporated quite fully into myth, ritual, and the standard theology of Ugarit. These dead kings were invoked alongside the main gods of the kingdom. They bring blessings to the nation and its people, and they are given offerings, with the other main gods (*KTU* 1.39, 48, 105, 106). *KTU* 1.108 may be a ritual celebrating the deification of the dead king. The beginning of the text can be read: "Lo! the *rap'u* [singular of *rapa'ūma*], the eternal king, has been established," referring to the dead king. Another text—perhaps a funeral liturgy—appears to treat the descent of the recently deceased king Niqmaddu to the netherworld (1.161). The *rapa'ūma* are invoked, offerings are made, and well-being is proclaimed for the new king and the kingdom.

Sacrifices and festivals were often for the benefit of the community or nation. A rather long text (*KTU* 1.40; cf. 1.84, 121, 122, 54) offers perspectives on sin and atonement (*npy,* sweeping away) for sin. At least two sheep and two donkeys, designated for "justification" (*mšr*), are offered for the sins of the men and women of Ugarit, the royal couple, and others, no matter what sin they may have committed.

Apart from sacrifice, humans made contact with the deities through prayer. A liturgy for the month *ib'lt* (*KTU* 1.119) prescribes the offering of sacrifices to Baal and other gods over a number of days. At the end it prescribes a prayer when the city is under attack: "O Baal, drive away the strong one from our gates . . . O Baal, we shall consecrate a bull [to you], we shall fulfill a vow. . . . We shall ascend to Baal's sanctuary, we shall walk the paths of Baal's temple." The result is that Baal will hear the prayer and ward off the enemy. The gods spoke to humans in dreams and symbolically through divination, specifically, through features present in animal innards, birth abnormalities, and astrological phenomena. A text giving instructions about curing a sick child may indicate that a cultic official of some sort was responsible for announcing an extended oracle (*KTU* 1.124; cf. 1.104). This curing of a sick child brings to mind other incantations against various evils, such as snakebite, demons, or the Evil Eye (*KTU* 1.100, 169, 96, respectively).

Excavations at Emar, located on the west side of the Euphrates where it takes its northward bend in Syria, have produced about 400 texts pertaining to religious matters and dating between 1340 and 1190 BCE. Most of these were found in a temple supervised by a diviner (LÚHAL). This diviner apparently was a cultic overseer of the larger region, and cultic practice proceeded rather independently of the monarchy. The documents include four major festival texts. The seven-day *zukru* rite was celebrated on the year's first new moon. It was performed for Emar's chief deity Dagan, whose main center of worship was in the middle Euphrates area. A main feature is a procession in which the god was taken outside the city. He passed between sacred stones anointed with oil and blood. These stones represented deities, constituting a council of the gods, as it were. The text includes a list of Emar's gods, nearly ninety lines long. Another festival is for the installation of the NIN.DINGIR, a priestess, in the temple service of the storm-god. This rite takes nine days and includes rites that transfer the woman from her father's domain to the temple. A third festival, lasting eight days, is for the installation of the *maš'artu* (another priestess) of Ashtart of Battle. Many of the activities take place at night, and the ritual is implicitly concerned with the idea of battle. Finally, many texts deal with *kissu* festivals for various deities. The one for Dagan lasted three days. These apparently are performed to acknowledge and honor the various deities.

There is some evidence that the people at Emar revered their dead ancestors by making offerings to them. This responsibility may be spelled out in legal documents, and a liturgy in the month of Abu may describe some of the offerings made to them. There is no clear evidence, however, that these ancestors were considered gods.

The fragmentary Hittite Elkunirsa myth (Hoffner 1998: 90–92), from the 13th century BCE, likely derives from a West Semitic original. It tells how the goddess Ashertu (= Athirat) asked the storm-god (= Baal) to sleep with her. He refused and told Elkunirsa, the husband of Ashertu. Elkunirsa is a Hittite transliteration of the West Semitic epithet of El, *qōnē'arṣ-* (creator/possessor of the earth) (e.g., *KAI* A iii 18). Baal disgraces her at Elkunirsa's instigation by killing dozens of her children. After a break in the text, Elkunirsa tells Ashertu to take Baal captive, but Anat-Astarte, Baal's sister, warns Baal. Nonetheless, Baal is injured and has to be magically healed and purified.

The religious tradition of the Phoenicians, the Northwest Semitic people whose homeland was on the Lebanon coast, begins to be firmly documented early in the 1st millennium BCE, although its roots go back into the 2nd millennium. Most of the Phoenician sources are dedicatory or building inscriptions that contain little information about religion. Some later non-Phoenician sources (e.g., the Hebrew Bible and classical, Hellenistic, and Christian writers) also contain information on Phoenician religion. The texts from the different cities in the Phoenician homeland reveal that each city had its own pantheon, continuing the tradition of particular gods being associated with particular cities. Two gods, a male and female pair, headed the pantheon of each city. The chief gods of Byblos were Baal-Shamem (perhaps identifiable with earlier Baal/Hadda) and Baalat (Lady of Byblos, perhaps identifiable with Anat) (*KAI* 4–7, 10); the chief gods of Sidon were Eshmun and Astarte (biblical Ashtoreth) (13–14); and the chief gods of Tyre were Melqart (the Tyrian form of Baal) and Astarte (see Esarhaddon's treaty with Tyre; *ANET* 533–34). Later classical tradition identified these with various Greek gods (e.g., Astarte = Aphrodite; Eshmun = Asclepius). Other gods were revered in each of the cities. The texts also reflect the Syro-Canaanite belief in a collectivity or assembly of gods (*KAI* 4). Phoenician religious ideas were carried throughout the

Mediterranean area and are found in Phoenician and Punic (i.e., the Phoenician language tradition of the Carthaginian Empire from the 5th century BCE on) inscriptions on the island and coastal sites.

Religious ideas were part of the royal ideology. A king may be described as legitimate "before the holy gods" (*KAI* 4). The gods make the kings rulers (10). Some kings were also priests (13), and some queens were also priestesses (14). Kings were responsible for building or rebuilding temples (14). Inscriptions on coffins of kings or officials show a concern about proper burial and respect for the dead (1, 10, 13–14, 30). The Tabnit inscription (13) describes opening the king's coffin as "an abomination of Astarte." Curses by the gods are often invoked against one who would open a sarcophagus, remove the body, or efface the accompanying inscription. These curses involve the destruction of one's posterity, not receiving a resting place with the shades (the *rp'm*, which are either the ghosts of all the dead or of the kings specifically, like the *rapa'ūma* at Ugarit), and not receiving proper burial. They imply a view of the afterlife where the dead are relatively inactive and where this life is the time of activity, reward, and punishment.

The tariffs speak of offerings and festivals. One text (*KAI* 37) lists expenditures for new moon festivals during two different months paid to officials and workers, such as the leader(?) of the new moon festival, masons, doorkeepers, singers, sacrificers, bakers, builders, and others. New moon and full moon festivals are mentioned in *KAI* 43. The 3rd-century BCE Marseilles Tariff (69; cf. 74–75), apparently originally made at Carthage and transported to France as ship ballast, describes animals used in different offerings in the temple of Baal-Saphon, a divine name known from Ugarit.

Many of the inscriptions are found in connection with objects devoted to the gods in fulfillment of a vow, as an offering to induce the god to bless the giver or as part of a building project. These objects include such things as statues of the giver (*KAI* 5–6, 43; Gibson 1982: 29), ornaments (*KAI* 25), maces (38), altars (43), walls (7), and various building structures (10). The gift of a throne to Astarte, flanked by two griffins (17), has been compared to the biblical ark of YHWH, mounted with two cherubim, which was considered a type of throne for that deity.

Child sacrifice was also practiced at times as part of Phoenician and Punic religion, especially at Carthage. Two inscriptions from Malta in the 6th century may be the earliest documentary evidence of the practice (*KAI* 61 A–B). The stelae were set up to Baal-Hammon (who became the chief god at Carthage; his consort was Tanit), the god generally associated with child sacrifice. This god appears to have been native to Phoenicia (*KAI* 24; Gibson 1982: 31) and later brought to Carthage, where he became the chief god (and identified with classical Cronus).

Roughly contemporary with early Phoenician texts are texts that provide data about the religion of the Arameans, the Northwest Semitic people of the area of ancient Syria. These sources are relatively meager, consisting mainly of royal building or dedicatory inscriptions from the 9th and 8th centuries BCE.

The chief deity of the Arameans was Hadad, the "thunderer" or storm-god, who can be identified with Baal (*KAI* 214, 222). Other chief deities included El, Shemesh (the sun-god), and Resheph (214). The inscription of Barhadad (201) found north of Aleppo from about 860 BCE venerates Melqart, a Phoenician deity. The inscription, in fact, follows a Phoenician model. Barhadad would have, nevertheless, officially worshiped Hadad.

The sparse inscriptions reflect the communication between deities and humans. The gods hear a king's prayer (*KAI* 201), and they communicate back to him. The Zakir (or Zakkur) Inscription describes how the king implored and received Baal-Shmayn's help against attacking enemies: "I lifted my hands to Baal-Sh[may]n; Baal-Shmay[n] answered me; Baal-Shmayn [spoke] to me by means of seers [*ḥzyn*] and prophets [*ʿddn*]; Baal-Shmayn [said to me]: 'Do not fear, for I have made you [king, and I will stan]d with you, and I will deliver you.'" This presupposes a rather elaborate way of ascertaining the divine will, with prophetic specialists and interpreters.

The texts show the intertwining of theology in royal ideology. The gods are the powers that make people kings and save them from enemies (*KAI* 202, 214). They bless the kings and fulfill their requests (214–17). They call upon kings to perform certain tasks (214). They enforce treaties made by kings (222–24). Aramean religion was taken up by foreigners who came to rule in the area (214–15). The Panammu text inscribed on a statue of Hadad (214) appears to refer to the veneration of dead kings, similar to the veneration of the *rapaʾūma* at Ugarit. It says that the person who sacrifices at the statue of Hadad is to "remember the ghost [*nbš*] of Panammu with [Ha]dad" by saying, "May [the gho]st of Panammu [eat] with you [Hadad], and may the [gh]ost of Panammu dri[nk] with you." Here the dead king receives sustenance along with the chief god.

Although the Aramaic texts say little about sacrifice, the Panammu text says that sacrifice was considered a meal given to the gods. The kings also give concrete objects to the gods. For example, Barhadad gives a statue of himself as a vow offering to Melqart (*KAI* 201). Other ritual practices included the enactment of analogical curses in a treaty ceremony. The Sefire Inscriptions (222–24), partly dependent upon Mesopotamian treaty forms, list hyperbolic descriptive curses to befall one who breaks the treaty stipulations. Then it lists simile curses that indicate that they were performed by the participants. For example, one clause says, "Just as this wax is burned with fire, so shall M[atiel] be burned [with fi]re."

The religion of Israel or the Hebrew Bible is another well-documented religious tradition of the 1st millennium BCE. It is important to realize that, although several cultural influences are discernable in Israelite/biblical religion, it is in the main an outgrowth of and part of Syro-Canaanite religion. The institutions and phenomena of temple, priesthood, sacrifice, sacrificial system, and prophecy are all Northwest Semitic in character. Even monotheistic Israelite monotheism may be seen as having a foundation in West Semitic religious notions, especially that where a city or national group recognized one deity as a chief among others. The Hebrew Bible retains the notion of multiple supernatural beings subordinate to and appearing in council with the chief god (1 Kings 22.19–23; Isa. 6.1–10). The Israelite god YHWH was given the attributes of Northwest Semitic gods and was identified, for example, as El.

Other traditions are less well attested in the 1st millennium. Only two important texts and traditions require mention here. The Mesha Inscription (ca. 850 BCE) is the major source of information about Moabite religion. It may have been written to celebrate the building of a shrine (or high place, *bmt*) to the chief Moabite god Chemosh, known already at Ebla and in the placename Carchemish. The text describes the ritual slaughter of enemies in battle (*ḥrm*) in dedication to the deity, also a biblical practice. Mesha places "before Chemosh" the "implements of YHWH" that he takes as booty. According to the Bible, Mesha sacrificed his son so that his god would save him from Israelite attack (2 Kings 3.27). Finally, the Mesha Inscription may imply an institutional means of conveying the divine word (prophecy?) when it says that Chemosh spoke to Mesha.

The other text is the difficult and fragmentary inscription from Deir Allah (about 700 BCE, found on the east side of the middle course of the Jordan River), written in a unique Northwest Semitic dialect (with similarities to Aramaic; see Hackett 1980; Levine 2000: 241–75). It tells of a vision of Balaam son of Beor, who was "seer of the gods" (cf. Num. 22–24). The gods visit Balaam at night in council, of whom El is chief. They tell him, and Balaam tells the people, that the gods will punish the land with darkness for the unnatural (i.e., socially inverted) behavior of people and animals. The second part of the text is hard to understand and may be independent of the first. It has been suggested, however, that it may deal with offering a child sacrifice in response to the gods' punishment in the first part of the text.

Syro-Canaanite religion can be best summed up as a belief in a group of deities or supernatural beings that were immanent in the natural world, although generally hidden from human view. Their powers were manifested through natural phenomena and in political and military acts of the rulers or kings whom they chose and supported. The gods and humans related in a master-servant relationship. The gods provided blessing and support to the people, and the people were expected to serve the deities, with various gifts and lavish praise. Offending the deities could anger them and bring catastrophe to humans. In large part, these religious ideas were a metaphorical construction from social and political relationships in the human world. This tradition is the heritage of modern Judaism and Christianity, whose theologies today continue to reflect aspects of Syro-Canaanite religion.

BIBL.: Mark W. Chavalas (ed.), *Emar: The History, Religion, and Culture of a Syrian Town in the Late Bronze Age* (Bethesda, Md.: CDL, 1996). J. Andrew Dearman (ed.), *Studies in the Mesha Inscription and Moab* (Society of Biblical Literature Archaeology and Biblical Studies 2; Atlanta: Scholars Press/ASOR, 1989). Daniel E. Fleming, *Time at Emar: The Cultic Calendar and the Rituals from the Diviner's House*

(Mesopotamian Civilizations 11; Winona Lake, Ind.: Eisenbrauns, 2000). Jonas Greenfield, "Aspects of Aramean Religion," in *Ancient Israelite Religion* (ed. Patrick D. Miller Jr., Paul D. Hanson, and S. Dean McBride; Philadelphia: Fortress, 1987), 67–78. Jo Ann Hackett, *Balaam Text from Deir 'Alla* (Harvard Semitic Monographs 31; Chico, Calif.: Scholars Press, 1980). Baruch Levine, *Numbers 21–36* (Anchor Bible 4A; New York: Doubleday, 2000). Glenn E. Markoe, *Phoenicians* (Peoples of the Past; Berkeley: University of California Press, 2000). Gregorio del Olmo Lete, *Canaanite Religion according to the Liturgical Texts of Ugarit* (trans. Wilfred G. E. Watson; Bethesda, Md.: CDL, 1999). Robert R. Stieglitz, "Ebla and the Gods of Canaan," in *Eblaitica: Essays on the Ebla Archives and Eblaite Language* (ed. Cyrus H. Gordon and Gary A. Rendsburg; Winona Lake, Ind.: Eisenbrauns, 1990), 2.79–89.

Israel

John J. Collins

*T*he religion of ancient Israel is known primarily from the Hebrew Bible, but archeological discoveries, as well as critical examination of the biblical text, suggest a different history of its development.

The biblical account

According to the Bible, Abraham came from Mesopotamia at some time in the 2nd millennium BCE and lived a seminomadic life in the land later known as Israel. He built altars in various places and worshiped the god El in various manifestations. In the fourth generation, his descendants went down to Egypt and were enslaved there, but escaped miraculously in the exodus under the leadership of Moses. Moses had already encountered the god of his forefathers on a mountain in Midian, south of Israel, under a new name, YHWH. In a revelation at Mount Sinai, this god gave Moses a code of laws that became the basis of a covenant. Israel was obligated to serve YHWH alone and to obey strict ethical and ritual commandments. After the death of Moses, the Israelites invaded the land of Israel and slaughtered its Canaanite inhabitants. With the rise of a monarchy (about 1000 BCE) the Mosaic religion was contaminated with customs and cults from the surrounding peoples. When the kingdom divided in two after the death of King Solomon, pagan influence was especially strong in the northern kingdom (Israel). Various prophets railed against the worship of deities other than YHWH. After the northern kingdom was destroyed by the Assyrians (722 BCE), the southern kingdom of Judah underwent a reform in the reign of King Josiah (621 BCE) and restored the observance of the law of Moses. This kingdom was brought to an end by the Babylonians in 586 BCE, and large numbers were deported to Babylon. Some fifty years later, however, the exiles were allowed to return and restore the religion of Moses in Judah.

Critical reconstruction

The consensus of archeologists at the beginning of the 21st century is that the early Israelites evolved within the land and culture of Canaan. There is no archeological evidence that they came from either Mesopotamia or Egypt. If the story of the exodus has a historical basis, it can account for only a small segment of the Israelite population. The god El, worshiped by Abraham and later identified with YHWH, was the high god of the Canaanite pantheon. It is clear from the Bible that many Israelites worshiped the Canaanite god Baal, who was YHWH's archrival. The theophanies of YHWH in the Bible (e.g., on Mount Sinai) are described in language that is very similar to descriptions of Baal in the Ugaritic texts. The biblical insistence that Israel serve only YHWH is highly unusual in the ancient world. Some scholars have supposed that it was influenced by the example of the 14th-century Egyptian pharaoh Akhenaten, who tried to suppress the worship of deities other than the sun-god Aten. There are some points of affinity between YHWH and Aten in the Bible, most notably in Ps. 104, which has many parallels to the Egyptian Hymn to Aten. But solar imagery is relatively rare in the Bible. YHWH is far more often depicted as a storm-god, in accordance with Canaanite imagery.

The earliest depictions of YHWH in the Hebrew Bible associate him with the region of Midian south of Israel. It may be that his cult was brought northward to Israel by people who had escaped slavery in Egypt, or it may have been spread by Midianite traders. In Israel, however, YHWH was no longer worshiped primarily as a storm-god, but as the god who brought the people Israel into existence. In northern Israel, his role was celebrated chiefly in connection with the exodus from Egypt. In contrast, the exodus became central to the Jerusalem cult only in the reform of Josiah in the 7th century BCE. The Jerusalem cult centered on the kingship of YHWH, which was reflected on earth in the rule of the Davidic Dynasty. YHWH had promised David that one of his sons would always sit on the throne in Jerusalem (2 Sam. 7). The Jerusalem temple was regarded as "the holy habitation of the Most High" (Ps. 46.4 [= 46.5 Hebrew]). The presence of YHWH in his temple ensured the protection of the city.

One of the distinctive features of Israelite religion in the biblical account is the absence of goddess worship. It now appears, however, that the goddess Asherah was worshiped widely, both in Israel and in Judah. An inscription from the 8th century BCE in a tomb at Khirbet el-Qom, near Hebron, south of Jerusalem, reads, "May Uriyahu be blessed by YHWH, from his enemies he has saved him by his Asherah." Another inscription from Kuntillet Ajrud, a stopover for caravans in the Sinai desert, has a blessing formula, ending with the words "by YHWH of Samaria and his Asherah." (Samaria was the capital of the northern kingdom of Israel.) Some scholars deny that Asherah is the name of a goddess in these inscriptions, since the possessive pronoun is not usually used with a proper name. They suggest that the reference is to a wooden image of some kind, a pole or tree, that is mentioned some forty times in the Hebrew Bible. But the wooden image was a symbol of the goddess, and so the inscriptions testify to the worship of Asherah in any case. Moreover, numerous figurines of a nude female figure, presumably a fertility-goddess, have been found by archeologists all over Israel and Judah. We also know that a goddess called Anatyahu (YHWH's Anat) was worshiped by a Jewish community in Elephantine in southern Egypt in the 5th century BCE. The Bible records that "the queen of heaven" was worshiped in Judah at the time of the Babylonian crisis in the early 6th century BCE (Jer. 7.18; 44.18).

The Bible does not deny that the people of Israel and Judah worshiped deities other than YHWH, including goddesses. It represents that worship, however, as violation of a covenant that had been formulated by Moses at the beginning of Israel's history. Scholars are divided, however, as to the antiquity of the Mosaic covenant. It finds its clearest expression in the Book of Deuteronomy, which was formulated at the time of King Josiah's reform in the late 7th century BCE. The 8th-century prophets (Amos, Hosea) presuppose that the exodus was being celebrated in northern Israel. The prophets clearly assume that the delivery from Egypt entailed obligations for the Israelites, but it is clear that most people did not share that view. Whether the prophets based their preaching on ancient traditions about a covenant or contributed to the development of the covenant idea is hard to decide. In any case, it is clear that during the period of the two kingdoms (approximately 922–722 BCE) only a small minority of Israelites restricted their worship to YHWH alone.

The phenomenon of prophecy was known throughout the ancient Near East, but the corpus of biblical prophecy has no parallel in the ancient world. There were hundreds of prophets in Israel and Judah at any given time. Most of these lent their support to the policies of the kings and to popular views. The prophets whose oracles are preserved in the Bible are exceptional. Not only do they flout popular opinion by railing against the worship of deities other than YHWH, but they also hold both king and people accountable to a strict moral standard. They are particularly outspoken on the subject of social justice and the abuse of the poor. They are also scathing on what they perceive as the abuse of cultic worship. For most people, the worship of a god was expressed through prayer and the offering of sacrifices. The more valuable the offering, the greater the devotion of the worshiper was assumed to be. Human sacrifice was practiced on occasion, even by kings. The prophets argued that all such gestures were empty if they did not lead to the practice of justice. "I hate, I despise your feasts," said Amos (5.21). "For I desire steadfast love and not sacrifice," said Hosea (6.6), "the knowledge of God, rather than burnt offerings." It is not clear whether these prophets thought that there should be no sacrificial cult. Such a view would have been extraordinary in the ancient world. But at least they thought that the cult as practiced was counterproductive. It gave people illusory confidence that they were serving God when in fact they were not.

Deuteronomic reform

The religion of Israel was transformed by the reform of King Josiah in 621 BCE (2 Kings 22–23). The central element in this reform was the centralization of the cult of YHWH. Henceforth no sacrifices were to be offered outside the Jerusalem temple. Josiah's troops tore down other altars that existed around the country. The worship of Canaanite deities (Baal, Asherah) was suppressed, and the place where human sacrifices were offered was destroyed. But even legitimate offerings to YHWH were no longer allowed outside Jerusalem. This reform was authorized by a "book of the law" allegedly found in the Jerusalem temple. This book evidently corresponded to some form of the Book of Deuteronomy. (See especially Deut. 12, which demands that sacrifice be restricted to one site, which YHWH would choose.) While this book purported to contain the laws of Moses, its formulation is influenced by the language and concepts of Assyrian treaties of the 7th century BCE, and it cannot have been composed before that time.

Josiah's reform laid the basis for great changes in the worship of YHWH. If sacrifice could be offered only in Jerusalem, then people who lived at a distance from the city could make offerings only on special occasions. The Jerusalem temple retained its importance, although Deuteronomic theology downplayed the presence of YHWH by saying that he made *his name* to dwell there. Since Jerusalem was now the only place of cultic worship, the temple was arguably more important than ever. New importance, however, was attached to "the book of the law." In earlier times, law (Torah) was taught orally by priests or was passed on by judges and elders in the gates of the cities. Now it was written in a book. Consequently, scribes became very important. These were the people who could read and write and who controlled what was actually contained in the book. Modern scholars hold that the book of the law was expanded several times in the century after Josiah's reforms. Even in antiquity, however, people were aware that scribes tampered with sacred writings. Less than a generation after Josiah's reform, the prophet Jeremiah complained bitterly: "How can you say, 'We are wise, and the law of the LORD is with us'? But, behold, the false pen of the scribes has made it into a lie" (Jer. 8.8).

Josiah's reforms were not immediately successful. He himself met an early death at the hands of the Egyptians in 609 BCE. The prophets Jeremiah and Ezekiel claimed that worship of other deities was widespread during the Babylonian crisis at the beginning of the 6th century. But the long-term impact of the reforms was ensured by the Babylonian exile. The exiles could not take their temple to Babylon, but they could take the book of the law. From this time forward, large numbers of people of Judean descent lived outside their native land. (This phenomenon is called the Diaspora.) Consequently Judaism developed as a religion that was independent of its geographical location. This development was greatly facilitated by the book of the law. Eventually, the synagogue (a house of prayer and study) and other community events would re-

place the temple as the focus of the religious life of most Jews. This development would not be complete for several centuries, but its root was already
present in the Babylonian exile.

Second Temple period

The Jerusalem temple was rebuilt approximately fifty years after its destruction. Life and religion in the period of the Second Temple, however, were different from what they had been before.

There was no longer a king in Jerusalem. Immediately after the restoration,
authority was shared by a governor and the high priest. Later, the high priest
was de facto ruler under the foreign overlord. While the high priests were often
quite worldly, their prominence guaranteed that the temple cult was a focal
point of Jewish religious life.

The concept of a normative "book of the law" had been introduced by
Josiah. During the exile, or in the following century, this Torah was expanded
to include the foundational traditions about the patriarchs and the exodus
and also to incorporate extensive priestly traditions. The priestly code, typified
by the Book of Leviticus, was concerned with ritual matters, such as regulations for sacrifices, and also with issues of purity. Many of these laws may have
been quite old, but they became much more prominent in the Second Temple
period. Matters that had primarily concerned priests at an earlier time were
now deemed to be binding on all Jews. After the Babylonian exile, some distinctive (though not all unique) observances came increasingly to define Judaism. These included the observance of the sabbath, the circumcision of male
children, dietary laws that forbade the eating of pork among other things, and
the prohibition of marriage with non-Jews (Gentiles).

The impact of the priestly legislation is seen most clearly in the reform of
Ezra, which should probably be dated to 458 BCE. Ezra was authorized by the
Persian king to implement the law of "the God of heaven" in Jerusalem (Ezra
1.2), in accordance with a Persian policy of codifying local laws and enforcing
them. (Ezra is sometimes regarded as the final editor of the Torah or Pentateuch, but this is uncertain.) He was horrified to discover that Jewish men, descendants of the exiles, had married women from outside the community, so
that "the holy race has mixed itself with the peoples of the lands" (9.2). Ezra
insisted that they divorce the foreign women and send them away, with their
children. Underlying this action was the concern for the preservation of a pure
and distinct community, which could be eroded by assimilation to the neighboring peoples. It was by such means that Judaism preserved its identity, while
neighboring peoples (Moabites, Edomites, etc.) gradually disappeared from
history.

Not all Judeans conformed to Ezra's strict interpretation of the Torah. Other
writings of the Second Temple period (Nehemiah, Malachi) complain of lax

observance and widespread abuses. Ezra represents one tendency in Second Temple Judaism that would become increasingly prominent in the Hellenistic period. But there was considerable diversity in Judaism throughout this period.

One source of diversity lay in different responses to neighboring cultures. After the conquests of Alexander the Great, Greek culture exercised a great fascination for many people in the Near East. In the 2nd century BCE, some people in Jerusalem set about promoting Greek culture in Jerusalem, with a view to breaking down the separation of Jew and Gentile. According to 2 Maccabees, this led to neglect of the temple cult, and some people even went so far as to disguise the marks of their circumcision. The motives of the reformers were not entirely idealistic. The leaders, Jason and Menelaus, outbid each other for the high priesthood and eventually engaged in civil war. At that point the king, Antiochus IV Epiphanes, intervened and attempted to suppress by force the observance of the traditional law. The religious persecution that resulted was a rare phenomenon in antiquity, and there is no consensus as to the king's motivation. The persecution led to the Maccabean revolt, which resulted in the establishment of a native Jewish kingship under the Hasmonean Dynasty, which lasted for a century. The Hasmonean kings also acted as high priests, despite severe criticism from some parties.

The conflict in the Maccabean era is often depicted as a clash between Judaism and Hellenism, as if Hellenistic customs were incompatible with Jewish religion. This is a misconception. The revolt was not provoked by the introduction of Greek customs (typified by the building of a gymnasium) but by the persecution of people who observed the Torah by having their children circumcised and refusing to eat pork. The Hasmoneans embraced Greek customs in many ways, even while forcing some conquered people to be circumcised. Moreover, while the Maccabees fought to defend the right of Jews to observe their traditional laws, they themselves were willing to make an exception to the law, by fighting on the sabbath. They were not, then, strict purists in the matter of legal observance.

After the Maccabean revolt, however, we see the rise of sectarian movements devoted to the strict observance of the Torah. The most influential of these were the Pharisees, who attached great importance to oral tradition, which specified how the law should be interpreted. The name Pharisee means "separated" and reflects their tendency to eat apart from less-observant Jews. A still-stricter form of Judaism is found in the Dead Sea Scrolls from Qumran, in writings that are usually attributed to the Essenes. These people went further than the Pharisees in separating themselves from the rest of Judaism, and they appear to have been bitter enemies of the Pharisees, although they shared many of the same concerns. Many of the reasons that led to the separation of the Essenes from the rest of Judaism had to do with purity, but they also seem to have had a different calendar, which made participation in the temple cult impossible.

Not all Jews of this era were preoccupied with purity, however. The Saddu-

cees rejected the oral Torah, and with it the stricter interpretations of the Pharisees, and continued to observe a more-traditional form of Judaism, centered on
the temple cult. Jews in the Diaspora, especially in Egypt, paid remarkably
little attention to purity issues, if we may judge by the writings that have survived. These writings enter into an extensive dialogue with Greek traditions
and sometimes present Judaism as a philosophical school, analogous to the
Stoics or the Platonists (so especially Philo of Alexandria, in the 1st century
CE). To a great degree, they emphasize the common ground shared by Jews
and Gentiles, but there remain some characteristic positions that set Jews
apart. Most fundamental of these is the rejection of idolatry and the insistence
that only the one God should be worshiped. Jewish authors typically inveigh
against homosexuality, which was widespread in the Hellenistic world. Only
rarely, however, do they mention the Jewish dietary laws, and when they do
they provide an allegorical interpretation to suggest that the laws are really
about the practice of virtue. We know from Philo that some Jews thought it
sufficient to pursue the allegorical meaning of these laws. Philo himself insisted
that they should also be observed in their literal sense. These writings, however, may reflect a rather rarified, intellectual, stratum of Jewish society. Greek
and Latin authors who comment on Judaism typically emphasize its distinctive
aspects: circumcision, sabbath observance, the dietary laws. It is likely, then,
that most Jews continued to observe the traditional practices, despite the attempts of people such as Philo to reinterpret the religion in philosophical
terms.

One other aspect of Second Temple Judaism should be noted: the development of apocalypticism. The apocalyptic writings first appear in the Hellenistic
period, especially around the time of the Maccabean revolt. They might be described as prophecy in a new key. They are not attributed to their actual authors, but to ancient figures such as Enoch and Daniel, who allegedly received
revelations in visions or in the course of guided tours of otherworldly regions.
The revelations include many mysteries of the heavenly world, but also concern the end of history and the judgment of the dead.

The apocalyptic writings are important for several reasons. It is here that we
first encounter a clear belief in the judgment of the individual dead in Jewish
tradition. (Another form of this belief developed separately a little later in the
Greek-speaking Diaspora, in connection with the philosophical idea of the immortality of the soul.) The idea that the end of history can be predicted had
long-lasting and fateful consequences in Western history and gave rise to numerous millenarian movements. Apocalyptic expectations played a major role
in the development of early Christianity. In the context of Second Temple Judaism, apocalyptic writings were often associated with sectarian movements,
which claimed to have a special revelation, above and beyond the Torah of
Moses. The community of the Dead Sea Scrolls (the Essenes) has often been
called an apocalyptic community, with considerable justification, as it too
claimed to have special revelations, which concerned both the heavenly world
and the end of history.

Rabbinic Judaism

Second Temple Judaism came to a disastrous end in the late 1st and early 2nd centuries CE in the course of three revolts against Roman rule. The first, in 66–70 CE, ended in the destruction of the Jerusalem temple, the great unifying symbol of Judaism, which has never been rebuilt. The second, in the years 115–18 CE, took place in Egypt and ended in the virtual annihilation of the Jewish community there. The third, in 132–35 CE, led by Bar Kochba, whom some people took for a messiah, was something of an aftershock. Any hopes that Jews might have had of regaining their independence had been dashed decisively in the earlier revolts.

The survival of Judaism as a religious way of life was due primarily to groups of rabbis in Galilee and Babylonia who devoted themselves to the study and elaboration of the scriptures. They accepted a limited canon of writings, which we now know as the Hebrew Bible. (This canon may have been held by the Pharisees before 70 CE, but the first references to a fixed number of writings come from the last decade of the 1st century CE.) The rabbinic canon included no apocalyptic writings except the Book of Daniel, although some others, such as the books of Enoch and Jubilees, appear to have enjoyed authority with the Dead Sea sect. Neither did the rabbis preserve numerous writings that survived in Greek and Latin translations and are now found in the Apocrypha, although some, such as 1 Maccabees and the Book of Ben Sira, were originally composed in Hebrew. Much of the religious diversity that characterized Second Temple Judaism was lost and survived only in translations preserved by Christians or in the scrolls hidden in caves by the Dead Sea.

The deliberations of the rabbis were eventually codified in the Mishnah (late 2nd century CE) and in the Babylonian and Jerusalem Talmuds, some centuries later. These are primarily legal expositions of the Torah, but they are not legalistic in the narrow sense. They preserve the debates among the rabbis and often include dissenting opinions. The kind of religion they represent has been well described as "covenantal nomism": the law is understood in the context of the whole relationship between God and Israel, not just as a measuring stick for individual performance. While rabbinic Judaism always has its starting point in the Torah, there is plenty of room for imagination and for the preservation of tradition in the biblical commentaries or midrashim, compiled between the 4th and 12th centuries CE. Even the mythological traditions associated with apocalyptic literature survived and reappear centuries later in the midrashim and in the mystical literature (Hekhalot). The main achievement of rabbinic Judaism, however, was to construct a body of commentary on the Torah that defined Judaism as a way of life that has endured down to the present day.

BIBL.: R. Albertz, *A History of Israelite Religion in the Old Testament Period* (2 vols.; Louisville: Westminster, 1994). F. M. Cross, *Canaanite Myth and Hebrew Epic* (Cambridge: Harvard University Press, 1973). P. D. Miller, *The Religion of Ancient Israel* (Louisville: Westminster John Knox, 2000). E. P. Sanders, *Judaism: Practice and Belief, 63 BCE–66 CE* (Philadelphia: Trinity, 1992).

Anatolia: Hittites

David P. Wright

*H*ittite religion is a blend of diverse cultural streams. While it includes features from the immigrant Indo-European peoples linguistically attested by the Hittite language, its main foundation consists of Hattian traditions, that is, of the people living in central Anatolia prior to the arrival of the Indo-Europeans. Furthermore, over time, it adopted beliefs and practices from Hurrian (the people of north Mesopotamia and Syria) as well as Akkado-Sumerian and Syrian religion. This amalgam is richly attested in the thousands of documents found at Bogazköy, Turkey, the site of Hattusha, the ancient Hittite capital. A large percentage of the six hundred plus individual works discovered pertain directly or indirectly to religious matters. The relevant genres include myths, hymns, prayers, festival prescriptions, rituals, divination texts, treaties, cultic inventories, and other administrative texts. Most of the texts date to the latest period of Hittite history (the Hittite Empire or New Kingdom, ca. 1350–1200 BCE), though there are many texts from the earlier periods (the so-called Middle Kingdom, ca. 1400–1350; and the Old Kingdom, ça. 1650–1400). This allows scholars to determine with some confidence the development of religious ideas and institutions. The textual evidence is complemented by archeological data, including the remains of temples, pictorial reliefs (especially at the Yazılıkaya shrine), seals, divine statues and symbols, and cult objects.

The Hittite pantheon grew in complexity over time, owing to the contributions from various cultural traditions. The Hittites were aware of the ethnic origin of their deities and provided them at times with worship in their native languages (Hattic, Hurrian, Luwian, Palaic, and Akkadian). The Hattian basis of the religious system is seen in the Old Hittite pantheon, which retained many Hattian deities. These include a storm-god (Taru), a sun-goddess (the "Sun-goddess of Arinna," later identified as Wurusemu), a sun-god (Estan), Inar (Hittite Inara), Telipinu (a vegetation-god), Halmasuit (a throne-goddess), Wurunkatte (a war-god), plus many other, lesser deities. The storm-god (called the Storm-god of Hatti) and the sun-goddess of Arinna presided as a divine pair over the pantheon. The prominence of a sun-goddess may be partly a reflection of a long-standing Anatolian tradition of a female fertility-goddess or mother-goddess, which is attested four millennia earlier at Çatal Höyük (south central Anatolia) and in the 1st millennium in Phrygia and Lycia. One early Hittite god was Sius, god of heaven and light, a term later used as the general Hittite word for god. This is cognate with Indo-European *diēu-s, which is found in the Greek word Zeus and Latin deus (god).

The Hittite pantheon grew by the addition of Hurrian as well as Mesopotamian deities (sometimes in Hurrian guise), especially starting around 1400 BCE (the time of Tudkhaliya II and his wife Nikkalmati, whose name is Hurrian) and mainly as a result of the campaigns of Shuppiluliuma I (ca. 1344–1322) into southern lands under Hurrian influence, including Syria. The main imported Hurrian gods included Teshub (the chief storm-god), Hepat (consort of Teshub), Kumarbi (a grain and fertility deity, also associated with the underworld), Sauska (a Hurrian Ishtar), and Simegi (sun-god). Hurrianized Mesopotamian gods who entered the pantheon include Ea, Damkina, Anu, and Enlil. In many cases borrowing was syncretistic. For example, Teshub was equated with the Storm-god of Hatti and Hepat with the sun-goddess of Arinna. Pudukhepa, wife of Hattushili III (ca. 1267–1237) and a priestess from the Hurrian-influenced land of Kizzuwatna, south of the Hittite homeland, explicitly makes the latter identification at the beginning of a prayer: "O Sun-goddess of Arinna, you are queen of all the lands. In the land of Hatti you go by the name of the Sun-goddess of Arinna, but in the land which you made cedar, you go by the name Hepat" (CTH 384; KUB 21.27 1.3–6; cf. ANET 393).

Treaties from the time of Shuppiluliuma I onward provide the most extensive list of deities and reflect a tendency toward theological systematization. The treaties show a fixed order in the deities, starting with the sun-god of heaven and the Sun-goddess of Arinna. These are followed by various storm-gods of various cult centers (e.g., Hattusha, Nerik, Samuha), followed in turn by various other groups of gods, including Babylonian gods, local deities, netherworld deities, and natural phenomena (mountains, rivers, springs). Despite the move toward a systematic listing of the gods, it was not complete. Some significant deities are missing, including the chief Storm-god of Hatti, whom one might expect to appear at the top of the list in association with the sun-goddess of Arinna. The inclusion of local pantheons in such lists shows that their maintenance was partly responsible for the multiplication of the Hittite gods. From about this time in Hittite history we begin to see the concept of "the thousand gods of Hatti," an indication of the compound nature of the pantheon (the actual number of known divine names is just over six hundred). The complexity of the Hittite pantheon at this period can be seen in the Prayer of Muwattalli II (ca. 1295–1272; CTH 381; cf. Singer 1996), which contains the longest list of deities in any single text (140 gods). Further systematization of the pantheon came with the development of male and female series (kalutis), mainly employed in the distribution of offerings. This bifurcated series is visually attested in the parade of deities carved into rock walls of the main chamber of the Yazılıkaya shrine. The reliefs date from the time of Tudkhaliya IV (ca. 1227–1209) and reflect the highly Hurrianized form of Hittite religion. The female gods are led by Hepat, and the male gods by Teshub. These two chief deities meet face to face.

Just as the pantheon derives in large part from Hattian and Hurrian sources, so too Hittite myths mainly derive from these two cultural sources, though there is a handful of myths with Hittite origins (the Tale of Kanes and Zalpa and the Tale of Appu). Both Hattian and Hurrian myths are, in general, concerned with negative and positive effects of deities on the cosmos. But they otherwise have distinct characteristics. The Hattian myths are generally simple and less artistic than the Hurrian myths, and they have connections with ritual performances or festivals. These include the Illuyanka myth, which is connected with the spring *purulli* festival. One version of this story tells how Inara, with the help of a human named Hupasiya, defeats a serpent who had defeated the storm-god. Many other myths deal with the disappearance of deities, such as Telipinu, the storm-god, the sun-god, and the moon-god. These myths are generally part of a ritual scheme in which offerings are made, often with the accompaniment of magical motifs and techniques, in order to find, appease, and return the deities. The mythical portions of these texts often describe the destructive effects of the gods' disappearance upon the land and the felicitous consequences of their return.

The Hurrian myths became part of Hittite culture mainly as part of the influx of Hurrian religious ideas from the Middle Kingdom and afterward. These are more artistic in character than the Hattian myths and are called songs. The Kumarbi Cycle of tales includes the Song of Kumarbi (also known as the Theogony or Kingship in Heaven), Song of the god LAMMA, Song of Silver, Song of Hedammu, and Song of Ullikummi. These myths describe the struggle for divine kingship between Kumarbi and Teshub, whom Kumarbi gave birth to as the result of biting off and swallowing the testicles of Anu, his older royal adversary. The stories are similar to the Ugaritic cycle of Baal myths, which describes Baal's struggle for divine power, and the Akkadian *Enuma Elish*, which describes Marduk's struggle for supremacy among the Babylonian gods. Indeed, Hurrian tradition appears indebted to Mesopotamian tradition for the idea of a theogony with successive generations of gods. Another myth-related text is the Song of Release, which exists in Hittite translation alongside the Hurrian (the Hurrian text may go back to a Syrian original). It begins with praise of Teshub, Allani (in Hittite called the sun-goddess of the underworld), and the Syrian goddess Ishhara. It also contains a series of ethical parables in the wisdom genre, a description of a feast for Teshub in the underworld, and Teshub's ordering the release of debts in Ebla (related to the Mesopotamian and biblical custom of releasing debts).

The gods were represented by images or by symbols, such as standing stones. Their images and symbols were generally housed in numerous temples throughout the kingdom. Temples were not just religious institutions, but integral parts of the economy because they employed a large number of people and held land. Temples contained storerooms for foods, valuables, and archived documents. In the capital city Hattusha several temples, large and small, have been discovered. The largest is devoted to the storm-god and contains a dual chamber for him and his consort the Sun-goddess of Arinna. Being the abode of the deities, the temples were to be kept pure. Priests, including the king during festivals, and other visitors were required to purify themselves before entering the sacred precincts. Certain animals could pollute the temple. For example, the Instructions for Temple Officials warn, "For you, let the place of broken bread be swept and sprinkled [i.e., purified]. Let not a pig or dog cross the threshold!" (*CTH* 264; KUB 13.4 3.59–60; cf. *ANET* 207–10). A bit later it warns kitchen personnel: "If the implements of wood and implements of fired clay which you hold—if a pig or dog ever approach [them], but the kitchen official does not throw them away [and] he gives to the god to eat from an unclean [vessel], then to him the gods will give excrement and urine to eat and drink" (3.64–68). Guards were posted to keep out such animals and unauthorized individuals.

A unique type of shrine is found at Yazılıkaya, three-quarters of a mile northeast of Bogazköy. It operated as a sanctuary from before the Old Kingdom and may have·been considered sacred in part because of a spring that flowed there. It gained particular prominence late in Hittite history under Tudkhaliya IV. The area consists basically of a rocky structure with crevices or open-air passages between rock walls. A temple was built in front of this natural maze. Reliefs carved on the walls of the passageways celebrate the gods as well as, implicitly, Tudkhaliya's kingship (his figure is found three times in the sculptures). The purpose of this shrine is not known, although it may have been used in the annual festivals. Some suggest that it was used specifically in new year ceremonies or that it was the mortuary temple of Tudkhaliya.

Offerings were mainly made to the gods at temples. These consisted of foods, for example, meats, breads, grain preparations, honey, oil, fermented drinks. As in most cases throughout the ancient Near East, offerings were a meal presented to the deities, to thank and praise them, to induce them to perform certain actions for the offerer's benefit, or to appease their wrath. This system operated on the analogy of feasting and offering gifts to a political superior to elicit his or her favor. The Instructions to Temple Officials make this metaphor clear: "Are the minds of man and the gods somehow different? No! Even here [in regard to their respective meals]? No! The[ir] minds are the same. When a servant stands up before his master he is washed and wears clean clothing, [then] either he gives him [the master] [something] to eat, or he gives him something to drink. Then when he, his master, eats [and] drinks, he is relieved in his mind" (KUB 13 1.21–26; *ANET* 207).

Killing the animal and manipulating its blood were generally unimportant in Hittite sacrifice, as opposed to biblical custom. Theories of sacrifice that focus on the killing of the animal as the central act or even a significant act therefore do not seem to help explain its meaning among the Hittites. Nevertheless, blood was occasionally offered to chthonic deities. Blood was also used for purification, such as to cleanse a temple and divine image (*CTH* 481; KUB 29.4 4.38–40) and apparently a new birth stool (*CTH* 476; KBo 5.1 1.25–26).

Festivals were occasions when offerings were made in great number. The importance of festivals can be partly seen in their making up the largest group of texts discovered at Bogazköy. Unfortunately we do not have a text that lays out the liturgical calendar systematically. The texts generally describe individual festivals. The main festivals were the AN.TAḪ.ŠUM (Festival of the Crocus Plant) in the spring and the *nutarriyashas* (Festival of Haste [?]) in the autumn. The former lasted thirty-eight days, and the latter lasted more than twenty-one. Other major festivals include the *purulli* (in the spring), the KI.LAM (season unknown, perhaps autumn), and the *(h)isuwas* (a late addition to the liturgy from Hurrian influence). The king, as chief priest, presided in the main festivals. Part of his responsibility included making procession to various local shrines at which ceremonies were held, as well as traveling to the several shrines in various cities to make offerings to the local gods. While the king's attention to cultic matters may appear to us to have been excessive, the purpose of the festivals was no doubt political in nature. By maintaining the various cults in the kingdom, the king shored up the unity of the kingdom and engendered support for his rule. Apart from offerings, festivals included purification rites to ensure the fitness of the king and other participants. They were also occasions for entertainment, including music and even competitive races and other athletic events. All of these activities helped secure the gods' attention, continuing presence, and favor.

The Hittite corpus contains a rather large number of rituals performed as occasion required. Several of these come from the later period and are of Hurrian and Luwian (another Indo-European people closely related to the Hittites) origin, mediated via the southern Luwian-populated province of Kizzuwatna, near Syria. The patients treated in these rites ranged from the king, queen, and the royal house down to unspecified individuals. Some of these rites were performed at the main transitions in life: birth, puberty, and death. Others sought to remove evils of various sorts, including uncleanness *(papratar)*, sorcery *(alwanzatar)*, curse *(hurtais)*, oath *(lingais)*, blood/murder *(eshar)*, evil tongue *(idalus lalas)*, sin *(wastul)*, plague, various sicknesses and infirmities, and also malevolent supernatural beings (including the ghosts of the dead).

Various means, usually symbolic, were used to remove these evils. Evils may be transferred to other objects or entities, and these may then be further disposed of or sent away in scapegoat fashion, sometimes with the accompanying notion that they are being banished to the underworld. According to one text, when a plague breaks out after a battle, one is to dress a foreign prisoner in the Hittite king's clothing and send the prisoner back to the enemy country as an "offering" to the attacking deity, to divert wrath from the Hittite country. The king or his representative says to the prisoner: "If some male god of the enemy land has caused this plague, behold, to him I have given the decorated man as a substitute. At his head this o[ne is gr]eat, at the heart this one is great, at the member this o[ne is gre]at. You, male god, be appeased with th[is dec]orated man. But to the king, the [leaders], the ar[my, and the] land of Hatti, tur[n yourself fai]thfully. . . . Let this prisoner b[ear] the plague and carry [it] ba[ck into the land of the enemy]" (*CTH* 407; KBo 15.1 1.14–21). Evils may also be placed on animals, providing interesting parallels to the biblical scapegoat ritual (Lev. 16). Other means of getting rid of evil include concretizing the evils by representing them with colored threads, certain types of clothing, or other objects. When these are removed, the evil is removed. The evils may also be purged by ritual "detergents," that is, by water, wine, clay, plants, flours, salt, blood, fire, and various mixtures.

An almost ubiquitous feature of Hittite ritual, found to some extent in other Near Eastern ritual, is the use of analogy. For example, in the ritual of Anniwiyani, which is performed to attract and appease a protecting deity, nine pebbles are heated. Anniwiyani, the female practitioner (the Old Woman), cools them off by pouring beer on them, saying: "Just as these have quenched their thirst, so you, protective god . . . , quench your thirst. For you let anger, wrath, and animosity vanish" (*CTH* 393 4.1–4). The analogy need not be dramatically enacted in every case. It may involve only reference to a natural or empirical fact that is brought to bear on the patient's situation. Analogy may be used not just to remedy evils, but also to impart blessing. An Old Woman ritual practitioner, Tunnawiya, grabs hold of the horn of a cow and says: "Sungod, my lord, just as this cow is fertile, and [is] in a fertile pen, and keeps filling the pen with bulls [and] cows, indeed, in the same way may the offerer be fertile! May she in the same way fill [her] house with sons [and] daughters" (*CTH* 409; KUB 7.53 4.8–13).

The maintenance of the many temples and the performance of the several-day and multiday festivals required an elaborate body of temple personnel. Functionally and conceptually, the highest priestly figure was the king, who presided at the main festivals and was responsible otherwise for maintaining good relations with the gods and securing their favor for the people and land at large. The primary priest was the ^{LÚ}SANGA (priest). Other priestly functionaries included the ^{LÚ}GUDU$_{12}$ ([anointed] priest) and the priestess ^{MUNUS}AMA.DINGIR (mother of the god). In addition, many cultic functionaries served at the temple: cooks, cupbearers, people who set out offerings, musicians, singers, people who cleaned, and those who cared for temple animals. The rituals of crisis performed for individuals employed a different set of practitioners. The performers of these rites are often mentioned by name. Often the performer is a female designated with the title "Old Woman" (perhaps meaning "Wise Woman"; Sumerian ^{MUNUS}U.GI = Hittite *hasawas*). Other participants in such rites include the ^{LÚ}A.ZU (physician), the ^{LÚ}HAL (seer), and the ^{LÚ}MUŠEN.DÙ (observer of birds).

Rituals of crisis may also include incantations and prayers. These spoken elements are relatively brief. The Hittite corpus also contains several texts that consist of lengthy prayers, sometimes with accompanying ritual description or prescription (*CTH* 371–89). These texts are virtually all spoken by the king or other members of the royal family and mostly date from the New Kingdom (e.g., the prayers by Queen Pudukhepa and King Muwattalli II). Another group of informative prayers is the Plague Prayers of Murshili II (ca. 1321–1295). In one prayer, the king petitions the gods to alleviate a plague that had been raging in the land since the end of the reign of his father, Shuppiluliuma I. He speaks of how his previous prayers for healing were ineffectual. He consequently inquired by oracle to find out why the gods were angry, the presupposition being that the plague was the result of divine anger. The oracles determined that offerings to a certain god had not been properly made and that a treaty oath made to the Storm-god of Hatti had been broken. Murshili promised to make proper offerings to appease the various deities angered. In addition to prayer texts, Hittite vocabulary contained its own terms for types of prayers, found in colophons or in the body of the texts themselves: *mugawar,* a petition for the god to attend to the plight of the one praying, often with an evocation ritual to attract the deity; *arkuwar,* a prayer defending against charges of wrongdoing; *walliyatar,* a hymn or prayer of praise; and *wekuwar,* a request or petition. The different genres may be mixed in any given prayer.

While humans spoke to the gods directly, the gods made their will known indirectly. A chief method was through dreams. These could come unexpectedly or be prepared for ritually or requested from the deities. In the prayer of Murshili II to relieve the plague, he asks the storm-god to send him a dream advising him of any other satisfaction he must provide to insure that he is making proper amends. External phenomena were also thought to convey the will of the gods. Heavenly occurrences, the behavior of birds or water snakes, birth defects, the drift of incense smoke, the disposition of oil on water, and the physical character of the liver, heart, gall bladder, and intestines of animals were examined and interpreted to discover divine intent. The Hittites also used a lot oracle (the KIN oracle), which may have been used in a gamelike fashion, to reveal the divine mind. As they did with respect to other cultural features, the Hittites borrowed some of their oracular techniques from the Mesopotamian world via Hurrian influence and even had their own editions of Babylonian divination texts. Since the divination techniques generally produced yes/no answers, the Hittites employed a series of oracular inquiries in order to arrive at a specific answer to a question. A good example of this is found in the text that recounts how Murshili II overcame the effects of a disability (perhaps a stroke) that resulted in his not being able to speak easily. After a dream, which may have aggravated his condition, he consulted a series of oracles to determine what he should do. The first oracle indicated that the storm-god of Manuzziya was responsible. A second oracle determined that he should give this god a substitute ox. A third oracle indicated that he should send the offering to the town of Kummanni, located just south of the main land of Hatti (*CTH* 486; see translation by Gary Beckman in Frantz-Szabó 1995: 2010).

Finally, most of what we know about the Hittite view of death concerns the king and royal family. At death the king "became a god," that is, a *sius.* This may mean that he became identified in some way, or entered into association with, the Indo-European deity Sius. One text preserves a fourteen-day funerary rite for the king (*CTH* 450; Otten 18–91; detailed summary in Haas 1995:

2024–27). The text begins by stating the circumstance for the ritual: "When a great calamity [lit., sin, *šalliš waštaiš*] occurs in Hattusha." This calamity is the king's death. On the third day the king is apparently cremated, a custom probably of Hurrian origin. On the sixth day his burned bones, which had earlier been wrapped in linen, were taken to a mausoleum or tomb called the "stone house." Offerings were presented to the deceased king and to the gods at various points. Other performances appear to symbolically outfit the dead with what he needs in the next life and to appease any anger he may have toward those who remain alive. The conception seems to be that life after death continues in a way similar to life during mortality. It is not entirely clear whether the ghost of the deceased was thought to live in the netherworld, the area under the physical earth. The netherworld figured significantly in the Hittite cosmological picture. Caves, springs, dug pits, and tombs provided passageways to the underworld. The sun traversed the sky during the day and crossed the underworld at night and therefore was the chief god of the netherworld. The netherworld (or the deep sea) was also conceptually the place where impurities were banished through elimination rituals. The ghosts of the kings could have resided here. Some have suggested that their habitation was in the west, where the sun entered the underworld.

BIBL.: Gary Beckman, *Hittite Birth Rituals* (Studien zu den Boğazköy-Texten 29; Wiesbaden: Harrassowitz, 1983). Gary Beckman, *Hittite Diplomatic Texts* (Society of Biblical Literature Writings from the Ancient World 7; Atlanta: Scholars Press, 1996). Gabriella Frantz-Szabó, "Hittite Witchcraft, Magic, and Divination," in *Civilizations of the Ancient Near East* (ed. Jack M. Sasson; New York: Scribner, 1995), 3.2007–19. O. R. Gurney, *Some Aspects of Hittite Religion* (Oxford: Oxford University Press, 1977). Volkert Haas, "Death and the Afterlife in Hittite Thought," in *Civilizations of the Ancient Near East* (ed. Jack M. Sasson; New York: Scribner, 1995), 3.2021–30. Volkert Haas and Gernot Wilhelm, *Hurritische und luwische Riten aus Kizzuwatna* (Hurritologische Studien 1; Alter Orient und Altes Testament Sonderreihe 3; Kevelaer: Butzon & Bercker/Neukirchen-Vluyn: Neukirchener Verlag, 1974). Harry A. Hoffner Jr., *Hittite Myths* (2nd ed.; Society of Biblical Literature Writings from the Ancient World 2; Atlanta: Scholars Press, 1998). Theo van den Hout, *The Purity of Kingship: An Edition of CTH 569 and Related Hittite Oracle Inquiries of Tuthaliya IV* (Documenta et monumenta orientis antiqui 25; Leiden: Brill, 1998). Alexei Kassian, Andrej Korolëv, and Andrej Sidel'tsev, *Hittite Funerary Ritual šalliš waštaiš* (Alter Orient und Altes Testament 288; Münster: Ugarit-Verlag, 2002). Jörg Klinger, *Untersuchungen zur Rekonstruktion der hattischen Kultschicht* (Studien zu den Boğazköy-Texten 37; Wiesbaden: Harrassowitz, 1996). R. Lebrun, *Hymnes et prières hittites* (Louvain-la-Neuve: Centre d'Histoire de Religions, 1980). Itamar Singer, *Muwatalli's Prayer to the Assembly of Gods through the Storm-God of Lightning (CTH 381)* (Atlanta: Scholars Press/ASOR, 1996). David P. Wright, "Analogical in Biblical and Hittite Ritual," in *Religionsgeschichtliche Beziehungen zwischen Kleinasien, Nordsyrien und dem Alten Testament* (ed. B. Janowski, K. Koch, and G. Wilhelm; Orbis biblicus et orientalis 129; Freiburg: Universitätsverlag/Göttingen: Vandenhoeck & Ruprecht, 1993), 473–506. David P. Wright, *The Disposal of Impurity: Elimination Rites in the Bible and in Hittite and Mesopotamian Literature* (Society of Biblical Literature Dissertation Series 101; Atlanta: Scholars Press, 1987).

Iran

William Malandra and Michael Stausberg

*I*n antiquity the Iranian cultural sphere extended over a large part of western Asia, far exceeding the borders of the modern state. It included the modern states of Iran, Afghanistan, western regions of Pakistan, the "republics" of the old Soviet central Asia, and areas within the Caucuses—all of them places where related dialects of the common Iranian language group were spoken and where many cultural and religious institutions were shared. Other peripheral areas came under strong Iranian influence at various times. Median, Persian, and Parthian dynasties extended their empires westward into the ancient Near East, the eastern Mediterranean, and Egypt and northward into Azerbaijan and Armenia. Commerce encouraged the expansion of Iranians along the trade routes to China. The Iranians living within such geographic diversity were not a monolithic people. The languages they spoke, although related, were often quite distinct from one another. For example, the Iranian Scythians (Saka) in central Asia spoke languages and carried out ways of life far different than Iranians living in the southwest on the borders of Mesopotamia.

Any historical study is limited by the nature and extent of the sources. This means that there are often long temporal and broad geographical gaps. There are subjects about which we would like to know more or at least something; yet the sources may be silent. Because we cannot interrogate the creators of the source material, we are frequently in the dark as to what something means. As one example, much of the collection of sacred poetry composed by Zarathustra is so obscure in its language and conceptual framework that we cannot always achieve a secure understanding of what the prophet wished to communicate. As another example, although we have the rich iconography of Achaemenid imperial art, no verbal testimony links an icon to its symbolic referent. While art and architectural remains provide some source material for religion, by far the most important sources are literary. Among the latter may be distinguished indigenous Iranian sources and foreign ones. The latter are predominantly Greek and Latin, with occasional references in Aramaic, Hebrew, and Neo-Babylonian. They all should be approached with caution. With the exception of lists of theophoric names in Elamite, all indigenous sources are in Iranian languages.

The most ancient Iranian literary sources are the inscriptions of the Achaemenid kings in Old Persian and the sacred texts of the Zoroastrian religion composed in the Avestan language. The inscriptions are easily dated to the 6th and 5th centuries BCE, to the reigns of Darius, Xerxes, and Artaxerxes. Although they serve the propagandistic ends of the rulers, they are rich in materials related to religion. The corpus of Zoroastrian texts known as the Avesta is a heterogeneous collection whose components were composed at various times and in various genres. Among them the most ancient are the five Gathas or songs attributed to Zarathustra, which comprise a total of seventeen chapters. Unfortunately no one knows when he lived. Some scholars place him at or just prior to the rise of Cyrus the Great (6th century BCE), while many prefer an earlier time between 1200 and 1000, and yet others seek an even earlier date. The large collection of hymns, the Yashts, which honor the deities, contains much material that may well be as ancient as the Gathas, yet the Yashts have been thoroughly edited by redactors who probably worked long after the fall of the Achaemenid Empire. The same may be said about the Yasna, a part of the Avesta which was, and is to this day, recited during the performance of the ritual of the same name. Another significant text is the Widewdad (Vendidad) which, for the most part, contains instruction on a variety of matters pertaining to questions of purity and pollution; parts of it seem to have been composed in the Arsacid period, as the Greek system of spatial measurement is presupposed. If we regard the Avesta as reflecting a period of antiquity that more or less ended with the conquest of Iran by Alexander of Macedon, it, together with the inscriptions, comprises almost all the source material for the most ancient forms of Iranian religion.

In the very extended period between Alexander and the 9th century CE, we have few extensive sources. Of the Sassanid inscriptions, the long inscription of the high priest Kirder is particularly important. But, apart from coin legends (especially those of the Kushans), minor inscriptions, and graffiti, nothing is preserved in significant volume until the renaissance of literary activity in the 9th century, after the coming of Islam to Iran. During this century, Zoroastrian scholars sought to preserve as much Sassanid learning as they could, and what they produced, for the most part, were digests, some very long, of older texts composed in the Pahlavi language. The main problem for the student of Iranian religion is how to sort out historical layers in these texts, for they quote extensively from Sassanid texts which themselves may be translations of lost Avestan texts or else contain more-ancient materials of unclear provenance. One could also include Manicheism in this survey, since Manichean sources in Middle Persian, Parthian, and Sogdian contain a great deal of material borrowed from Iranian (and other) religious traditions. It follows from the foregoing survey of the sources for ancient Iranian religion that the largest part of what we know is mediated by Zoroastrianism.

During the middle of the 2nd millennium BCE there was a gradual migration of nomadic or seminomadic peoples from the steppes into the eastern Mediterranean, the Near East, the Iranian plateau, and the Indian subcontinent. These peoples spoke languages belonging to the Indo-European family. Within that broad family of related languages were two closely related groups collectively identified by linguists as Indo-Iranian. As the name implies, one group settled in India (but also Anatolia and part of the Near East), the other in greater Iran. Not only in language but also in culture and religious ideology did they share a common heritage. Central to both was the sacrificial worship (Old Indic *yajñá*, Old Iranian *yasna*) of the gods (Old Indic *devá*, Avestan *daēwa*, Old Persian *daiwa*, proto-Indo-European *deiwó-s*) in which an essential element was the preparation of the sacred drink (Old Indic *sóma*, Avestan *haoma*, Old Persian *haumd*). They worshiped deities, some of whom bore the same or nearly identical names, for example, Mitra/Mithra, Vayu/Wayu, Tvastar/Thworeshtar, and some of whom represented common concepts of divine functions, for example, Indra/Werethragna (Warrior), Prthivi/Spenta Armaiti (Earth), Agni/Atar (Fire). The most ancient Indian texts, the Vedas, are extremely important for the study of Iranian religion, as they contain a volume and richness of material far beyond what survived in Iran. Nevertheless, both branches of the family exhibit such divergent evolution that they cannot simply be superimposed upon each other.

At the head of the Iranian pantheon stood Ahura Mazda. He was a creator *(dātar)* in the sense that he exercised dominion over creation in establishing order and putting *(dā-)* everything in its proper place. The actual crafting of the creation was the work of the demiurge, Thworeshtar (Craftsman). Ahura Mazda's consort was the Earth, known by the name Spenta Armaiti, although he seems to have had other wives, the Ahuranis (wives of Ahura). Ahura Mazda had a particular connection to the cosmic principle of order and truth called Rta (Avestan *aša*, Old Persian *arta*), and, like the supreme Vedic god Varuna, was a source of insight into truth for poets, the divinely inspired creators of sacred hymns. Two male deities were closely associated with Ahura Mazda. One was Rashnu (Judge), who had a limited judicial function, analogous to that exercised by Varuna, in serving as the divine judge presiding over the oaths sworn by humans. The other was Mithra. While Mithra was a complex deity, the essence of his being was that he was foremost the god Covenant. That is, he presided over all treaties between nations and covenants between people. The image of him as a mighty warrior riding in his chariot full of weapons reflects his ability to enforce the sanctity of covenants. As a warrior he shares much in common with another powerful deity: Werethragna (Victory), whose name etymologically means "the smashing of resistance." As such he embodied the ideal of the Iranian warrior who was capable of smashing the defenses of all enemies. Warriors invoked both Mithra and Werethragna as they went into battle, yet when it came to the exercise of legitimate temporal power and the success of the ruler in wielding that power, two other forces came into play. The Iranians developed a unique concept of an impersonal force called

X^warnah, conceived as a fiery presence that attached itself to legitimate rulers, but remained unseizable by illegitimate usurpers. Without this royal glory one could not hope to hold power. Whereas X^warnah was an impersonal power, victory to the legitimate ruler and righteous warrior was granted by a goddess, Aredwi Sura Anahita. Like Athena and Ishtar, she dispensed success in arms.

The cosmos was basically three-tiered, consisting of earth, atmosphere, and heaven. The earth was divided into six concentric continents *(karšwar)* surrounding the central continent, X^wainiratha, where *aryana waējah* (the Iranian Expanse) is located. At the center of the earth was the cosmic mountain, Hara Berezaiti, the Elburz, which acted as the axis mundi. At its southern flank was the sacred Wouru-kasha sea, in the middle of which grew the Tree of Life. Over the earth and expanse of sky arched the stone vault of heaven *(asman)*, beyond which was the realm of the Infinite Lights *(anagra raocah)*, the heavenly abode called the Best Existence *(wahišta ahu)*, and the House of Song *(garō-nmāna)*. Below the earth was the realm of Infinite Darkness *(anagra temah)*. The entire earth rested upon and was surrounded by the waters of chaos. Fresh water flowed down Hara in the river goddess Aredwi Sura (Strong Moist), into the Wouru-kasha, and from it the various rivers of the world flowed, accumulating pollutants in their courses to the salt sea, called Puitika (Filterer), from which the hydrological cycle repeated itself.

As far as one can reconstruct on the basis of Pahlavi sources, the temporal dimension of the cosmos was a system of four world ages, analogous to the yuga system of ancient India and the four metallic ages of Greece, with each lasting three thousand years. One can guess that there was degradation of the cosmos over the course of the ages and that a complete cycle would have ended with a cataclysm and subsequent creation that renewed the cycle, although in its present form the cycle has been thoroughly transformed into a myth of creation, a battle of good and evil, with the final triumph of the good and establishment of the eternal kingdom of God, Ohrmazd. The yearly cycle was punctuated by various sacred festivals, which probably varied from region to region. The most important was the spring festival celebrating the New Year (Pahlavi *Nōg Rōz*), preceded by a liminal time marking the return of the spirits of the dead, the *frawašis*.

The ancient Iranian cultic practices seem to have been very similar to those referred to in the Vedic literature. Men with special training were required, and, as at later periods, the priestly functions may have been hereditary. The presiding priest was the *zaotar* (Old Indic *hótar*) (the one who offers libations) and was attended by various functionaries. Another functional title, *athaurwan* (cf. Old Indic *átharvan*), became the name for the sacerdotal caste, though originally it may have designated those priests charged with the care of the sacred fire, *ātar*, both the element and a deity. Worship of the deities was ritually performed through the *yasna*. Originally this was a complex ritual that involved the offering of a victim (food) and the sacred *haoma* (drink). Modeled on rites of hospitality, the *yasna* was an elaborate festive meal to which a deity or deities were invited as honored guests. The deity was offered food and drink and was entertained through the recitation of poetry created for the occasion to magnify the divine guest(s). The poet was called a *mạthrān* (cf. Old Indic *mantrín*), that is, one who creates sacred poetry *(mạthra)*. The Yashts of the Avesta are collections of such poetry. Since hospitality is part of the complex social interaction of gift exchange, the *yasna* placed the deities under an obligation to present the host with a gift. Thus, beyond the general desire to maintain favorable relations with the powers controlling the world, the sacrificer could hope for specific boons.

Our picture of ancient Iranian religion is colored by the prophet Zarathustra (Zoroaster). His specific dates and place of activity are unknown, though we may say with imprecision that he lived between the 12th and 6th centuries BCE somewhere in the northeastern Iranian cultural sphere. We assume that his religious milieu was that sketched above. He was both a *zaotar* and a *mathran*. The only reliable biographical information about him is contained in his Gathas, preserved by the oral tradition, of which he was a part, for centuries and then continued to the present in oral and written priestly transmission. Zarathustra had a particularly close relationship with Ahura Mazda, from whom he received revelatory visions *(daēnā)*. His vision, expressed in the Gathas, included a radical transformation of traditional beliefs. In place of the pantheon he elevated Ahura Mazda to a position of supremacy that approaches monotheism and surrounded him with a group of abstract entities, the Amesha Spentas, all of whom perpetuate key concepts of Iranian religion as hypostases of Ahura Mazda. At the heart of the vision, however, was an ethical dualism that saw the principles of *aša* (Old Persian *arta,* Old Indic *r̥tá*), Truth, and *druj* (Old Persian *dranga,* Old Indic *dróha*), Falsehood, in fundamental opposition. In Zarathustra's thought dualism is not primordial, as it appears in later Sassanid theology, but arose out of the right and wrong choices made by twin spirits, who stand in paradigmatic relationship to human beings in the exercise of free will. As a result, the world could be divided between the followers of Truth (*ašawan-;* cf. Old Persian *artāwan,* Old Indic *r̥tā́varn*) and the followers of the Lie *(drugwant).* His dualistic theology also led to the polarization of the traditional classes of deities, the *ahuras* and the *daēwas.* A *zaotar,* Zarathustra was concerned with proper cultic practice, especially the proscription of violence upon the sacrificial victim as carried out by the *daiwic* priests. He may have modified the *haoma* cult, but certainly did not ban it. Finally, Zarathustra articulated the kernel of the idea of a savior figure, the Saoshyant, who would arrive in the future to redeem the world. (Further on Zarathustra and his religious innovations, see the Appendix to this essay.)

The history of Iranian religion after Zarathustra is very difficult to reconstruct. In the course of his ministry in eastern Iran, he converted a local ruler *(kawi)* named Wishtaspa, who became his patron and protector. For convenience scholars call the religion of the prophet Zarathustrianism or Zoroastrianism. We can only assume that the religious community that Zarathustra founded continued and thrived after his death. With the consolidation of greater Iran under the Achaemenids, his religion, into whatever form it had evolved, made its way to western Iran. There it encountered forms of Iranian religion different not only from itself, but also from non-Zarathustrian religions of the East. In particular, there was the politically entrenched priestly caste of the Magi who, according to Herodotus (1.132), presided at all religious ceremonies, at which they recited "theogonies," presumably Yasht-like hymns. There is no consensus among scholars over the question of whether the early great kings, Cyrus, Darius, Xerxes, were influenced by Zarathustrianism. They certainly believed in the absolute supremacy of Ahura Mazda and probably in the dichotomy of *ahura/daiwa*. But, beyond that all is speculation. Neither the Achaemenids themselves nor Herodotus mention Zarathustra, and Gathic quotations that some see in the inscriptions may merely reflect phrases common to the shared (Indo-)Iranian poetic diction.

In any case, what emerges during the Achaemenid period is an eclectic Iranian religion, called by scholars Zoroastrianism, which contains elements of Zarathustrianism, apocryphal legends of the prophet, a full pantheon of deities almost entirely absent from the Gathas, an overriding concern over purity and pollution, the establishment of fire temples. Curiously, the extant Avesta remains thoroughly eastern Iranian in its geographic and linguistic orientation. One assumes that radical concessions to traditional beliefs had already taken place after Zarathustra's death and before Zoroastrianism became pan-Iranian.

After the conquest by Alexander, Iran fell under the superficial influence of Hellenism. Apart from fragmentary evidence it is difficult to formulate a cohesive history from Alexander to the foundation of the Sassanid Dynasty in the 3rd century CE. The Pahlavi books hint at a Zoroastrian revival under Vologases I (ca. 51–80 CE) in which some sort of collection and codification of the Avesta took place. Kushan coins of the same period from the northeast show a pantheon of Iranian deities. From Gandhara Mahayana, Buddhism gained strength throughout the region, traveling along the trade routes to China. Jews, Christians, and eventually Manicheans also entered the religious mix. With the founding of the Sassanid Dynasty around 224 CE under Ardashir, there was a revival of Iranian nationalism that consciously harkened back to the glory of the Old Persian Empire. Part of this was the creation of a centralized Zoroastrian ecclesiastical structure that was inseparable from the royal authority of the state. After an initial struggle over the patronage of Shapuhr I (240–72 CE), the high priest Kirder overcame his rival Mani and established Zoroastrianism *(dēn mazdēsn)* throughout the empire, while persecuting religious minorities. Zoroastrianism remained the state religion until the Arab-Islamic conquest in the latter part of the 7th century CE.

W. W. M.

Appendix: Zoroastrianism

The name Zoroastrianism is a product of modern colonial discourse. It goes back to a Greek rendering (Zoroastres) of the Iranian name Zarathustra, which refers to the key individual, the founder, or prophet of this religion. The designations of the religion found in most premodern primary sources, on the other hand, draw attention either to the (supposed) quality of the religion—the "pure/good religion"—or to the name of its dominant male divinity, Ahura Mazda. This is an ancient Iranian (Avestan) term that can be rendered either as "the Wise Lord" or as "Lord Wisdom."

Together both names—Zarathustra and Ahura Mazda—occur in the Gathas. These are five hymns that are often assumed to be part of the oldest layer of the corpus of ritual texts written in Avestan, an ancient Iranian language. Many scholars nowadays believe that the Gathas were composed by Zarathustra himself, whereas others argue that Zarathustra as a person belongs to the realm of myth. While many linguists distinguish between two or even more historical layers of the Avestan language—Old and Young Avestan—others reject that distinction, opting instead for a distinction between Gathic and Standard Avestan.

There is disagreement about virtually everything in the study of Zoroastrianism, not the least on the question of origins. There are dozens of theories, mostly mere speculative assumptions, about the homeland of the religion (or of its prophet), generally held to be somewhere east of what is modern Iran. It is not clear when Zarathustra lived (if there ever was such a person). While some scholars argue that he must have lived in remote antiquity, even going back as far as 1700 BCE, some place him in the 6th or 5th century BCE, whereas the majority puts the date around 1000 BCE. Some later Zoroastrian texts in Middle and New Persian recount "biographies" of Zarathustra. These biographies focus on his miraculous birth and childhood, his divine revelations and encounters, and his eventually successful campaign at the court of a king.

Whatever their origin, the Gathas came to be orally transmitted in ritual contexts. Although many translations of the Gathas are available, most of them disagree about fundamental issues, and the Gathas are still obscure in many ways. It is difficult to avoid the suspicion that one finds in the Gathas whatever one may be looking for. By way of example, Zoroastrian scholars have "discovered" such modern ideas as gender equality, ecology, and human rights in the Gathas. To the eyes of many modern Zoroastrians, especially in Iran and the West, the Gathas are the normative model of religious scripture, while the later (or Standard) Avestan texts containing more-straightforward material of praise to the divinities and divine prescriptions are disregarded as secondary elaborations.

The issues of monotheism and dualism are a major concern of both modern Western orientalists and Zoroastrian theologians. These often (erroneously) have been presented as an either-or argument. It can easily be understood that modern Zoroastrians living in a world dominated by Christian and Islamic patterns have insisted on their religion being regarded as a pure monotheism; and for many scholars monotheism has served as a bridge linking Zoroastrian and Jewish religious history. (Some scholars hold that Zoroastrianism had a profound influence on Jewish traditions.) In the Avestan texts, however, one can easily find support for monotheist, dualist, and polytheist interpretations. Whereas monotheism, dualism, and polytheism are different sets of classification in Western thought, no such distinctions seem to have existed in the Avestan mentality. To stretch things into a schematic pattern: Ahura Mazda—the most powerful of the gods, who set the creation into place and motion, together with the other male and female divinities and divine beings, most prominently the Amesha Spentas (Bountiful Immortals), a group that came to consist of six divinities closely allied to or created by Ahura Mazda and thought to represent moral virtues and cosmic elements (such as fire, water, earth, etc.)—is held to be actively involved in a continuous struggle against impure demons and demonic agents of varying degrees of power. Humanity is involved in this struggle in a number of ways. Ideally, humankind is expected to support the divinities by properly performing rituals and by a virtuous conduct of life implementing truth, purity, the right measure, and god-given order, the latter also containing submission to elders and gender rules. While females play an important role in that struggle, they are assumed to be more easily affected by demonic forces and thus need to be held under tight male, patriarchal control. From the Achaemenian period onward in Iran, similar forms of dualist rhetoric were also employed in order to foster political claims for legitimacy, loyalty, and empire.

According to more systematic accounts transmitted in the Middle Persian (Pahlavi) books, the struggle between the forces of good and evil evolved out of an original opposition between Ohrmazd (i.e., Ahura Mazda) and his main adversary Ahriman (i.e., Angra Mainyu) in the early stages of the history of creation, which then had obtained two dimensions: a spiritual, invisible, meta-empirical level *(menog)* and an equally good material, tangible, empirical level *(getig)*. The Zoroastrian version of dualism, monotheism, and polytheism is thus closely linked to a vision of cosmic history. Events culminate in a process often referred to as *frašgird,* the final transfiguration of the cosmos, when the forces of evil (and hence dualism) will be eliminated. This process is instigated by the arrival of a future hero who is regarded as a posthumous son of Zarathustra.

The climax of cosmic history can be expressed in terms of a final ordeal or a final judgment. In a way, this can be regarded both as the culmination and a reversal of the eschatological judgment that each and every human being is expected to face after death. The number of merits and sins that each person has gathered in the course of his or her life are held to be decisive for the progress of the soul on its journey, which may lead to paradise, hell, or a place in between. Probably, fear of hell and the promise of heaven were major factors promoting religious commitment and ritual practice.

At least starting from the reign of the Achaemenians (6th to 4th centuries BCE), Zoroastrianism was the dominant set of religious traditions in pre-Islamic Iranian history. The link between the religion and the land of Iran has been given particular importance, especially since the Sassanian period (3rd to 7th centuries CE). Recent scholarship draws attention to many—partly local,

popular, and lay—varieties of the traditions, while premodern written Zoroastrian sources as products of male, priestly, and partly local discourse draw only
a partial picture of religious practices and mentalities. In the aftermath of the
Arabic invasion of Iran, groups of Zoroastrians have relocated to western India, where they are known as Parsis (derived from the name Persia). Nowadays, Zoroastrianism has around 125,000 adherents, mostly in India, Iran,
and North America.

M.ST.

BIBL.: Mary Boyce, *A History of Zoroastrianism* (3 vols.; Leiden, 1975–91). Albert
de Jong, *Traditions of the Magi* (Leiden, 1997). *The Cambridge History of Iran* (ed.
I. Gershevitch; Cambridge, 1985), 2.640–97. Michael Stausberg, *Die Religion
Zarathushtras: Geschichte, Gegenwart, Rituale* (3 vols.; Stuttgart, 2002–2003).

Minoan and Mycenaean Civilizations

Nanno Marinatos

Minoan Religion

Minoan culture flourished on the island of Crete from the 3rd to the 1st millennium BCE and from the 2nd millennium onward as a palatial society. At that time, its writing system, its religious symbols, and its material culture spread beyond the boundaries of Crete to encompass most of the islands of the Aegean and the southern part of mainland Greece. Scholars debate whether this spread of Minoan art, writing, and religion was only superficial and indicates nothing more than trade connections or whether it reveals the network of an empire. Whatever the case, the ubiquity of Minoan religious symbols is certainly a result of power, perhaps even colonialism.

The basic mythology and theology of Minoan religion cannot be reconstructed on the basis of texts. Such literary documents as have been left behind, consisting of clay tablets inscribed in a language we call Linear A, are inaccessible because the writing system is only partially understood and the language itself is unknown. This leaves us with only archeological remains and images; still, they yield a great deal of information.

Contemporary ideas about the Minoans go back to Sir Arthur Evans, who excavated the palace of Knossos on Crete during the first decades of the 20th century. Many of his observations were keen and have stood the test of time; others need revision. One of the fallacies introduced by Evans into Minoan religion is the dominant role of a Great Minoan Mother Goddess, with its concomitant matriarchal society. A close scrutiny of the iconography of the numerous extant rings and seals shows that the Minoan pantheon consisted of several deities, among whom a youthful male god armed with a spear features prominently. On a ring imprint found at Chania, a god is shown towering over

Figure 1

a town (Fig. 1). The hierarchy and relationship of gods within the pantheon is difficult to decode from the images alone. On a ring impression from Knossos (Fig 2.), the dominant deity is female, flanked by lions. She faces a male who is probably a god rather than a worshiper. They may be a divine couple. On a wall painting from the island of Thera (modern Santorini), a seated goddess receives an offering of saffron from young girls.

Evans also overemphasized fertility as a central concern of Minoan cult, and he characterized Minoan religious mentality as conceptually primitive; these ideas were further developed in the middle of the 20th century by A. W. Persson and the sober and systematic M. P. Nilsson. The unfortunate consequence of this is that Minoan religion is still classified as primitive.

In reality, Minoan religion was the religion of a sophisticated and urbanized palatial culture with a complex social hierarchy. It was not dominated by fertility any more than any religion of the past or present has been, and it addressed gender identity, rites of passage, and death. It is reasonable to assume that both the organization and the rituals, even the mythology, resembled the religions of Near Eastern palatial civilizations.

The palaces seem to have been at the core of a religious system that can be termed theocratic. On the Knossos seal impression (Fig. 2), the palace is depicted behind a goddess. It is multitiered and topped by "horns of consecration." Evans recognized that the horns were a symbol of sacred authority as well as political power. The diffusion of this symbol outside Crete testifies to the function of Minoan emblems as carriers of ideology.

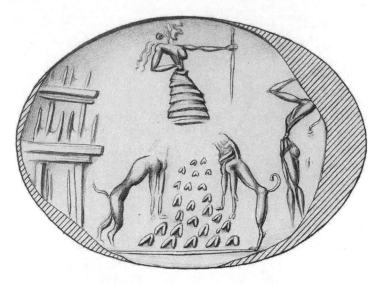

Figure 2

There are no temples in Minoan Crete, although buildings associated with cult have been found on mountaintops ("peak sanctuaries"). They were apparently controlled by the palaces, but the varying quality of the votives shows that common people and rural folk congregated there. Typical offerings are statuettes of humans and animals, libation vessels, and portable offering tables.

The fall of the palatial system in Crete sometime after 1400 BCE caused some changes in the archeological record of religion. Rooms with benches and statues make their appearance, which structurally resemble shrines both on mainland Greece and in Syria and Palestine. Many terra-cotta statues of goddesses date to this era; they stood on the benches, and offerings were made to them.

Mycenaean religion

The inhabitants of Greece during the 2nd millennium BCE are called Mycenaeans after the famous and impressive citadel of Mycenae, which was excavated by Heinrich Schliemann at the end of the 19th century. Many similar citadels existed in Greece, and there is enough homogeneity among them that we are justified to speak of a Mycenaean culture. Mycenaean religion shares many symbols with Minoan religion, from the period of the Shaft Graves in the 16th century BCE to the end of its existence. For example, Mycenaean palaces were also topped by horns. One generally assumes that the borrowing of symbols of authority demonstrates that the Mycenaean palaces took over the enHtire theocratic Minoan system and adapted it to their culture. We also suspect that there were dynastic links. After the 14th century BCE, the Mycenaean writing system, Linear B (most probably a derivative of Minoan Linear A), is also found on Crete. The decipherment of this system revealed its language as an early form of Greek; its syllabic structure, however, cannot have been intrinsic to Greek, because the numerous consonant clusters that are characteristic of Greek translate rather clumsily into Linear B.

There were other differences, as well, between the two cultures. Mycenaean palaces included a *megaron*, a large central rectangular room with a hearth in the center where offerings were made; only one palace on Crete, that of Galatas, contained a hearth. Apart from the *megaron* in the palaces, modest bench sanctuaries are found within the citadels and the towns. On the benches of these small shrines were found terra-cotta figures of varying sizes; normally there was a hearth in the center, showing that offerings took place there as well. The bench sanctuary seems to have been a prevalent type throughout the Aegean and the Levant in the 13th and 12th centuries BCE. Sanctuaries existed outside the Mycenaean palaces as well, on mountaintops (as on a hill near Epidaurus) and within settlements. Recently such a settlement sanctuary has been excavated on the peninsula of Methana (Saronic Gulf). Its main feature was a hearth and the usual benches. Typical offerings in all Mycenaean sanctuaries are terra-cotta figurines of varying sizes.

Linear B tablets of the 13th century BCE, found in Thebes and Pylos on the mainland and in Chania and Knossos on Crete, attest that the Mycenaeans had an elaborate pantheon. These tablets were clay scrapbooks that survived decomposition because they were accidentally burned when the palaces were destroyed. The tablets record offerings to various gods, the titles of religious officials, and the dispensation of various goods to diverse sanctuaries. Among the gods mentioned are Poseidon, Zeus, Dionysus (attested only on Crete), and Marineus. Goddesses named include Potnija, Ifimedia, Diwija, and Posidaeja —the latter two being the female equivalents of Zeus and Poseidon, respectively.

Many names correspond closely to those of the later Greek gods of the 1st millennium. Yet, the danger of projecting the Greek religious system backward onto the Mycenaean world must be resisted; some divine names are unattested later, while prominent Greek gods, such as Apollo and Aphrodite, seem to be absent. Minoan and Mycenaean theocracies can be understood best as a subcategory of Near Eastern theocracies. The archeological evidence suggests that the Minoan and Mycenaean religions, despite their differences, had many common elements: palace-centered cults, absence of temples, hearths, and animal bones attesting to banqueting. Neither foreshadows the Greek polis religion.

BIBL.: Robin Hägg, "Mycenaean Religion: The Helladic and the Minoan Components," in *Linear B: A 1984 Survey* (ed. Anna Morpurgo-Davies and Yves Duhoux; Louvain-la-Neuve: Peeters, 1985), 203–25. Nanno Marinatos, *Minoan Religion: Ritual, Image, and Symbol* (Columbia: University of South Carolina Press, 1993). Helène Whittaker, *Mycenaean Cult Buildings: A Study of Their Architecture and Function in the Context of the Aegean and the Eastern Mediterranean* (Monographs from the Norwegian Institute at Athens; Bergen: Norwegian Institute at Athens, 1997).

Greece

Jon Mikalson

*F*or the student of antiquity, Greek religion seems, like Athena from the head of Zeus, to spring forth suddenly, mature, and fully developed. And it does so in the epic poetry of Homer and Hesiod, commonly dated by scholars to the mid- to late-8th century BCE. In these poems appear most of the fundamental features of Greek religion as we know them from later sources: polytheism; anthropomorphism; the names, functions, and iconography of individual gods; the forms, language, rituals, and occasions of sacrifices, prayers, and dedications; the nature and forms of sanctuaries, altars, cult statues, and temples; the nature and role of priests and priestesses; the rituals and purposes of oath taking; divine concern with the guest/host relationship *(xenia)*; and the forms and occasions of divination by seers, bird augury, omens, oracles, and dreams.

These elements of Greek religion are treated in Homeric and Hesiodic poetry with such familiarity and consistency that one may assume that they had already become conventional in this oral epic tradition. Moreover, if we view this "epic" religion retrospectively in terms of what we know of later practiced Greek religion from nonpoetic sources, it would appear that even this early epic religion had already been subjected to considerable patterning, simplification in some areas, expansion in others, and, in general terms, to a process of Panhellenization. For example, the poet-singers selected and featured a few from the hundreds of gods worshiped throughout Greece. They then largely stripped the chosen few of their local identities and of many of the epithets and peculiarities of ritual, cult, and even mythology that they would have had in the individual cities in which they were originally worshiped. And, by expansion, the poets constructed for the chosen few personal histories and an elaborate Olympian family structure—with the result best exemplified in Hesiod's *Theogony*. And it is in this sense that Herodotus, who had no notion of an oral epic tradition prior to these poets, could say that Hesiod and Homer "created a divine genealogy for Greeks, gave their epithets to the gods, distributed their offices and their skills, and marked out their outward appearances" (2.53.2).

The deities favored by the poetic tradition, now freed from limitations and particularities of their local cults, could serve—within the poetic tradition—as gods for all Greek audiences. Rituals in the epics were similarly stylized. The ritual sequence for the sacrifice of a cow is firmly set in the Homeric tradition: the gilding of the horns, the barley-corn preliminary offering, the ritual throat cutting, the butchering, the burning of the thigh pieces on the altar, the eating of the vital organs, the cooking, and the feast. But we know from later sources that many major variations were possible, depending on the occasion, the deity, and local traditions. In sacrifice, as in other rituals, the epic tradition selected or created one ritual set, generalized it, and made it into a set scene.

We must assume a period of maturation for this "epic" portrayal of Greek religion, to be measured perhaps in centuries. And that would bring us back to the Greek Dark Ages (ca. 1125 to ca. 700 BCE) at least, perhaps even to the end of the Mycenaean age. And, second, if the development of epic religion is somewhat as I have described, then the relationship of the Greek religion known from the Homeric epics to practiced religion of Homeric or later times is very complex. Homeric religion would ultimately derive from practiced cult and would preserve many of its features, but it would also differ from it in some major elements. And so the religion that springs upon us in such a full, complete, and appealing form in the 8th-century BCE epics is a religion significantly different from that practiced by the Greek peoples of that or any time. And, to further complicate the issue, the epics enjoyed such popularity among the Greeks that they, in turn, could influence local cults and certainly shaped later literary and artistic representations and philosophical discussions of what was considered to be Greek religion.

If we attempt to look beyond the Homeric period, to the prehistory of Greek religion, some isolated details emerge, enough to suggest that some defining elements of Greek religion do in fact reach back to the Mycenaean period. Zeus alone of the gods is unmistakably Indo-European, etymologically linked with the Roman Jupiter and the Dyaus pitar of the Rig Veda. Some aristocratic Greeks claimed genealogies that went back to a divine ancestor in the 16th century BCE. And the Linear B tablets from Knossos, Mycenae, Chania, and Pylos (all probably from about 1200 BCE) contain the familiar names of Zeus, Athena, Poseidon, Hera, Hermes, and Dionysus intermixed with deities unfamiliar to us. For the Dark Ages, there has been considerable speculation about what archeological finds at scattered places may or may not reveal about change or continuity in Greek religious concepts and about the social and political meaning of the placing and design of sanctuaries and the changing types of dedications. Much of this discussion attempts to place religion in the equally theoretical models for the social and political development of the early city-state. The sites are few, the interpretations of finds often uncertain, and the theories many and strongly contested.

Archeological finds do, however, indicate a sharp increase in religious buildings and dedications at the end of the Dark Ages. As one example among many possible, 10 apparently religious dedications from Olympia are dated to the 11th and 10th centuries BCE, 21 to the 9th century, and 837 to the 8th century.

Monumental temples begin to appear only in the second half of the 8th century, with that of Hera on Samos, of Apollo at Eretria, and those of Artemis and Hera on Delos. Perhaps the earliest surviving cult statues—seemingly distinct from the usual votive dedications—come from Dreros on Crete, about 700 BCE. Religion shared in the renaissance of Greek culture in the 8th century, and it is noteworthy that many of the elements appearing first in the archeological record then—temples, demarcated sanctuaries, altars, dedications, and cult statues—are also well-established features in the *Iliad* and *Odyssey*. This may suggest that what appears in the archeological record at this time had antecedents—how far back it is impossible to know—in more-perishable materials such as wood and mud-brick. But it is unmistakable that the most distinctive features of Greek religion take their definitive form—in both literature and material remains—as part of the 8th-century BCE renaissance.

Pollution and purification

The Greek concept of pollution—an impure state resulting from murder, sexual intercourse, childbirth, or contact with the dead, negatively affecting relations with the divine world and requiring purification by time or through rituals—is at best latently apparent in concerns for physical "cleanliness" before ritual activities and the exclusion of murderers from society in Homeric epic and in the injunctions of Hesiod's *Works and Days*. Ritual purification for murder is first unmistakably attested in literature in Achilles' purification in the *Aethiopis* (mid-7th century BCE[?]). The concept that the dead cause pollution of the sacred is first documented in Pisistratus's exclusion of tombs from areas even overlooking Apollo's sanctuary on Delos in the mid-6th century. Both presume preexisting traditions, and the question remains open whether purification rituals did not exist in Homeric times or were, for some reason, suppressed by the epic poets. Whenever introduced, pollution remained a live issue until the end of the Hellenistic period and beyond, with only pollution concerning murder apparently beginning to lose some of its efficacy in the 4th century BCE.

Heroes

Heroes, individuals who received public cult after their deaths, form a second class of deities in the Greek tradition, and the first cults of named heroes date to the end of the 8th century and are associated with Homeric heroes, the best examples being those of Menelaus and Helen near Sparta. Hero cults have been claimed for a few 10th- and 9th-century sites, and some scholars see traces of them in the *Iliad* (e.g., 2.546–51). But the real development of these cults is in the period 750–650 BCE, a movement perhaps influenced by the increasing spread and popularity of the Homeric epics. Many, perhaps most, such cults were not, however, devoted to Homeric heroes, and some cultic heroes and heroines even remained nameless. It is unknown whether these cults were antecedents, by-products, or parallel developments with the cults of the Homeric heroes. Some heroes were linked with Olympian deities, as Erechtheus with Athena at Athens, Hyacinthus with Apollo at Sparta, and Pelops with Zeus at Olympia, and in some cases the hero may have been established first. Hero cults were highly localized, closely bound to the presumed tomb of the hero, and a hero's cult could be moved only by the transfer of his bones. A few heroes such as Heracles and Asclepius broke local boundaries and became Panhellenic, usually in the process becoming assimilated to gods in cult and ritual. Once established, these hero cults persisted throughout antiquity. In classical times occasional individuals, such as the "tyrant slayers" Harmodius and Aristogeiton in Athens or the athlete Cleomedes of Astypalaea, were given such cults, usually for outstandingly beneficial or fearsome actions. Heroes might be benefactors, but theirs was still a cult of the dead, and about many of them, particularly the old ones, lingered an atmosphere of fear and uncanniness—well reflected in the cult that Sophocles creates for Oedipus at Athens in his *Oedipus at Colonus*.

Polis religion

It is not until the mid-6th century that we have sufficient historical, archeological, and epigraphical records to develop a sense of the underlying structure of state religion in a Greek polis, and that polis is Athens. We find cults in the urban center: that of Athena Polias, patroness of the city, associated with the hero Erechtheus in her temple on the Acropolis; that of Athena Nike with her altar, also on the Acropolis; that of Dionysus with the very beginnings of tragedy, now or soon to be situated in the Dionysus sanctuary and theater on the south slope of the Acropolis; in the "old city" southwest of the Acropolis, a sanctuary of Apollo with ties to Delphi and, under construction, a major temple of Zeus Olympios. In the developing new Agora northwest of the Acropolis was placed the altar of the twelve gods, at the imagined geographical center of Athens. In the Agora were also sanctuaries of Zeus Soter/Eleutherios and of Apollo Patroös, the putative ancestor of Athenians and all Ionian Greeks. Some cults in the rural areas of Athens were now assuming statewide importance, for example, the cult of Artemis Brauronia in the township Brauron and that of Demeter at Eleusis with its annual Mysteries, and there are indications of the state laying claim to these by building subsidiary sanctuaries of each on or near the Acropolis. And, after the establishment of democracy in 508/507 BCE, ten from one hundred local heroes were selected by the Delphic Oracle to give their names and protection to each of the ten tribes into which the Athenian polity was now divided. Part of the democratizing process was to bring into the state administrative structure the 139 individual townships (demes) that made up Athens, and later calendars and records of their sacrifices and festivals suggest that already in the 6th century rural demes had, for their residents, a rich program of religious activities. Some centered on local gods and heroes, others mirrored the cults of state deities.

Festivals

In the 6th century, statewide religious festivals *(heortai)* are introduced or elaborated in Athens. Among them, the Panathenaia for Athena and the City Dionysia included processions, sacrifices, hymns, and dances. Athena's festival featured a variety of athletic, equestrian, and musical competitions, and at the City Dionysia competitions in dithyrambic poetry, tragedy, and, later, comedy were held. Only citizens could fully participate in most such festivals, but the Panathenaia was truly Panathenian, with designated roles for male and female citizens of different ages, resident aliens, and even slaves. Such festivals, ranging over several days, combined communal worship of the deity with the pleasures of holiday feasting and the entertainment that the games offered, and they remained a feature of Greek religion throughout antiquity.

Priests

In these times and for centuries to come, most religious (in contrast to financial) matters of individual cults, even those of the state on the Acropolis, remained largely in the control of aristocratic families, with the priesthood of the cult passed from generation to generation within each family. Except at major religious centers such as Delphi and Eleusis, a Greek priest served part time, on occasions of sacrifices and festivals, with some responsibility for cult affairs, but possessing no esoteric religious knowledge and not subject to special restrictions on his daily life. In democratic Athens, priests of new cults were selected by lot for annual terms, and in several Asia Minor Greek cities priesthoods were auctioned off annually. Greek religion is distinguished by a lack of a central authority based on either a canonical text or a professional priesthood. State supervision, when it existed, consisted largely of lay committees overseeing the financial affairs of individual cults, of the legislative assembly approving the introduction of new cults, and of the courts prosecuting cases of impiety.

Diversity

We have the most knowledge about Athens, but the particular alignment of deities and their functions at Athens cannot serve as a model for all states. Epigraphical and historical evidence indicates that, in matters small and large, religion developed in various different ways in other Greek cities. On Naxos, for example, the patron deity of the state was Dionysus, not Athena, and the

Naxians would have had a quite different religious calendar featuring some-what different kinds of festivals at different times of the year. Rare was the cult, such as that of Demeter Thesmophoros, that was practiced in much the same form by all Greeks. As ethnic, cultural, political, and economic conditions var-ied from city to city over the centuries reaching back to the Dark Ages, so too, in these relatively isolated little countries, the specific deities worshiped, the rit-uals of this worship, and the functions of these deities came to differ, or, per-haps better, original differences were maintained.

The local nature and diverse functions of Greek deities are often revealed by the epithets attached to their names. The Athenian Artemis Brauronia (of the deme Brauron) differed in major respects from Artemis Ephesia (of Ephesus) in cult, function, and appearance. In Athens, Zeus Ktesios (of the stores) was rep-resented in the storeroom of each house as a pot wrapped in wool, but Zeus Eleutherios/Soter had a state sanctuary and statue in the Agora and protected the "freedom" of the city as a whole. Sanctuaries of Zeus Katabaites (coming down) marked spots hit by lightning, and Zeus Meilichios, a chthonic figure, was pictured as a bearded snake. Each was worshiped as a distinct deity at a separate place and time and with a separate function and ritual. How they each became associated with Zeus in Athens is unknown, but for Zeus and all Greek deities the epithet often reveals more than the Homeric name about their cults and functions.

Relationships between human and divine

To judge by prayers and dedications, what the Greeks sought from their gods, in general terms, was fertility of crops, animals, and selves; economic prosper-ity; good health; and safety of self, family, and country. These purposes were accomplished by establishing with the deities a relationship based on *charis*. A *charis* was a "favor" that was expected to be repaid, and the mutual exchange of favors or gifts is at the heart of successful human / divine relationships. This is a subtler and more complex relationship—based on aristocratic rather than mercantile values—than the formula *do ut des* (I give so that you may give), of-ten used to describe this relationship, implies. The model for the relationship of a human to a god is that of a good subject to a beneficent king, a relation-ship in which "gifts" of very different types and values might be exchanged for a variety of purposes. The gifts that the Greek gods give are successes in those areas listed above. The gifts that humans give include sanctuaries, sacri-fices, dedications, hymns, and dances. These gifts are intended to reflect the "honor" *(timē)*, not "love" or "fear," in which the humans hold these deities for the power they have and for the gifts they give. The gods, in turn, "rejoice" *(chairein)* in these honoring gifts. These gifts of humans are, in addition, "adornment" *(kosmos)* for the deities and their sanctuaries, and much of the finest Greek art, architecture, and poetry results from the Greek inclination to make their gifts to the gods beautiful.

In epic and tragedy, the relationships between humans and gods are often fractured, by gross impieties on the human side or by capricious and unjust behavior on the divine side. In everyday life, however, the Greeks seem remarkably confident that a good relationship between humans and gods is the normal situation, interrupted only temporarily by occasions of pollution or minor religious oversights, both of which can be corrected by rituals or additional gifts acknowledging the worth of the deity. The foundation myths of cults usually stress two elements: the power of the deity and the specific benefit that the god, of his or her own accord, is offering to humans, for Apollo of Delphi the oracle, for Dionysus of Thebes wine, and for Eleusinian Demeter grain. And in return, the gods expect "honor" in the form of cult. Some etiological myths, as for Artemis, put more stress on the dangerous side of the deity who, when offended, demands cultic acts as appeasement. But in both cases the humans, through cult, establish and maintain with the deity a mutually beneficial relationship based on *charis* and *timē*. And, finally, a human's relationships with the deities worshiped in life are severed by death. Apart from a few mythical figures of massive impiety, individuals were neither rewarded nor punished in the afterlife for religious behavior in this life. If such rewards and punishments did not fall on individuals during their lifetimes, they fell on their descendants, if on anyone. The hundreds of surviving Greek epitaphs suggest that the Greeks expected little of the afterlife, but the concept of a blessed afterlife was known to some: initiates into the Eleusinian Mysteries were said to have "sweeter hopes concerning the end of life and all eternity," and from the 6th century on, some private cults, associated with the historical Pythagoras and the legendary Orpheus, promised to their devotees a more blessed afterlife as a reward for following prescribed behavior in this life. It is unknown, however, how widely such beliefs about the afterlife were held.

Transmission, transformation, and conservation

From about the mid-8th to the early 6th century BCE, the "old" Greek cities sent throughout the Mediterranean colonies of their own citizens, and these colonies then often sent out colonies of their own. These colonists, for example, Corinthians to Syracuse in Sicily and Therans (themselves colonists of Sparta) to Cyrene in North Africa, initially transplanted some cults and festivals from their homelands in their new cities, and this was the prime cause of the spread of Greek religion throughout the Aegean and Mediterranean areas. But in the move some elements changed. Some cults, especially those of heroes and of deities with connections to local springs and such things, could not be transferred from the motherland. In place of the hero cults of their homelands, the colonists established hero cults of their founders. The colonists also encountered in their new lands indigenous cults, some of which they brought into the pantheon of their new state, such as the hero cult of the Argonaut Idmon at Herakleia Pontika. After their own period of development, the cults of a colony would come to differ in significant ways from those of the motherland. And so we have, even at this early stage, two types of state religion: that long established in the "old" Greek cities, with a multitude of well-entrenched heroes, local cults, and Olympian deities, and that in colonies, perhaps initially with fewer cults but surely more open to innovation and integration with indigenous cults.

Once established, the religious structures, particularly in the old cities, appear remarkably resistant to change. In part, this was due to a high degree of religious conservatism, often expressed in the necessity to worship the gods "in the ancestral ways." These ancestral ways would be in part preserved by the aristocratic families that controlled these cults and, for the state, from Solon's time in Athens, in official calendars of religious activities and sacred laws, often inscribed in stone. Contributing to this stability was the characteristic that deities and cults were not closely identified with one economic or social, or political faction within the city and hence were remarkably unaffected by economic and political tribulations that most Greek cities experienced. The priests and priestesses of most cults were aristocrats, but these same cults provided benefits, not only good relations with the divine world but also banquets and games, to the whole citizenry. And the costs of these benefits were paid sometimes by the wealthy, sometimes from the state treasury. Each citizen group thus benefited in some significant way, and hence the cults remained outside the clashes among these groups.

The greatest physical danger to religious cults came from outside the city-state, from foreign invaders such as the Persians Darius and Xerxes in the early 5th century and Philip V of Macedon in the 2nd century BCE. Darius promised revenge on Greek sanctuaries for the Greek burning of the temple of Kubaba in Sardis in 498, and for the next eighteen years he and his successor Xerxes ravaged and burned all Greek sanctuaries that came under the control of their armies, including most of the sanctuaries in Asia Minor, many of those in central Greece, and, of course, all those of Athens. In 200 BCE, the Macedonian king Philip V ravaged the Athenian countryside as he had other areas in Greece, apparently destroying beyond repair the hundreds, perhaps thousands of sanctuaries there. Within two generations of the Persian Wars most of the Greek sanctuaries had been rebuilt, often with considerably greater splendor. Times were, however, much worse in 2nd century BCE Greece, and the sanctuaries destroyed by Philip V disappear from the historical and epigraphical record.

Many have seen a threat to the foundations of Greek religion in the speculations concerning religion in the late 6th and 5th centuries by the pre-Socratic philosophers such as Xenophanes and the Sophists such as Prodicus. They and their successors in philosophy offered criticisms of the gods in terms of morality, proposed euhemeristic or other theories about the origins of gods, and theorized new types of deities more abstracted from human life. One could also include here the criticisms of deities found in Athenian tragedy (as in Euripides' *Hippolytus* and *The Trojan Women*) and old comedy (e.g., Aristophanes' *Birds*). But these criticisms of both philosophy and literature were directed almost solely against the gods of Homeric epic and rarely if ever touched the gods and rites of local cult. There is no indication from the historical evidence for practiced cult in Athens that family, local, or state cults suffered any loss of attention or support as a result.

The changes we see in classical and early Hellenistic Greek religion are incremental and not revolutionary. Cities with extensive trading interests often set up small sanctuaries in other countries for their own traveling or temporarily resident citizens to use, as the Samians did of their Hera in the Egyptian trading center of Naucratis, or as the Athenians allowed the Thracians to do in Piraeus for their goddess Bendis. In the late 5th and the 4th centuries, Asclepius, who offered new and welcome means of physical healing, was imported from Epidaurus into many cities, among them Athens in 420 BCE, just five years after the end of the plague that had devastated Athens. And a few new hero cults were created, as we have seen. In a typical Greek city the pantheon thus grew, but very slightly and very slowly, without any apparent neglect of preexisting cults.

The rise and dominance of the Macedonian kings, beginning with Philip II and Alexander the Great in the mid-4th century BCE and continuing with the line of their successors in Macedonia, Anatolia, Syria, and Egypt, brought major changes to the Greek world, and religion in the Hellenistic period reflected some of these changes. These Macedonian monarchs patronized Greek religious centers and in most of the hundreds of cities under their control received divine honors, with cults, priests, statues, and often elaborate festivals in their names. Through these cults the individual cities could express their gratitude for the favors large and small that these new kings, almost greater than human to their contemporaries, bestowed. These new cults did not displace, but apparently were added to or linked to existing cults and festivals. The Ptolemies, Alexander's successors in Egypt, seem most systematically to have manipulated cult for political purposes, with the Hellenization of the indigenous Sarapis to unify their subjects of Greek, Macedonian, and Egyptian origin and then with the exportation of this deity to international centers.

Foreign cults

So long as Greek citizens were bound to their cities, religion for individuals and cities remained quite stable. But the social, economic, military, and political conditions under Macedonian and then Roman domination broke down national barriers and caused or allowed the movement and temporary or permanent relocation of many Greeks throughout the Aegean and Mediterranean areas. As traders, sailors, mercenary soldiers, governmental officials, performing artists, and refugees, Greeks were exposed to and participated in "foreign" cults, either cults of other Greek cities or, more commonly, Egyptian, Syrian, and other non-Greek cults—cults of peoples who now too were moving freely around the Mediterranean world. Delos, which became a major international

trading center after 167/166 BCE, epitomizes this development. Apollo's island was soon filled with a bewildering variety of Egyptian, Syrian, Anatolian,
local Greek, and Roman cults, and Delos provides extensive epigraphical evidence of Greeks of many cities now participating and officiating in Egyptian
cults, Syrians in Greek cults, and Romans in cults of all nationalities. International centers such as Delos and the new cities founded by Macedonian kings
with heterogeneous populations, such as Antioch, became the melting pots for
Greek religion, breaking down distinctions between Greek and foreign deities
and rituals and between nationalities of worshipers. In these cities Greek deities were assimilated to foreign deities (what is often called syncretism), foreign
deities were given Greek names, and foreign cult structures were adopted by
some Greek cults. As traveling and emigrant Greeks returned to their home cities, they brought with them their new deities, and these were gradually added
to the pantheon of their homelands. Again, the "old" Greek cities of the mainland seem most resistant to the changes, but Greek cities in Asia Minor, physically closer to the homelands of these "new" foreign cults and more open to influences from indigenous peoples, appear more readily and completely to have
accepted the new mix of foreign cults that came to characterize late Hellenistic
and Greco-Roman religion.

BIBL.: W. Burkert, *Greek Religion* (Cambridge, Mass., 1985). F. Graf, "Religion und
Mythologie im Zusammenhang mit Homer: Forschung und Ausblick," in *Zweihundert
Jahre Homer-Forschung* (ed. J. Latacz; Stuttgart/Leipzig, 1991), 331–62. J. D.
Mikalson, *Religion in Hellenistic Athens* (Berkeley, 1998). M. P. Nilsson, *Geschichte
der griechischen Religion* (2 vols.; 2nd/3rd ed.; Munich, 1961–67).

Etruria

Olivier de Cazanove

*E*truria is, geographically, the region of Italy that lies between the Tyrrhenian Sea to the west, the Apuan Alps to the north, and the river Tiber to the east and south. On the left bank of the river lie Umbria, Sabine territory, and Latium. Within this boundary—but also, to some extent, in adjacent areas temporarily under Etruscan influence, the Po Plain and Campania—there developed, starting in the archaic period, a group of flourishing city-states. These were independent, but linked by a common cultural identity cemented among other things by a shared language. Etruscan is a non-Indo-European language whose interpretation still poses serious problems. It is clearly distinguished not only from Latin (and related dialects, such as Faliscan) but also from the three "Sabellic" languages, South Picenian, Umbrian, and Oscan. All these local languages disappeared once Italy was incorporated by Rome (between the Social War in the early 1st century BCE and the Principate of Augustus). But the military submission of Etruria (as of the rest of Italy) to Rome had been achieved long before Tarquinia, Veii, and Volsinii (Orvieto) were decisively defeated in the period 273–264 BCE, at the same time as Rome extended its power over south Italy (capture of Tarentum, 272 BCE).

The history of Etruria, and especially its religion, presents formidable problems of analysis for modern scholars. There is no surviving Etruscan literature. We are therefore dependent on Roman authors who wrote after (sometimes long after) Etruria had come under Roman control. As a result they possibly committed anachronisms or even outright errors. Their accounts were strongly influenced by various factors in Rome's relations with Etruria, among other things by the tradition of Etruscan kings of Rome. Partly as a result of this, the Romans themselves projected the origin of many of their own religious institutions onto the Etruscans, while at the same time also presenting Etruscan religion and culture as significantly different from their own. Etruscans, for example, were often assumed to have particular expertise in divination, and the Etruscan diviners known as haruspices were still being consulted by the Romans for specialized divinatory advice far into the period of the Roman Empire.

Modern studies of Etruscan religion have for a long time been dominated by the idea that it was a religion not so much "of the book," but "of books": *libri haruspicini, libri fulgurales,* and *libri rituals*—that is, books of haruspicy, which concerned the practice of divination by the examination of entrails; books concerning the religious interpretation of lightning; and books concerning religious ceremonies. This *disciplina Etrusca* (Etruscan discipline or Etruscan religious science) comprised the systematic account of techniques of divination and of the interpretation of different kinds of divine signs. It was supposed to originate from divine revelation, brought to humankind by the mythical infant Tages, who emerged from the furrow of a plowed field in the territory of the Etruscan town Tarquinia; he was preternaturally wise and, although newborn, had a paradoxically elderly appearance. However, we now possess only fragments of the *disciplina Etrusca,* mostly summaries or later elaborations given by Roman writers, and modern scholars have tried to reconstruct these books. In the past, scholars often tried to make links between them and what was known of divination in the ancient Near East, an idea based on the theory (suggested by the Greek historian Herodotus, but now largely abandoned) that the origin of the Etruscans went back to Lydia, in Asia Minor. They also tried to elucidate the fragmentary textual evidence through visual images and material objects—for example, a famous bronze mirror with an engraved design showing the prophet Chalcas (= Greek Calchas) examining the liver of an animal or the bronze model of a liver from Piacenza, which is of relatively late date (2nd to 1st century BCE) but seems to summarize the traditional knowledge of the Etruscan haruspices (one side of the model marks forty sections of the liver, each containing the name of a divinity).

This line of research, which has been intensively investigated for more than a century, does not seem likely, for the moment, to produce any radically new insights, since there is little possibility of new literary evidence. There are a few major epigraphical texts. Most significant, longest, and most frequently cited are the so-called Capua Tile and the wrapping of the Zagreb mummy: the Capua Tile comprises some sixty lines of text inscribed on terra-cotta, found at Capua in south Italy and probably dating to the first half of the 5th century BCE; the mummy wrapping, now in the collection of the Zagreb Museum, in Croatia, was made out of an Etruscan linen book *(liber linteus),* most likely of the 3rd or 2nd century BCE, which was cut into strips and reused in the 1st century BCE or CE to wrap an Egyptian mummy. Recent advances in the decipherment of the Etruscan language has helped our understanding of both these texts, but there is still no definitive interpretation. It is generally agreed that both the Capua Tile and the Zagreb mummy wrapping contain Etruscan religious calendars, including details of prescribed offerings, but there are still many uncertainties about their precise translation and significance. There is also evidence of numerous Etruscan images (relief sculptures, mirrors, tomb paintings) representing gods and myths; but these can be tricky to interpret because they appear largely to follow Greek iconographic conventions.

Future advances in our knowledge of Etruscan religion are most likely to come from archeology. There is increasing interest in the physical settings in which religious cult took place. This approach has the advantage of pinning down rituals and divinities to spatial contexts and of showing that they cannot be understood outside the city (and its territory) whose identity they helped to define. It follows from this that there is no single Etruscan religion, but a multiplicity of Etruscan religions, each one belonging to its own community: Caere, Tarquinia, Vulci, Veii, and so on. True, various "federal" cults linked the different cities, such as the sanctuary of Voltumna ("the principal deity of Etruria" according to the Roman writer Varro) in the territory of Volsinii, which also served as the setting for the annual assembly of the various Etruscan peoples (sometimes referred to as the "twelve peoples of Etruria"). And the same major divine figures were certainly to be found in various cities (Tinia [identified as the equivalent of Roman Jupiter], Uni-Juno, Turan-Venus)—the names of some clearly betraying traces of borrowing from the Greek world (Aritmi-Artemis, Charun-Charon) or from the Italic (Menrva-Minerva). But they also appear to have had a distinctive role in each of the cities where they were worshiped. Graffiti on vases, for example, refer to *Fufluns Pachies Velclthi* (Fufluns Bacchius of Vulci): these give the god Fufluns a Greek epithet, defining him as Dionysus, the master of the *thiasos;* but the reference to the city, Velclthi, also ties the god to that particular location.

Important recent work is also being carried out in the excavation or the reexamination of major sanctuaries that put a particular monumental stamp on the urban spaces of Etruria and the territories of the cities with a characteristic form of monumental religious building—notably the great "Tuscan" temples with three *cellae* (cult chambers), later codified in Vitruvius's typology of architecture. But at the same time, some of these sanctuaries were widely attended by people who came from every part of the Mediterranean world and its different religious traditions: Greeks from Ionia and Aegina at Gravisca, the Greek *emporion* (port of trade) at Gravisca, Carthaginians at Pyrgi, the *emporion* at Caere. The cultural complexity is illustrated by the Carthaginians calling the patron deity of Pyrgi "Astarte," the Etruscans "Uni," and Greek sources "Leucothea" or "Eileithyia." The archeological investigation of the sanctuaries and cemeteries of Etruria—the layout of temples, altars and associated structures, iconography, the distribution of votive offerings, analysis of bone remains—has brought advances in our understanding of public and private ritual (although the evidence has sometimes been overinterpreted).

The state of the evidence and recent directions in research are similar if we turn to the religion of the other early Italic peoples on the peninsula of Italy outside Rome. Here too there can be no question of reducing the many different systems into one single religion. Of course, there were similarities between them (especially in the case of adjacent areas where cultures were in general

closely related); but they also had their own distinct and independent characteristics. A striking illustration of this independence, from the Roman perspective, is found in Rome's official refusal to consult the oracle of Fortuna at
Praeneste (only twenty-three miles from Rome) until 241 BCE; that would have
meant having recourse to a "foreign" oracle.

The literary sources (which are rarely earlier than the reign of the first Roman emperor Augustus, 31 BCE–14 CE) tend to reflect the distorting view of
Greeks and Romans on the native cults of Italy; these writers almost always reduce indigenous religion to a series of natural curiosities—the sulfurous waters
of the sanctuary of the goddess Mefitis at Ampsanctus in Hirpine country in
southern Italy; or the "floating island" of Aquae Cutiliae in Sabine territory,
consecrated to the deity "Victory." This represents very much the point of view
of ancient travelers ("tourists" might almost be the best term) or of learned an-
tiquarians; one thinks, for example, of the Roman poet Ovid participating in
the traditional procession in honor of Juno in the country of the Falisci, between Etruria and Sabine territory (*Amores* 3.13).

Inscriptions give rather more information on rituals and the structure of local pantheons: the seven tablets from Gubbio (ancient Iguvium), commonly
known as the Iguvine Tables, written in Umbrian between 200 and 70 BCE; the
bronze tablet, written in Oscan, "of the enclosed garden [*hurz*])" of Kerres
(Ceres) near Agnone in Samnium; the fifty-eight votive inscriptions from a
cult site of Mefitis at Rossano di Vaglio in Lucania, which flourished between
the mid-4th century BCE and the 1st century BCE or CE—all of these reveal
hierarchized systems of divine power, in which divinities were defined, one
against the other, in a complicated and sometimes obscure series of epithets.
We find, for example, at Agnone a "Cererian" Hercules and at Rossano a
"Mefitanian" Mamers (= Mars); presumably these two major Italic divinities,
Hercules and Mamers, were here the "guests" of Ceres and Mefitis, and so
in some senses subordinated to the titular deity of the sanctuary. But some formulations are even more complicated. At Gubbio, among the twenty-nine divinities cited, are two, Prestota and Torsa, defined as "Cerfian of Martian
Cerfus." This expression links them to the god Cerfus and indirectly to Mars—
although it is hard now to unravel what exactly this double dependence entails.
The Iguvine Tables also document a set of rituals (taking the auspices, sacrifice)
that took place usually at the gates of the city on behalf of either the community as a whole *(touta)* or the Brotherhood of the Atiedii (often compared to
the Arval Brethren at Rome).

As in Etruria, the excavation of sanctuaries has multiplied our knowledge of
the religious systems. Cult places were often open to the sky, as in the paved
courtyard closed off by a long altar at Rossano di Vaglio. Major temples were
built, in Samnium for example, notably at Pietrabbondante; but these were a
relatively late phenomenon, occurring between the second Punic War and the
Social War (late 3rd to early 1st century BCE). After the Social War, when most
of Italy was incorporated within the Roman state, some elements of the cults
of the erstwhile Italic allies of Rome survived in the towns *(municipia)* and col-

onies of Italy—although restricted and controlled both politically and religiously. "What we used to call 'municipal cults' [*municipalia sacra*]," noted the Roman writer Festus, "are those that the peoples concerned used always to practice, before receiving Roman citizenship, and which the [sc. Roman] *pontifices* wanted them to continue to observe and practice in the traditional way." It was at this price that the cults of independent Italy enjoyed a sort of survival. But in fact they had become Roman.

BIBL.: O. de Cazanove, "La penisola italiana prima della conquista romana," in *Storia dell'Italia religiosa*, vol. 1: *L'antichità e il medioevo* (ed. A. Vauchez; Rome/Bari, 1993), 9–39. G. Colonna (ed.), *Santuari d'Etruria* (Milan, 1985). F. Gaultier and D. Briquel (eds.), *Les plus religieux des hommes: État de la recheche sur la religion étrusque (Actes du colloque international, Paris 1992)* (Paris, 1997). J.-R. Jannot, *Devins, dieux et démons: Regards sur la religion de l'Étrurie antique* (Paris, 1998). A. Prosdocimi, "Le religioni degli Italici," in *Italia: Omnium terrarum parens* (Milan, 1989), 477–545. G. Radke, *Die Götter Altitaliens* (2nd ed.; Münster, 1979). H. Rix, *Sabellische Texte* (Heidelberg, 2002).

Rome

John North

Rome and the development of its empire

In the centuries before the lifetime of Julius Caesar (100–44 BCE), what we now call Italy was a patchwork of different languages, cultures, and traditions. When Rome was founded, perhaps nine centuries before Caesar's birth, the first inhabitants of the site shared a common language and cultural tradition with just a handful of similar communities (we should say villages) in part of what we now call Latium. Around them, both at the time and for at least three centuries afterward, there were more powerful and numerous groups in central Italy: tribes speaking Oscan (a language related to Latin but distinct) to the east and south, Etruscans to the north, Greeks in new cities founded in the south and Sicily from the 8th and 7th centuries BCE onward. The history of Rome's early development and expansion was scarcely recorded at the time, and all but the barest outlines had been long forgotten when Roman history began to be written up in the 2nd century BCE, although Greek historians had noticed the rise of this new power in the west in the previous century.

We can reconstruct, with a good deal of help from the archeology of the region and from a handful of surviving documents, some of the key turning points. By the 6th century BCE, Rome was a substantial power with a developed urban center and contacts widely spread through Italy and beyond. In common with other parts of Italy, the Romans abolished their original system of kingship and by the 5th century BCE were being ruled through officials elected for annual terms of office. This is the system called "the Republic," which lasted until the 1st century BCE. It allowed all citizens to have a limited say in decision-making, although its working was dominated by an oligarchy, largely hereditary, drawn from rich and powerful family groups. By the early 3rd century BCE, the Romans had established a highly successful military system and were in control of a large Italian empire, including south and much of central Italy, though not yet the Po Valley. At this stage, they were sending colonies—newly created cities—into many parts of Italy, but other areas were still self-governing, maintaining their own traditions and obliged only to provide troops to fight in Rome's ever-increasing wars.

The Roman Empire, as we think of it today, was created in a long series of wars with Carthage in North Africa, with the great kingdoms of the Hellenistic world, and with the local peoples of Spain. By the time of Caesar's birth, Roman power, sometimes direct, sometimes indirect, was established around much of the Mediterranean and deep into Asia Minor. In an astonishing period of sustained aggression from about 70 BCE until the turn of the era, Rome came to control militarily and to impose methodical government over the whole of western, central, and eastern Europe and the Near and Middle East as far as Syria and Iraq. Three men dominated this history of expansion: Caesar's great rival Pompey, who imposed Roman rule in much of the East (66–61 BCE); Caesar himself, who campaigned in France (58–49 BCE); and his adopted son Caesar Octavianus, who took the title Augustus, whom we think of as the first emperor of Rome, and who supervised the pushing of Roman boundaries to the Rhine and the Danube.

So far, the story is one of ruthless and highly successful imperialism. For the historian of Roman religion this tale of triumph and expansion from humble beginnings creates major problems. First, our knowledge of the early stages of the history is hopelessly inadequate, since our sources of information come from hundreds of years later than the religious situation we are trying to reconstruct; second, as the empire expands from Latium to Italy and from Italy to the greater part of the ancient world, the impact on the nature of Roman society, on their cultural inheritance, and even on their identity as Romans is profound. To take the most obvious example, the population of the city of Rome evidently expanded dramatically in the last three centuries BCE; processions and rituals that once would have been known to all citizens must have been virtually inaccessible to many by the time that Rome had a million inhabitants. We can find areas of continuity and trace the sequence of changes to a limited extent. But, all too often, theories depend on an a priori decision as to what should be thought traditionally Roman and what should not, about which scholars have continuing debates and divisions.

A further complication is implied by the political transformation that accompanied the growth of the empire. The republican system was believed to have lasted since the late 6th century BCE, though much changed in the course of centuries; but the last century BCE saw not only an unprecedented rate of expansion, but also the rise of increasingly severe conflict and divisions within the ruling oligarchy. The system had always depended on the leading men accepting restraints on their ambition, but the men of the 1st century were no longer willing to limit their desire for money, power, and fame. The result was civil conflict and the emergence, in the end, of a single dominant family led by a single dominant ruler. Augustus sought to veil this dominance by operating through republican traditions and powers. But historians, both ancient and modern, have treated the result as a monarchy and have called Augustus and his successors "emperors," with the result that the word *empire* came to mean both the vast territories over whom the Romans had come to rule and the new regime in Rome that had replaced the old Republic.

The city and its gods

The gods and goddesses of Rome, like those of many other cities of the ancient world, were closely identified with the life of the city. This local divine role seems not to have been compromised in the eyes of ancient people by the existence of the worship of the same gods and goddesses in other cities near and far, sometimes by allies, sometimes by enemies. So Jupiter, Mars, and Juno were worshiped under those or similar names very widely throughout Italy; but that did not stop the Romans from treating them as their own. They participated, almost like divine citizens, in the life of the city and all its activities. They were consulted before actions; they sent messages and warnings; they received honors and sacrifices in the event of successes; they had spaces in the city devoted to them; and their images attended processions and games.

There were many channels through which communications could pass between deities and humans, and much ritual activity was determined by these channels. Some messages were sought from the gods by divination, originally from the flight of birds, later from a variety of techniques, including the study of the entrails of sacrificed animals and lightning in the sky; others came unbidden, as when extraordinary happenings were reported from Roman territory (the birth of monsters, groanings from the earth, flashings in the sky), taken as signs from the gods and dealt with regularly by ritual action on priestly advice. The authorities also sought the advice of prophetic books preserved by a special priestly college, whose task was to consult the books and recommend action, sometimes to appease established deities, sometimes to introduce new ones. Messages are passed from humans to gods by prayer (which usually goes with sacrifice) and vows, which specify ritual or gifts in return for divine support. Surviving records of dedications made in gratitude for the fulfillment of such vows leave no doubt about the enduring importance of these transactions throughout the Roman world.

In some respects at least, the religious situation of pagan Rome strikes a modern observer as familiar enough. Holy places had to be consecrated and cared for. Texts for prayers and vows had to be carefully preserved and pronounced. Processions were made through the streets, and divine images were paraded from their temples on special occasions. Prophetic texts were preserved and consulted for advice. The divine beings were conceived of as concerned about human welfare and powerful enough to intervene on behalf of their loyal worshipers. Inherited rituals were respected in the case of birth, marriage, and death within the family. Other aspects, although still practiced in some parts of the world today, would be regarded as deeply "alien" by much modern opinion: the central rite consisted of the killing of animals. This was not a simple ceremony—complex rules determined the nature of the victim for a particular god or goddess, and the sequence of events consisted of procession, sanctification of the victim, prayer, killing, and cooking, leading to a feast for the participants.

On closer examination, however, the differences from almost any modern religion seem to become more profound. The religious identity of a Roman was precisely to be a Roman and to worship the gods of Rome. There was no option of losing this identity or replacing it by becoming a member of some other religion. There were no other religions in competition for the adherence of Roman citizens, nor could they be members of anything corresponding to a "church," to which a citizen might or might not belong. There were various kinds of religious groupings, some open to particular areas or professions, many dedicated to a particular god or goddess. Individuals must have made choices according to their ranks, needs, or preferences; but such choices were within the religious life accepted by the city and caused no problem as to loyalty to the city. In other words, religion did not constitute an autonomous area with the city's life. In the same way, the priests, of whom there were many types, did not represent a rival source of authority to that of the state or its officials. It can be argued plausibly that the same institution in Rome—the Senate, whose members were all who had held annual offices in the past—was the highest authority on religious and nonreligious issues alike, although they respected the advice of the priests.

At all dates for which we have any substantial knowledge, the religious life of the Romans was deeply implicated with their political life. This is a feature of which they were themselves aware, at least in the later republican period. Cicero (the great orator and writer on politics; born 106 BCE) is even proud of it. He himself and his great contemporaries were not just politicians (and, many of them, warriors) but also priests, members of the powerful groups that supervised the different aspects of public and to some extent private religious observance. The state maintained a complicated ritual program, consisting partly of an annual fixed cycle of festivals, partly of rituals to mark specific occasions in public life, and partly of an elaborate system for the consultation of the gods and goddesses of the city before any action was taken. It followed that almost all actions, in civilian as well as in military life, were perceived as involving divine as well as human agents. The priests were responsible for the supervision of the ritual; they did not themselves carry out most of it, but characteristically they dictated the formulas, adjudicated if there were any problems, and were consulted after the event if there was any challenge to the validity.

Modern interpretations have sometimes emphasized this aspect of public life in Rome and argued, consequently, that religion had been reduced to the level of a tool in the hands of the politicians, who found it useful long after they had ceased to put their faith in its claims; during earlier periods, they imply, the Romans would have been genuinely pious and not abused religious rules in this way. In fact, there is no independent evidence for the supposed period of either piety or cynicism, and almost certainly, the whole interpretation rests on a misunderstanding of the fundamental relationships. So far as Romans were concerned, there was no question of choosing between religious objectives and political objectives, between church interests and state interests; most activities were involved with rituals of some kind, and their validity was automatically wrapped up with religious issues.

Another negative perception is that the religion described above was a public ritual system, which ignored or destroyed the needs of individuals for "real" religious experience. Previous scholars reacted to this state of affairs either by vilifying the whole religion as impoverished or by assuming that private religious needs were satisfied in private or family cults about which we know very little. The strong version of this second position is to say that all religions must cater to individual emotional needs; where there are no records of the means used, we must assume that the records are defective. There can, in fact, be little doubt that our knowledge of the religion of the Romans is partial and concentrates on the affairs of the state and public institutions. But forcing all religions into the same mold ignores the possibility that different societies can operate in profoundly different ways. "They *must* have been like us" is not a good principle for writing religious history.

Origins and development of the Roman religious system

Our understanding of the whole Roman religious system is essentially derived from information about its character in the 2nd and 1st centuries BCE and the 1st century CE, from writers of the late Republic and early imperial periods. To a limited extent, we can be confident in projecting this picture backward in time to earlier periods: the names of gods, rituals, festivals, priests, and so on were seen by the Romans as of the greatest antiquity, and we know that they were sedulous in preserving all the details they could of their religious formulas and rituals. But over the course of centuries we also know that the society of Rome and its physical appearance were radically transformed. However conservative they sought to be about the details, religion must have changed as the life of the Romans changed.

In some respects it is quite clear how such changes might have come about. Given the close connection between the religious order and the political system, it must always have been likely that political changes would produce religious consequences. Thinking along these lines, it can be seen that the religious system of the later republican period echoed the political system in having no sharply established focus of consistent authority. Religious decisions were split between the Senate and the priestly colleges; and, although the colleges had senior members, they acted in important matters as a corporation; no priest was normally in more than one college, so an accumulation of authority was difficult if not impossible. But once the position of emperor was established by Augustus and his successors, then the emperor began to acquire an irresistible concentration of religious authority; he became *pontifex maximus* (senior priest of the college of *pontifices*), held all the other priesthoods as well, and combined these with an unprecedented degree of political authority, both formal and informal. The image of the emperor sacrificing to the gods becomes the most common representation of religious action, the key expression of the relationship of humans to the divine.

When we try to go back to still earlier periods, rational speculation becomes difficult. It is a possibility, although no more, that at this early stage religion was a more separate area of life than in later periods, and consequently the religious personnel were more professionally dedicated to their religious tasks than were Caesar and his contemporaries. On the other hand, we have little understanding of the real character of the early monarchy of Rome, and it is also possible that the kings combined in themselves authority over all areas of life and that the priests were no more than their religious advisers on their particular areas of expertise. But it seems that, when the monarchy was abolished, the king's ritual role was handed on to a priest known as the King of Sacrifices (rex sacrorum), who was far from being a high priest. Meanwhile the various colleges of priests continued to be autonomous, keeping their own rules and records and making decisions according to their own traditions within their own defined area of concern. The state intervened only to widen their membership.

One subject on which we do have a good deal of information over the republican years is the regular practice of importing new cults and new rituals from outside the city—from elsewhere in Italy, from Greek cities, and later still from Asia Minor. The importations were triggered by a wide range of circumstances, but often by vows taken in the face of defeat or disaster or by recommendations from the priests. New cults were also sometimes created internally by recognizing as a deity what had previously been seen as a quality—Hope, Honor, Piety. For the Romans themselves, these innovations seem not to have been seen as problematic: they themselves recognized deities without number and were willing enough to worship and honor still more. The long-established custom perhaps throws light on a contentious area, namely, their willingness to add more deities still in the form of their own emperors.

Within the city of Rome itself, this custom of deification took place after the emperor's death and only when the Senate approved the transition from human to divine honors, so that emperors whom the senators disliked (Caligula, Nero, Domitian) never achieved the status at all. Outside Rome, no such reticence applied. The living emperors received temples, sacrifices, festivals, and priests exactly as the old gods and goddesses did, although their role stayed consistently in the public sphere and they never received vows or dedications from individuals, as did their divine predecessors. The cult was not standardized through the empire, though it must have been encouraged from the center. But everywhere it provided dignified roles for prominent local dignitaries, who both formed a link between Rome and the cities and also gained high status in the eyes of their fellow citizens at home.

It is important to remember that the overwhelming majority of the empire's inhabitants, not just Greeks and Romans but most of the original peoples of the whole area, were (in modern terms) polytheists, who were willing enough to accept the mutual identity of their gods and goddesses. In many ways, this provided great advantages for the empire: those who moved from one area to another found beliefs and rituals they could understand; it could be assumed that "the gods" were the patrons of all the peoples of the empire, although called by different names in different areas; the worship of the emperor could be accepted everywhere in terms of the local cult practice, without raising too much conflict. There was of course one locality that provided a famous exception: the cult violated the religious principles of the Jews.

Religions in the Roman Empire

As we turn from the story of the Romans and their city to that of the empire that the Romans created, it becomes harder still to agree on the right material for a historical analysis, let alone on the main lines of religious development. But it is at least clear that profound changes in the whole nature of religious life occurred between the lifetime of Caesar and that of Augustine in the 4th and 5th centuries CE. By this later date, individuals (sometimes with their whole family) could choose from radically different religious groups to which they might adhere: orthodox Christians, other Christians considered heretical by the orthodox, Manicheans, Jews, pagans, and so on. They could and did identify themselves by their religion as well as by their city or their family, in a way that earlier centuries would not have understood at all. In terms of religious history, it is hard to exaggerate the importance of this change in the location of religion in society and in the lives of individuals.

One effect of the change was to introduce a new level of hostility and conflict into the relationships of the adherents of the different systems. The most obvious and celebrated sign of this hostility within the Roman Empire was the persecution of Christians by the authorities both of Rome itself and of the cities of the eastern and western provinces. There had been a great deal of strife between the Greek and Jewish inhabitants of the cities of the eastern provinces in the Hellenistic period and the early years of Roman rule; but this, although it certainly had its religious aspects, was essentially intercommunal conflict within a city, not the attempt to eliminate a particular religious form. Moreover, the Jews were recognized as an ethnic group, and this explained why they would have different religious values, profoundly eccentric to pagan eyes, but at least inherited and not adopted. Christians were often pagans choosing to abandon the true religion and hence deeply suspect.

It is important, however, not to exaggerate this element of conflict. The persecutions were occasional and local, their memory being preserved for the most part by the Christians themselves in the promotion of their new cults of martyrs. General persecution throughout the empire was attempted for only two quite brief periods during the second half of the 3rd century CE. For most of the time, through most of the empire, pagans and Christians occupied the same cities peaceably enough. We know of families that included both pagan and Christian members; we find Christian and pagan places of worship close together. The official position of the emperors of the 2nd century CE was normally to take no inquisitorial action, but act only if there were complaints from pagan informers. There was no toleration in principle, but little action in practice.

There is no doubt about the importance of this process of religious change, but little agreement as to its origins, although it is clear that the existence of the empire between 200 BCE and 200 CE must have been a factor giving conditions of relative tranquility and ease of travel throughout the Mediterranean area and also deep into central Europe and the Near and Middle East. Whether it was easy to move around, it is clear that much movement of population did take place and that the cities of the whole empire came to consist not just of locally based communities, but mixtures of different kinds; in many cases, their religious cults and practices traveled together with these mobile groups. We find Greek communities in the west, Egyptian communities and Jewish communities everywhere. The Romans promoted this process themselves, first, by importing and subsequently freeing very large numbers of slaves from all over the eastern world; second, they both exported Roman citizens into the provinces and gave the rights of citizenship to members, especially influential members, of the local elites. Later still, citizenship was conferred on free people throughout the empire.

The coexistence of these different ethnic groups certainly led to a religious life of rich variety in many parts of the empire, and the evidence proves not only that a wide range of cults existed, but also that individuals joined them on the basis of religious preferences and a desire for particular kinds of experience. Thus the Egyptian cult of Isis spread far outside Egypt; the cult of Mithras, perhaps from Persia, but heavily adapted to Western tastes, became widespread in frontier areas of the empire; non-Jews attached themselves to Jewish practices although there was little encouragement from the Jewish authorities to do so. Much of this movement would have consisted of pagans joining groups within the boundaries of paganism and attracted little or no resistance from the authorities, though we do sometimes hear strong disapproval from conservative Roman commentators, particularly when women become the devotees.

These developments must have provided the context within which profound religious changes came about. The outcome is also reasonably clear: by the end of the 3rd century CE, many sharply defined religious options were in existence, which differed deeply from one another in the ideas and value systems they advocated and in their whole conception of the place of human beings in the cosmos. There were still practicing pagans throughout the Roman world, as there continued to be for many generations; but increasingly they were forced to defend their position by argument and by resistance to Christian and other rival claims. It was a struggle for which pagan religious life had given little preparation.

BIBL.: Mary Beard, John North, and Simon Price, *Religions of Rome* (2 vols.; Cambridge, 1998).

Early Christianity

Harold W. Attridge

A mutation in ancient religiosity, Christianity began as a revitalization movement within Judaism. The movement was inspired by the preaching of an itinerant charismatic, Jesus of Nazareth, who proclaimed the "reign of God" as a future reality anticipated by his own healing, exorcism, and provocative teaching. His claims about his own status in that reign of God remain unclear. It is highly unlikely that he claimed to be divine, as his followers would later assert. He probably did understand himself in prophetic terms, as a divine emissary, but not without irony. He may have spoken of his role allusively, with images such as "Son of Man" from the Hebrew scriptures (Dan. 7.13). His teaching utilized images from daily life in Galilee, farmers sowing, mustard seeds growing, householders entertaining, parents dealing with problem children, a Samaritan helping a stranger. Such images combined with injunctions to nonviolence, and a practice of openness with conventionally defined "sinners." The use of language of divine kingship involved at least an implicit threat to the current political and social order. When such preaching was coupled with a dramatic prophetic gesture, for example, the "cleansing" of the temple of Jerusalem (Mark 11), Roman authorities reacted forcefully.

After Jesus's crucifixion, his followers experienced him triumphant over death, raised from the netherworld, and enthroned at God's right hand. Expectations of the imminent reign of God grounded new readings of Israelite scripture and the formation of new social groups. Inspired by prophetic visions (Isa. 42.6; 43.6–9), some disciples hoped that scattered Israelites would be reassembled, in the company of people from all nations, to worship Israel's God. Followers of Jesus recruited adherents to this vision from non-Israelites throughout the eastern Mediterranean. Jesus's shameful death remained a scandal, but followers explained it as a sacrifice for the sins of humankind (Rom. 3.25), the vehicle for the inauguration of a "new covenant" between God and humanity (Heb. 8–10).

The missionary success of Saul of Tarsus, who also bore the Roman name

Paul, provoked a crisis over conditions of membership within the movement. A conference of leading disciples in Jerusalem around 49 CE confirmed Paul's essential claim that non-Israelites could join the messianic fellowship without undertaking the covenantal sign of circumcision (Acts 15; Gal. 2). The presence of Gentiles within Christianity continued to increase, until by the 2nd century they came to dominate the movement.

During the 50s, Paul and his collaborators continued evangelizing in Asia Minor, Macedonia, and Achaea and planned further work in Rome and Spain (Rom. 15.24). Paul called his new communities the *ekklēsia*, a traditional term for the popular "assembly" in a Greek polis and for the people of Israel (Deut. 4.10; 18.16). Neither political expediency nor genetic affinity united Paul's communities, but the conviction that they possessed a new *pneuma* (spirit) that transformed the present and offered a foretaste of future bliss (Rom. 8). Emissaries (2 Cor. 8–9) bearing letters knit together the scattered and sometimes fractious Christian communities. Paul's own letters, probably collected by the late 1st century, eventually formed an important part of Christian scriptures.

Despite the Jerusalem Council, controversy over entry requirements continued. Paul argued for the equality of Jews and Gentiles because both needed rescue from the power of sin, to which God responded by a gracious act of justification (Rom. 3–7). Paul strove to bridge the divide through a monetary collection from his Gentile congregants for Jerusalem's "poor" (1 Cor. 16; 2 Cor. 8–9; Rom. 15.25–27). The fate of Paul's offering is unknown, but he himself was arrested, sent to Rome, and executed under Nero in the early 60s.

At Paul's death, Christianity consisted of small, mainly urban communities, organized in the households of well-to-do patrons. Members celebrated the memory of the death and resurrection of Jesus at communal meals, enhanced with various spiritual displays (1 Cor. 12–14). Set liturgical forms and hierarchical organization were yet to emerge.

Two sets of events marked the end of the movement's first phase. The deaths of leading apostles such as Paul and Peter, who was also, according to tradition, martyred in Rome under Nero, signaled the passing of the founding generation. The Jewish revolt against Rome, begun in 66 and culminating with the destruction of Jerusalem in 70, eliminated the Christian presence in Israel's ancient symbolic center.

The late 1st century saw the emergence of new literary forms. The first apostolic generation had preached a gospel of "good news" about the new era inaugurated by Jesus's life, death, and resurrection. These traditions now coalesced into narratives combining images of Jesus as wonderworker and teacher with accounts of his noble death and divinely engineered triumph over death. Three such narratives are closely related. The Gospel according to Mark, probably composed around the time of the Jewish revolt, reflects that period's tension, while it admonishes disciples to follow Jesus's way to the cross. The Gospel according to Matthew, probably from the 80s, insists on the ongoing validity of the Torah and portrays the person of Peter as its authoritative interpreter. The Gospel according to Luke, probably written in the 90s along with the Acts of the Apostles, portrays a compassionate Jesus, preaching repentance and forgiveness. Both Matthew and Luke evidence rivalry from leaders of Jewish communities, which probably intensified in the postrevolt period. The last gospel eventually included in the Christian canon, the Gospel according to John, probably achieved its final form around the turn of the century. Even more than Matthew and Luke, it displays an extreme animosity toward Jewish rivals, while trying to inspire a deeper understanding of the significance of Jesus as the incarnate Word of God who fulfills all that temple and Torah promised.

In the late 1st and early 2nd centuries, Christians composed other forms of the "good news." These texts include collections of sayings of Jesus (such as the *Gospel of Thomas*) and apocalyptic visions (such as the canonical Book of Revelation, which tells of the ultimate defeat of satanic powers by the Lion of Judah/Slain Lamb), all of which respond to pressures being placed on followers of the Jewish Messiah in the late 1st century. This literary tradition continued in the 2nd century with *Shepherd of Hermas* and many other "revelations" of eschatological and heavenly realities. Other Christians imitated the work of the previous generation and produced didactic exercises in the names of revered apostles *(Didache)* or romances recounting the missionary adventures of various apostles *(Acts of Peter, Acts of Paul and Thecla)*.

New organizational forms accompanied the literary creativity. The loose associations of house churches of the earliest communities organized into local and regional assemblies, under various forms of leadership. Councils of elders *(presbyteroi)* were the norm in many areas in the late 1st century. By the early 2nd century, one of the elders, designated bishop or overseer *(episkopos)*, began to take on special leadership functions. The trend first becomes apparent in the letters of Ignatius of Antioch, martyred in Rome under the emperor Trajan around 110. On his way to battle the beasts, Ignatius composed a series of letters to communities in Asia Minor and Greece, emphasizing the importance of episcopal authority, as well as belief in the incarnation of Christ.

The institution of the monarchical episcopacy came more slowly to important sites such as Rome. The *First Epistle of Clement* attests to the situation of the late 1st century. Written around the end of the century from Rome to Corinth to resolve a local dispute, it appears to be the work of a Roman presbyteral council, perhaps recorded by its secretary or convener. Although not yet committed to episcopal leadership, the letter offers an early indication of the claims of the Roman community to broader leadership. It also presages later developments by describing the leadership of the Roman community in Jewish sacerdotal terms (*1 Clement* 40).

While hierarchical organization dominated in some locales, looser organizational principles obtained elsewhere. Little evidence survives from Christian communities in Egypt in the late 1st and early 2nd centuries, but later documents suggest that Christians there developed a variation on the "house church" model attested in Pauline communities. What apparently emerged, at least in the urban environment of Alexandria, were small "study circles." Under the guidance of a spiritual master, these groups, like their Platonic and Hermetic counterparts, engaged in the interpretation of texts and comparison of their own traditions with other religious and philosophical sources. Out of such groups emerged, in the mid- to late 2nd century, the phenomenon known as Gnosticism, led by charismatic teachers such as Basilides and Valentinus. Their disciples formed groups with distinctive interpretations of received traditions, both from scripture and the early stages of the Jesus movement.

Gnostics would eventually pose challenges to Christian self-definition, but the first major figure who convulsed the 2nd-century Christian world was Marcion. A successful merchant from Pontus, in the north of Asia Minor, he came to Rome in the late 130s, made a significant benefaction to the community, but was soon expelled on dogmatic grounds. Marcion advocated recognizing one authoritative source for Christian teaching, a collection of the letters of Paul and the Gospel of Luke, duly expurgated of problematic "Judaizing" additions. This first "canon" of scripture supported a theology sharply differentiating the loving God of Jesus from the merely just, and thus inferior, God of the Old Testament. The rejection of Marcion's position guaranteed that Christians would continue to revere the God of Israel as Creator and Redeemer and would continue to read Israel's scriptures as revelatory.

As Christians emerged from obscurity, they encountered opposition and occasional persecution, attested in the correspondence between Pliny the Younger and the emperor Trajan, while the former served as governor of Bithynia in northern Asia Minor. While Trajan approved Pliny's policy of executing recalcitrant Christians, the governor's testimony shows that there was not a settled official policy on the matter and that Christianity was beginning to have a larger social impact.

While governors such as Pliny took sporadic action against Christians, some members of the community offered apologetic responses. In Rome, Justin (a teacher martyred in 165), Tatian (his pupil), Theophilus of Antioch, and others published tracts refuting various charges, for example, of incest (men and women exchanging "kisses of peace" in darkened rooms by night) and cannibalism (devotees consuming Christ's "body and blood"). On the offensive, they excoriated the immorality of traditional Greek and Roman mythologies with their stories of lascivious and sensual deities.

Apologists also reveal Christian practice in the mid-2nd century. Thus Justin describes (*Apology* 1.59–61) the weekly meetings of his community with their readings of scripture and eucharistic celebrations. His report indicates that the rudiments of the central Christian ritual were in place. Yet ritual practice did not develop at the same pace in all quarters. The *Didache*, a document from Syria dating probably from the late 1st or early 2nd century, records a "eucharist" that lacks elements later considered essential: the remembrance of Christ's death and presence in the elements of the meal.

By the end of the 2nd century, Christianity had been sown from the western Mediterranean, through Gaul, Italy, North Africa, Asia Minor, Syria (including the hinterland of Edessa and Nisibis), and Mesopotamia. Christians had even traveled as far away as the Malabar coast of India, which missionaries had already visited when a teacher from Alexandria, Pantaenus, made the journey in the late 2nd century (Eusebius, *Church History* 5.10). Some of these early non-Greek Christian communities have left only scattered traces. Others were more influential. Syrian Christians, for example, composed the exuberant *Odes of Solomon* and developed a rigorously ascetical practice, evident, for instance, in the *Acts of Thomas*.

As Christianity expanded, it adapted in various ways to the ambient culture. In the process it began to deal with the reality that sin remained within the community of the saved. A 2nd-century visionary text from Rome, the *Shepherd of Hermas,* calls the community to renewed moral vigor, but holds out the promise of forgiveness, at least once, for serious sinners such as adulterers. Not all Christians were so lax. As some moved toward accommodation, movements arose to return the church to the purity of its origins. Montanism, a rekindling of apocalyptic prophecy in Asia Minor in the last half of the 2nd century, was precisely such a reaction. While hoping for a literal fulfillment of eschatological hopes, it also insisted on the moral rigor of the movement. If some Christians laid the foundations for a penitential system, others, such as the North African polemicist Tertullian, found the rigorism of the "new prophecy" of Montanism attractive and denounced lax confreres. Disputes between rigorist and accommodating forms of Christianity would mark much of the 3rd century and, in 4th-century North Africa, would lead to the division between Donatists and Catholics.

In the first two centuries, forms of organization and ritual practice exhibited considerable local variation. While Christians generally negotiated the boundaries of their communities and the requirements of membership, debates about the intellectual content of the faith continued. Troublesome questions about the nature of Jesus and his relationship to the God of Israel continued. Apologists explored ways of explaining the mediatorial role of Jesus, developing the category of the Logos (Word) found in the Fourth Gospel. Thus, as the ordinary human word has two forms, in the mind *(endiathetos)* and on the lips *(prophorikos),* so the Word of God has two forms: in the mind of God and in the person of Jesus. This description of Christ's significance dominated Christian theological discourse for the next three centuries, and theologians wrestled with the strengths and weaknesses of the image.

Equally troubling were questions about the nature of the godhead itself and the structure and fate of the cosmos. One set of answers came from the "gnostic" teachers, who explored mythical accounts of the origin of evil in divine complexity. Their work combined radically literal readings of Jewish scriptures and elaborate metaphysical schemes at least partially inspired by Platonic cosmologies. The result was a distinction between an inferior god of creation, the Demiurge, equivalent to YHWH of the Old Testament, and a transcendent spiritual entity, sometimes named the Silent Depth, from whom emanated the revealing Wisdom or Logos that briefly inhabited Jesus. Their writings, such as the Valentinian *Gospel of Truth,* which was found at Nag Hammadi in Egypt in 1945, also offered a powerful vision of what Jesus came to do, namely to awaken in all the spark of divinity sown into matter by a primordial fault in the godhead itself. Once awoken, that spark would find its way back to its transcendent source, with little need of episcopal supervision or sacramental practice. Thinkers of this sort united their metaphysics with a distinctive inter-pretation of scripture, particularly the cosmogony of Genesis. Their literal reading found evidence of a vengeful and ignorant deity inimical to human welfare. Salvation lay not through that Demiurge, but by escaping his realm.

The theological construal of Christianity offered by such gnostic teachers met resistance from thinkers who defended both the God of Israel, the moral law, and the contemporary ecclesiastical organization that taught it. Irenaeus of Lyons attempted a refutation of gnostic teachers in a massive heresiological work, *Against Heresies*. In addition to mocking denunciations of particular claims of Valentinians and others, Irenaeus articulated an influential vision of orthodox Christianity. For him, the normative scriptures, of both Old and New Testaments, correctly interpreted by bishops whose succession guaran-teed their authority, grounded the life of faith. That episcopally guaranteed faith came to expression in creedal form, the "rule of faith."

Other heresiologists followed Irenaeus, including Hippolytus, an early-3rd-century teacher who formed a rigorist schismatic faction within the Roman church. The most significant intellectual of 3rd-century Christianity was un-doubtedly Origen. Born in Alexandria in the late 2nd century, he gained prominence as a catechist preparing neophytes for baptism. After tensions arose with his bishop, he moved to Caesarea in Palestine, in 230. Enormously prolific, Origen wrote many tracts on exegetical, apologetic, and dogmatic issues, although his masterpiece was a major work of systematic theology, the *De principiis* or *On First Principles*. The work matched the comprehensive sweep of the imaginative systems of the 2nd-century gnostics, although it re-jected their controversial claims about the relationship between the God of cre-ation and the transcendent God of salvation. Like the gnostics, Origen's work was steeped in the Platonic tradition, and some of his platonizing moves, his flirting with metempsychosis, for example, would later elicit criticism.

Despite the apologists' efforts, 2nd- and 3rd-century Christians remained on the periphery of society. Accounts celebrating their heroic deaths (*Martyrdom of Polycarp,* from around 155; *Martyrdom of Perpetua and Felicitas,* early 3rd century) braced others to follow in their footsteps but also reinforced their sense of alienation. The political crisis of the mid-3rd century created more martyrs. The first empire-wide persecution under the emperor Decius (251) tried to solve the "Christian problem" by systematically suppressing the move-ment. Although intense, the persecution was relatively short. Subsequent spo-radic attempts at suppression culminated in the persecution under Diocletian and Galerius, rulers of the eastern half of the empire in the first decade of the 4th century. Persecution ended with the death of Galerius. The subsequent Edict of Milan of 313, issued by the two Augusti, Constantine and Licinius, guaranteed the freedom of Christians to assemble and worship without fear.

Constantine's victory over Licinius in 324 inaugurated the ascendancy of the Christian church as an instrument in the administration of the empire, Shortly after his assumption of supreme authority, Constantine summoned a synod of bishops at Nicea to resolve a festering dispute over the nature of Christ. Although not immediately successful, the council laid the foundation for later orthodoxy. More importantly perhaps, it inaugurated the process of unification of political and religious forces, leading to Christianity's eventual establishment as the empire's formal religion under Theodosius (379–95).

The 4th century marked a period of consolidation, after considerable controversy, of doctrine and organizational form, the fixation of scripture, and the elaboration of liturgical expression. From that point onward Christianity was not simply one religious force among many, but the dominant religious force of the late antique world.

BIBL.: W. H. C. Frend, *The Early Church, from the Beginnings to 461* (London: SCM, 2003). Helmut Koester, *Introduction to the New Testament* (2 vols.; New York: Walter De Gruyter, 1995–2000). Ramsay MacMullen, *Christianizing the Roman Empire A.D. 100–400* (New Haven: Yale University Press, 1984).

Epilogue

Bruce Lincoln

A certain tension is manifest in the preceding articles of this volume, in which extremely knowledgeable specialists address issues of enormous complexity with a maximum of efficiency and economy. Being both learned and scrupulous, they struggle to select a few choice examples from the countless possibilities available to them, after which they are forced to abbreviate and simplify even these. Toward the end of their articles, as they move to summarize, generalize, and distill, they suffer once more as they sacrifice diversity, nuance, complexity, and prudent qualifications on the conjoined altars of the Big Picture and the Short Article. *Sic semper est* with encyclopedias, even the sainted Pauly-Wissowa. The problem is more acute still for one charged (or cursed) with writing the final article: summary of summaries, epitome of epitomes, thinnest, blandest, most superficial, most simplistic, and therefore inevitably—also, quite rightly—most open to objection.

Admittedly insuperable difficulties can be liberating, however, since one is free to err in the manner of one's choosing, all possible approaches being wrong. Accordingly, I will frame the following discussion with two broad sets of questions. First, what do we mean by "the ancient world"? What constitutes the ancient and separates it from that which follows (a category I will, for the sake of convenience and provocation, call the "post-ancient")? Second, what forms does religion take and what roles does it play in the ancient? In the post-ancient? And how do changes in the religious contribute to the change from one era to the other?

As an initial attempt to engage these questions—one that is admittedly inadequate and destined for further refinement—let me advance the proposition that "the ancient" is that situation in which religion is not one system of culture coexisting among many others, but occupies the central position and plays a unique role—informing, inflecting, integrating, stabilizing, even at times controlling and determining all others (a position that has had some currency at least since Fustel de Coulanges 1864). Such a formulation carries a Hegelian danger, of course, threatening to turn into its opposite. For were religion to be found everywhere, there would be no borders to delimit and define it. Indeed, its very ubiquity might render it unrecognizable, rather like "culture" or life itself. That many, perhaps most ancient languages have no term to match the semantics of English "religion" (Latin is only a partial exception) lends support to this suspicion. It also raises the possibility that the emergence of the term and category "religion" is itself a product of the cultural transformation effected by the Reformation and Enlightenment, making this concept a particularly anachronistic instrument for understanding the situation of the premodern (compare the discussions of W. C. Smith 1963 and Asad 1993).

Although this argument has the merit of making us cautious, it errs by way of overstatement. To say that nothing in antiquity was free of religion—not war, disease, erotic love, science, the arts, poetry, or the state; not the landscape, the family, the meat on the table, or the fire on the hearth—is to say not that everything "was" religious, only that religious concerns were a part of all else, and a part that remains—to us, at least—analytically recognizable. Proceeding thus, we might theorize "the ancient" as that situation where, to cite just a few examples, one treats toothache by reciting the account of creation, reads the organs of sacrificial victims before waging battle, secures the verity of speech acts with sacred oaths, and conducts international diplomacy through appeals to mythic genealogy (Pritchard 1969, 100–101; Cicero, *On Divination* 1.95; Hesiod, *Theogony* 782–806; Herodotus 7.150, e.g.).

Scholars have often worked with such a model, although often it remains subtextual and implicit (Loew 1967, Eliade 1954, Frankfort 1948). Correlated with this model (whether as consequence or motive is hard to tell) is an understanding that "the ancient" ended with a "Greek miracle" that anticipated the Enlightenment by breaking with myth, tradition, and puerile superstition to achieve a critical view of religion (Nestle 1940, Cornford 1912, Vernant 1982). Xenophanes, Heraclitus, and Socrates are often singled out in this respect and accorded particular credit. Closer reading, however, makes clear that these thinkers were hardly critics of religion as such, but only critics of specific forms. Thus, for all that Xenophanes chided Homer and Hesiod for telling scandalous tales about the gods, and notwithstanding his sly suggestion that cattle imagined gods in bovine form, he also maintained, apropos of proper etiquette at drinking parties: "It is fitting, above all, for men of good cheer to hymn the god with well-spoken *mythoi* and pure *logoi,* having poured libations and prayed to be able to accomplish just things" (Xenophanes, DK 21B11 and 21B112; 21B15, cf. 21B16; 21B1, ll. 13–16). He made clear in the same passage, which represents the longest excerpt we have of his work, his concern that religion should promote decorum, well-being, grace, and harmony. As a negative complement, he did maintain "there is nothing useful" in beliefs that promote violent disorders *(stasias sphedanas),* but this is hardly a critique of religion *per se* (ll. 21–23).

Similarly, Socrates claimed to have grounded his incessant critical activity on an oracle received from the Delphic Pythia, and he took pains to assure the jury that tried him for impiety *(asebēia)* that he was incapable of this offense, since a personal *daimōn* supervised his conduct and he always heeded this deity's advice (Plato, *Apology* 20e–23c, 40a–c). Plato's valuation of reasoned knowledge *(epistēmē)* over faith *(pistis)* and opinion *(doxa)* also involved less criticism of religion than is normally supposed. Thus, he maintained that the philosophical disposition which makes it possible for a very small elite to acquire such knowledge is itself the product of postmortem experiences before the soul's reincarnation. In that heavenly realm, ultimate reality is revealed to all, but its true nature is remembered only by those who have cultivated exceptional powers of self-control by their prior training and *askesis* (Plato, *Phaedrus* 246d–249d, *Republic* 614b–621d). Ultimately, Plato's epistemology is inseparable from his theory of the soul and its fate (psychology in the most literal sense and eschatology), also his metaphysics and soteriology. In a word, his philosophy incorporates and depends on religion, albeit a form of religion that eschews civic cult, while drawing on dissident strains of speculation current among Orphics, Pythagoreans, and others.

"The ancient" does break down, of course, but it does so gradually, not through any "miracle" (itself a surprisingly religious trope, as is that of "genius," which often attends it). Earlier, to characterize "the ancient," I cited a set of examples that gestured toward medicine (the Babylonian toothache charm), warfare (Roman divination before battle), law (Greek oaths), and diplomacy (Persian use of genealogies to court potential allies). Change, however, can be seen in all these domains, as when epilepsy ("the sacred disease") is said to derive from natural causes and when generals repeat divinatory consultations until they get the results they want or proceed in defiance of the readings (Hippocratic corpus, *On the Sacred Disease*; Cicero, *On Divination* 2.52). The same shift toward a "post-ancient" less thoroughly encompassed by religion can be perceived when statements are secured by signing a contract, rather than swearing an oath; or when threats and bribes, rather than invocations of shared ancestors, are used to enlist allies (Thucydides 5.89). Such changes come piecemeal, however, so that antiquity ends—if the model we are currently entertaining permits us to conclude that it ends at all—only in fits and starts. Indeed, the model allows the view that "the ancient" reasserts itself (or simply persists) whenever oaths are sworn in a court of law, wherever prayers are said for the sick or for soldiers in battle, and whenever nations make common cause on the basis of shared beliefs.

Our first attempt sought to resolve all problems at once by identifying "the ancient" with the omnipresence of religion, while paying no attention to complexities internal to the latter term. The result was a critical instrument too blunt for the Gordian knot. It is time to back up and seek a sharper blade.

Elsewhere, in quite a different context, I have sought to define religion as a polythetic entity involving at least four domains: (1) a discourse whose concerns transcend the human, temporal, and contingent, and that claims for itself a similarly transcendent status; (2) a set of practices whose goal is to produce a proper world and/or proper human subjects, as defined by the religious discourse to which these practices are connected; (3) a community whose members construct their identity with reference to a religious discourse and its attendant practices; (4) an institution that regulates discourse, practices, and community, reproducing them over time and modifying them as necessary, while asserting their eternal validity and transcendent value (Lincoln 2003: 5–7). Accordingly, I would suggest that the transition from ancient to post-ancient might better be studied with reference to these four variables, rather than to the one that is their sum and product, "religion" *tout court*.

As a starting point, one might observe that the most authoritative discourses of antiquity tended to be acts of speech that understood—and represented—themselves to be inspired. Not simply human utterances, these were pronouncements in which some divine agency was felt to be at work, speaking through select human instruments and channels. Mantic, oracular, and prophetic speech regularly enjoyed such status, as did royal proclamations and poetic performance. Poetry was extraordinarily important, and the reasons for this must be assessed from two complementary perspectives, technological and ideological. Prior to the emergence of alphabetic script and the consequent spread of literacy, poetry was the most effective technique of memory. Any proposition or narrative that could be put in poetic language was thereby rendered more memorable than in any other linguistic form and therefore more likely to be transmitted across space and time. Such encoding was reserved for those cultural contents that were (or better: were judged and became, as a result of this judgment) most important. Reflecting and compounding this practical advantage was the claim of divine status that poets regularly made for themselves and their art. As Hesiod put it, the very breath with which he spoke—the material substance of his speech—was placed in his lungs by the Muses themselves, who were daughters of Zeus and Memory (Mnemosynē) (Hesiod, *Theogony* 31–32: *enepneusan de moi audēn thespin*). The Delphic Pythia, by contrast, gave oracles only in trance, when possessed by Apollo. The proof that the god spoke through her came not only from the state of her body and visage, but also because she spoke in perfect hexameters (Plutarch, *On the Obsolescence of Oracles*). Similar constructions of poetic discourse as sacred and of poets as "masters of truth" (Detienne 1996) are to be found among the Hebrew prophets, Vedic seers, Roman sibyls, and the hymns attributed to Zarathustra (Kugel 1990).

With the spread of literacy and alphabetic script, written prose gradually displaced oral poetry as the most effective mnemonic technique, and widespread cultural changes followed (Havelock 1963, Goody 1987, Ong 1982). In the realm of religion, sacred books came to enjoy higher status than did inspired utterances. Growing awareness that the latter might not be what they claimed and were open to manipulation by their human agents also served to undercut their authority. This authority might be preserved, however, when the utterances in question were textualized and reconstituted as revealed scripture, as in the case of the biblical prophets and the Sibylline books.

So bibliocentric (initially in the broad, and later in the narrow sense) did religious discourse become that the danger emerged of excess production and oversupply. To control this danger, priestly bodies assumed the power to impose limits through canon formation and the closure of prophecy, sometimes with the backing of state power, as when Augustus had the Sibylline Books collected, purged of suspicious content, and placed in the temple of his patron deity, where they were kept under lock and key, accessible only to authorized priests (Suetonius, *Augustus* 31.1). Similar processes, if less dramatic and under less direct state control, elsewhere produced restricted bodies of scripture that were invested with authoritative status. Energies were directed toward the interpretation of these texts rather than the production of new ones. Reading rather than speaking became the privileged moment of religious discourse, and innovation no longer came through the claim of inspiration, but through the practice of shrewd hermeneutics. To put it in slightly different terms, as Jeremiah yielded to the rabbis, John the Baptist to the Church Fathers, Muhammad to the *qadis* and *ulama*, one can see not only Weber's routinization of charisma, but also the historic shift from a prophetic ethos associated with orality to the scholarly ethos of the text.

Religious practices also changed significantly from the ancient to the post-ancient. Two sorts of practice fell into relative desuetude, both of which purported to mediate between the sacred and profane in direct, material fashion. The first of these was a whole complex of behaviors involving the statues of deities. Most commonly, the presence of such statues in temples constituted the sanctuaries as the site of a god's residence on earth, thereby cementing the relation of a specific city and people to a specific deity. Thus, to cite but one example, the statue of Marduk in the temple Esagila at Babylon marked the city as this god's special domain and the god as this city's patron, also as the dominant member of the pantheon when the city's power expanded. For as was true with other Mesopotamian cities, when the Babylonians were victorious in warfare, they often captured (the statues of) other cities' deities as tokens of subordination and risked similar capture of their own god should they in turn be conquered. The priests of this temple were charged with the care, feeding, decoration, and worship of Marduk's resident statue, which is to say his virtual, palpable presence. This was not mere servitude, however, since deity and people were engaged in an ongoing mutually beneficial exchange. The flow of benefits to humanity was particularly dramatized at the *Akitu* (New Year) festival, when the king clasped the hands of Marduk's image and thereby had his legitimacy and power renewed by the god himself, with consequences for the prosperity of the land and people:

> [Marduk], exalted among the gods,
> [Who dwells in the temple Esag]il, who creates the laws,
> [Who . . .] to the great gods,
> [. . .] I praise your heroism.

[May] your heart [be sympathetic] to whoever seizes your hands.
"Temple Program for the New Year's Festival at Babylon," ll. 396–400, trans. A.
Sachs, in Pritchard, *Ancient Near Eastern Texts*, p. 334

Other peoples developed different practices. Sometimes access to the statues was restricted to the priesthood or its high-ranking members. Sometimes worshippers were permitted to make contact by entering an inner sanctum of the temple where the statue/deity was housed. In other cases, images were brought forth to outer chambers on festal occasions or even paraded through the streets of the city. Some of the statues represented benevolent, nurturing deities who brought blessings to their people; others were demanding and jealous figures, who threatened those they found inadequately devoted or attentive. But in all instances, these blocks of material substance were the site where relations between the human and the divine were transacted, the point of conjuncture between sacred and profane.

At least equal in importance was the practice of sacrifice, the most common and also the most significant form of ritual among virtually all ancient peoples. Countless theories of sacrifice have been offered (W. R. Smith 1889, Hubert and Mauss 1964, Burkert 1983, Thieme 1957, Detienne and Vernant 1989, Girard 1977, Grottanelli 1999) and the practice itself could be infinitely varied in its performance. Ordinarily, it involved the immolation of an animal or vegetable offering (much more rarely a human victim), the spiritual portion of which was believed to pass to the divine, while the material portion became the basis of a feast enjoyed by the human performers, with the gods as their honored guests, thereby restoring a commensality lost in the mythic primordium. All details of the performance could be invested with symbolic content—for instance, the division of the victim's body might provide analysis of the categoric distinctions between divine, human, and animal levels of existence (Vernant 1989, Grottanelli and Parise 1988)—or the ritual might replicate events recounted in cosmogonic myth that homologize the body to the world as microcosm to macrocosm (Lincoln 1986). Sacrifice also provided a means to invest bloody and violent acts with sacral significance and avoid the charge that one killed just to obtain food. Rather, one assumed the burden and awesome responsibility of caring for the gods and the cosmos, which meant performing each minute part of the action in perfectly controlled, symbolically appropriate fashion. Preparation of the feast and disposal of the remains, no less than actual dispatch of the victim, were subject to the same regulation and scrutiny, since all aspects of sacrificial ritual were "good to think" and therefore subject to symbolic elaboration.

Destruction of the Second Temple in 70 CE made it impossible for the priests of Israel to continue their performance of sacrifice. The resulting reorganization of cult and thought led to the emergence of that which we know as Judaism(s). In other traditions, no such dramatic events were responsible, but over time sacrifice and the use of statues ceased to form the center of ritual practice, and material mediations of every sort diminished in their import. They were displaced—although never completely—by practices that relocated the prime site of interest and action inside the human subject. Prayer; the cultivation of certain valorized dispositions, sentiments, and states of being; the habit of monitoring one's progress toward these ethical and existential ideals; and reporting flaws and slips to spiritual advisors, while submitting to their guidance and discipline, became privileged aspects of religious practice with the move toward the post-ancient.

Clearly, these developments correlated with shifts in the nature of religious community. In the ancient, religion was a shared concern of groups existing at familial, civic, ethnic, and national levels of integration. The collective identity of such groups was strongly overdetermined, being based simultaneously on territory, language, polity, kinship, and laws, as well as the religion that members held in common and that, in turn, held them. One's neighbors were thus one's fellow citizens and also one's co-religionists, who spoke the same language, shared the same norms, celebrated the same festivals, and worshiped at the same altars, seeking favor of the same gods for the group of which they were all a part. The post-ancient, by contrast, saw the emergence of communities based primarily—and also most explicitly and emphatically—on religious considerations, integrating persons who might be divided by geography, language, culture, or citizenship.

This development had begun as early as the 6th century BCE with the Pythagoreans. Among its contributing factors was the formation of great empires that brought disparate populations into a single political entity and tax structure, but left subject peoples only very imperfectly integrated by religion and culture. At the same time, expanded trade and improved communications permitted relatively wide circulation of religious tenets, texts, and teachers, all of which gradually refashioned themselves in broader, less localized idioms as they engaged—and absorbed feedback from—a disparate international audience (Grottanelli 1982). At times, imperial powers sought to introduce aspects of their native religion to the provinces, or at least to the elite strata therein (e.g., Seleucid policy at the time of the Maccabean revolt). At other times, the imperial center imported religious forms from the periphery as a conscious policy (e.g., the Roman *evocatio* ritual that appropriated gods of conquered enemies); as a means to indulge growing taste for the exotic (e.g., the introduction of Isis and Cybele at Rome); or as part of the backwash that inevitably accompanies conquest (e.g., Mithraism). The diaspora of various groups (such as the Magi and the Jews) and the proselytizing activities of others (the missions recounted in the Acts of the Apostles and related apocrypha) also contributed to the de-territorialization of religious community characteristic of the post-ancient.

In contrast to older groups focused on a specific temple, city, cult place, or sacred locale, which they served and from which they took their identity, the increasingly international, multiethnic, and geographically dispersed population of post-ancient religious communities was held together not only by shared symbols, beliefs, and practices, but also by itinerant leaders and mobile texts such as the epistles of the New Testament, the polemic exchanges among Church Fathers, the corpora assembled at Qumran and Nag Hammadi, or the rabbinic responsa. Inclusion or exclusion in such amorphous communities was not ascribed by birth in a given place, lineage, or social stratum, but was elective. One joined by conversion, that is, by accepting the beliefs, practices, texts, and leadership that constituted the group and were central to their self-understanding. The promise of salvation provided a prime inducement to convert and the conviction that one's faith offered salvation to others (whose contributions would sustain and renew the group) provided a prime motive to proselytize. Soteriological concerns thus figured prominently in the life of post-ancient religions, whose members sought—and promised others—escape from a world they experienced as hostile, bewildering, and finite to an alternative realm of eternal bliss. Such escape was prefigured by the move from one social group, identity, and set of loyalties to another: abandoning one's family, for instance, to join one's new brothers-and-sisters-in-Christ (Matthew 10.37, Luke 14.26). This shift further correlates to a change from "locative" worldviews concerned with the proper emplacement of all things and persons (since being-in-place is what renders them sacred) to "utopian" orientations that valorize mobility as transcendence and liberation (J. Z. Smith 1978).

One final point about religious community in the post-ancient context: In groups that made shared beliefs and practices their chief criteria of inclusion, deviation from these had serious consequences and could provoke not only debate and discussion, but also power struggles and schism. Accordingly, issues of heterodoxy and orthodoxy, heteropraxy and orthopraxy, heresy and heresiology all rose to prominence, along with the institutional means to frame and resolve them—and also to enforce the hierarchic elevation of victors over vanquished.

This brings us to institutions. In the ancient, specifically religious institutions—priesthoods, temples, cult sites, and so on—were typically subordinate to institutions of the state, be these civic, national, or imperial, democratic, oligarchic, or royal. Smaller and weaker than their political counterparts, religious institutions served and were dependent on them for protection, financial support, and personnel. As examples, consider Athenian interest in Eleusis, the temples of the Acropolis, and the Panathenaea; the haoma sacrifices at Persepolis (Bowman 1970); or the integration of priestly and magisterial offices in the Roman *cursus honorum*. Only in a very few cases, where religious institutions possessed extraordinary prestige and authority such that they attracted an international clientele and rich contributions, were they able to sustain themselves and achieve a situation of relative autonomy. Delphi is the paradigmatic case, alongside only a handful of others.

In the post-ancient, some religious institutions such as the rabbinate attained a certain measure of autonomy from the states to which they were subject, but from which they maintained a cautious distance. In other situations—Byzantium and the Islamic caliphate, in particular—religious and political organizations and concerns interpenetrated each other so thoroughly as practically to merge. The most dramatic development, however, occurred in the West, where events beginning with the conversion of Constantine and the Edict of Milan (313 CE) produced a centralized, well-staffed and well-funded, hierarchic religious establishment that became the senior partner in the collaborations of church and state subsequent to the fall of Rome (476 CE). In all these forms and locales, however, religious bodies secured considerable control over such vital arenas of activity as education (general and professional), social welfare (charity and counseling), record keeping, rites of passage (the crucial moments of subject and family formation), and moral scrutiny and control (through preaching, confession, absolution, and pastoral care). Gradually, they perfected the ability to extract revenue from the faithful through a variety of mechanisms. Thus, in addition to contributions (tithing, *zakkat*) that were often voluntary in name only, bequests intended to secure salvation were also an important source of income, as was commerce in spiritual goods and services of varied sorts: blessings, indulgences, relics, charms, mystic knowledge, magic formulas, and so forth.

As ancient religion gave way to post-ancient, a discourse based on canonic corpora of sacred texts displaced inspired performances of sacred verse; practices of prayer, contemplation, and self-perfection displaced mediations through sacrifice and statues of the deity; de-territorialized elective communities constructed on the basis of religious adherence displaced multi-stranded groups within which ties of geography, politics, kinship, culture, and religion were all isomorphic and mutually reinforcing; and institutions that, with some exceptions, had better funding, a wider range of activities, and more autonomy from the state displaced their weaker, more localized predecessors.

Although these sweeping generalizations call for extended treatment that would attend to the nuances and particularities of a thousand specific cases, the constraints of a concluding article point in the opposite direction, toward a summation whose oversimplifications serve chiefly to prompt objections, further inquiry, and debate. And so, here it is: The transition yields Christianity. Or, to put it a bit more cautiously, the ancient ends and the post-ancient begins with Christianity(ies), Judaism(s), and Islam(s), with the westernmost form of Christianity as the extreme case.

Bibliography

Asad, Talal. *Genealogies of Religion: Discipline and Reasons of Power in Christianity and Islam*. Baltimore: Johns Hopkins University Press, 1993.
Assmann, Jan, ed. *Die Erfindung des inneren Menschen: Studien zur religiösen Anthropologie*. Gütersloh: G. Mohn, 1993.

Bianchi, Ugo, and Martin Vermaseren, eds. *La soteriologia dei culti orientali nell'Impero romano.* Leiden: Brill, 1982.

Bowman, Raymond. *Aramaic Ritual Texts from Persepolis.* Chicago: University of Chicago Press, 1970.

Brown, Peter. *Society and the Holy in Late Antiquity.* Berkeley: University of California Press, 1982.

Burkert, Walter. *Homo necans: The Anthropology of Ancient Greek Sacrificial Ritual and Myth,* trans. Peter Bing. Berkeley: University of California Press, 1983. [German original 1972.]

Cornford, Francis Macdonald. *From Religion to Philosophy: A Study in the Origins of Western Speculation.* London: E. Arnold, 1912.

Detienne, Marcel. *The Masters of Truth in Archaic Greece,* trans. Janet Lloyd. New York: Zone Books, 1996. [French original 1967.]

Detienne, Marcel, and Jean-Pierre Vernant. *The Cuisine of Sacrifice among the Greeks,* trans. Paula Wissing. Chicago: University of Chicago Press, 1989. [French original 1979.]

Dodds, E. R. *Pagan and Christian in an Age of Anxiety: Some Aspects of Religious Experience from Marcus Aurelius to Constantine.* Cambridge: Cambridge University Press, 1965.

Eliade, Mircea. *The Myth of the Eternal Return,* trans. Willard R. Trask. Princeton: Princeton University Press, 1954. [French original 1949.]

Frankfort, Henri. *Kingship and the Gods: A Study of Ancient Near Eastern Religion as the Integration of Society and Nature.* Chicago: University of Chicago Press, 1948.

Fustel de Coulanges, Numa Denis. *The Ancient City: A Study on the Religion, Laws, and Institutions of Greece and Rome.* Baltimore: Johns Hopkins University Press, 1980. [French original 1864.]

Girard, René. *Violence and the Sacred,* trans. Patrick Gregory. Baltimore: Johns Hopkins University Press, 1977. [French original 1972.]

Goody, Jack. *The Interface between the Written and the Oral.* Cambridge: Cambridge University Press, 1987.

Grottanelli, Cristiano. "Healers and Saviors of the Eastern Mediterranean," in Bianchi and Vermaseren 1982.

———. *Il sacrificio.* Rome: Laterza, 1999.

Grottanelli, Cristiano, and Nicola Parise. *Sacrificio e società nel mondo antico.* Rome: Laterza, 1988.

Havelock, Eric Alfred. *Preface to Plato.* Cambridge, Mass.: Harvard University Press, 1963.

Hubert, Henri, and Marcel Mauss. *Sacrifice: Its Nature and Function.* Chicago: University of Chicago Press, 1964. [French original 1899.]

Kippenberg, Hans, ed. *Die vorderasiatischen Erlösungsreligionen in ihrem Zusammenhang mit der antiken Stadtherrschaft.* Frankfurt am Main: Suhrkamp, 1991.

Kugel, James, ed. *Poetry and Prophecy: The Beginnings of a Literary Tradition.* Ithaca: Cornell University Press, 1990.

Lincoln, Bruce. *Holy Terrors: Thinking about Religion after September 11.* Chicago: University of Chicago Press, 2003.

———. *Myth, Cosmos, and Society: Indo-European Themes of Creation and Destruction.* Cambridge, Mass.: Harvard University Press, 1986.

Loew, Cornelius. *Myth, Sacred History, and Philosophy: The Pre-Christian Religious Heritage of the West.* New York: Harcourt, Brace & World, 1967.

Momigliano, Arnaldo. *Alien Wisdom: The Limits of Hellenization.* Cambridge: Cambridge University Press, 1975.

———. *On Pagans, Jews, and Christians.* Middletown, Conn.: Wesleyan University Press, 1987.

Nestle, Wilhelm. *Vom Mythos zum Logos: Die Selbstentfaltung des griechischen Denkens von Homer bis auf die Sophistik und Sokrates.* Stuttgart: A. Kröner, 1940.

Ong, Walter. *Orality and Literacy: The Technologizing of the Word.* London: Methuen, 1982.

Pritchard, James, ed. *Ancient Near Eastern Texts Relating to the Old Testament,* 3rd ed. Princeton: Princeton University Press, 1969. "A Cosmological Incantation: The Worm and the Toothache," trans. E. A. Speiser, pp. 100–101.

Smith, Jonathan Z. *Drudgery Divine: On the Comparison of Early Christianities and the Religions of Late Antiquity.* Chicago: University of Chicago Press, 1990.

———. *Map Is Not Territory: Studies in the History of Religions.* Leiden: Brill, 1978.

Smith, Wilfred Cantwell. *The Meaning and End of Religion: A New Approach to the Religious Traditions of Mankind.* New York: Macmillan, 1963.

Smith, William Robertson. *Lectures on the Religion of the Semites: First series, The Fundamental Institutions.* New York: Appleton, 1889.

Stroumsa, Guy. "Les mutations religieuses de l'antiquité tardive," lectures given at the Collège de France, Spring 2004 (publication forthcoming).

Thieme, Paul 1957. "Vorzarathustrisches bei den Zarathustriern und bei Zarathustra," *Zeitschrift der Deutschen Morgenländischen Gesellschaft* 107 (1957): 67–104.

Vernant, Jean-Pierre. "At Man's Table: Hesiod's Foundation Myth of Sacrifice," in Detienne and Vernant 1989, pp. 21–86. [French original 1979.]

———. *The Origins of Greek Thought.* Ithaca, N.Y.: Cornell University Press, 1982. [French original 1962.]

Contributors

Jan Assmann, University of Heidelberg

Harold W. Attridge, Divinity School, Yale University

Mary Beard, Faculty of Classics and Newnham College, Cambridge University

Paul-Alain Beaulieu, Department of Near Eastern Languages and Civilizations, Harvard University

Jan Bremmer, Faculty of Theology and Religious Studies, University of Groningen

Olivier de Cazanove, Department of Ancient History, University of Paris I

John J. Collins, Divinity School, Yale University

David Frankfurter, Religious Studies Program, Department of History, University of New Hampshire

Fritz Graf, Department of Greek and Latin, The Ohio State University

Sarah Iles Johnston, Department of Greek and Latin, The Ohio State University

Bruce Lincoln, Divinity School, University of Chicago

William Malandra, Department of Asian Studies, University of Texas

Nanno Marinatos, Department of Classics and Mediterranean Studies, University of Illinois at Chicago

Jon Mikalson, Department of Classics, University of Virginia

John North, Department of Ancient History, University College London

Eckart Otto, Institut für Alttestamentliche Theologie, University of Munich

John Scheid, Collège de France, Paris

Michael Stausberg, Department of the History of Religions, University of Bergen

David P. Wright, Department of Near Easter and Judaic Studies, Brandeis University

Index